P9-DGL-476

Taste of Home WINNING RECIPES

REIMAN MEDIA GROUP, INC. • GREENDALE, WISCONSIN

Taste of Home Reader's Digest

A TASTE OF HOME/READER'S DIGEST BOOK

Editor: Janet Briggs
Art Directors: Edwin Robles, Jr., Lori Arndt
Layout Designers: Catherine Fletcher, Nancy Novak
Proofreaders: Linne Bruskewitz, Jean Steiner
Editorial Assistant: Barb Czysz
Food Director: Diane Werner RD
Recipe Testing and Editing: Taste of Home Test Kitchen
Food Photography: Reiman Photo Studio
Cover Photo Photographers: Rob Hagen, Dan Roberts
Cover Food Stylists: Jennifer Janz, Jim Rude
Cover Set Stylists: Dolores Schaefer, Grace Sheldon

Senior Editor, Retail Books: Jennifer Olski
Creative Director: Ardyth Cope
Vice President, Executive Editor/Books: Heidi Reuter Lloyd
Senior Vice President, Editor in Chief: Catherine Cassidy
President, Food & Entertaining: Suzanne M. Grimes
President and Chief Executive Officer: Mary G. Berner

Pictured on the front cover, clockwise from top left: Hearty Hamburger Soup (p. 84), Very Veggie Lasagna (p. 264), Sweet Raspberry Muffins (p. 313), Stovetop Pot Roast (p. 157), Freeze-and-Bake Rolls (p. 344), Baked Chicken and Acorn Squash (p. 222) and Granny's Rhubarb Pie (p. 429).

International Standard Book Number (10): 0-89821-694-X
International Standard Book Number (13): 978-0-89821-694-3
Library of Congress Control Number: 2007942728

For other Taste of Home books and products, visit www.tasteofhome.com.
For more Reader's Digest products and information, visit
www.rd.com (in the United States)
www.rd.ca (in Canada)

Printed in China
3 5 7 9 10 8 6 4 2

Table of Contents

Top-Honor Recipes
Guaranteed to Win You Raves!

Imagine the time you'll save—and the praises you'll earn—when you start your cooking with recipes already judged the best of the best!

You can count on these 645 recipes for delicious results every time. Why? Because each one of these kitchen-tested, family-approved taste sensations is a real winner from a national cooking contest sponsored by the Taste of Home Test Kitchen.

Home cooks just like you sent in their very best recipes, the ones that friends and family ask for again and again, hoping their contest entries would be judged number 1. Our professional home economists sorted through the stacks of mail we received, looking for recipes with interesting flavors, innovative uses of ingredients or unique twists on old favorites. They selected recipes that had accurate measurements for the ingredients, showcased good cooking techniques and met the contest guidelines.

Then the Test Kitchen team prepared the top contenders for our taste-test panel of experienced food editors, fellow home economists and magazine and book editors with a knack for picking winners. After much sampling, the panel had the difficult task of deciding which recipes were the absolute best. The ones that made the grade were then declared contest winners and published in our magazines and books.

Taste of Home Winning Recipes compiled the grand-prize winners and runners-up from dozens and dozens of contests. These scrumptious recipes include everything from appealing appetizers to mouth-watering main dishes to delectable desserts.

You'll find some of the top picks from contests, such as Luscious Lasagna, Pork Parade, Chock-full of Chips, Tempting Turkey, Comforting Casseroles, Brownie Bonanza, Regal Roasts, Fantastic Fruit Pies, Ground Beef Roundup, Say Cheesecake, 30-Minute Side Dishes, Easy Chocolate Desserts, Great Grilled Fare, Sunny Citrus, Chili Cook-Off, Favorite Cookie Collection and so many more! Look for the 1st prize icon for best of the best—the first-place winners from these and other contests.

What's more, every recipe in this collection features easy-to-follow directions and a full-color photograph. And because each one has been tasted and approved by our Test Kitchen staff, you can be confident that you're serving your family the best-tasting dishes. Now you know why you'll come out a winner with *Taste of Home Winning Recipes*. You be the judge of which fabulous recipe to try first!

APPETIZERS & BEVERAGES

CLAM FRITTERS, pg. 16

Appetizers & Beverages

Taco Meatball Ring

While it looks complicated, this attractive meatball-filled ring is really very easy to assemble. My family loves tacos, and we find that the crescent roll dough is a nice change from the usual tortilla shells or chips. There are never any leftovers when I serve this at a meal or as a party appetizer!

—Brenda Johnson, Davison, Michigan

2 cups (8 ounces) shredded cheddar cheese, *divided*
2 tablespoons water
2 to 4 tablespoons taco seasoning
1/2 pound ground beef
2 tubes (8 ounces *each*) refrigerated crescent rolls
1/2 head iceberg lettuce, shredded
1 medium tomato, chopped
4 green onions, sliced
1/2 cup sliced ripe olives
Sour cream
2 small jalapeno peppers, seeded and sliced
Salsa, optional

In a bowl, combine 1 cup cheese, water and taco seasoning. Crumble beef over mixture and mix well. Shape into 16 balls. Place 1 in. apart in an ungreased 15-in. x 10-in. x 1-in. baking pan. Bake, uncovered, at 400° for 12-15 minutes or until meat is no longer pink.

Drain meatballs on paper towels. Reduce heat to 375°. Unroll crescent roll dough and separate into triangles. Place triangles on a 14-in. pizza pan, forming a ring with pointed ends facing outer edge of pan and wide ends overlapping. Lightly press wide ends together. Place a meatball on each roll; fold point over meatball and tuck under wide end of roll (meatballs will be visible). Bake for 15-20 minutes or until rolls are golden brown.

Taco Meatball Ring

Fill the center of ring with the lettuce, tomato, onions, olives, remaining cheese, sour cream, jalapenos and salsa if desired. **Yield: 8 servings.**

Editor's Note: When cutting or seeding hot peppers, use rubber or plastic gloves to protect your hands. Avoid touching your face.

Appetizer Roll-Ups

Cream cheese and a variety of herbs and vegetables make even deli cold cuts a fancy and filling appetizer. Bite-size pieces look so pretty set on a platter in a circle. But the arrangement never stays complete for long once this snack is served.

—Marcella Funk, Salem, Oregon

ROAST BEEF:

- **4 ounces cream cheese, softened**
- **1/4 cup minced fresh cilantro**
- **2 to 3 tablespoons minced banana peppers**
- **1 garlic clove, minced**
- **1/2 pound thinly sliced cooked roast beef**

HAM AND TURKEY:

- **12 ounces cream cheese, softened**
- **1/2 cup shredded carrot**
- **1/2 cup shredded zucchini**
- **4 teaspoons dill weed**
- **1/2 pound thinly sliced fully cooked ham**
- **1/2 pound thinly sliced cooked turkey**

In a bowl, combine the cream cheese, cilantro, peppers and garlic. Spread about 2 tablespoons on each slice of beef. Roll up tightly and wrap in plastic wrap.

In another bowl, combine cream cheese, carrot, zucchini and dill. Spread about 2 tablespoons on each slice of ham and turkey. Roll up tightly; wrap in plastic wrap. Refrigerate overnight. Slice into 1-1/2-in. pieces. **Yield: 6-7 dozen.**

Appetizer Roll-Ups

Rye Party Puffs 1st prize

I can't go anywhere without taking along my puffs. They're pretty enough for a wedding reception yet hearty enough to snack on while watching football on television. A platterful of these will disappear even with a small group.

—Kelly Williams, La Porte, Indiana

- **1 cup water**
- **1/2 cup butter**
- **1/2 cup all-purpose flour**
- **1/2 cup rye flour**
- **2 teaspoons dried parsley flakes**
- **1/2 teaspoon garlic powder**
- **1/4 teaspoon salt**
- **4 eggs**

Caraway seeds

CORNED BEEF FILLING:

- **2 packages (8 ounces *each*) cream cheese, softened**
- **2 packages (2-1/2 ounces *each*) thinly sliced cooked corned beef, chopped**
- **1/2 cup mayonnaise**
- **1/4 cup sour cream**
- **2 tablespoons minced chives**
- **2 tablespoons diced onion**
- **1 teaspoon spicy brown *or* horseradish mustard**
- **1/8 teaspoon garlic powder**
- **10 small stuffed olives, chopped**

In a large saucepan, bring water and butter to a boil over medium heat. Add the flours, parsley, garlic powder and salt all at once; stir until a smooth balls forms. Remove from the heat; let stand for 5 minutes. Add eggs, one at a time, beating well after each addition. Continue beating until mixture is smooth and shiny.

Drop by rounded teaspoonfuls 2 in. apart onto greased baking sheets. Sprinkle with caraway. Bake at 400° for 18-20 minutes or until golden brown. Remove to wire racks. Immediately cut a slit in each puff to allow steam to escape; cool.

In a large mixing bowl, combine first eight filling ingredients. Stir in olives. Split puffs; add filling. Refrigerate. **Yield: 4-1/2 dozen.**

Rye Party Puffs

Sweet-Hot Sausage Meatballs

These good-tasting sausage meatballs seem to disappear before anything else on the table. They have a delightful tang with a bit of crunch from the water chestnuts. I've used the recipe for over 20 years because it's so easy to do and comes out perfect every time.
—Claire Stryker, Boulder City, Nevada

- 2 cans (8 ounces *each*) water chestnuts, drained
- 1 pound bulk pork sausage
- 1 pound bulk spicy pork sausage
- 1/4 cup cornstarch
- 1 cup maple syrup
- 2/3 cup cider vinegar
- 1/4 cup soy sauce

In a blender or food processor, process water chestnuts until minced. Transfer to a bowl; add sausage. Mix well. Shape into 1-in. balls. Place in ungreased 15-in. x 10-in. x 1-in. baking pans. Bake, uncovered, at 350° for 20-25 minutes or until meat is no longer pink.

Meanwhile, in a saucepan, combine the cornstarch, syrup, vinegar and soy sauce until smooth. Bring to a boil; cook and stir for 2 minutes or until thickened. Drain meatballs; add to sauce and heat through. **Yield: 12-14 servings.**

Sweet-Hot Sausage Meatballs

Ground Beef Snack Quiches

Hawaiian Egg Rolls

Ground Beef Snack Quiches

My husband, Cory, farms, so supper can sometimes be quite late. A hearty appetizer like these meaty mini quiches is a perfect way to start the meal. They taste super made with ground beef, but I sometimes substitute bacon, ham, ground pork or sausage.
—Stacy Atkinson, Rugby, North Dakota

- **1/4 pound ground beef**
- **1/8 to 1/4 teaspoon garlic powder**
- **1/8 teaspoon pepper**
- **1 cup biscuit/baking mix**
- **1/4 cup cornmeal**
- **1/4 cup cold butter**
- **2 to 3 tablespoons boiling water**
- **1 egg**
- **1/2 cup half-and-half cream**
- **1 tablespoon chopped green onion**
- **1 tablespoon chopped sweet red pepper**
- **1/8 to 1/4 teaspoon salt**
- **1/8 to 1/4 teaspoon cayenne pepper**
- **1/2 cup finely shredded cheddar cheese**

In a saucepan, cook the beef, garlic powder and pepper over medium heat until meat is no longer pink; drain and set aside. In a small bowl, combine the biscuit mix and cornmeal; cut in the butter until the mixture is crumbly. Add enough water to form a soft dough. Press onto bottom and up the sides of 18 greased miniature muffin cups. Place teaspoonfuls of beef mixture into each shell.

In a small bowl, combine the egg, cream, onion, red pepper, salt and cayenne; pour over beef mixture. Sprinkle with cheese. Bake at 375° for 20 minutes or until a knife inserted near the center comes out clean. **Yield: 1-1/2 dozen.**

Hawaiian Egg Rolls

An avid cook, I am constantly trying to come up with recipes for leftovers. This one gives a whole new twist to extra ham. My two children think these egg rolls are great, and they freeze well. I thaw as many as needed and bake them.
—Terri Wheeler, Vadnais Heights, Minnesota

10 fresh spinach leaves, julienned
1/2 teaspoon ground ginger
2 tablespoons olive oil
1/2 pound fully cooked ham, coarsely ground (2 cups)
4 water chestnuts, chopped
1/4 cup undrained crushed pineapple
2 tablespoons chopped green onions
1 tablespoon soy sauce
7 egg roll wrappers
Vegetable oil for frying
Sweet-and-sour sauce

In a saucepan, saute spinach and ginger in oil for 1-2 minutes. In a small bowl, combine the ham, water chestnuts, pineapple, onions and soy sauce. Stir in the spinach mixture.

Place 3 tablespoons of ham mixture in the center of each egg roll wrapper. Fold bottom corner over filling. Fold sides toward center over filling. Moisten remaining corner with water; roll up tightly to seal.

In an electric skillet, heat 1 in. of oil to 375°. Fry egg rolls for 2 minutes on each side or until golden brown. Drain on paper towels. Serve with sweet-sour sauce. **Yield: 7 egg rolls.**

Sausage Wonton Stars

These cute, crunchy cups are ideal when entertaining large groups. Kids even enjoy them. We keep a few in the freezer so we can easily reheat them for late-night snacking. —Mary Thomas, North Lewisburg, Ohio

Sausage Wonton Stars

1 package (12 ounces) wonton wrappers
1 pound bulk pork sausage
2 cups (8 ounces) shredded Colby cheese
1/2 medium green pepper, chopped
1/2 medium sweet red pepper, chopped
2 bunches green onions, sliced
1/2 cup ranch salad dressing

Lightly press wonton wrappers onto the bottom and up the sides of greased miniature muffin cups. Bake at 350° for 5 minutes or until edges are browned.

In a large skillet, cook sausage over medium heat until no longer pink; drain. Stir in the cheese, peppers, onions and salad dressing. Spoon a rounded tablespoonful into each wonton cup. Bake for 6-7 minutes or until heated through. **Yield: about 4 dozen.**

Sausage Quiche Squares

Sausage Quiche Squares

Having done some catering, I especially appreciate interesting, appetizing finger foods. I'm constantly asked to make these popular squares to serve at parties. They're almost like a zippy quiche.
—Linda Wheeler, Middleburg, Florida

- 1 pound bulk pork sausage
- 1 cup (4 ounces) shredded cheddar cheese
- 1 cup (4 ounces) shredded Monterey Jack cheese
- 1/2 cup finely chopped onion
- 1 can (4 ounces) chopped green chilies
- 1 tablespoon minced jalapeno pepper, optional
- 10 eggs
- 1 teaspoon chili powder
- 1 teaspoon ground cumin
- 1 teaspoon salt
- 1/2 teaspoon garlic powder
- 1/2 teaspoon pepper

In a large skillet, cook sausage over medium heat until no longer pink; drain. Place in a greased 13-in. x 9-in. x 2-in. baking dish. Layer with the cheeses, onion, chilies and jalapeno if desired. In a large bowl, beat eggs and seasonings. Pour over cheese.

Bake, uncovered, at 375° for 18-22 minutes or until a knife inserted near the center comes out clean. Cool for 10 minutes; cut into 1-in. squares. **Yield: about 8 dozen.**

Editor's Note: When cutting or seeding hot peppers, use rubber or plastic gloves to protect your hands. Avoid touching your face.

Sesame Chicken Strips

These tasty chicken strips dipped in the lightly sweet sauce are a wonderful finger food. They go over really well at outdoor summer gatherings. This recipe puts a new twist on fried chicken—a staple at most picnics.
—Teri Rasey, Cadillac, Michigan

- 1 cup mayonnaise
- 2 teaspoons dried minced onion
- 2 teaspoons ground mustard
- 1 cup crushed butter-flavored crackers (about 25 crackers)
- 1/2 cup sesame seeds
- 2 pounds boneless skinless chicken breasts

SAUCE:

- 1 cup mayonnaise
- 2 tablespoons honey

In a small bowl, combine the mayonnaise, onion and mustard. In a shallow dish, combine crackers and sesame seeds. Cut chicken lengthwise into 1/4-in. strips. Dip strips into mayonnaise mixture, then into the sesame seed mixture.

Place in a single layer on a greased 15-in. x 10-in. x 1-in. baking pan. Bake at 425° for 15 to 18 minutes or until juices run clear.

Combine the sauce ingredients and serve with chicken strips. **Yield: 10-12 appetizer servings.**

Maple-Glazed Chicken Wings

Some wonderful maple syrup I brought back from a trip to Vermont inspired my recipe. These wings have been a hit with family and friends. They can be used for snacks, hors d'oeuvres for parties or showers, or appetizers—or double or triple the recipe and make the wings a main dish you can serve with a salad or corn on the cob on the side.

—Janice Henck, Clarkston, Georgia

- **2 to 3 pounds whole chicken wings**
- **1 cup maple syrup**
- **2/3 cup chili sauce**
- **1/2 cup finely chopped onion**
- **2 tablespoons Dijon mustard**
- **2 teaspoons Worcestershire sauce**
- **1/4 to 1/2 teaspoon crushed red pepper flakes**

Cut chicken wings into three sections; discard wing tip section. In a large resealable plastic bag, combine the remaining ingredients. Set aside 1 cup for basting and refrigerate. Add chicken to remaining marinade. Seal bag and turn to coat; refrigerate for 4 hours, turning occasionally.

Drain and discard marinade from wings. Grill chicken, covered, over medium heat for 12-16 minutes, turning occasionally. Brush with reserved marinade. Grill, uncovered, for 8-10 minutes or until juices run clear, basting and turning several times. **Yield: 6-8 servings.**

Editor's Note: 3 pounds of uncooked chicken wing sections (wingettes) may be substituted for the whole chicken wings. Omit the first step.

Sesame Chicken Strips

Maple-Glazed Chicken Wings

Sweet-Sour Chicken Dippers

Chickaritos

Sweet-Sour Chicken Dippers

Since you can chop up all the ingredients the night before, this can be ready in about 30 minutes. You can serve it as a snack, an appetizer or a great after-work dinner. —*Kari L. Caven, Post Falls, Idaho*

- 1 can (8 ounces) crushed pineapple
- 1-1/2 cups sugar
- 1 can (14-1/2 ounces) diced tomatoes, undrained
- 1/2 cup cider vinegar
- 1/2 cup chopped onion
- 1/2 cup chopped green pepper
- 1 tablespoon soy sauce
- 1/4 teaspoon ground ginger
- 1 tablespoon cornstarch

BATTER:

- 1 cup all-purpose flour
- 1 cup cornstarch
- 2 teaspoons baking powder
- 2 teaspoons baking soda
- 2 teaspoons sugar
- 1-1/3 cups cold water
- Oil for deep-fat frying
- 1-1/2 pounds boneless skinless chicken breasts, cut into chunks

Drain pineapple, reserving juice. In a large saucepan, combine the sugar, tomatoes, vinegar, onion, green pepper, soy sauce, ginger and pineapple. Bring to a boil. Reduce heat; simmer, uncovered, for 20 minutes.

In a bowl, combine cornstarch and reserved pineapple juice until smooth; stir into tomato mixture. Bring to a boil; cook and stir for 2 minutes or until slightly thickened. Remove from the heat; set aside.

In a large bowl, combine the flour, cornstarch, baking powder, baking soda, sugar and water until smooth.

In a deep-fat fryer, heat oil to 375°. Dip chicken pieces, a few at a time, in batter, then

Orange-Pecan Hot Wings

fry for about 5 minutes or until golden brown and juices run clear. Remove to paper towels to drain. Serve immediately with sweet-sour sauce. **Yield: 4 dozen appetizers.**

Chickaritos 1st prize

This recipe is a great way to use leftover chicken. Chickaritos are easy to make and can be prepared ahead of time. Just bake right before serving.
—Nancy Coates, Oro Valley, Arizona

- 3 cups finely chopped cooked chicken
- 1-1/2 cups (6 ounces) shredded sharp cheddar cheese
- 1 can (4 ounces) chopped green chilies
- 1/2 cup finely chopped green onions
- 1 teaspoon hot pepper sauce
- 1 teaspoon garlic salt
- 1/4 teaspoon pepper
- 1/4 teaspoon ground cumin
- 1/4 teaspoon paprika
- 1 package (17-1/4 ounces) frozen puff pastry sheets, thawed *or* pie pastry for double-crust pie (10 inches)

Salsa
Guacamole

In a large bowl, combine the chicken, cheese, chilies, onions and seasonings. Cover and refrigerate until ready to use.

Remove half of the pastry from refrigerator at a time. On a lightly floured surface, roll to a 9-in. x 12-in. rectangle. Cut into nine small rectangles. Place about 2 tablespoons of filling widthwise on each rectangle. Wet edges of pastry with water and roll pastry around filling. Crimp ends with a fork to seal. Repeat with remaining pastry and filling. Place seam side down on a lightly greased baking sheet. Refrigerate until ready to bake.

Bake at 425° for 20-25 minutes or until golden brown. Serve warm with salsa and guacamole. **Yield: 18 appetizers.**

Orange-Pecan Hot Wings

We like to use oranges and orange juice in lots of different ways—we even have an orange tree in our backyard. These chicken wings are a fun appetizer that our friends are very fond of.
—June Jones, Hudson, Florida

- 3 pounds whole chicken wings
- 3 eggs
- 1 can (6 ounces) frozen orange juice concentrate, thawed
- 2 tablespoons water
- 1 cup all-purpose flour
- 1/2 cup finely chopped pecans
- 1/2 cup butter, melted
- 2 cups ketchup
- 3/4 cup packed brown sugar
- 2 to 3 tablespoons hot pepper sauce

Cut chicken wings into three pieces; discard wing tips. In a small bowl, whisk the eggs, orange juice concentrate and water. In a shallow dish or a resealable plastic bag, combine flour and pecans. Dip wings in egg mixture, then coat with flour mixture.

Pour butter into a 15-in. x 10-in. x 1-in. baking pan. Arrange wings in a single layer in pan. Bake, uncovered, at 375° for 25 minutes.

Meanwhile, combine remaining ingredients. Spoon half over wings; turn. Top with remaining sauce. Bake 30 minutes longer or until meat juices run clear. **Yield: 8-10 servings.**

Editor's Note: 3 pounds of uncooked chicken wing sections (wingettes) may be substituted for the whole chicken wings. Omit the first step.

Salmon Appetizers

Salmon Appetizers

As a cook for a commercial salmon fishing crew, I found this recipe to be a wonderful variation for using salmon. I often rely on these pretty pinwheels when entertaining. They're easy to prepare, and they prove to be popular at parties and other get-togethers.
—Evelyn Gebhardt, Kasilof, Alaska

- 1 can (14-3/4 ounces) salmon *or* 2 cups cooked salmon, flaked
- 1 package (8 ounces) cream cheese, softened
- 4 tablespoons salsa
- 2 tablespoons chopped fresh parsley
- 1 teaspoon dried cilantro
- 1/4 teaspoon ground cumin, optional
- 8 flour tortillas (8 inches)

Drain salmon; remove any bones. In a small bowl, combine the salmon, cream cheese, salsa, parsley and cilantro. Add cumin if desired. Spread about 2 tablespoons of the salmon mixture over each tortilla.

Roll each tortilla up tightly and wrap individual with plastic wrap. Refrigerate for 2 to 3 hours. Slice each tortilla into bite-size pieces. **Yield: about 48 appetizers.**

Clam Fritters

We had clam fritters every time we went to Rhode Island. I looked for a recipe and finally found this one. Now we have them whenever we want.
—Cecelia Wilson, Rockville, Connecticut

- 2/3 cup all-purpose flour
- 1 teaspoon baking powder
- 1/4 teaspoon salt
- 1/8 teaspoon pepper
- 1 can (6-1/2 ounces) minced clams
- 1 egg
- 3 tablespoons milk
- 1/3 cup diced onion
- Oil for deep-fat frying
- Tartar sauce *and/or* lemon wedges, optional

In a small bowl, combine the flour, baking powder, salt and pepper; set aside. Drain clams, reserving 2 tablespoons juice; set clams aside. In a small bowl, beat the egg, milk and reserved clam juice; stir into dry ingredients just until moistened. Add the clams and onion.

In an electric skillet or deep-fat fryer, heat oil to 375°. Drop batter by tablespoonfuls into oil. Fry for 2-3 minutes, turning occasionally, until golden brown. Drain paper towels. Serve with tartar sauce and/or lemon if desired. **Yield: 14-16 servings.**

Colorful Crab Appetizer Pizza

If you're looking for a really easy and special appetizer, this one stands out. It's a fresh-tasting and lovely variation on a cold vegetable pizza. I make it as a snack for parties all the time and even for a light main dish with a soup or salad.

—Diane Caron, Des Moines, Iowa

- 1 tube (8 ounces) refrigerated crescent rolls
- 1 package (8 ounces) cream cheese, softened
- 1-1/2 cups coarsely chopped fresh spinach, *divided*
- 1 green onion, thinly sliced
- 1-1/2 teaspoons minced fresh dill *or* 1/2 teaspoon dill weed
- 1 teaspoon grated lemon peel, *divided*
- 1/2 teaspoon lemon juice
- 1/8 teaspoon pepper
- 1-1/4 cups chopped imitation crabmeat
- 1/4 cup chopped ripe olives

Unroll the crescent roll dough and place on an ungreased 12-in. pizza pan. Flatten dough, sealing seams and perforations. Bake at 350° for 8-10 minutes or until lightly browned; cool.

In a small mixing bowl, beat cream cheese until smooth. Stir in 1 cup spinach, onion, dill, 1/2 teaspoon lemon peel, lemon juice and pepper. Spread over the crust. Top with the crab, olives and remaining spinach and lemon peel. Cut into bite-size squares. **Yield: 8-10 servings.**

Clam Fritters

Colorful Crab Appetizer Pizza

Marinated Shrimp

Picnic Stuffed Eggs

Marinated Shrimp

Seafood is a staple here in Florida. This recipe is quick and easy to make and can be prepared well in advance. I always seem to get a lot of requests for the recipe when I make it for a party or special occasion.
—Margaret DeLong, Gainesville, Florida

- 2 pounds cooked medium shrimp, peeled and deveined
- 1 medium red onion, cut into rings
- 2 medium lemons, cut into slices
- 1 cup pitted ripe olives, drained
- 1/2 cup olive oil
- 1/3 cup minced fresh parsley
- 3 tablespoons lemon juice
- 3 tablespoons red wine vinegar
- 1 garlic clove, minced
- 1 bay leaf
- 1 tablespoon minced fresh basil *or* 1 teaspoon dried basil
- 1 teaspoon salt
- 1 teaspoon ground mustard
- 1/4 teaspoon pepper

In a 3-qt. glass serving bowl, combine the shrimp, onion, lemons and olives. In a jar with a tight-fitting lid, combine the remaining ingredients; shake well. Pour over shrimp mixture and stir gently to coat.

Cover and refrigerate for 24 hours, stirring occasionally. Discard bay leaf before serving. **Yield: 14 servings.**

Picnic Stuffed Eggs

My dad loves these stuffed eggs, which are a Southern favorite. I've been cooking since I became a teenager, and this is one of my original recipes.
—Rebecca Register, Tallahassee, Florida

- 12 hard-cooked eggs
- 1/2 cup mayonnaise
- 1/4 cup sweet pickle relish, drained
- 1 tablespoon honey mustard
- 1 teaspoon garlic salt
- 1/2 teaspoon Worcestershire sauce
- 1/4 teaspoon pepper
- Fresh parsley sprigs, optional

Slice eggs in half lengthwise; remove yolks and set whites aside. In a small bowl, mash yolks with a fork. Add the mayonnaise, pickle relish, mustard, garlic salt, Worcestershire sauce and pepper; mix well.

Stuff or pipe into the egg whites. Refrigerate until serving. Garnish with parsley if desired. **Yield: 2 dozen.**

Mozzarella Sticks

I'm fond of these tasty snacks because they're baked, not fried. Cheese is one of my family's favorite foods. Being of Italian descent, I often use ricotta and mozzarella cheeses.
—Mary Merchant, Barre, Vermont

- 2 eggs
- 1 tablespoon water

Mozzarella Sticks

- 1 cup dry bread crumbs
- 2-1/2 teaspoons Italian seasoning
- 1/2 teaspoon garlic powder
- 1/8 teaspoon pepper
- 12 sticks string cheese
- 3 tablespoons all-purpose flour
- 1 tablespoon butter, melted
- 1 cup marinara *or* spaghetti sauce, heated

In a small bowl, beat eggs and water. In a plastic bag, combine the bread crumbs, Italian seasoning, garlic powder and pepper. Coat cheese sticks in flour, dip in egg mixture, then coat with bread crumb mixture. Repeat egg and bread crumb coatings. Cover and chill for at least 4 hours or overnight.

Place on an ungreased baking sheet; drizzle with butter. Bake, uncovered, at 400° for 6-8 minutes or until heated through. Let stand for 3-5 minutes before serving. Serve with marinara or spaghetti sauce for dipping. **Yield: 4-6 servings.**

Editor's Note: Regular mozzarella cheese, cut into 4-in. x 1/2-in. sticks, can be substituted for the string cheese.

Country Cheese Snacks

Country Cheese Snacks

This is one of my favorite appetizers for family and friends. They take just minutes to prepare.
—Sandy Thorn, Sonora, California

- 1 cup mayonnaise
- 1 cup grated Parmesan cheese
- 1 package (8 ounces) cream cheese, softened
- 2 green onions with tops, minced

Snack-size rye bread slices *or* toasted English muffins *or* bagels

Parsley sprigs

Stuffed green olives, sliced

In a small bowl, combine the mayonnaise, Parmesan cheese, cream cheese and green onions. Spread on bread; place on a baking sheet.

Broil 4 in. from the heat until golden and bubbly, about 1-2 minutes. Garnish with parsley and olives. Serve immediately. **Yield: 2 cups spread.**

Garden Focaccia

Frozen bread dough is the convenient base for this herb-flavored flat Italian bread. These savory slices are a super appetizer at a summer gathering. It's a fun and delicious way to use up abundant garden tomatoes and fresh zucchini.
—Mary Ann Ludwig, Edwardsville, Illinois

- 1 loaf (1 pound) frozen bread dough, thawed
- 1 tablespoon olive oil
- 1 tablespoon minced fresh rosemary *or* 1 teaspoon dried rosemary, crushed
- 1 tablespoon minced fresh thyme *or* 1 teaspoon dried thyme
- 1 package (8 ounces) cream cheese, softened
- 1/4 cup finely chopped onion
- 1 garlic clove, minced
- 4 large fresh mushrooms, sliced
- 3 medium tomatoes, sliced
- 1 small zucchini, thinly sliced
- 1/4 cup grated Parmesan cheese

On a lightly floured surface, roll dough into a 15-in. x 10-in. rectangle. Place in a greased 15-in. x 10-in. x 1-in. baking pan. Cover and let rise for 30 minutes.

Using your fingertips, press indentations in the dough. Brush with oil; sprinkle with rosemary and thyme. Bake at 400° for 12-15 minutes or until golden brown. Cool slightly.

In a small mixing bowl, combine the cream cheese, onion and garlic. Spread over crust. Top with the mushrooms, tomatoes and zucchini; sprinkle with Parmesan cheese. Bake 12-15 minutes longer or until lightly browned. Cool for 5 minutes before cutting. **Yield: 20 slices.**

Feta Bruschetta

You won't believe the compliments you'll receive when you greet guests with these warm appetizers. Each crispy bite offers the savory tastes of feta cheese, tomato, basil and garlic. They're terrific for holiday parties or most any gathering.

—Stacey Rinehart, Eugene, Oregon

- 1/4 cup butter, melted
- 1/4 cup olive oil
- 10 slices French bread (1 inch thick)
- 1 package (4 ounces) crumbled feta cheese
- 2 to 3 garlic cloves, minced
- 1 tablespoon minced fresh basil *or* 1 teaspoon dried basil
- 1 large tomato, seeded and chopped

In a small bowl, combine butter and oil; brush onto both sides of bread. Place on a baking sheet. Bake at 350° for 8-10 minutes or until lightly browned on top.

Combine the feta cheese, garlic and basil; sprinkle over toast. Top with tomato. Bake 8-10 minutes longer or until heated through. Serve warm. **Yield: 10 appetizers.**

Feta Bruschetta

Garden Focaccia

Taco Tater Skins

Cheesy Asparagus Bites

Taco Tater Skins

My family often makes a meal out of these skins. But they're also great for parties as appetizers.
—Phyllis Douglas, Fairview, Michigan

- **6 large russet potatoes**
- **1/2 cup butter, melted**
- **2 tablespoons taco seasoning**
- **1 cup (4 ounces) shredded cheddar cheese**
- **15 bacon strips, cooked and crumbled**
- **3 green onions, chopped**

Salsa *and/or* sour cream, optional

Bake the potatoes at 375° for 1 hour or until tender. Reduce heat to 350°. When cool enough to handle, cut the potatoes lengthwise into quarters. Scoop out pulp, leaving a 1/4-in. shell (save pulp for another use).

Combine the butter and taco seasoning; brush over both sides of potato skins. Place skin side down on a greased baking sheet. Sprinkle with cheese, bacon and onions.

Bake for 5-10 minutes or until the cheese is melted. Serve with salsa and/or sour cream if desired. **Yield: 2 dozen.**

Cheesy Asparagus Bites

When I managed a cafeteria, I would cook up snacks for the staff. These tiny squares with a big asparagus flavor never lasted long and prompted lots of recipe requests. —*Lois McAtee, Oceanside, California*

- 1/2 cup diced onion
- 1 garlic clove, minced
- 2 tablespoons vegetable oil
- 2 cups (8 ounces) shredded sharp cheddar cheese
- 1/4 cup dry bread crumbs
- 2 tablespoons minced fresh parsley
- 1/4 teaspoon salt
- 1/4 teaspoon pepper
- 1/8 to 1/4 teaspoon dried oregano
- 1/8 teaspoon hot pepper sauce
- 4 eggs, beaten
- 1 pound fresh asparagus, trimmed and cut into 1/2-inch pieces

In a skillet, saute onion and garlic in oil until tender. Combine cheese, bread crumbs, parsley, salt, pepper, oregano and hot pepper sauce. Stir in the onion mixture and eggs.

Place 1/2 in. of water in a large saucepan; add asparagus. Bring to a boil. Reduce heat; cover and simmer for 3-5 minutes or until crisp-tender. Drain well. Stir into cheese mixture. Pour into a greased 9-in. square baking pan.

Bake at 350° for 30 minutes or until a knife inserted near the center comes out clean. Let stand for 15 minutes. Cut into small squares; serve warm. **Yield: 5 dozen.**

Jalapeno Pepper Appetizers

Jalapeno Pepper Appetizers

These appetizers are so easy to make and they taste so good. I have to warn you that eating them is habit-forming! —*Peggy Roberts, Lockney, Texas*

- 10 medium fresh jalapeno peppers
- 4 ounces cream cheese, softened
- 10 bacon strips, halved

Cut peppers in half lengthwise; remove seeds, stems and center membrane. Stuff each half with about 2 teaspoons of cream cheese. Wrap with bacon and secure with toothpick.

Place on a broiler rack coated with nonstick cooking spray. Bake at 350° for 20-25 minutes or until bacon is crisp. Remove toothpicks. Serve immediately. **Yield: 20 appetizers.**

Editor's Note: When cutting or seeding hot peppers, use rubber or plastic gloves to protect your hands. Avoid touching your face.

Sausage-Stuffed Mushrooms

Sausage-Stuffed Mushrooms

Pennsylvania is often referred to as the "Mushroom Capital of the World." This recipe's a delicious appetizer and is always the hit of the party.
—Beatrice Vetrano, Landenberg, Pennsylvania

- 12 to 15 large fresh mushrooms
- 2 tablespoons butter, *divided*
- 2 tablespoons chopped onion
- 1 tablespoon lemon juice
- 1/4 teaspoon dried basil

Salt and pepper to taste

- 4 ounces bulk Italian sausage
- 1 tablespoon chopped fresh parsley
- 2 tablespoons dry bread crumbs
- 2 tablespoons grated Parmesan cheese

Remove stems from the mushrooms. Chop stems finely; reserve caps. Place stems in paper towel and squeeze to remove any liquid.

In a skillet, heat 1-1/2 tablespoons butter. Cook stems and onion until soft. Add the lemon juice, basil, salt and pepper; cook until almost all the liquid has evaporated. Cool.

Combine mushroom mixture with sausage and parsley. Stuff into mushroom caps. Combine the crumbs and cheese; sprinkle over stuffed mushrooms. Dot each with remaining butter.

Place in a greased baking pan. Bake, uncovered, at 400° for 20 minutes. Baste occasionally with pan juices. Serve hot. **Yield: 12-15 servings.**

Spinach Turnovers

The flaky cream cheese pastry adds sensational texture to these hot appetizers—and just wait until you taste the wonderful filling. I usually fix a double batch and freeze some to have on hand in case unexpected guests drop by.
—Jean von Bereghy, Oconomowoc, Wisconsin

- 2 packages (8 ounces *each*) cream cheese, softened
- 3/4 cup butter, softened
- 2-1/2 cups all-purpose flour
- 1/2 teaspoon salt

FILLING:

- 5 bacon strips, diced
- 1/4 cup finely chopped onion
- 2 garlic cloves, minced
- 1 package (10 ounces) frozen chopped spinach, thawed and well drained
- 1 cup small-curd cottage cheese
- 1/4 teaspoon salt
- 1/4 teaspoon pepper
- 1/8 teaspoon ground nutmeg
- 1 egg, beaten

Salsa, optional

In a mixing bowl, beat cream cheese and butter until smooth. Combine flour and salt; gradually add to creamed mixture (dough will be stiff). Turn onto a floured surface; gently knead 10 times. Cover and refrigerate at least 2 hours.

In a skillet, cook bacon over medium heat until crisp. Using a slotted spoon, remove bacon to paper towels to drain, reserving 1 tablespoon drippings. Saute onion and garlic in drippings until tender. Remove from the heat; stir in the spinach, cottage cheese, seasonings and reserved bacon. Cool.

On a lightly floured surface, roll dough to 1/8-in. thickness. Cut into 3-in. circles; brush edges with egg. Place 1 heaping teaspoon of filling on each circle. Fold over; seal edges. Prick tops with a fork. Brush with egg.

Place 1 in. apart on a greased baking sheet. Bake at 400° for 10-12 minutes or until golden brown. Serve with salsa if desired. **Yield: about 4 dozen.**

Toasted Zucchini Snacks

I added green pepper to this recipe I got years ago from a friend. I prepared this rich snack for company when zucchini is plentiful. Everyone seems to enjoy it—even those who say they don't care for zucchini.
—Jane Bone, Cape Coral, Florida

- 2 cups shredded zucchini
- 1 teaspoon salt
- 1/2 cup mayonnaise
- 1/2 cup plain yogurt
- 1/4 cup grated Parmesan cheese
- 1/4 cup finely chopped green pepper
- 4 green onions, thinly sliced
- 1 garlic clove, minced
- 1 teaspoon Worcestershire sauce
- 1/4 teaspoon hot pepper sauce
- 36 slices snack rye bread

In a small bowl, toss the zucchini and salt; let stand for 1 hour. Rinse and drain, pressing out excess liquid. Add the mayonnaise, yogurt, Parmesan cheese, pepper, onions, garlic, Worcestershire and hot pepper sauce; mix well.

Spread a rounded teaspoonful on each slice of bread; place on a baking sheet. Bake at 375° for 10-12 minutes or until bubbly. Serve warm. **Yield: 3 dozen.**

Toasted Zucchini Snacks

Spinach Turnovers

Apricot Wraps

Cucumber Party Sandwiches

Apricot Wraps

I accumulated a large recipe collection from around the world while my husband served in the Air Force for 25 years. This mouth-watering appetizer is one of our favorites, and we enjoy sharing it with friends.
—Jane Ashworth, Beavercreek, Ohio

- 1 package (14 ounces) dried apricots
- 1/2 cup whole almonds
- 1 pound sliced bacon
- 1/4 cup plum *or* apple jelly
- 2 tablespoons soy sauce

Fold each apricot around an almond. Cut bacon strips into thirds; wrap a strip around each apricot and secure with a toothpick.

Place on two ungreased 15-in. x 10-in. x 1-in. baking pans. Bake, uncovered, at 375° for 25 minutes or until bacon is crisp, turning once.

In a small saucepan, combine jelly and soy sauce; cook and stir over low heat for 5 minutes or until warmed and smooth.

Remove apricots to paper towels; drain. Serve with sauce for dipping. **Yield: about 4-1/2 dozen.**

Cucumber Party Sandwiches

This is one of my favorite appetizers. We have lots of pig roasts in Kentucky, and these small sandwiches are perfect to serve while the pig is roasting.
—Rebecca Rose, Mt. Washington, Kentucky

- 1 package (8 ounces) cream cheese, softened
- 1/2 envelope (2 teaspoons) dry Italian salad dressing mix
- 2 tablespoons mayonnaise
- 30 slices snack rye bread
- 30 thin slices cucumber
- Fresh dill sprigs

In a small bowl, combine the cream cheese, dressing mix and mayonnaise. Let stand for at least 30 minutes.

Spread on rye bread. Top with a slice of cucumber and a sprig of dill. Cover and refrigerate until serving time. **Yield: 30 appetizers.**

Fried Onion Rings

Here's a yummy snack that's also a great side dish. Try it as an accompaniment to hamburgers or fried fish, or with steaks on the grill. The recipe's from my mom, and it's one of her most popular.
—Marsha Moore, Poplar Bluff, Missouri

- 2 large sweet onions
- 1 egg, lightly beaten
- 2/3 cup water
- 1 tablespoon vegetable oil
- 1 teaspoon lemon juice

Fried Onion Rings

- 1 cup all-purpose flour
- 1-1/2 teaspoons baking powder
- 1 to 1-1/4 teaspoons salt
- 1/8 to 1/4 teaspoon cayenne pepper
- Oil for deep-fat frying

Cut onions into 1/2-in. slices; separate into rings. Place in a bowl; cover with ice water and soak for 30 minutes.

Meanwhile, combine the egg, water, oil and lemon juice in a bowl; mix well. Combine the flour, baking powder, salt and cayenne; stir into egg mixture until smooth.

Drain onion rings; dip into batter. In an electric skillet or deep-fat fryer, heat 1 in. of oil to 375°. Fry onion rings, a few at a time, for 1 to 1-1/2 minutes per side or until golden brown. Drain on paper towels. **Yield: 4-6 servings.**

Editor's Note: Onion rings may be kept warm in a 200° oven while frying remainder of batch.

Mushroom Bacon Bites

Mushroom Bacon Bites

This is the perfect appetizer for most any occasion. The tasty bites are easy to assemble and brush with prepared barbecue sauce. When we have a big cookout, they're always a hit, but they make a nice little "extra" for a family dinner, too.
—Gina Roesner, Ashland, Missouri

- 24 medium fresh mushrooms
- 12 bacon strips, halved
- 1 cup barbecue sauce

Wrap each mushroom with a piece of bacon; secure with a toothpick. Thread onto metal or soaked bamboo skewers; brush with barbecue sauce.

Grill, uncovered, over indirect medium heat for 10-15 minutes or until the bacon is crisp and the mushrooms are tender, turning and basting occasionally with remaining barbecue sauce. **Yield: 2 dozen.**

Cheddar Bacon Dip

Both children and adults enjoy this dip. I like it, too—it's so quick to prepare. I make it for special occasions.
—Carol Werkman, Neerlandia, Alberta

- 1 package (8 ounces) cream cheese, softened
- 1 cup (8 ounces) sour cream
- 5 green onions, thinly sliced
- 4 medium tomatoes, chopped
- 1 large green pepper, chopped
- 1 jar (16 ounces) taco sauce
- 2 cups (8 ounces) shredded cheddar cheese
- 1 pound sliced bacon, cooked and crumbled

Tortilla *or* taco chips

In a mixing bowl, beat cream cheese and sour cream. Spread in an ungreased 13-in. x 9-in. x 2-in. dish or on a 12-in. plate. Combine onions, tomatoes and green pepper; sprinkle over the cream cheese layer.

Pour taco sauce over the vegetables. Sprinkle with cheddar cheese. Refrigerate. Just before serving, sprinkle with bacon. Serve with tortilla or taco chips. **Yield: 10-12 servings.**

Hot Kielbasa Dip

I like to look for simple, speedy ways to cook. This thick cheesy dip, with the unusual addition of sausage, goes together in a jiffy. Accompanied by crackers or fresh veggies, it's a hearty appetizer for a football party or family gathering.
—Mary Bondegard, Brooksville, Florida

- 1 package (8 ounces) cream cheese
- 1/2 cup sour cream
- 1/3 cup milk
- 1 tablespoon mayonnaise
- 1/2 teaspoon Worcestershire sauce
- 1/2 pound fully cooked kielbasa *or* Polish sausage, finely chopped

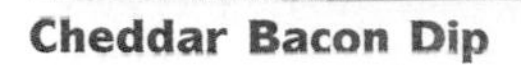

Cheddar Bacon Dip

1/2 cup sliced green onions, *divided*

1/4 cup grated Parmesan cheese

Assorted crackers *or* raw vegetables

In a 1-1/2-qt. microwave-safe bowl, heat the cream cheese, uncovered, on high for 1 minute. Stir in sour cream, milk, mayonnaise and Worcestershire sauce. Add kielbasa, 1/4 cup onions and Parmesan cheese; mix well.

Microwave, uncovered, on high for 3-4 minutes or until heated through, stirring once. Sprinkle with remaining onions. Serve with crackers or vegetables. Store in the refrigerator. **Yield: about 3 cups.**

Editor's Note: This recipe was tested with an 850-watt microwave.

Hot Kielbasa Dip

Creamy Caramel Dip

Hot Macadamia Spread

Creamy Caramel Dip

Because I feed three hungry "men" (my husband and our two boys), I love satisfying snacks that are easy to make like this dip. We sure appreciate this cool, light treat in the summertime.
—Karen Laubman, Spruce Grove, Alberta

- 1 package (8 ounces) cream cheese, softened
- 3/4 cup packed brown sugar
- 1 cup (8 ounces) sour cream
- 2 teaspoons vanilla extract
- 2 teaspoons lemon juice
- 1 cup cold milk
- 1 package (3.4 ounces) instant vanilla pudding mix
- Assorted fresh fruit

In a large mixing bowl, beat cream cheese and brown sugar until smooth. Add the sour cream, vanilla, lemon juice, milk and pudding mix, beating well after each addition.

Cover and refrigerate for at least 1 hour. Serve as a dip for fruit. **Yield: 3-1/2 cups.**

Creamy Crab Cheesecake

Hot Macadamia Spread

While my husband was in the Army, I'd get together with other wives for snacks and to exchange favorite recipes. I still enjoy serving this rich spread because most guests can't quite put their finger on the zippy ingredient—horseradish.

—Naomi Francis, Waukesha, Wisconsin

- 1 package (8 ounces) cream cheese, softened
- 2 tablespoons milk
- 1/2 cup sour cream
- 2 teaspoons prepared horseradish
- 1/4 cup finely chopped green pepper
- 1 green onion, chopped
- 1/2 teaspoon garlic salt
- 1/4 teaspoon pepper
- 1/2 cup chopped macadamia nuts *or* blanched almonds
- 2 teaspoons butter

Assorted crackers

In a small mixing bowl, beat cream cheese and milk until smooth. Stir in the sour cream, horseradish, green pepper, onion, garlic salt and pepper. Spoon into an ungreased shallow 2-cup baking dish; set aside.

In a small skillet, saute the nuts in butter for 3-4 minutes or until lightly browned. Sprinkle over the cream cheese mixture.

Bake, uncovered, at 350° for 20 minutes. Serve with crackers. **Yield: 6-8 servings.**

Creamy Crab Cheesecake

A savory appetizer cheesecake such as this one is sure to grab the attention and tempt the taste buds of party guests. It's an elegant spread that you make ahead, so there's no last-minute fuss.

—Cathy Sarrels, Tucson, Arizona

- 1 cup crushed butter-flavored crackers (about 25 crackers)
- 3 tablespoons butter, melted
- 2 packages (8 ounces *each*) cream cheese, softened
- 3/4 cup sour cream, *divided*
- 3 eggs
- 2 teaspoons grated onion
- 1 teaspoon lemon juice
- 1/4 teaspoon seafood seasoning
- 2 drops hot pepper sauce
- 1/8 teaspoon pepper
- 1 cup crabmeat, drained, flaked and cartilage removed

Additional seafood seasoning, optional

In a small bowl, combine cracker crumbs and butter. Press onto the bottom of the greased 9-in. springform pan. Bake at 350° for 10 minutes. Cool on a wire rack. Reduce heat to 325°.

In a mixing bowl, beat cream cheese and 1/4 cup sour cream until smooth. Add eggs; beat on low just until combined. Add the onion, lemon juice, seafood seasoning, hot pepper sauce and pepper; beat just until blended. Fold in crab. Pour over crust. Bake for 35-40 minutes or until center is almost set.

Cool on a wire rack for 10 minutes. Carefully run a knife around edge of pan to loosen. Cool 1 hour longer. Spread remaining sour cream over top. Refrigerate overnight.

Remove sides of pan. Let stand at room temperature for 30 minutes before serving. Sprinkle with seafood seasoning if desired. **Yield: 20-24 appetizer servings.**

Taco Joe Dip

Taco Joe Dip

This recipe was given to us by our daughter. My husband and I love it. Because it's made in a slow cooker, it's great for parties or busy days.
—Lang Secrest, Sierra Vista, Arizona

- 1 can (16 ounces) kidney beans, rinsed and drained
- 1 can (15-1/4 ounces) whole kernel corn, drained
- 1 can (15 ounces) black beans, rinsed and drained
- 1 can (14-1/2 ounces) stewed tomatoes
- 1 can (8 ounces) tomato sauce
- 1 can (4 ounces) chopped green chilies, drained
- 1 envelope taco seasoning
- 1/2 cup chopped onion
- Tortilla chips

In a 3-qt. slow cooker, combine the first eight ingredients. Cover and cook on low for 5-7 hours. Serve with tortilla chips. **Yield: about 7 cups.**

Editor's Note: To make Taco Joe Soup, add a 29-ounce can of tomato sauce to the slow cooker. **Yield: 6-8 servings.**

Corn and Bacon Dip

More than 20 years ago, a friend gave me the recipe for this creamy appetizer or snack dip. It becomes a favorite wherever I share it. People are constantly asking me for the recipe. Sometimes, I simply serve it with corn chips.
—Carolyn Zaschak, Corning, New York

- 1 package (8 ounces) cream cheese, softened
- 1 cup (8 ounces) sour cream
- 1/4 cup mayonnaise
- 2 garlic cloves, minced
- 1/4 teaspoon hot pepper sauce
- 1 can (15-1/4 ounces) whole kernel corn, drained
- 8 bacon strips, cooked and crumbled
- Assorted raw vegetables *and/or* crackers

In a small mixing bowl, combine the cream cheese, sour cream, mayonnaise, garlic and hot pepper sauce. Stir in corn and bacon. Cover and refrigerate for several hours. Serve with vegetables and/or crackers. **Yield: 3 cups.**

Three-in-One Cheese Ball

Every Christmas, I make these cheese balls for our get-together. They aren't only for the holidays, however. You'll find they freeze well and will last for a week in the refrigerator. I have even re-formed leftovers into smaller balls for snacks.
—Mary Anne Marston, Almonte, Ontario

- 4 cups (16 ounces) shredded cheddar cheese
- 1 package (8 ounces) cream cheese, softened
- 2 tablespoons milk
- 2 tablespoons minced onion
- 2 tablespoons Worcestershire sauce
- Coarsely cracked black pepper
- 1/2 cup (2 ounces) crumbled blue cheese
- Minced fresh parsley

Corn and Bacon Dip

1/4 teaspoon garlic powder
Finely chopped pecans
Assorted crackers

Place the cheddar cheese in a large mixing bowl and let stand at room temperature for 30 minutes. Add the cream cheese, milk, onion and Worcestershire sauce; beat until mixture is fluffy. If a smoother spread is desired, process in a food processor until creamy.

Divide into thirds (about 1 cup each). Shape first portion into a ball; roll in cracked pepper. Add the blue cheese to the second portion; mix well. Shape into a ball; roll in parsley. Add garlic powder to the remaining portion; mix well. Shape into a ball; roll in nuts.

Cover and refrigerate. Let stand at room temperature 30 minutes before serving. Serve with crackers. **Yield:** 3 cheese balls.

Three-in-One Cheese Ball

Beefy Taco Dip

Salmon Cheese Spread

Beefy Taco Dip

This taco dip is a combination of several different recipes I received from friends. I experimented until I came up with my favorite! It's always a hit wherever I bring it. —*Faye Parker, Bedford, Nova Scotia*

- 1 package (8 ounces) cream cheese, softened
- 1 cup (8 ounces) sour cream
- 3/4 cup mayonnaise
- 1 pound ground beef
- 1 envelope taco seasoning
- 1 can (8 ounces) tomato sauce
- 2 cups (8 ounces) shredded cheddar *or* taco cheese
- 4 cups shredded lettuce

2 medium tomatoes, diced
1 small onion, diced
1 medium green pepper, diced
Tortilla chips

In a small mixing bowl, beat the cream cheese, sour cream and mayonnaise until smooth. Spread on a 12- to 14-in. pizza pan or serving dish. Refrigerate for 1 hour.

In a saucepan over medium heat, cook beef over medium heat until no longer pink; drain. Add taco seasoning and tomato sauce; cook and stir for 5 minutes. Cool completely. Spread over cream cheese layer. Cover and refrigerate.

Just before serving, sprinkle with cheese, lettuce, tomatoes, onion and green pepper. Serve with chips. **Yield: 16-20 servings.**

Salmon Cheese Spread

Here's a delightful hors d'oeuvre that's excellent for any occasion. The combination of salmon, cream cheese and curry powder gives it terrific flavor.
—Raymonde Bernier, St. Hyacinthe, Quebec

2 packages (3 ounces *each*) cream cheese, softened
3 tablespoons mayonnaise
1 tablespoon lemon juice
1/2 teaspoon salt
1/2 teaspoon curry powder
1/4 teaspoon dried basil
1/8 teaspoon pepper
1 can (7-1/2 ounces) salmon, drained, bones and skin removed
2 green onions, thinly sliced
Crackers

In a small mixing bowl, combine the cream cheese, mayonnaise and lemon juice. Add the salt, curry powder, basil and pepper; mix well. Gently stir in salmon and onions. Cover and refrigerate for at least 1 hour. Serve with crackers. **Yield: 1-1/2 cups.**

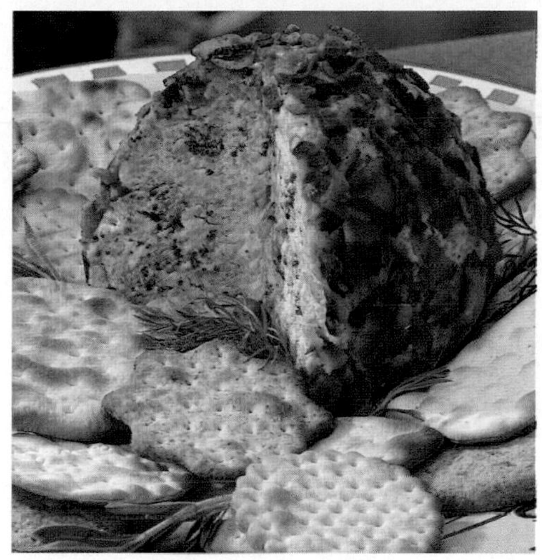

Bacon-Broccoli Cheese Ball

Bacon-Broccoli Cheese Ball

Needing a quick appetizer one night when dinner was running late, I combined a few leftovers into this easy cheese ball. For variety, you can shape it into a log, or substitute your favorite herbs for the pepper.
—Tamara Rickard, Bartlett, Tennessee

1 package (8 ounces) cream cheese, softened
1 cup (4 ounces) finely shredded cheddar cheese
1/2 teaspoon pepper
1 cup finely chopped broccoli florets
6 bacon strips, cooked and crumbled
Assorted crackers

In a mixing bowl, beat cream cheese, cheddar cheese and pepper until blended. Stir in broccoli. Shape into a ball and roll in bacon. Cover and refrigerate.

Remove from refrigerator 15 minutes before serving. Serve with crackers. **Yield: 2-1/2 cups.**

Festive Appetizer Spread

Festive Appetizer Spread

Our state is known for its cranberries, and there are many bogs in our area. I won first place with this recipe in a contest sponsored by our local newspaper.
—Edith Howe, Woburn, Massachusetts

- 1 cup water
- 1 cup sugar
- 1 package (12 ounces) fresh *or* frozen cranberries
- 1/2 cup apricot preserves
- 2 tablespoons lemon juice
- 1/3 cup slivered almonds, toasted
- 1 package (8 ounces) cream cheese

Assorted crackers

In a saucepan, bring water and sugar to a boil over medium heat without stirring; boil for 5 minutes. Add cranberries, cook for 10-15 minutes or until berries pop and sauce is thickened. Remove from the heat.

Cut apricots in the preserves into small pieces; add to cranberry mixture. Stir in lemon juice. Cool. Add almonds.

Spoon over cream cheese; serve with crackers. Store leftovers in the refrigerator. **Yield: about 3 cups.**

Editor's Note: This sauce may also be served as an accompaniment to poultry or pork.

Avocado Salsa

When I found this recipe, I was planning a party and thought it might be a fun, different salsa to set out with chips. It was an absolute success. People love the garlic, corn and avocado combination.
—Susan Vandermeer, Ogden, Utah

- 1-2/3 cups frozen corn, thawed
- 2 cans (2-1/4 ounces *each*) sliced ripe olives, drained
- 1 medium sweet red pepper, chopped
- 1 small onion, chopped
- 5 garlic cloves, minced
- 1/3 cup olive oil
- 1/4 cup lemon juice
- 3 tablespoons cider vinegar
- 1 teaspoon dried oregano
- 1/2 teaspoon salt
- 1/2 teaspoon pepper
- 4 medium ripe avocado, peeled

Tortilla chips

In a large bowl, combine the corn, olives, red pepper and onion. In a small bowl, combine the garlic, oil, lemon juice, vinegar, oregano, salt and pepper. Pour over corn mixture and toss to coat. Cover and refrigerate overnight.

Just before serving, chop avocados and stir into salsa. Serve with tortilla chips. **Yield: about 7 cups.**

Four-Tomato Salsa

A variety of tomatoes, onions and peppers makes this chunky salsa so good. Whenever I try to take a batch to a get-together, it's hard to keep my family from finishing it off first! It's a super snack with tortilla chips.
—Connie Siese, Wayne, Michigan

- 7 plum tomatoes, chopped
- 7 medium tomatoes, chopped
- 3 medium yellow tomatoes, chopped
- 3 medium orange tomatoes, chopped

Avocado Salsa

1 teaspoon salt
2 tablespoons lime juice
2 tablespoons olive oil
1 medium white onion, chopped
2/3 cup chopped red onion
2 green onions, chopped
1/2 cup *each* chopped sweet red, orange, yellow and green pepper
3 pepperoncinis, chopped
3 pickled sweet banana wax peppers, chopped
1/2 cup minced fresh parsley
2 tablespoons minced fresh cilantro
1 tablespoon dried chervil
Tortilla chips

In a colander, combine tomatoes and salt. Let drain for 10 minutes. Transfer to a large bowl.

Stir in lime juice, oil, onions, peppers, parsley, cilantro and chervil. Serve with tortilla chips. Refrigerate or freeze leftovers. **Yield: 14 cups.**

Editor's Note: Look for pepperoncinis (pickled peppers) in the pickle and olive section of your grocery store.

Four-Tomato Salsa

Ranch Snack Mix

Popcorn Caramel Crunch

Ranch Snack Mix

This is a wonderful, fast-to-fix munchie. The recipe makes a generous 24 cups and doesn't involve any cooking. It's a cinch to package in individual snack bags, keeps its crunch and is a savory alternative to the cakes and pies usually offered at bake sales.
—Linda Murphy, Pulaski, Wisconsin

- 1 package (12 ounces) miniature pretzels
- 2 packages (6 ounces *each*) Bugles
- 1 can (10 ounces) salted cashews
- 1 package (6 ounces) bite-size cheddar cheese fish crackers
- 1 envelope ranch salad dressing mix
- 3/4 cup vegetable oil

In two large bowls, combine the pretzels, Bugles, cashews and crackers. Sprinkle with

Sugar 'n' Spice Nuts

dressing mix; toss gently to combine. Drizzle with oil; toss until well coated. Store in airtight containers. **Yield: 6 quarts.**

Popcorn Caramel Crunch

For munching or gift-giving, this popcorn snack is chock-full of goodies. Store in airtight containers to keep the popcorn crisp.
—Lucille Hermsmeyer, Scotia, Nebraska

- 4 cups popped popcorn
- 1 cup dry roasted peanuts
- 1 cup chow mein noodles
- 1/2 cup raisins
- 1 cup sugar
- 3/4 cup butter
- 1/2 cup light corn syrup
- 2 tablespoons water
- 1 teaspoon ground cinnamon

In a large greased bowl, combine the popcorn, peanuts, chow mein noodles and raisins. Set aside.

In a large saucepan, combine the sugar, butter, corn syrup and water. Cook over medium heat until mixture reaches soft crack stage (280°-290°) with a candy thermometer, stirring occasionally. Remove from the heat. Stir in cinnamon.

Pour over popcorn mixture; stir until all ingredients are evenly coated. Immediately pour onto a greased 15-in. x 10-in. x 1-in. pan.

When cool enough to handle, break into pieces. Store in covered containers to enjoy later or to give as gifts. **Yield: about 8 cups.**

Editor's Note: We recommend that you test your candy thermometer before each use by bringing water to a boil; the thermometer should read 212°. Adjust your recipe temperature up or down based on your test.

Sugar 'n' Spice Nuts

To tell the truth, I can't recall where I found this recipe. It's been a regular in my holiday baking, though, for many years. Between Thanksgiving and New Year's, I hand these out to almost everybody—even the mailman's been known to find a batch in the mailbox! *—Debbi Baker, Green Springs, Ohio*

- 3 cups lightly salted mixed nuts
- 1 egg white
- 1 tablespoon orange juice
- 2/3 cup sugar
- 1 tablespoon grated orange peel
- 1 teaspoon ground cinnamon
- 1/2 teaspoon ground ginger
- 1/2 teaspoon ground allspice

Place nuts in a large bowl. In a small bowl, beat egg white and orange juice with a fork until foamy. Add the sugar, orange peel, cinnamon, ginger and allspice; mix well. Pour over nuts and stir to coat.

Spread into an ungreased 15-in. x 10-in. x 1-in. baking pan. Bake at 275°, stirring every 15 minutes, for 45-50 minutes or until nuts are crisp and lightly browned.

Cool completely. Store in an airtight container. **Yield: 4 cups.**

Spiced Nut Mix

Spiced Nut Mix

When we were newlyweds, our first Christmas was pretty lean. I usually made presents, but that year I had no idea what I could afford to put together. A good friend gave me a special gift—this recipe and a sack of ingredients. I think of her every time I stir up this mix. —*Patti Holland, Parker, Colorado*

- 3 egg whites
- 2 teaspoons water
- 2 cans (12 ounces *each*) salted peanuts
- 1 cup whole blanched almonds
- 1 cup walnut halves
- 1-3/4 cups sugar
- 3 tablespoons pumpkin pie spice
- 3/4 teaspoon salt
- 1 cup raisins

In a large mixing bowl, beat egg whites and water until foamy. Add nuts; stir gently to coat. Combine the sugar, pie spice and salt; add to nut mixture and stir gently to coat. Fold in raisins. Spread into two greased 15-in. x 10-in. x 1-in. baking pans.

Bake, uncovered, at 300° for 20-25 minutes or until lightly browned, stirring every 10 minutes. Cool. Store in an airtight container. **Yield:** about 10 cups.

Orange Sherbet Party Punch

This punch is always a big hit with everyone. You can make the base for it several days ahead and chill. Before serving, add the sherbet and ginger ale.
—*Lannis Blunk, Mascoutah, Illinois*

- 4 cups water, *divided*
- 1 package (6 ounces) strawberry gelatin
- 1-1/2 cups sugar
- 1 can (46 ounces) pineapple juice
- 1 can (46 ounces) orange juice
- 1 cup lemon juice
- 1/2 gallon orange sherbet, softened
- 1 liter ginger ale, chilled

Heat 2 cups water to boiling; add gelatin and sugar, stirring until dissolved. Add 2 cups cold water and fruit juices. Chill until ready to serve.

Just before serving, spoon in sherbet and pour in ginger ale. Chill with an ice ring. **Yield: 6-1/2 quarts.**

Tangy Fruit Punch

The fruity flavors mingle in this rosy, refreshing punch. Since its versatile, sweet-tart taste goes wonderfully with all kinds of foods, it's a popular beverage for a brunch. —*Ann Cousin, New Braunfels, Texas*

- 1 can (46 ounces) pineapple juice
- 1 can (12 ounces) frozen orange juice concentrate, thawed
- 3/4 cup lemonade concentrate
- 1 cup water, *divided*

Orange Sherbet Party Punch

- 1/2 cup sugar
- 2 large ripe bananas
- 1 package (20 ounces) frozen unsweetened whole strawberries, thawed
- 2 liters ginger ale, chilled

In a punch bowl or large container, combine the pineapple juice, orange juice concentrate, lemonade concentrate, 1/2 cup water and sugar.

In a blender, cover and process the bananas, strawberries and remaining water until smooth. Stir into the juice mixture. Cover and refrigerate. Just before serving, stir in ginger ale. **Yield: 25-30 servings (about 5 quarts).**

Tangy Fruit Punch

Mocha Punch

Spicy Cranberry Warmer

Mocha Punch

I first tried this smooth, creamy punch at a friend's Christmas open house. It was so special and distinctive I didn't leave until I had the recipe. Having a frosty glass of this chocolate punch is almost like sipping a chocolate shake.

—Yvonne Hatfield, Norman, Oklahoma

- 6 cups water
- 1/2 cup instant chocolate drink mix
- 1/2 cup sugar
- 1/4 cup instant coffee granules
- 1/2 gallon vanilla ice cream
- 1/2 gallon chocolate ice cream
- 1 cup heavy whipping cream, whipped

Chocolate curls, optional

In a large saucepan, bring water to a boil. Remove from the heat. Add the drink mix, sugar and coffee; stir until dissolved. Transfer to a large bowl. Cover and refrigerate for 4 hours or overnight.

About 30 minutes before serving, pour mixture into a large punch bowl. Add scoops of ice cream; stir until partially melted. Garnish with dollops of whipped cream and chocolate curls if desired. **Yield: 20-25 servings (about 5 quarts).**

Spicy Cranberry Warmer

This drink tastes great in winter when sitting in front of the fireplace. It warms you up, plus the kitchen smells so good!

—Marlene Cartwright, Sierra City, California

- 3 whole cloves
- 2 cinnamon sticks
- 2 whole allspice
- 4 cups apple cider
- 1/3 cup packed brown sugar
- 4 cups cranberry juice
- Additional cinnamon sticks, optional

Place the first three ingredients in a double thickness of cheesecloth. Bring up corners of cloth and tie with a kitchen string. Place with cider in a large saucepan. (Or, if desired, place loose spices in saucepan and strain before serving.)

Bring to a boil. Reduce heat; cover and simmer for 5 minutes. Stir in sugar and simmer 5 minutes longer. Add cranberry juice and heat through. Serve hot in mugs. Garnish with cinnamon sticks if desired. **Yield: 8-10 servings.**

Two-Fruit Frosty

Two-Fruit Frosty

This is a refreshing and colorful drink to serve for brunch. The cinnamon and nutmeg give it just the right amount of zing.

—Angie Hansen, Gildford, Montana

- 1-1/2 cups fresh *or* frozen blueberries *or* huckleberries
- 1 cup frozen unsweetened sliced peaches, thawed
- 1 cup milk
- 1 cup (8 ounces) vanilla yogurt
- 1/4 to 1/3 cup honey
- 1/2 teaspoon ground cinnamon
- 1/2 teaspoon ground nutmeg
- Cinnamon sticks, optional

In a blender; cover and process the blueberries, peaches and milk until blended. Add yogurt, honey, cinnamon and nutmeg; blend well.

Pour into chilled tall glasses. Garnish with cinnamon sticks if desired. Serve immediately. **Yield: 4 (1-cup) servings.**

Old-Fashioned Strawberry Soda

Old-Fashioned Strawberry Soda

With just a quick pulse of the blender, you will have what I call a refreshing sipper—you'll be asked for more! —*Ginger Hubbard, Anderson, Missouri*

- 1 cup milk
- 1/2 cup fresh *or* frozen strawberries
- 1/2 cup vanilla ice cream, softened
- 2 tablespoons sugar
- 2 to 3 drops red food coloring, optional
- 1 cup ginger ale, chilled

In a blender container, combine the milk, strawberries, ice cream, sugar and food coloring if desired; cover and process until smooth.

Pour into two tall glasses. Add ginger ale and serve immediately. **Yield: 2 servings.**

Orange Lemonade

I was looking for a way to sweeten lemonade without using more sugar when I came up with the recipe. I make it more often in summer, but we enjoy it year-round. —*Wendy Masters, Grand Valley, Ontario*

- 1-3/4 cups sugar
- 2-1/2 cups water
- 1-1/2 cups fresh lemon juice (about 8 lemons)
- 1-1/2 cups fresh orange juice (about 5 oranges)
- 2 tablespoons grated lemon peel
- 2 tablespoons grated orange peel
- Water

In a medium saucepan, combine sugar and water. Cook over medium heat until sugar is dissolved, stirring occasionally. Cool.

Add juices and peels to cooled sugar syrup. Cover and let stand at room temperature for 1 hour. Strain syrup; cover and refrigerate.

To serve, fill glasses or pitcher with equal amounts of fruit syrup and water. Add ice and serve. **Yield: 12 servings.**

Orange Lemonade

SALADS

ORTELLINI CAESAR SALAD, pg. 59

Salads

Grilled Chicken Pasta Salad

During the summer, my family often requests this dish. Simply add garlic bread for a great meal. It's wonderful, too, for a picnic or any gathering.
—Lori Thon, Basin, Wyoming

- 1-1/2 cups Italian salad dressing
- 1/2 cup cider vinegar
- 1/3 cup honey
- 2 teaspoons dried oregano
- 1 teaspoon dried basil
- 1/2 teaspoon pepper
- 6 boneless skinless chicken breast halves (4 ounces *each*)
- 1 package (12 ounces) fettuccine
- 1-1/2 cups broccoli florets
- 3 medium carrots, thinly sliced
- 2 celery ribs, thinly sliced
- 1 cup chopped green pepper
- 2 cans (2-1/4 ounces *each*) sliced ripe olives, drained

DRESSING:

- 1-1/2 cups Italian salad dressing
- 1 teaspoon garlic salt
- 1 teaspoon dried oregano
- 1 teaspoon Italian seasoning

In a large resealable plastic bag, combine the first six ingredients. Cut each chicken breast into four strips; add to dressing mixture. Seal bag and turn to coat; refrigerate for 2-3 hours.

Drain and discard marinade. Grill chicken, uncovered, over medium heat for 4-5 minutes on each side or until juices run clear.

Grilled Chicken Pasta Salad

Meanwhile, cook fettuccine according to package directions; drain and cool. Cut chicken into bite-size pieces; set aside. In a large bowl, combine the vegetables, olives and fettuccine. Combine dressing ingredients in a jar with a tight-fitting lid; shake well. Pour over salad and toss to coat. Top with chicken. **Yield: 6 servings.**

Lemony Chicken Fruit Salad

Lemony Chicken Fruit Salad

Back in the 1950s, I was a home economist for the electric company, which is how I came across this recipe. During spring and summer, when it is hot here, my family especially likes it. I've also found this chicken salad is good for women's luncheons and covered-plate meals since it's so different.
—Johnece Stuard, Mansfield, Texas

- 2 cans (8 ounces *each*) pineapple chunks
- 1 medium apple, diced
- 3 cups cubed cooked chicken
- 1 cup seedless grapes, halved
- 3 tablespoons butter
- 3 tablespoons all-purpose flour
- 1/4 cup sugar
- 1 teaspoon salt
- 1/2 cup lemon juice
- 2 egg yolks, lightly beaten
- 1/2 cup heavy whipping cream
- Lettuce leaves
- 1/2 cup slivered almonds, toasted

Drain pineapple, reserving the juice. Set aside pineapple and 1/2 cup juice. Toss remaining juice with apple; drain. In a large bowl, combine the chicken, grapes, pineapple and apple. Cover and refrigerate.

In a saucepan, melt butter. Stir in the flour, sugar and salt until smooth; gradually add lemon juice and the reserved pineapple juice. Cook and stir over medium-high heat until thickened and bubbly. Reduce heat; cook and stir 2 minutes longer. Remove from the heat. Stir a small amount of hot filling into egg yolks; return all to pan, stirring constantly. Bring to a gentle boil; cook and stir 2 minutes longer. Remove from the heat. Chill for 10-15 minutes.

Beat cream until stiff peaks form; fold into cooled dressing. Pour over chicken mixture; gently stir to coat. Cover and refrigerate for 1 hour. Serve in a lettuce-lined bowl. Sprinkle with almonds. **Yield: 6-8 servings.**

Nectarine Chicken Salad

When guests are coming for lunch or dinner in the warm summer months, I like to serve this attractive, colorful salad. The dressing is refreshingly tart. A neighbor shared the recipe years ago and I've passed it on many times. —Cathy Ross, Van Nuys, California

- 1/4 cup lime juice
- 1 tablespoon sugar
- 1 tablespoon minced fresh thyme *or* 1 teaspoon dried thyme
- 1 tablespoon olive oil
- 1 garlic clove, minced
- 6 cups torn mixed salad greens

- 1 pound boneless skinless chicken breasts, cooked and sliced
- 5 medium ripe nectarines, thinly sliced

In a jar with a tight-fitting lid, combine the lime juice, sugar, thyme, oil and garlic; shake well.

On a serving platter, arrange salad greens, chicken and nectarines. Drizzle with dressing. Serve immediately. **Yield: 4 servings.**

Nectarine Chicken Salad

Chicken Chopped Salad

Lime dressing gives lively flavor to this crunchy salad tossed with peaches, peppers and peanuts. The unusual combination is a great way to use up leftover chicken or turkey, and it packs well for lunches or picnics. It's also terrific with the addition of grapefruit sections or pineapple tidbits.

—Diane Halferty, Corpus Christi, Texas

- 2 cups chopped or torn mixed salad greens
- 2 cups chopped cooked chicken
- 1 cup chopped celery
- 1 can (15-1/4 ounces) peaches, drained and chopped
- 1 cup chopped sweet red *or* yellow pepper
- 1/3 cup limeade concentrate
- 1/4 cup vegetable oil
- 2 tablespoons cider vinegar
- 2 to 3 tablespoons minced fresh cilantro
- 1-1/2 teaspoons minced fresh gingerroot
- 1/4 teaspoon salt
- 1/2 cup dry roasted peanuts

In a large salad bowl, combine the first five ingredients. In a jar with a tight-fitting lid, combine the limeade concentrate, oil, vinegar, cilantro, ginger and salt; shake well. Pour over salad and toss to coat. Sprinkle with peanuts. Serve immediately. **Yield: 6 servings.**

Chicken Chopped Salad

Tropical Turkey Salad

BLT Chicken Salad

Tropical Turkey Salad

Forever on the lookout for simple dishes to prepare, I tried this delicious salad while on a trip. It's lovely and satisfying with a mixture of turkey, fruit and vegetables.
—Rosalind Canada, White Bluff, Tennessee

- 5 cups torn fresh spinach
- 3 cups torn lettuce
- 2 cups cooked cubed turkey
- 2 slices red onion, separated into rings
- 1/2 cup chopped green pepper
- 1/2 cup mandarin oranges
- 1/2 cup sliced celery
- 1/2 cup pineapple chunks
- 1/3 cup vegetable oil
- 1/4 cup raspberry syrup
- 2 tablespoons red wine vinegar
- 1-1/2 teaspoons honey

- 1/2 teaspoon celery seed
- 1/2 cup sliced almonds, toasted
- 1/4 cup flaked coconut, toasted

Line a large salad bowl with spinach and lettuce. Combine next six ingredients; spoon into bowl.

In a jar with tight-fitting lid, combine the oil, raspberry syrup, vinegar, honey and celery seed; shake well. Pour over the salad. Top with almonds and coconut. Serve immediately. **Yield: 6 servings.**

Hot Chicken Salad

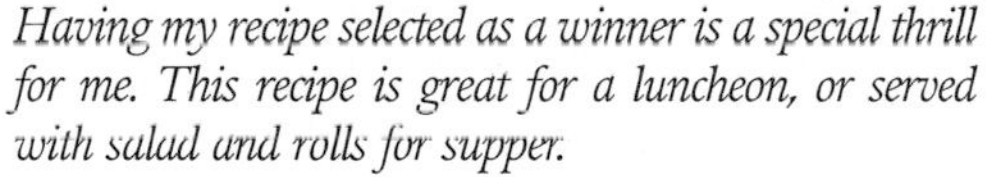

Having my recipe selected as a winner is a special thrill for me. This recipe is great for a luncheon, or served with salad and rolls for supper.

—Michelle Wise, Spring Mills, Pennsylvania

- 2-1/2 cups diced cooked chicken
- 1 cup diced celery
- 1 cup sliced fresh mushrooms
- 1 tablespoon minced onion
- 1 teaspoon lemon juice
- 1/2 teaspoon crushed rosemary
- 1/4 teaspoon pepper
- 1 can (8 ounces) sliced water chestnuts, drained
- 2 cups cooked rice
- 3/4 cup mayonnaise
- 1 can (10-3/4 ounces) cream of chicken soup, undiluted

TOPPING:

- 3 tablespoons butter
- 1/2 cup cornflake crumbs
- 1/2 cup slivered almonds

In a large bowl, combine the first nine ingredients. Blend mayonnaise and soup. Pour over chicken mixture; stir gently to coat. Spoon into a greased 2-qt. baking dish.

In a skillet, melt butter. Stir in cornflakes and almonds. Sprinkle over casserole. Bake, uncovered, at 350° for 30-35 minutes or until heated through. **Yield: 6 servings.**

Hot Chicken Salad

BLT Chicken Salad

Barbecue sauce in the dressing gives a different taste to this green salad that features the fun fixings for a BLT chicken sandwich.

—Cindy Moore, Mooresville, North Carolina

- 1/2 cup mayonnaise
- 3 to 4 tablespoons barbecue sauce
- 2 tablespoons finely chopped onion
- 1 tablespoon lemon juice
- 1/4 teaspoon pepper
- 8 cups torn salad greens
- 2 large tomatoes, chopped
- 1-1/2 pounds boneless skinless chicken breasts, cooked and cubed
- 10 bacon strips, cooked and crumbled
- 2 hard-cooked eggs, sliced

In a small bowl, combine the first five ingredients. Cover and refrigerate until serving.

Place salad greens on a large serving platter. Sprinkle with the tomatoes, chicken and bacon; garnish with eggs. Drizzle with dressing. **Yield: 8 servings.**

Pasta Salad with Steak

While there are quite a few ingredients in this recipe, it doesn't take too long to make—and cleanup afterward's a snap. —*Julie DeRuwe, Oakville, Washington*

- 3/4 cup olive oil
- 2 tablespoons lemon juice
- 2 teaspoons dried oregano
- 1 tablespoon Dijon mustard
- 2 teaspoons cider vinegar
- 1 teaspoon sugar
- 1/2 teaspoon salt
- 1/2 teaspoon pepper
- 3 cups cooked small pasta shells
- 1 boneless beef sirloin steak (1 pound)

RUB:

- 1 tablespoon olive oil
- 3 garlic cloves, minced
- 2 teaspoons dried oregano
- 2 teaspoons pepper
- 1 teaspoon sugar

SALAD:

- 2/3 cup diced cucumber
- 1/2 cup crumbled feta *or* blue cheese
- 1/4 cup sliced ripe olives
- 1/4 cup chopped red onion
- 1/4 cup minced fresh parsley
- 1 jar (2 ounces) diced pimientos, drained

Iceberg *or* romaine lettuce

Combine the first eight ingredients; set half of the dressing aside. Place pasta in a bowl; add remaining dressing. Toss to coat; cover and refrigerate.

Pierce steak with a fork. Combine rub ingredients; rub over steak. Cover and refrigerate for at least 15 minutes.

Grill steak, uncovered, over medium heat for 9-10 minutes on each side or until meat reaches desired doneness (for medium-rare, a meat thermometer should read 145°; medium, 160°; well-done, 170°). Let stand for 10 minutes.

Pasta Salad with Steak

Meanwhile, add the cucumber, cheese, olives, onion, parsley and pimientos to pasta; mix well. Spoon onto a lettuce-lined platter. Slice steak and arrange over salad. Serve with reserved dressing. **Yield: 4 servings.**

Mexican Garden Salad

When I found this salad, I knew it would taste as good as it looks. Although similar to a traditional taco salad, this recipe adds tasty extras like broccoli and shredded carrot. —*Dianne Esposite, New Middletown, Ohio*

- 1 pound ground beef
- 1 jar (16 ounces) thick and chunky salsa, *divided*
- 1/4 cup water
- 1 envelope taco seasoning
- 1-1/2 heads iceberg lettuce, torn
- 3 cups broccoli florets (about 1/2 pound)
- 1 small red onion, thinly sliced into rings
- 1 medium carrot, shredded
- 1 large tomato, chopped
- 1 can (4 ounces) chopped green chilies, drained
- 1/2 to 1 cup shredded cheddar cheese
- 1 cup (8 ounces) sour cream

Tortilla chips, optional

In a skillet, cook beef over medium heat until no longer pink; drain. Add 1 cup salsa, water and taco seasoning; bring to a boil. Reduce heat and simmer, uncovered, for 20 minutes; cool.

In a 3- or 4-qt. glass bowl, layer vegetables in order given. Top with chilies, beef mixture and cheese. Combine sour cream and remaining salsa; serve with salad and tortilla chips if desired. **Yield: 6-8 servings.**

Spicy Beef Salad

This recipe was inspired by my love of spicy flavors and light, nutritious entrees. I make it year-round because it's fast and easy to prepare after a long day at work. —Peggy Allen, Pasadena, California

- 1/2 pound boneless beef sirloin steak
- 1/3 cup fresh lime juice
- 1 tablespoon brown sugar
- 1 tablespoon soy sauce
- 1 tablespoon minced fresh basil
- 2 teaspoons minced fresh mint
- 1 jalapeno pepper, minced
- 2 to 3 garlic cloves, minced
- 1 teaspoon grated fresh gingerroot
- 1 large sweet red pepper, julienned
- 1/2 medium cucumber, chopped
- 6 cups torn mixed salad greens

Partially freeze beef. Slice across grain into thin strips; set aside. For dressing, combine lime juice, sugar, soy sauce, basil and mint; set aside.

In a nonstick skillet coated with nonstick cooking spray, saute the jalapeno, garlic and ginger for 30 seconds. Add beef; stir-fry until beef reached desired doneness. Remove beef mixture from pan; gently toss with red pepper and cucumber.

Place greens in a large bowl; top with beef mixture. Add dressing to pan and bring to a boil; remove from the heat and drizzle over salad. Toss to coat. **Yield: 4 servings.**

Editor's Note: When cutting or seeding hot peppers, use rubber or plastic gloves to protect your hands. Avoid touching your face.

Mexican Garden Salad

Spicy Beef Salad

Southwestern Pork Salad

Layered Ham and Spinach Salad

Layered Ham and Spinach Salad

Here's a delicious salad that's sure to be a favorite with your family and friends. It's very easy to make.
—Beverly Sprague, Baltimore, Maryland

- 16 cups torn fresh spinach
- 1 teaspoon sugar
- 1 teaspoon pepper
- 1/4 teaspoon salt
- 6 hard-cooked eggs, chopped
- 1-1/2 cups cubed fully cooked ham
- 1 medium red onion, sliced
- 1 envelope ranch salad dressing mix
- 1-1/2 cups mayonnaise
- 1 cup (8 ounces) sour cream
- 2 cups (8 ounces) shredded Swiss cheese
- 1/2 pound sliced bacon, cooked and crumbled

Place two-thirds of the spinach in a 4-qt. salad bowl. Sprinkle with half of sugar, pepper and salt. Top with the eggs, ham and remaining spinach. Sprinkle with remaining sugar, pepper and salt. Arrange onion slices on top.

In a bowl, combine the dressing mix, mayonnaise and sour cream. Spread over onions. Sprinkle with the cheese and bacon. Refrigerate until serving. **Yield: 8-10 servings.**

Southwestern Pork Salad

As pork producers, we're proud to cook and serve the delicious product we raise. This tempting salad is refreshing and colorful. I know your family will enjoy it as much as we do.
—Sue Cunningham, Prospect, Ohio

- 2 cups cooked pork strips
- 1 can (16 ounces) kidney beans, rinsed and drained

Ham Salad Puff

- 1/2 cup sliced ripe olives
- 1 medium onion, chopped
- 1 large green pepper, chopped
- 1 large tomato, chopped
- 2 tablespoons sugar
- 1/4 cup cider vinegar
- 1/4 cup vegetable oil
- 1 teaspoon ground mustard
- 1 teaspoon ground cumin
- 1 teaspoon dried oregano
- 1/2 teaspoon salt
- 2 tablespoons minced fresh parsley

In a large bowl, toss the pork, beans, olives, onion, green pepper and tomato. Combine remaining ingredients in a jar with tight-fitting lid; shake well.

Pour over pork mixture; toss gently. Cover and refrigerate for 4-6 hours, stirring occasionally. **Yield: 4 servings.**

Ham Salad Puff

Rarely do I come home with leftovers when I take this appetizing salad to family gathering and potlucks at work. It's hearty yet refreshing, and the edible "bowl" makes it fun to serve. Our two sons consider it a treat.
—Cheryl McGarva, Taber, Alberta

- 1 cup water
- 1/2 cup butter
- 1 cup all-purpose flour
- 1/4 teaspoon salt
- 4 eggs
- 1-1/2 cups cubed fully cooked ham
- 2 celery ribs, chopped
- 1/2 cup cooked small shrimp
- 1/2 cup chopped green pepper
- 1/2 cup sliced green onions
- 1/2 cup mayonnaise
- 1 teaspoon dill weed

Salt and pepper to taste
Lettuce leaves
Additional dill weed, optional

In a large saucepan, bring water and butter to a boil. Add flour and salt all at once, stirring until smooth ball forms. Remove from the heat; let stand for 5 minutes. Add eggs, one at a time, beating well after each addition. Continue beating until mixture is smooth and shiny.

Spread dough onto the bottom and up the sides of a greased 9-in. pie plate. Bake at 400° for 30-35 minutes or until puffed and golden brown. Prick the puff with a fork. Cool on a wire rack.

In a bowl, combine the ham, celery, shrimp, green pepper, onions, mayonnaise, dill, salt and pepper. Line puff with lettuce; fill with ham mixture. Garnish with dill if desired. Refrigerate leftovers. **Yield: 4 servings.**

Hearty Eight-Layer Salad

Hearty Eight-Layer Salad

I have been making this delicious salad for years. This is my most requested recipe for family gatherings. It's simple to make ahead of time and looks lovely with all of its tasty layers. Dijon mustard gives a nice kick to the dressing. —Noreen Meyer, Madison, Wisconsin

- 1-1/2 cups uncooked small pasta shells
- 1 tablespoon vegetable oil
- 3 cups shredded lettuce
- 3 hard-cooked eggs, sliced
- 1/4 teaspoon salt
- 1/8 teaspoon pepper
- 1 cup julienned deli ham
- 1 cup julienned hard salami
- 1 package (10 ounces) frozen peas, thawed
- 1 cup mayonnaise
- 1/4 cup sour cream
- 1/4 cup chopped green onions
- 2 teaspoons Dijon mustard
- 1 cup (4 ounces) shredded Colby *or* Monterey Jack cheese
- 2 tablespoons minced fresh parsley

Cook pasta according to package directions; drain and rinse with cold water. Drizzle with oil; toss to coat.

Place the lettuce in a 2-1/2-qt. glass serving bowl; top with macaroni and eggs. Sprinkle with salt and pepper. Layer with the ham, salami and peas. Combine the mayonnaise, sour cream, green onions and mustard. Spread over the top.

Cover and refrigerate for several hours or overnight. Just before serving, sprinkle with cheese and parsley. **Yield: 10 servings.**

Shrimp Taco Salad

I created this main-dish salad to satisfy our family's love of shrimp. It has lots of contrasting textures, including firm taco-seasoned shrimp, crispy tortilla strips and hearty black beans. A convenient bag of salad greens cuts down on prep time, so I can have this meal ready in half an hour.

—Ellen Morrell, Hazleton, Pennsylvania

- 1 pound uncooked large shrimp, peeled and deveined
- 1 envelope taco seasoning, *divided*
- 1/2 cup plus 3 tablespoons olive oil, *divided*
- 1 small onion, finely chopped
- 3 tablespoons cider vinegar
- 2 tablespoons diced green *or* sweet red pepepr
- 6 garlic cloves, minced
- 1/2 teaspoon ground coriander
- 1/4 teaspoon sugar
- 3 corn tortillas (6 inches), cut into 1/4-inch strips
- 1 package (8 ounces) ready-to-serve salad greens
- 1 medium tomato, chopped
- 1 can (8 ounces) black beans, rinsed and drained
- 2 cups (8 ounces) finely shredded Colby-Monterey Jack cheese

Remove shrimp tails if desired. Place shrimp in a bowl; sprinkle with half of the taco seasoning. Set aside. In another bowl, combine 1/2 cup oil, onion, vinegar, green pepper, garlic, coriander and sugar; set aside.

In a skillet, stir-fry tortilla strips in remaining oil; drain on paper towels. Sprinkle with remaining taco seasoning. In the same skillet, saute shrimp for 8-10 minutes or until pink.

In a large bowl, combine the greens, tomato, beans, shrimp and tortilla strips. Drizzle with dressing. Sprinkle with cheese; toss. **Yield: 6-8 servings.**

Shrimp Taco Salad

Eastern Shore Seafood Salad

We live just a short distance from the Chesapeake Bay area, so crabmeat dishes are very popular here. This is a new recipe I came across that I think is extra special.
—Kimberly Brennan, Clear Spring, Maryland

- 1 pound cooked medium shrimp
- 3 cups cooked *or* canned crabmeat, drained, flaked and cartilage removed
- 1 small onion, chopped
- 1 celery rib, thinly sliced
- 1/2 cup mayonnaise
- 2 teaspoons seafood seasoning
- 1 teaspoon lemon juice
- 1/2 teaspoon salt
- 1/8 teaspoon pepper
- Leaf lettuce, optional
- 1 hard-cooked egg, sliced, optional

In a large bowl, combine the shrimp, crab, onion and celery. In a small bowl, combine the mayonnaise, seafood seasoning, lemon juice, salt and pepper; add to the shrimp mixture and mix gently.

Cover and refrigerate for at least 1 hour. If desired, serve in a lettuce-lined bowl and garnish with egg. **Yield: 6 servings.**

Eastern Shore Seafood Salad

Crab Pasta Salad

Tortellini Caesar Salad

Crab Pasta Salad

This salad has a very good blend of flavors. It's easy to make and especially delicious on a hot day.
—Kathryn Anderson, Wallkill, New York

- 2 cups uncooked medium shell pasta
- 1-1/2 cups imitation crabmeat, chopped
- 1 cup broccoli florets
- 1/2 cup diced green pepper
- 1/2 cup quartered cherry tomatoes
- 1/4 cup chopped green onions

DRESSING:

- 1/2 cup mayonnaise
- 1/4 cup creamy Italian salad dressing
- 1/4 cup grated Parmesan cheese

Cook pasta according to package directions; drain and rinse in cold water. Place in a large bowl. Stir in the crab, broccoli, green pepper, tomatoes and onions.

Combining dressing ingredients; pour over salad and toss gently to coat. Cover and refrigerate for 2-4 hours before serving. **Yield: 4-6 servings.**

Tortellini Caesar Salad

This salad was served at a dear friend's baby shower by a health-conscious friend, who suggested the dressing be prepared with low-fat or fat-free ingredients. Either way, the creamy dressing has plenty of garlic flavor and coats the pasta, romaine and croutons nicely.
—Tammy Steenbock, Sembach Air Base, Germany

- 1 package (9 ounces) frozen cheese tortellini
- 1/2 cup mayonnaise
- 1/4 cup milk
- 1/4 cup plus 1/3 cup shredded Parmesan cheese, *divided*
- 2 tablespoons lemon juice
- 2 garlic cloves, minced
- 8 cups torn romaine
- 1 cup seasoned salad croutons
- Halved cherry tomatoes, optional

Cook tortellini according to package directions. Meanwhile, in a small bowl, combine the mayonnaise, milk, 1/4 cup Parmesan cheese, lemon juice and garlic; mix well.

Drain tortellini and rinse in cold water; place in a large bowl. Add the romaine and remaining Parmesan.

Just before serving, drizzle with dressing and toss to coat. Top with croutons and tomatoes if desired. **Yield: 10 servings.**

Spicy Ravioli Salad

You'll be sitting down to dinner in no time when you prepare this main-dish salad. A convenient combination of frozen ravioli and pantry staples, including

Spicy Ravioli Salad

canned tomatoes, corn and olives, is dressed with easy taco sauce for tangy, fresh-tasting results.
—Paula Marchesi, Lenhartsville, Pennsylvania

- 1 package (25 ounces) frozen beef, sausage *or* cheese ravioli
- 1 can (10 ounces) diced tomatoes and green chilies, undrained
- 1 can (8-3/4 ounces) whole kernel corn, drained
- 1 bottle (8 ounces) taco sauce
- 1 can (2-1/4 ounces) sliced ripe olives, drained
- 1 small cucumber, peeled, seeded and chopped
- 1 small red onion, sliced
- 2 garlic cloves, minced
- 1/4 teaspoon ground cumin
- 1/4 teaspoon salt
- 1/4 teaspoon pepper

Cook ravioli according to package directions. Meanwhile, combine remaining ingredients in a large bowl. Drain ravioli; stir into tomato mixture. Cover and refrigerate for at least 2 hours. **Yield: 8-10 servings.**

Summer Spinach Salad

Summer Spinach Salad 1st prize

Guests always request the recipe for this fabulous spinach salad. Tossed with ripe banana chunks, fresh strawberries and toasted almonds, it looks and tastes special enough for company. The tangy poppy seed dressing is a snap to combine in the blender.
—Callie Berger, Diamond Springs, California

- 1/2 cup vegetable oil
- 1/4 cup chopped onion
- 2 tablespoons plus 2 teaspoons red wine vinegar
- 2 tablespoons plus 2 teaspoons sugar
- 1-1/2 teaspoons ground mustard
- 1/2 teaspoon salt
- 1-1/2 teaspoons poppy seeds
- 8 cups torn fresh spinach
- 3 green onions, sliced
- 2 pints fresh strawberries, sliced
- 3 large ripe bananas, cut into 1/2-inch slices
- 1/2 cup slivered almonds, toasted

Place the first six ingredients in a blender or food processor; cover and process until the sugar is dissolved. Add the poppy seeds; process just until blended.

In a salad bowl, combine the remaining ingredients. Drizzle with dressing; toss to coat. Serve immediately. **Yield: 14 servings.**

Lettuce with Hot Bacon Dressing

I plant lettuce in my garden, so this is a recipe I make often. It's a nice change from a regular tossed salad.
—Myra Innes, Auburn, Kansas

- 5 bacon strips
- 8 cups torn salad greens
- 2 hard-cooked eggs, chopped
- 2 green onions, sliced
- 1/2 cup sugar
- 1/2 cup cider vinegar
- 1/2 teaspoon seasoned salt
- 1/2 teaspoon garlic powder
- 1/4 teaspoon ground mustard

In a skillet, cook bacon over medium heat until crisp. Remove to paper towels; drain, reserving 1/4 cup drippings. Crumble bacon and set aside.

In a large bowl, combine the greens, eggs, onions and bacon. Add remaining ingredients to the drippings; bring to a boil. Drizzle over the salad and toss to coat. Serve immediately. **Yield: 8 servings.**

Festive Tossed Salad

This is a delightful salad that has a wonderful blend of flavors. It has a crunchy texture and looks good, too, with its variety of colors.
—Isabell Burrows, Livermore, California

- 1 cup coarsely chopped walnuts
- 3 tablespoons butter
- 1/4 cup sugar
- 1 teaspoon coarsely ground pepper
- 1/4 teaspoon salt
- 12 cups torn mixed salad greens
- 3/4 cup dried cranberries
- 4 ounces crumbled feta cheese

DRESSING:

- 1/4 cup red wine vinegar
- 1/4 cup vegetable oil
- 1/2 cup loosely packed fresh parsley sprigs
- 1/4 cup chopped red onion
- 2 garlic cloves, peeled
- 1 tablespoon sugar
- 1/2 teaspoon dried oregano
- 1/8 teaspoon salt
- 1/8 teaspoon pepper

In a skillet, cook and stir walnuts in butter over medium-low heat until toasted, about 5 minutes. Remove from the heat; stir in the sugar, pepper and salt.

In a salad bowl, toss the greens, cranberries, cheese and walnuts. Place the dressing ingredients in a blender or food processor; cover and process until smooth.

Drizzle desired amount over salad; toss to coat. Serve immediately. Refrigerate leftover dressing. **Yield: 12 servings.**

Lettuce with Hot Bacon Dressing

Festive Tossed Salad

Green Salad with Onion Dressing

Spinach Salad with Spicy Honey Dressing

Green Salad with Onion Dressing

This is such an elegant salad. It will dress up any table. The caramelized onion in the dressing tastes fantastic. It's never failed to be a hit whenever I've served it. —Cara Bonnema, Painesville, Ohio

- 1 large onion, peeled and cut into eighths
- 8 tablespoons olive oil, *divided*
- 1-1/2 teaspoons sugar
- 1/4 cup chicken broth
- 2 tablespoons white wine vinegar
- 1/4 teaspoon salt
- 14 cups torn salad greens
- 1 cup chopped walnuts, toasted
- 1/2 cup thinly sliced red onion

Place onion in a baking dish. Drizzle with 1 tablespoon oil; sprinkle with sugar. Bake, uncovered, at 400° for 30 minutes. Turn and bake 25-30 minutes longer, stirring several times, until the onion is tender and lightly browned. Cool for 30 minutes.

Place onion in a blender or food processor; add the broth, vinegar, salt and remaining oil. Cover and process until smooth (mixture will be thick). Cover and refrigerate.

Just before serving, toss the greens, walnuts, red onion and dressing in a large salad bowl. **Yield: 12 servings.**

Spinach Salad with Spicy Honey Dressing

Here's a salad with some zip to it. I've also served the spicy dressing with mixed vegetables, fruit and tossed salads. —Barbara Martineau, Hudson, Wisconsin

Mandarin-Cashew Tossed Salad

4 cups torn fresh spinach
1 cup minced fresh parsley
1 cup sliced fresh mushrooms
2 medium tomatoes, cut into wedges
2 celery ribs, chopped
1 cup canned bean sprouts, rinsed and drained
1-1/2 cups (6 ounces) shredded cheddar cheese
1 cup salted sunflower kernels
1/4 teaspoon *each* salt, pepper and garlic salt

DRESSING:

1/2 cup vegetable oil
1/4 cup honey
1/4 cup cider vinegar
1/4 cup chopped onion
3 tablespoons chili sauce
1-1/2 teaspoons Worcestershire sauce
1/4 teaspoon salt

In a large salad bowl, combine the spinach, parsley, mushrooms, tomatoes, celery, bean sprouts, cheese, sunflower kernels and seasonings.

In a jar with a tight-fitting lid, combine the dressing ingredients; shake well. Drizzle desired amount over salad and toss to coat. Serve immediately. Refrigerate any leftover dressing. **Yield: 12 servings.**

Mandarin-Cashew Tossed Salad

Mandarin oranges and chopped red onion add a touch of color to mixed greens and sweet roasted cashews in this refreshing salad. You're sure to be handing out the recipe once friends and family get a taste of the tangy honey dressing.

—Sheri Shaffer, Northfield, Ohio

5 cups torn red leaf lettuce
5 cups torn iceberg lettuce
3 cups torn Boston lettuce
2 cans (11 ounces *each*) mandarin oranges, well drained
3/4 cup chopped green pepper
1 celery rib, thinly sliced
1/4 cup chopped red onion

HONEY LIME DRESSING:

1/4 cup vegetable oil
1/4 cup honey
1/2 teaspoon ground mustard
1/2 teaspoon grated lime peel
1/4 teaspoon paprika
1/8 teaspoon salt
Dash white pepper
1 cup honey roasted cashews

In a large salad bowl, combine the lettuces, oranges, green pepper, celery and onion.

In a small bowl, whisk together the oil, honey, mustard, lime peel, paprika, salt and pepper. Drizzle over salad. Add cashews; toss to coat. Serve immediately. **Yield: 10-12 servings.**

Artichoke Heart Salad

In a bowl, combine the artichokes, olives if desired, green pepper and onions. Add dressing and toss to coat.

Cover and refrigerate for at least 30 minutes. Serve with a slotted spoon. **Yield: 3-4 servings.**

Nutty Broccoli Slaw

My daughter gave me the recipe for this delightful salad. The sweet dressing nicely coats a crisp blend of broccoli slaw mix, carrots, onions, almonds and sunflower kernels. Crushed ramen noodles provide even more crunch. It's a smash hit wherever I take it.
—Dora Mae Clapsaddle, Kensington, Ohio

- 1 package (3 ounces) chicken ramen noodles
- 1 package (16 ounces) broccoli coleslaw mix
- 2 cups sliced green onions (about 2 bunches)
- 1-1/2 cups broccoli florets
- 1 can (6 ounces) ripe olives, drained and halved
- 1 cup sunflower kernels, toasted
- 1/2 cup slivered almonds, toasted
- 1/2 cup sugar
- 1/2 cup cider vinegar
- 1/2 cup olive oil

Set aside the noodle seasoning packet; crush the noodles and place in a large bowl. Add the slaw mix, onions, broccoli, olives, sunflower kernels and almonds.

In a jar with a tight-fitting lid, combine the sugar, vinegar, oil and contents of seasoning packet; shake well. Drizzle over salad and toss to coat. Serve immediately. **Yield: 16 servings.**

Artichoke Heart Salad

I put together this fast, five-ingredient salad after sampling a similar mixture from a salad bar. Bottled Italian dressing gives robust flavor to this simple treatment for canned artichoke hearts. It is a snap to make as a last-minute side dish.
—Elizabeth Birkenmaier, Gladstone, Missouri

- 1 can (14 ounces) water-packed artichoke hearts, rinsed, drained and quartered
- 1 can (2-1/4 ounces) sliced ripe olives, drained, optional
- 1/3 cup chopped green pepper
- 1/3 cup thinly sliced green onions
- 3/4 cup Italian salad dressing

Nutty Broccoli Slaw

Broccoli Slaw

Here's a new twist on traditional coleslaw. It's easy to make and so delicious.

—Kimmy Thomas, Citrus Heights, California

- 4 cups broccoli florets
- 1 medium carrot, shredded
- 2 cups shredded red cabbage
- 1/2 cup raisins
- 1 small sweet onion, chopped
- 1 bottle (16 ounces) coleslaw dressing

In a serving bowl, combine all the ingredients. Cover and refrigerate for at least 2 hours. Stir before serving. **Yield: 6 servings.**

Broccoli Slaw

Sweet Floret Salad

Carrot Broccoli Salad

Sweet Floret Salad

Everywhere I take this crunchy, fresh-tasting salad with its sweet creamy dressing, people invariably want the recipe. It's perfect for a potluck—best made the night before you serve it and easy to transport.
—Kathi Lavier, Hillsboro, Oregon

- 1/2 cup mayonnaise
- 1/3 cup sugar
- 1/4 cup vegetable oil
- 1/4 cup cider vinegar
- 1 medium head cauliflower, broken into florets
- 1-3/4 pounds fresh broccoli, broken into florets
- 1 medium red onion, sliced
- 1 medium sweet yellow pepper, cut into 1-inch pieces, optional
- 1/2 pound sliced bacon, cooked and crumbled

In a small saucepan, combine the mayonnaise, sugar, oil and vinegar. Bring to a boil, whisking constantly. Cool to room temperature.

In a large bowl, combine the remaining ingredients. Add dressing and toss to coat. Cover and refrigerate for several hours or overnight, stirring occasionally. **Yield: 10-12 servings.**

Carrot Broccoli Salad

I created this salad for last summer's round of family reunions and picnics. My in-laws provided me with all the fresh vegetables from their garden.
—Heather Hibbs, Middleburg, Pennsylvania

- 6 medium carrots, shredded
- 1 small bunch broccoli (about 12 ounces), chopped
- 1 cup raisins
- 1 small onion, chopped
- 1 garlic clove, minced

- 2/3 to 1 cup mayonnaise
- 1/2 cup sugar
- 1 teaspoon ground mustard
- 1/2 pound sliced bacon, cooked and crumbled

In a large bowl, combine the first five ingredients. In another bowl, combine the mayonnaise, sugar and mustard. Add to vegetable mixture and gently stir to coat. Cover and refrigerate. Stir in bacon just before serving. **Yield: 6 servings.**

Citrus Pineapple Coleslaw

A blue-ribbon recipe, this slaw was a winner in our state fair competition. Alaska is famous for its giant cabbages, but any garden-variety head will taste yummy dressed in marshmallow bits and citrusy pineapple. —*Carol Ross, Anchorage, Alaska*

- 1/3 cup sugar
- 1/4 cup cornstarch
- 1/4 teaspoon salt
- 1 cup unsweetened pineapple juice
- 1/4 cup orange juice
- 3 tablespoons lemon juice
- 2 eggs, lightly beaten
- 2 packages (3 ounces *each*) cream cheese, softened
- 1 medium head cabbage, shredded
- 2 large carrots, shredded
- 1 can (8 ounces) crushed pineapple, drained
- 1 cup miniature marshmallows

Carrot curls, optional

In a saucepan, combine the first six ingredients until smooth. Bring to a boil over medium heat; cook and stir for 2 minutes or until thickened. Stir a small amount into the eggs. Return all to saucepan, stirring constantly. Cook and stir until mixture reaches 160°. Cool for 5 minutes. Stir in cream cheese until melted. Cover and chill.

In a large salad bowl, combine the cabbage, carrots, pineapple and marshmallows. Add dressing; toss to coat. Garnish with carrot curls if desired. **Yield: 8-12 servings.**

Citrus Pineapple Coleslaw

Crunchy Corn Medley

Crunchy Corn Medley

This recipe came from my husband's aunt, who's an excellent cook, friend and mentor. The salad's crunchy, colorful and combined with a light tasty dressing. I've shared it with friends and relatives, who think it's a great addition to their recipe collection.
—Meredith Cecil, Plattsburg, Missouri

- 2 cups frozen peas, thawed
- 1 can (15-1/4 ounces) whole kernel corn, drained
- 1 can (15-1/4 ounces) white *or* shoepeg corn, drained
- 1 can (8 ounces) water chestnuts, drained and chopped
- 1 jar (4 ounces) diced pimientos, drained
- 8 green onions, thinly sliced
- 2 celery ribs, chopped
- 1 medium green pepper, chopped
- 1/2 cup cider vinegar
- 1/2 cup sugar
- 1/4 cup vegetable oil
- 1 teaspoon salt
- 1/4 teaspoon pepper

In a large bowl, combine the first eight ingredients. In a small bowl, combine the vinegar, sugar, oil, salt and pepper; whisk until sugar is dissolved. Pour over corn mixture; mix well.

Cover and refrigerate for at least 3 hours. Stir just before serving; serve with a slotted spoon. **Yield: 10 servings.**

Chili Corn Bread Salad

A co-worker brought this wonderful dish to a potluck several years ago. She had copies of the recipe next to the pan. Now I make it for get-togethers and also supply copies of the recipe. I never have any leftover salad or recipes. —Kelly Newsom, Jenks, Oklahoma

- 1 package (8-1/2 ounces) corn bread/muffin mix
- 1 can (4 ounces) chopped green chilies, undrained
- 1/8 teaspoon ground cumin
- 1/8 teaspoon dried oregano
- Pinch rubbed sage
- 1 cup mayonnaise
- 1 cup (8 ounces) sour cream
- 1 envelope ranch salad dressing mix
- 2 cans (15 ounces *each*) pinto beans, rinsed and drained
- 2 cans (15-1/4 ounces *each*) whole kernel corn, drained
- 3 medium tomatoes, chopped
- 1 cup chopped green pepper
- 1 cup chopped green onions
- 10 bacon strips, cooked and crumbled
- 2 cups (8 ounces) shredded cheddar cheese

Prepare corn bread batter according to package directions. Stir in the chilies, cumin, oregano and sage. Spread in a greased 8-in. square baking dish. Bake at 400° for 20-25 minutes or until a toothpick inserted near the center comes out clean. Cool in pan on a wire rack.

In a small bowl, combine the mayonnaise, sour cream and dressing mix; set aside. Crumble half of the corn bread into a 13-in. x 9-in. x 2-in. dish. Layer with half of the beans, mayonnaise mixture, corn, tomatoes, green pepper, onions, bacon and cheese. Repeat layers (dish will be very full). Cover and refrigerate for 2 hours. **Yield: 12 servings.**

Chili Corn Bread Salad

German Cucumber Salad

This recipe came from a friend who ran his own inn in Germany. The salad's very cool and light with an exhilarating taste that's delicious any time of the year—especially when made with fresh-from-the-garden cucumbers and tomatoes.

—Julie Koren, Kennesaw, Georgia

- 2 medium cucumbers, thinly sliced
- 4 green onions, thinly sliced
- 3 small tomatoes, sliced
- 2 tablespoons minced fresh parsley

DRESSING:

- 1/4 cup sour cream
- 1/4 teaspoon prepared mustard
- 2 tablespoons minced fresh dill
- 1 tablespoon cider vinegar
- 1 tablespoon milk
- 1/8 teaspoon pepper

In a bowl, combine the cucumbers, onions, tomatoes and parsley. Combine dressing ingredients; pour over cucumber mixture and toss gently. Cover and refrigerate for at least 1 hour. **Yield: 4-6 servings.**

German Cucumber Salad

Grilled Three-Pepper Salad

Deluxe German Potato Salad

Grilled Three-Pepper Salad

I have been cooking since my mother taught me how at an early age. I enjoy it, and I'm always trying new recipes. This one's both flavorful and colorful.
—Ruth Wickard, York, Pennsylvania

- 2 *each* large green, sweet red and yellow peppers, cut into 1-inch pieces
- 1 large red onion, halved and thinly sliced
- 1 pound part-skim mozzarella cheese, cut into bite-size cubes
- 1 can (6 ounces) pitted ripe olives, drained and halved

VINAIGRETTE:

- 2/3 cup olive oil
- 1/3 cup cider vinegar
- 2/3 cup red wine vinegar
- 2 tablespoons lemon juice
- 2 tablespoons Dijon mustard
- 1 tablespoon minced fresh basil *or* 1 teaspoon dried basil
- 1/2 teaspoon cayenne pepper
- 1/2 teaspoon garlic powder

Thread peppers onto metal or soaked wooden skewers; grill or broil for 10-12 minutes or until edges are browned. Remove from skewers and place in a large bowl. Add the onion, mozzarella and olives; toss gently. Cover and refrigerate.

Combine the vinaigrette ingredients in a jar with tight-fitting lid; shake well. Just before serving, pour over the pepper mixture; toss to coat. **Yield: 10-12 servings.**

Deluxe German Potato Salad 1st prize

I often take this salad to potlucks, and there's never any left over. The celery, carrots and ground mustard are a special touch not usually found in traditional German potato salad. —Betty Perkins, Hot Springs, Arkansas

- 1/2 pound sliced bacon
- 1 cup thinly sliced celery
- 1 cup chopped onion
- 1 cup sugar
- 2 tablespoons all-purpose flour
- 1 cup cider vinegar
- 1/2 cup water
- 1 teaspoon salt
- 3/4 teaspoon ground mustard
- 5 pounds unpeeled red new potatoes, cooked and sliced
- 2 carrots, shredded
- 2 tablespoons minced fresh parsley

Additional salt to taste

In a large skillet, cook bacon over medium heat until crisp. Remove to paper towels; drain, reserving 1/4 cup drippings. Crumble bacon and set aside. Saute the celery and onion in drippings until tender.

Combine sugar and flour; stir into skillet until blender. Stir in the vinegar, water, salt and mustard. Bring to a boil; cook and stir for 2 minutes or until thickened. Cook, stirring constantly, until mixture thickens and bubbles.

In a large bowl, combine the potatoes, carrots and parsley; pour the sauce over and stir gently to coat. Season to taste with additional salt. Spoon into a serving dish; garnish with crumbled bacon. Serve warm. **Yield: 14-16 servings.**

Green Bean Potato Salad

I have a taste for beans and find them a great companion to potatoes. This makes a versatile side dish—or, add ham to make the salad a meal in itself.
—Bea Vrsalijko, Belle Chasse, Louisiana

- 1-1/2 pounds small red potatoes, quartered
- 1 garlic clove, peeled and halved
- 2 cups cut fresh green beans (1-1/2-inch pieces)
- 1 can (14-1/2 ounces) chicken broth

Green Bean Potato Salad

TARRAGON DRESSING:

- 3 tablespoons olive oil
- 3 tablespoons cider vinegar
- 1 garlic clove, minced
- 1 tablespoon minced fresh parsley
- 1 to 1-1/2 teaspoons minced fresh tarragon
- 1/2 teaspoon ground mustard
- 1/2 teaspoon salt
- 1/4 teaspoon pepper
- 1/4 teaspoon Creole *or* Cajun seasoning

Lettuce leaves, optional

In a saucepan, cook potatoes and garlic in boiling salted water for 5 minutes. Add beans; cook 10-14 minutes longer or until vegetables are tender. Drain; discard garlic. Place vegetables in a bowl. Warm broth; pour over vegetables. Cover and refrigerate for at least 2 hours, stirring several times.

In a small bowl, combine the oil, vinegar and seasonings; mix well. Drain vegetables; add dressing and toss to coat. Serve in a lettuce-lined bowl if desired. **Yield: 6-8 servings.**

Warm Mustard Salad

Warm Mustard Potato Salad 1st prize

This tangy mixture is wonderful and so different from traditional potato salads. The Dijon mustard and dill spark the flavor.
—Tiffany Mitchell, Susanville, California

- 2 pounds small red potatoes
- 1 cup mayonnaise
- 1/4 cup Dijon mustard
- 1/2 to 3/4 cup chopped red onion
- 2 green onions with tops, sliced
- 2 garlic cloves, minced
- 3 tablespoons snipped fresh dill
- 1/2 teaspoon salt
- 1/2 teaspoon pepper
- 1/4 teaspoon lime juice

Place the potatoes in a saucepan and cover with water. Bring to a boil. Reduce heat; cover and cook for 20-25 minutes or until tender. Drain thoroughly and cool slightly.

Meanwhile, combine the remaining ingredients. Cut potatoes into chunks; place in a bowl. Add the mustard mixture and toss to coat. Serve warm. **Yield: 8-10 servings.**

Creamy Sliced Tomatoes

Creamy Sliced Tomatoes

This is a family favorite that's also popular with friends. It's a pretty presentation, perfect as a side dish. The basil and cool creamy dressing make the dish tasty.
—Doris Smith, Woodbury, New Jersey

- 1 cup mayonnaise
- 1/2 cup half-and-half cream
- 1-1/2 teaspoons chopped fresh basil, *divided*
- Lettuce leaves
- 6 medium tomatoes, sliced
- 1 medium red onion, thinly sliced into rings

Herbed Cherry Tomatoes

In a small bowl, combine mayonnaise, cream and half of the basil. Cover and chill.

Just before serving, arrange the lettuce, tomatoes and onion on individual salad plates. Drizzle with dressing. Sprinkle with remaining basil. **Yield: 12 servings.**

Herbed Cherry Tomatoes 1st prize

My recipe's a good one for when you want a little fancier salad dish but one that's still quick to fix. I find it's especially popular served with grilled steak, baked potatoes and corn on the cob.
—Dianne Bahn, Yankton, South Dakota

1 pint cherry tomatoes, halved
1/4 cup vegetable oil
3 tablespoons cider vinegar
1/4 cup minced fresh parsley
1-1/2 teaspoons minced fresh basil
1-1/2 teaspoons minced fresh oregano
1/2 teaspoon salt
1/2 teaspoon sugar
Leaf lettuce, optional

Place tomatoes in a medium bowl; set aside. In a small bowl, combine oil and vinegar. Add the parsley, basil, oregano, salt and sugar; mix well. Pour over the tomatoes.

Cover and refrigerate for at least 3 hours. Drain; serve on lettuce if desired. **Yield: 4-6 servings.**

Creamy Summer Vegetable Salad

My mother made this salad whenever we barbecued. It's easy to fix, goes well with meat or chicken and is a good way to utilize garden vegetables.
—Barbara Arneson, Creston, Washington

- 4 medium tomatoes, chopped
- 3 large cucumbers, seeded and chopped
- 1 medium onion, chopped
- 10 radishes, sliced
- 2 cups (16 ounces) sour cream
- 1/4 cup lemon juice
- 1 teaspoon seasoned salt
- 1/2 teaspoon pepper
- 3/4 teaspoon celery seed, optional

In a large bowl, combine the tomatoes, cucumbers, onion and radishes. In a small bowl, combine the remaining ingredients. Add to vegetables and toss to coat.

Cover and refrigerate for at least 2 hours. Serve with a slotted spoon. **Yield: 16 servings.**

Creamy Summer Vegetable Salad

Dilly Veggie Pasta Salad

I got the recipe for this fresh, crunchy salad seasoned with dill from my sister. It's handy because you can assemble and eat it right away, or cover and refrigerate it to take to a picnic or potluck the next day. The longer it chills, the more tangy it is.
—Anna Emory-Royal, Murfreesboro, Tennessee

- 2-3/4 cups uncooked medium shell pasta
- 1 cup halved cherry tomatoes
- 1 cup sliced green pepper
- 1 cup (4 ounces) shredded cheddar cheese
- 1/2 cup chopped green onions
- 1/2 cup sliced ripe olives

DRESSING:

- 1/4 cup olive oil
- 2 tablespoons lemon juice
- 2 tablespoons white wine vinegar
- 1 teaspoon dill weed
- 1 teaspoon dried oregano
- 1 teaspoon salt
- 1/8 teaspoon pepper

Cook pasta according to package directions; drain and rinse in cold water. Place in a large bowl. Add the tomatoes, green pepper, cheese, onions and olives.

In a small bowl, whisk together the dressing ingredients. Pour over salad and toss to coat. Cover and chill until serving. **Yield: 8 servings.**

Italian Pasta Salad

This zesty recipe combines vegetables and pasta in a creamy dressing. Refreshing and filling, this change-of-pace salad is perfect as a side dish, and it's always popular at a potluck.
—Tina Dierking, Skohegan, Maine

Dilly Veggie Pasta Salad

- 3/4 cup uncooked spiral pasta
- 1-1/2 cups halved cherry tomatoes
- 1 cup sliced fresh mushrooms
- 1/4 cup chopped sweet red pepper
- 1/4 cup chopped green pepper
- 3 tablespoons thinly sliced green onions
- 1-1/2 cups zesty Italian salad dressing
- 3/4 cup mayonnaise
- 1/2 cup grated Parmesan cheese
- 1/3 cup cubed provolone cheese
- 1 can (2-1/4 ounces) sliced ripe olives, drained

Leaf lettuce, optional

Cook pasta according to package directions; rinse with cold water and drain. Place in a bowl; add the tomatoes, mushrooms, peppers, onions and salad dressing. Cover and refrigerate for at least 4 hours or overnight; drain.

In a bowl, combine the mayonnaise and Parmesan cheese; stir in the provolone cheese and olives. Gently fold into the pasta mixture. Serve in a lettuce-lined bowl if desired. **Yield: 6 servings.**

Italian Pasta Salad

Spiced Peach Salad

Fruity Green Salad

Spiced Peach Salad

This fruity gelatin salad is my most requested recipe. A touch of cinnamon makes it taste like peach pie.
—Karen Hamilton, Ludington, Michigan

- 1/2 cup sugar
- 3 tablespoons cider vinegar
- 2 cups water
- 1 tablespoon whole cloves
- 4 cinnamon sticks (3 inches *each*)
- 2 packages (3 ounces *each*) peach *or* apricot gelatin
- 1 can (29 ounces) peach halves

In a medium saucepan, combine the sugar, vinegar and water. Place cloves and cinnamon on a double thickness of cheesecloth; bring up corners of cloth and tie with kitchen string to form a bag. Place in saucepan. Bring to a boil. Reduce heat; simmer, uncovered, for 10 minutes.

Remove from the heat and discard spice bag. Add gelatin; stir until dissolved. Drain

Layered Fresh Fruit Salad

peaches, reserving syrup; set peaches aside. Add water to syrup to measure 2 cups. Add to gelatin mixture; stir well.

Refrigerate until slightly thickened. Thinly slice peaches; add to gelatin. Pour into a 2-qt. glass bowl; chill until firm. **Yield: 8-10 servings.**

Editor's Note: If desired, 1/2 teaspoon ground cinnamon and 1/4 teaspoon ground cloves may be substituted for the whole spice; combine with the gelatin before adding to sugar mixture.

Fruity Green Salad

My family enjoys this fast and refreshing salad. It's jazzed up with a beautiful blend of red apple, pear, dried cranberries, toasted pecans and Swiss cheese. No matter when I serve it, the lemon dressing and fruity flavor remind me of springtime.

—Helen Petisi, Palm Coast, Florida

- 2/3 cup vegetable oil
- 1/3 cup lemon juice
- 1/4 cup sugar
- 2 teaspoons chopped green onions
- 3/4 teaspoon salt
- 1 teaspoon poppy seeds
- 8 cups torn mixed salad greens
- 1 medium red apple, chopped
- 1 medium pear, chopped
- 1 cup chopped pecans, toasted
- 1 cup (4 ounces) shredded Swiss cheese
- 1/4 cup dried cranberries

In a jar with a tight-fitting lid, combine the first six ingredients; shake well. In a large bowl, combine the remaining ingredients. Drizzle with dressing and toss to coat. Serve immediately. **Yield: 16 servings.**

Layered Fresh Fruit Salad

People always pass on compliments when I take this salad to covered-dish suppers. It's nice on a hot day with a winter meal or as a dessert!

—Page Alexander, Baldwin City, Kansas

- 2/3 cup fresh orange juice
- 1/3 cup fresh lemon juice
- 1/3 cup packed brown sugar
- 1 cinnamon stick (3 inches)
- 1/2 teaspoon grated orange peel
- 1/2 teaspoon grated lemon peel

FRUIT SALAD:

- 2 cups cubed fresh pineapple
- 1 pint fresh strawberries, hulled and sliced
- 2 kiwifruit, peeled and sliced
- 3 medium firm bananas, sliced
- 2 oranges, peeled and sectioned
- 1 red grapefruit, peeled and sectioned
- 1 cup seedless red grapes

In a saucepan, bring the first six ingredients to a boil. Reduce heat; simmer, uncovered, for 5 minutes. Cool.

Meanwhile, in a large glass salad bowl, layer fruit in order listed. Remove cinnamon stick from the sauce and pour sauce over fruit. Cover and refrigerate several hours. **Yield: 10-12 servings.**

Pecan-Pear Tossed Salad

Pecan-Pear Tossed Salad

To save time, I prepare the ingredients and dressing the day before, then combine them just before serving. Once, when I forgot to bring this salad, dinner was postponed so I could go home and get it!
—Marjean Claassen, Sedgwick, Kansas

- 2 tablespoons fresh raspberries
- 3/4 cup olive oil
- 3 tablespoons cider vinegar
- 2 tablespoons plus 1 teaspoon sugar
- 1/4 to 1/2 teaspoon pepper

SALAD:

- 4 medium ripe pears, thinly sliced
- 2 teaspoons lemon juice
- 8 cups torn salad greens
- 2/3 cup pecan halves, toasted
- 1/2 cup fresh raspberries
- 1/3 cup (2 ounces) crumbled feta cheese

Press raspberries through a sieve, reserving juice. Discard seeds. In a jar with a tight-fitting lid, combine the oil, vinegar, sugar, pepper and reserved raspberry juice; shake well.

Toss pear slices with lemon juice; drain. In a salad bowl, combine the salad greens, pears, pecans and raspberries. Sprinkle with cheese. Drizzle with dressing. **Yield: 8 servings.**

Minted Melon Salad

People can't resist digging into a salad made with colorful summer fruits. The unique mint is what makes this salad a crowd-pleaser. I get compliments whenever I serve it, especially when I put it on the table in a melon boat. It's a warm-weather treat.
—Terry Saylor, Vermillion, South Dakota

- 1 cup water
- 3/4 cup sugar
- 3 tablespoons lime juice
- 1-1/2 teaspoons chopped fresh mint
- 3/4 teaspoon aniseed

Pinch salt

- 5 cups cubed watermelon (about 1/2 melon)
- 3 cups cubed cantaloupe (about 1 medium melon)
- 3 cups cubed honeydew (about 1 medium melon)
- 2 cups peach slices (about 2 peaches)
- 1 cup fresh blueberries

In a small saucepan, bring the first six ingredients to a boil. Boil for 2 minutes; remove from the heat. Cover, cool syrup completely.

Combine the fruit in a very large bowl; add syrup and stir to coat. Cover and chill for at least 2 hours, stirring occasionally. Drain before serving. Spoon into watermelon bowl or 8-qt. serving bowl. **Yield: 12-14 servings.**

Creamy Celery Seed Dressing

I like this recipe because of its versatility. It's wonderful with potatoes, hot or cold sliced meat or vegetables.
—Patricia Dougherty, Dunkirk, New York

- 1/2 cup butter
- 1 cup cider vinegar
- 3 eggs, lightly beaten

Minted Melon Salad

1-1/2	teaspoons celery seed
1	teaspoon salt
1/4	teaspoon white pepper
2	cups mayonnaise
3/4	cup Italian salad dressing
1/2	cup sugar

In a saucepan, melt butter. Meanwhile, combine the vinegar, eggs, celery seed, salt and pepper. Gradually add to butter, stirring constantly. Cook and stir over medium heat for 5 minutes or until slightly thickened and a thermometer reads 160°.

Remove from the heat and allow to cool. Mix in the mayonnaise, Italian dressing and sugar. Cover and refrigerate for at least 1 hour. Serve over coleslaw, vegetables or pasta. **Yield: 4-1/2 cups.**

Creamy Celery Seed Dressing

Cranberry Orange Vinaigrette

Cranberry Orange Vinaigrette

I eat a lot of salad, and this is one of my favorite dressings. Living in Florida, I like using orange products produced in our state. —Toni Serpe, Dania, Florida

- 1/4 cup cranberry juice concentrate
- 1/4 cup orange juice concentrate
- 1/4 cup red wine vinegar
- 1/4 cup olive oil
- 1 teaspoon Dijon mustard
- 1/2 teaspoon salt
- 1/2 teaspoon pepper
- Torn salad greens
- Sliced radishes and sweet yellow and orange peppers *or* vegetables of your choice

In a jar with a tight-fitting lid, combine the first seven ingredients; shake well. Serve over greens and vegetables. Store in the refrigerator. **Yield: 1 cup.**

Blue Cheese Dressing

Blue Cheese Dressing

I tasted this tangy dressing at a friend's house, and she gave me the recipe. It tastes much better than bottled blue cheese dressing. —Barbara Nowakowski North Tonawanda, New York

- 1-1/2 cups mayonnaise
- 1/2 cup sour cream
- 1/4 cup cider vinegar
- 4 teaspoons sugar
- 1/2 teaspoon ground mustard
- 1/2 teaspoon garlic powder
- 1/2 teaspoon onion powder
- 1 cup (4 ounces) crumbled blue cheese

In a bowl, combine the first seven ingredients. Stir in the blue cheese. Cover and refrigerate for at least 2 hours. Store in the refrigerator. **Yield: 2 cups.**

EARTY HAMBURGER SOUP, pg. 84

Soups & Chili

Chunky Beef Noodle Soup

My husband and I lived for 11 years in the Arctic, where there was very little fresh produce and I had to order nonperishable groceries for a year ahead of time. This hearty soup—a meal in itself served with warm rolls—became a staple in our diet because it calls for ingredients I could easily find.

—Lil Morris, Emerald Park, Saskatchewan

- **1** **pound boneless round steak, cut into 1/2-inch cubes**
- **1** **medium onion, chopped**
- **2** **garlic cloves, minced**
- **1** **tablespoon vegetable oil**
- **2** **cups water**
- **1** **can (14-1/2 ounces) diced tomatoes, undrained**
- **1** **can (10-1/2 ounces) condensed beef consomme, undiluted**
- **1** **to 2 teaspoons chili powder**
- **1** **teaspoon salt**
- **1/2** **teaspoon dried oregano**
- **1** **cup uncooked spiral pasta**
- **1** **medium green pepper, chopped**
- **1/4** **cup minced fresh parsley**

In a large saucepan, cook the round steak, onion and garlic in oil until the meat is browned and the onion is tender, about 5 minutes. Stir in water, tomatoes, consomme and seasonings; bring to a boil. Reduce heat; cover and simmer for 1-1/2 hours or until meat is tender.

Stir in pasta and green pepper. Simmer, uncovered, until noodles are tender, about 8 minutes. Add parsley. **Yield: 8 servings (2 quarts).**

Chunky Beef Noodle Soup

Meatball Mushroom Soup

Meatball Mushroom Soup

This creamy, super-thick soup is hearty with meatballs, mushrooms, barley, macaroni and rice. With dinner rolls or breadsticks, it's a simple and satisfying meal for my husband and me on a rainy day. Leftovers easily reheat for a fast, filling lunch or dinner. —JoAnn Abbott, Kerhonkson, New York

- **1/2 pound ground beef**
- **2 cans (10-3/4 ounces *each*) condensed cream of mushroom soup, undiluted**
- **1-1/3 cups milk**
- **1-1/3 cups water**
- **1 teaspoon Italian seasoning**
- **1 teaspoon dried minced onion**
- **1/2 teaspoon dried minced garlic**
- **1/4 cup quick-cooking barley**
- **1/4 cup uncooked elbow macaroni**
- **1/4 cup uncooked long grain rice**
- **1 medium carrot, shredded**
- **1 jar (4-1/2 ounces) sliced mushrooms, drained**
- **2 tablespoons grated Parmesan cheese**

Shape beef into 1-in. balls; set aside. In a large saucepan, combine the soup, milk and water; bring to a boil. Add the Italian seasoning, onion, garlic, barley, macaroni and rice. Reduce the heat; simmer, uncovered, for 15 minutes.

Meanwhile, brown meatballs in a nonstick skillet until no longer pink. Stir carrot into soup; cover and simmer for 5 minutes. Use a slotted spoon to transfer meatballs to soup. Stir in mushrooms and Parmesan cheese; heat through. **Yield: 6 servings.**

Hearty Hamburger Soup

At family get-togethers, our children always request this spirit-warming soup along with a fresh loaf of homemade bread and tall glasses of milk. It has robust flavor, plenty of fresh-tasting vegetables and is easy to make. —Barbara Brown, Janesville, Wisconsin

- **1 pound ground beef**
- **4 cups water**
- **1 can (14-1/2 ounces) diced tomatoes, undrained**
- **3 medium carrots, sliced**
- **2 medium potatoes, peeled and cubed**
- **1 medium onion, chopped**
- **1/2 cup chopped celery**
- **4 beef bouillon cubes**
- **1-1/2 teaspoons salt**
- **1/4 teaspoon pepper**
- **1/4 teaspoon dried oregano**
- **1 cup cut fresh *or* frozen green beans**

In a large saucepan, cook beef over medium heat until no longer pink; drain. Add the next 10 ingredients; bring to a boil. Reduce heat;

cover and simmer for 15 minutes or until potatoes and carrots are tender. Add beans. Cover and simmer 15 minutes longer or until the beans are tender. **Yield: 8 servings (2 quarts).**

Hearty Hamburger Soup

Stuffed Sweet Pepper Soup

Tomatoes, peppers, garlic and onions are the mainstays of my garden. Being the oldest of seven children, I acquired a knack for cooking from my mom.
—Joseph Kendra, Coraopolis, Pennsylvania

- 1 pound ground beef
- 2 quarts water
- 1 quart tomato juice
- 3 medium sweet red peppers, diced
- 1-1/2 cups chili sauce
- 1 cup uncooked long grain rice
- 2 celery ribs, diced
- 1 large onion, diced
- 2 teaspoons browning sauce, optional
- 3 chicken bouillon cubes
- 2 garlic cloves, minced
- 1/2 teaspoon salt

In a Dutch oven, cook beef over medium heat until no longer pink; drain. Add the remaining ingredients; bring to a boil. Reduce heat; simmer, uncovered, for 1 hour or until the rice is tender. **Yield: 16 servings (4 quarts).**

Stuffed Sweet Pepper Soup

Hungarian Goulash Soup

Swedish Meatball Soup

Hungarian Goulash Soup 1st prize

I taught with the Defense Department in Germany where goulash soup is common. I pieced this together once I got back and am pleased with the results.
—Betty Kennedy, Alexandria, Virginia

- 3 bacon strips, diced
- 1 small green pepper, seeded and chopped
- 2 medium onions, chopped
- 1 large garlic clove, minced
- 1-1/2 pounds beef stew meat, cut into 1/2-inch cubes
- 2 tablespoons paprika
- 1-1/2 teaspoons salt
- Pepper to taste
- Dash sugar
- 1 can (14-1/2 ounces) diced tomatoes
- 3 cups beef broth
- 2 large potatoes, peeled and diced
- 1/2 cup sour cream, optional

In a Dutch oven, cook bacon over medium heat until almost crisp. Add the green pepper, onions and garlic; cook until tender. Add the beef cubes and brown on all sides. Sprinkle with the paprika, salt, pepper and sugar; stir and cook for 2 minutes. Add the tomatoes and broth.

Cover and simmer for about 1-1/2 hours or until beef is tender. About 30 minutes before serving, add the potatoes and cook until tender. Garnish each serving with a dollop of sour cream if desired. **Yield: 8 servings (about 2 quarts).**

Swedish Meatball Soup

To me, this is a very comforting, filling, homey soup. I especially like cooking it during winter months and serving it with hot rolls, bread or muffins.
—Debora Taylor, Inkom, Idaho

- 1 egg
- 2 cups half-and-half cream, *divided*
- 1 cup soft bread crumbs
- 1 small onion, finely chopped
- 1-3/4 teaspoons salt, *divided*
- 1-1/2 pounds ground beef
- 1 tablespoon butter
- 3 tablespoons all-purpose flour
- 3/4 teaspoon beef bouillon granules
- 1/2 teaspoon pepper
- 1/8 to 1/4 teaspoon garlic salt
- 3 cups water
- 1 pound red potatoes, cubed
- 1 package (10 ounces) frozen peas, thawed

In a bowl, beat egg; add 1/3 cup cream, bread crumbs, onion and 1 teaspoon salt. Crumble beef over mixture and mix well. Shape into 1/2-in. balls. In a Dutch oven, brown meatballs in butter, half at a time. Remove from the pan; set aside. Drain fat.

Stir in the flour, bouillon, pepper, garlic salt and remaining salt into pan until blended. Gradually stir in water. Bring to a boil, stirring often. Add potatoes and meatballs. Reduce heat; cover and simmer for 25 minutes or until the potatoes are tender. Stir in peas and remaining cream; heat through. **Yield: 8 servings (about 2 quarts).**

Beefy Wild Rice Soup

Beefy Wild Rice Soup

Living in central Wisconsin, we experience many days of snow and cold temperatures. I like to prepare soup often, especially this one. My family loves it.
—Marilyn Chesbrough, Wautoma, Wisconsin

- 1 pound ground beef
- 1/2 teaspoon Italian seasoning
- 8 cups water, *divided*
- 2 large onions, chopped
- 3 celery ribs, chopped
- 1 cup uncooked wild rice
- 2 teaspoons beef bouillon granules
- 1/2 teaspoon pepper
- 1/4 teaspoon hot pepper sauce
- 3 cans (10-3/4 ounces *each*) condensed cream of mushroom soup, undiluted
- 1 can (4 ounces) mushroom stems and pieces, drained

In a Dutch oven or soup kettle, cook beef and Italian seasoning over medium heat until meat is no longer pink; drain. Add 2 cups water, onions, celery, rice, bouillon, pepper and hot pepper sauce; bring to a boil.

Reduce heat; cover and simmer for 45 minutes. Stir in the soup, mushrooms and remaining water. Cover and simmer for 30 minutes. **Yield: 10-12 servings (3 quarts).**

Pronto Taco Soup

Pronto Taco Soup

When out-of-state friends dropped by, I invited them to stay for dinner, knowing that I could put together this mild, chili-flavored soup in a jiffy. I served it with cornmeal muffins and a crisp salad for a filling meal everyone loved. My guests even asked for a copy of the recipe before leaving for home!
—Priscilla Gilbert, Indian Harbour Beach, Florida

- 1 pound ground beef
- 1 medium onion, chopped
- 2 garlic cloves, minced
- 2 cans (14-1/2 ounces *each*) beef broth
- 1 can (14-1/2 ounces) diced tomatoes, undrained
- 1-1/2 cups picante sauce
- 1 cup uncooked spiral *or* small shell pasta
- 1 medium green pepper, chopped
- 2 teaspoons chili powder
- 1 teaspoon dried parsley flakes

Shredded cheddar cheese and tortilla chips

In a large saucepan, cook beef, onion and garlic over medium heat until meat is no longer pink; drain. Add the broth, tomatoes, picante sauce, pasta, green pepper, chili powder and parsley. Bring to a boil, stirring occasionally.

Reduce heat; cover and simmer for 10-15 minutes or until pasta is tender. Garnish with cheese and tortilla chips. **Yield: 8 servings (2 quarts).**

Stir-Fried Pork Soup

Especially to guests who enjoy the variety of Chinese cooking, this is a treat. I like it partnered with fried noodles or rice as a side dish.
—Louise Johnson, Harriman, Tennessee

- 2/3 pound boneless pork loin, cut into thin strips
- 1 cup sliced fresh mushrooms
- 1 cup chopped celery
- 1/2 cup diced carrots
- 2 tablespoons vegetable oil
- 6 cups chicken broth
- 1/2 cup chopped fresh spinach
- 2 tablespoons cornstarch
- 3 tablespoons cold water
- 1 egg, lightly beaten

Pepper to taste

In a large saucepan, stir-fry the pork, mushrooms, celery and carrots in oil until pork is browned and vegetables are tender. Add broth and spinach.

Combine cornstarch and water until smooth; stir into soup. Return to a boil; cook and stir for 1 minute. Quickly stir in egg. Add pepper. Serve immediately. **Yield: 4-6 servings.**

Corn and Sausage Soup

I created this recipe years ago when I received an abundance of fresh sweet corn from friends. The soup is easy to make and has always been a big hit with family and friends. I usually serve it with bread and a tossed salad. —Rebecca Clark, Hammond, Louisiana

- 2-1/2 cups chopped onions
- 1/2 cup *each* chopped green pepper, sweet red pepper and celery
- 6 tablespoons butter
- 1-1/2 pounds smoked sausage, cut into 1/4-inch pieces
- 3 garlic cloves, minced

Stir-Fried Pork Soup

- 4 cans (15 ounces *each*) Italian-style tomato sauce
- 3 packages (16 ounces *each*) frozen corn
- 2 cans (14-1/2 ounces *each*) Italian diced tomatoes, undrained
- 2 cups water
- 3 bay leaves
- 1-1/2 teaspoons *each* dried basil, oregano and thyme
- 1/2 teaspoon pepper
- 1/4 teaspoon dried marjoram
- 1/4 teaspoon hot pepper sauce, optional

In a Dutch oven or soup kettle, saute the onions, peppers and celery in butter until tender. Add sausage and garlic; cook for 8-10 minutes or until heated.

Stir in the remaining ingredients. Bring to a boil. Reduce heat; simmer, uncovered, for 1 hour, stirring occasionally. Discard bay leaves. **Yield: 16-18 servings (about 5 quarts).**

Corn and Sausage Soup

Sausage Potato Soup

Sausage Broccoli Chowder

Sausage Potato Soup

After a full day of teaching and coaching, I'm often too tired to spend a lot of time preparing dinner. So I rely on this thick, chunky blend that I can have on the table in 30 minutes. The whole family enjoys the wonderful flavor of the smoked sausage.
—Jennifer LeFevre, Hesston, Kansas

- 1/2 pound smoked kielbasa *or* Polish sausage, diced
- 6 medium potatoes, peeled and cubed
- 2 cups frozen corn
- 1-1/2 cups chicken broth
- 1 celery rib, sliced
- 1/4 cup sliced carrot
- 1/2 teaspoon garlic powder
- 1/2 teaspoon onion powder
- 1/2 teaspoon salt
- 1/4 teaspoon pepper
- 1-1/2 cups milk
- 2/3 cup shredded cheddar cheese
- 1 teaspoon minced fresh parsley

In a large saucepan, brown sausage over medium heat; drain. Set sausage aside. In the

same pan, combine the potatoes, corn, broth, celery, carrot and seasonings. Bring to a boil. Reduce heat; cover and simmer for 15 minutes or until vegetables are tender.

Add the milk, cheese, parsley and sausage. Cook and stir over low heat until cheese is melted and soup is heated through. **Yield: 6 servings.**

Sausage Broccoli Chowder

In New England, we frequently have cool fall evenings that call for a dinner that warms you all over. This chowder does that. I must admit I don't care too much for the taste of broccoli, but I really like this chowder.
—Donald Roberts, Amherst, New Hampshire

- 1 pound bulk Italian sausage
- 1 medium onion, chopped
- 3 garlic cloves, minced
- 1/2 pound fresh mushrooms, sliced
- 2 tablespoons butter
- 2 cups broccoli florets
- 2 to 3 carrots, diced
- 2 cans (14-1/2 ounces *each*) chicken broth
- 1 can (10-3/4 ounces) condensed cream of mushroom soup, undiluted
- 9 ounces cheese tortellini, cooked and drained
- 1/2 teaspoon pepper
- 1/2 teaspoon dried basil
- 1/2 teaspoon dried thyme
- 2 quarts half-and-half cream
- 1/2 cup grated Romano cheese

Crumble sausage into a skillet; cook over medium heat until no longer pink. Using a slotted spoon, remove to paper towels to drain; set aside. In the same skillet, saute onion, garlic and mushrooms in butter until tender; set aside.

Tasty Reuben Soup

In a Dutch oven, cook the broccoli and carrots in chicken broth until tender. Stir in sausage and the mushroom mixture. Add the soup, tortellini, pepper, basil and thyme; heat through. Stir in cream and Romano cheese; heat through. **Yield: 12-16 servings (4 quarts).**

Tasty Reuben Soup

I'm a working mom with limited time to feed my hungry family, so I'm always looking for quick recipes. This speedy soup, which may remind you of a Reuben sandwich, is a favorite of ours.
—Terry Ann Brandt, Tobias, Nebraska

- 4 cans (14-1/2 ounces *each*) chicken broth
- 4 cups shredded cabbage
- 2 cups uncooked medium egg noodles
- 1 pound smoked kielbasa *or* Polish sausage, halved and cut into 1-inch slices
- 1/2 cup chopped onion
- 1 teaspoon caraway seeds
- 1/4 teaspoon garlic powder
- 1 cup (4 ounces) shredded Swiss cheese

In a large saucepan, combine the first seven ingredients; bring to a boil. Reduce heat; cover and simmer for 15 minutes or until cabbage and noodles are tender. Garnish with cheese. **Yield: 10 servings (2-1/2 quarts).**

Turkey Dumpling Soup

Turkey Dumpling Soup

Simmering up a big pot of this soup is one of my favorite holiday traditions. This is a variation on a recipe my mom made while I was growing up. My husband and children can't get enough of the tender dumplings.—Debbie Wolf, Mission Viejo, California

- 1 meaty leftover turkey carcass (from an 11-pound turkey)
- 6 cups chicken broth
- 6 cups water
- 2 celery ribs, cut into 1-inch slices
- 1 medium carrot, cut into 1-inch slices
- 1 tablespoon poultry seasoning
- 1 bay leaf
- 1/2 teaspoon salt
- 1/2 teaspoon pepper

SOUP INGREDIENTS:

- 1 medium onion, chopped
- 2 celery ribs, chopped
- 2 medium carrots, sliced
- 1 cup fresh *or* frozen cut green beans
- 1 package (10 ounces) frozen corn
- 1 package (10 ounces) frozen peas
- 2 cups biscuit/baking mix
- 2/3 cup milk

In a large Dutch oven, combine the first nine ingredients. Slowly bring to a boil. Reduce heat; cover and simmer for 3 hours.

Remove carcass and allow to cool. Remove meat from bones; discard bones. Cut meat into bite-size pieces; set aside 4 cups for soup (refrigerate any remaining meat for another use). Strain broth, discarding vegetables and bay leaf.

Return broth to Dutch oven; add the onion, celery, carrots and beans. Bring to a boil. Reduce heat; cover and simmer for 10 minutes or until vegetables are tender. Add the corn, peas and reserved turkey. Bring to a boil; reduce heat.

Combine biscuit mix and milk. Drop by teaspoonfuls onto simmering broth. Cover and simmer for 10 minutes or until a toothpick inserted in a dumpling comes out clean (do not lift the cover while simmering). **Yield: 16 servings (4 quarts).**

Southern Chicken Rice Soup

A favorite at soup night at our church, this recipe's one my husband concocted after he retired. I frequently find it on the table when I get home from work.
—Rosalie Biar, Thorndale, Texas

- 1 broiler/fryer chicken (about 3 pounds)
- 10 cups water
- 2 teaspoons salt
- 1/2 cup uncooked long grain rice
- 1/2 cup chopped onion
- 1/2 cup chopped celery
- 1/2 cup thinly sliced carrots
- 1/2 cup sliced fresh *or* frozen okra
- 1 can (14-1/2 ounces) stewed tomatoes, diced
- 1 tablespoon chopped green chilies
- 1 garlic clove, minced
- 1-1/2 teaspoons chili powder
- 1 teaspoon seasoned salt
- 1/2 teaspoon lemon-pepper seasoning
- 1/2 teaspoon Creole seasoning

Place chicken, water and salt in a Dutch oven. Slowly bring to a boil; skim foam from broth. Reduce heat; cover and simmer for about 1 hour or until the chicken is tender.

Remove chicken; when cool enough to handle, remove meat from bones. Discard bones. Cut meat into bite-size pieces; set aside.

Skim fat from broth. Add the rice, vegetables and seasonings. Cook, uncovered, over medium heat for 30 minutes. Add the chicken. Simmer, uncovered, 30 minutes longer or until vegetables are tender. **Yield: 10 servings (about 2-1/2 quarts).**

Southern Chicken Rice Soup

New England Clam Chowder

I wasn't satisfied with other recipes I came across for clam chowder, so I devised this one. Everyone who's tried it raves about it. The dish is great on a cold day.
—Rachel Nydam, Uxbridge, Massachusetts

- 4 medium potatoes, peeled and cubed
- 2 medium onions, chopped
- 1/2 cup butter
- 3/4 cup all-purpose flour
- 2 quarts milk
- 3 cans (6-1/2 ounces *each*) chopped clams, undrained
- 2 to 3 teaspoons salt
- 1 teaspoon ground sage
- 1 teaspoon ground thyme
- 1/2 teaspoon celery salt
- 1/2 teaspoon pepper
- Minced fresh parsley

Place potatoes in a saucepan and cover with water; bring to boil. Reduce heat; cook, covered, until potatoes are tender, about 15 minutes.

Meanwhile, in a Dutch oven, saute onions in butter until tender. Stir in flour until blended. Gradually add milk. Bring to a boil over medium heat; cook and stir for 2 minutes or until thickened.

Drain potatoes; add to Dutch oven. Add clams and the remaining ingredients; heat through. **Yield: 10-12 servings (3 quarts).**

New England Clam Chowder

Northwest Salmon Chowder

Creamy Carrot Parsnip Soup

Northwest Salmon Chowder

I have a big garden, and by the end of fall, my cellar shelves are full of canned fruits and vegetables. This recipe uses some of the root vegetables I grow, along with the delicious salmon that is so plentiful here.
—Josephine Parton, Granger, Washington

- 1/2 cup *each* chopped celery, onion and green pepper
- 1 garlic clove, minced
- 3 tablespoons butter
- 1 can (14-1/2 ounces) chicken broth
- 1 cup uncooked diced peeled potatoes
- 1 cup shredded carrots
- 1-1/2 teaspoons salt
- 1/2 teaspoon pepper
- 1/4 to 3/4 teaspoon dill weed
- 1 can (14-3/4 ounces) cream-style corn
- 2 cups half-and-half cream
- 1-3/4 to 2 cups fully cooked salmon chunks *or* 1 can (14-3/4 ounces) salmon, drained, flaked, bones and skin removed

In a large saucepan, saute the celery, onion, green pepper and garlic in butter until the vegetables are tender. Add the broth, potatoes, carrots, salt, pepper and dill; bring to a boil. Reduce heat; cover and simmer for 40 minutes or until the vegetables are nearly tender.

Stir in the corn, cream and salmon. Simmer for 15 minutes or until heated through. **Yield: 8 servings (2 quarts).**

Creamy Carrot Parsnip Soup 1st prize

This creamy concoction tastes like it's fresh from the garden. A hint of horseradish and ginger sparks every steaming spoonful.

—Phyllis Clinehens, Maplewood, Ohio

- 8 cups chopped carrots
- 6 cups chopped peeled parsnips
- 4 cups chicken broth
- 3 cups water
- 2 teaspoons sugar
- 1 teaspoon salt
- 1 medium onion, chopped
- 4 garlic cloves, minced
- 1 teaspoon peeled grated horseradish
- 1 teaspoon minced fresh gingerroot
- 3 tablespoons butter
- 2 cups buttermilk
- 2 tablespoons sour cream
- Fresh dill sprigs, optional

In a Dutch oven, combine the carrots, parsnips, broth, water, sugar and salt; bring to a boil. Reduce heat; cover and cook for 25-30 minutes or until vegetables are tender.

In a skillet, saute the onion, garlic, horseradish and ginger in butter until tender. Add to the carrot mixture and cool slightly.

Transfer soup to a blender in batches; cover and process until smooth. Return to the pan. Stir in buttermilk; heat through (do not boil).

Rich French Onion Soup

Garnish servings with sour cream and dill if desired. **Yield: 12 servings (3 quarts).**

Rich French Onion Soup

When entertaining guests, I bring out this savory soup while we're waiting for the main course. It's simple to make—just saute the onions early in the day and let the soup simmer until dinnertime. In winter, big bowls of it make a warming supper with a salad and biscuits.

—Linda Adolph, Edmonton, Alberta

- 6 large onions, chopped
- 1/2 cup butter
- 6 cans (10-1/2 ounces *each*) condensed beef broth, undiluted
- 1-1/2 teaspoons Worcestershire sauce
- 3 bay leaves
- 10 slices French bread, toasted
- Shredded Parmesan cheese and part-skim mozzarella cheeses

In a large skillet, saute onions in butter until crisp-tender. Transfer to a 5-qt. slow cooker. Add the broth, Worcestershire sauce and bay leaves. Cover and cook on low for 5-7 hours or until the onions are tender. Discard bay leaves. Top each serving with French bread and cheeses. **Yield: 10 servings.**

Creamy Asparagus Chowder

Creamy Asparagus Chowder 1st prize

While this soup's good with fresh asparagus, it can also be prepared with frozen or canned. In fact, I like to blanch and freeze asparagus in portions just right for the recipe—this way, I can make our favorite chowder all year. —*Shirley Beachum, Shelby, Michigan*

- 1/4 cup butter
- 2 medium onions, chopped
- 2 cups chopped celery
- 1 garlic clove, minced
- 1/2 cup all-purpose flour
- 1 large potato, peeled and cut into 1/2-inch cubes
- 4 cups milk
- 4 cups chicken broth
- 1/2 teaspoon dried thyme
- 1/2 teaspoon dried marjoram
- 4 cups chopped fresh asparagus, cooked and drained
- Salt and pepper to taste
- Sliced almonds
- Shredded cheddar cheese
- Chopped fresh tomato

In a Dutch oven, melt butter; saute the onions, celery and garlic until tender. Stir in flour. Add the potato, milk, broth and herbs; cook over low heat for 20-30 minutes or until potato is tender and soup is thickened, stirring occasionally.

Add the asparagus, salt and pepper; heat through. To serve, sprinkle with the almonds, cheese and chopped tomato. **Yield: 8-10 servings (2-1/2 quarts).**

Parmesan Potato Soup

Even my husband, who's not much of a soup eater, likes this. Our two boys do, too. With homemade bread and a salad, it's a satisfying meal.
—*Tami Walters, Kingsport, Tennessee*

- 4 medium baking potatoes (about 2 pounds)
- 3/4 cup chopped onion
- 1/2 cup butter, cubed
- 1/2 cup all-purpose flour
- 1/2 teaspoon dried basil
- 1/2 teaspoon seasoned salt
- 1/4 teaspoon celery salt
- 1/4 teaspoon garlic powder
- 1/4 teaspoon onion salt
- 1/4 teaspoon pepper
- 1/4 teaspoon rubbed sage
- 1/4 teaspoon dried thyme
- 4-1/2 cups chicken broth
- 6 cups milk
- 3/4 to 1 cup grated Parmesan cheese
- 10 bacon strips, cooked and crumbled

Pierce potatoes with a fork; bake in the oven or microwave until tender. Cool, peel and cube; set aside.

In a large Dutch oven, cook onion in butter over medium heat until tender. Stir in flour and seasonings until blended. Gradually add broth, stirring constantly. Bring to a boil; cook and stir for 2 minutes.

Add potatoes; return to a boil. Reduce heat; cover and simmer for 10 minutes. Add milk and cheese; heat through (do not boil). Stir in bacon. **Yield: 10-12 servings.**

Hearty Vegetable Soup

A friend gave me the idea to use V8 juice in soup because it provides more flavor. This soup is great to make on a crisp autumn afternoon.

—Janice Steinmetz, Somers, Connecticut

- 8 medium carrots, sliced
- 2 large onions, chopped
- 4 celery ribs, chopped
- 1 large green pepper, seeded and chopped
- 1 garlic clove, minced
- 1 tablespoon olive oil
- 4 cups water
- 1 can (28 ounces) diced tomatoes, undrained
- 2 cups V8 juice
- 2 cups chopped cabbage
- 2 cups frozen cut green beans
- 2 cups frozen peas
- 1 cup frozen corn
- 1 can (15 ounces) garbanzo beans *or* chickpeas, rinsed and drained
- 2 teaspoons chicken bouillon granules
- 1-1/2 teaspoons dried parsley flakes
- 1 teaspoon salt
- 1 teaspoon dried marjoram
- 1 teaspoon dried thyme
- 1 bay leaf
- 1/2 teaspoon dried basil
- 1/4 teaspoon pepper

In a Dutch oven, saute the carrots, onions, celery, green pepper and garlic in oil until crisp-tender. Stir in remaining ingredients. Bring to a boil. Reduce heat; cover and simmer for 1 to 1-1/2 hours or until vegetables are tender. Discard bay leaf before serving. **Yield: 14-16 servings (4 quarts).**

Parmesan Potato Soup

Hearty Vegetable Soup

Southwestern Tomato Soup

Red Pepper Soup

Southwestern Tomato Soup

This smooth, flavorful tomato soup is unbeatable when the season's ripest tomatoes are available and the weather starts to cool. Each delicious, fresh-tasting bowlful will warm you from the inside out.
—Sherri Jackson, Chillicothe, Ohio

- 10 plum tomatoes, halved lengthwise
- 1 to 2 Anaheim peppers, halved and seeded
- 1/2 cup chopped onion
- 2 garlic cloves, minced
- 1 tablespoon olive oil
- 2 cans (14-1/2 ounces *each*) chicken broth
- 1 tablespoon minced fresh cilantro
- 2 teaspoons ground cumin
- 1/2 teaspoon sugar
- 1/2 teaspoon salt
- 1/4 teaspoon pepper
- Vegetable oil for frying
- 8 corn tortillas (6 inches), cut into 1/4-inch strips
- Sour cream, optional

Place tomatoes cut side down on a broiler pan; broil 3-4 in. from the heat for 15-20 minutes. Peel and discard skins. Repeat with peppers, broiling for 5-10 minutes.

In a skillet, saute onion and garlic in oil until tender. Transfer to a food processor or blender; add the tomatoes and peppers. Cover and process until smooth. Pour into a large saucepan; cook and stir over medium heat for 2 minutes.

Press mixture through a strainer with a spoon; discard seeds. Return tomato mixture to the pan. Add the broth, cilantro, cumin, sugar, salt and pepper. Cover and cook on low for 15-20 minutes or until heated through.

Meanwhile, heat 1/2 in. of oil in a skillet to 375°. Fry tortilla strips, in batches, for 3-5 minutes or until golden brown; drain on paper towels. Garnish bowls of soup with tortilla strips. Serve with sour cream if desired. **Yield: 6 servings.**

Editor's Note: When cutting or seeding hot peppers, use rubber or plastic gloves to protect your hands. Avoid touching your face.

Red Pepper Soup 1st prize

While I don't have scientific proof of it, Red Pepper Soup works for me as a head cold remedy! It is a good gift to take when visiting a sick friend, too. For a pretty touch, top the soup with grated cheese and parsley. —Barb Nelson, Victoria, British Columbia

- 6 medium sweet red peppers, chopped
- 2 medium carrots, chopped
- 2 medium onions, chopped
- 1 celery rib, chopped
- 4 garlic cloves, minced
- 1 tablespoon olive oil
- 2 cans (one 49-1/2 ounces, one 14-1/2 ounces) chicken broth
- 1/2 cup uncooked long grain rice
- 2 tablespoons minced fresh thyme *or* 2 teaspoons dried thyme
- 1-1/2 teaspoons salt
- 1/4 teaspoon pepper
- 1/8 to 1/4 teaspoon cayenne pepper
- 1/8 to 1/4 teaspoon crushed red pepper flakes

In a large Dutch oven, saute the red peppers, carrots, onions, celery and garlic in oil until tender. Stir in the broth, rice, thyme, salt, pepper and cayenne; bring to a boil. Reduce heat; cover and simmer for 20-25 minutes or until the vegetables and rice are tender.

Cool for 30 minutes. Puree in small batches in a blender; return to pan. Add red pepper flakes; heat through. **Yield: 10-12 servings (about 3 quarts).**

Best-Ever Potato Soup

Best-Ever Potato Soup

You'll be surprised at the taste of this rich, cheesy concoction—it's not a typical potato soup. I came up with the recipe after enjoying baked potato soup at one of our favorite restaurants.
—Coleen Morrissey, Sweet Valley, Pennsylvania

- 6 bacon strips, diced
- 1 can (14-1/2 ounces) chicken broth
- 3 cups cubed peeled potatoes
- 1 small carrot, grated
- 1/2 cup chopped onion
- 1 tablespoon dried parsley flakes
- 1/2 teaspoon *each* celery seed, salt and pepper
- 3 tablespoons all-purpose flour
- 3 cups milk
- 8 ounces process American cheese, cubed
- 2 green onions, thinly sliced, optional

In a large saucepan, cook bacon over medium heat until crisp. Using a slotted spoon, remove to paper towels; drain. Add the broth, vegetables and seasonings. Bring to a boil. Reduce heat; cover and simmer for 15 minutes or until potatoes are tender.

Combine flour and milk until smooth; add to soup. Bring to a boil; cook and stir for 2 minutes. Add cheese; stir until cheese is melted and the soup is heated through. Garnish with green onions if desired. **Yield: 8 servings (2 quarts).**

Cream of Cauliflower Soup

Cream of Cauliflower Soup 1st prize

Generally, my husband isn't a soup fan—but his spoon's poised and ready for this version. I adapted this rich and creamy concoction from a recipe I tasted at a local restaurant, and it's since become a popular item on my menu at home.

—Carol Reaves, San Antonio, Texas

- 2 medium onions, chopped
- 2 medium carrots, grated
- 2 celery ribs, sliced
- 2 garlic cloves, minced
- 1/4 cup plus 6 tablespoons butter, *divided*
- 1 medium head cauliflower, chopped
- 5 cups chicken broth
- 1/4 cup minced fresh parsley
- 1 teaspoon salt
- 1 teaspoon coarsely ground pepper
- 1/2 teaspoon dried basil
- 1/2 teaspoon dried tarragon
- 6 tablespoons all-purpose flour
- 1 cup milk
- 1/2 cup heavy whipping cream
- 1/4 cup sour cream

Fresh tarragon, optional

In a soup kettle or Dutch oven, saute the onions, carrots, celery and garlic in 1/4 cup butter until tender. Add the cauliflower, broth, parsley, salt, pepper, basil and tarragon. Cover and simmer for 30 minutes or until the vegetables are tender.

Meanwhile, in a saucepan, melt the remaining butter. Stir in flour until smooth. Gradually stir in the milk and whipping cream. Bring to a boil; cook and stir for 2 minutes or until thickened, stirring frequently. Remove from the heat; stir in sour cream. Garnish with tarragon if desired. **Yield: 8 servings (about 2 quarts).**

Sizzling Rice Soup

My family enjoys food with flair like this unique Oriental soup. Whenever I serve it, it's such a hit that no one has much room for the main course. The children get a real kick out of watching the rice sizzle when it gets added to the soup.

—Mary Woodke, Gardiner, New York

- 1 cup uncooked long grain rice
- 8 cups chicken broth
- 2 cups cubed cooked chicken
- 2 cups sliced fresh mushrooms
- 1/4 cup chopped green onions
- 1 can (8 ounces) bamboo shoots, drained
- 1 can (8 ounces) sliced water chestnuts, drained
- 4 chicken bouillon cubes
- 1/2 teaspoon garlic powder
- 1 package (10 ounces) frozen peas
- 1/4 cup vegetable oil

Cook the rice according to package directions. Spread on a greased 15-in. x 10-in. x 1-in. baking pan. Bake at 325° for 2 hours or until dried and browned, stirring occasionally; set rice aside.

In a Dutch oven, combine the broth, chicken, mushrooms, onions, bamboo shoots, water chestnuts, bouillon and garlic powder. Cover and simmer for 1 hour. Add peas; cook for 15 minutes.

Just before serving, heat oil in a skillet. Fry rice in hot oil until it is slightly puffed. Ladle soup into serving bowls. Immediately spoon some hot rice into each bowl and it will sizzle. **Yield: 10-12 servings (3 quarts).**

Sizzling Rice Soup

Wild Rice Soup

As the oldest of eight girls growing up on the farm, I began cooking at an early age! This soup—which I first had at my sister's house—brings me compliments no matter where I serve it.

—Elienore Myhre, Balaton, Minnesota

- 1/3 cup uncooked wild rice
- 1 tablespoon vegetable oil
- 1 quart water
- 1 medium onion, chopped
- 1 celery rib, finely chopped
- 1 medium carrot, finely chopped
- 1/2 cup butter
- 1/2 cup all-purpose flour
- 3 cups chicken broth
- 2 cups half-and-half cream
- 1/2 teaspoon dried rosemary, crushed
- 1 teaspoon salt

In a medium saucepan, combine the rice, oil and water; bring to a boil. Reduce heat; cover and simmer for 30 minutes.

Meanwhile, in a Dutch oven, cook the onion, celery and carrot in butter until vegetables are almost tender. Stir in flour until blended. Gradually add the broth; stir in undrained rice. Bring to a boil; cook and stir for 2 minutes or until slightly thickened.

Reduce heat; stir in the cream, rosemary and salt. Simmer, uncovered, for about 20 minutes or until rice is tender. **Yield: 8 servings (about 2 quarts).**

Wild Rice Soup

Savory Cheese Soup

Lentil Barley Soup

Savory Cheese Soup 1st prize

This delicious soup recipe was shared by a friend and instantly became a hit with my husband. Its big cheese flavor blends wonderfully with the vegetables. I first served this creamy soup as part of a holiday meal, but now we enjoy it throughout the year.
—Dee Falk, Stromsburg, Nebraska

- 1/4 cup chopped onion
- 3 tablespoons butter
- 1/4 cup all-purpose flour
- 1/4 teaspoon salt
- 1/8 teaspoon pepper
- 1/8 teaspoon garlic powder
- 2 cups milk
- 1 can (14-1/2 ounces) chicken broth
- 1/2 cup shredded carrot
- 1/2 cup finely chopped celery
- 1-1/2 cups (6 ounces) shredded cheddar cheese
- 3/4 cup shredded part-skim mozzarella cheese

Fresh *or* dried chives, optional

In a large saucepan, saute onion in butter until tender. Stir in the flour, salt, pepper and garlic powder until smooth. Gradually add milk. Bring to a boil over medium heat; cook and stir for 2 minutes or until thickened.

Meanwhile, bring chicken broth to a boil in a small saucepan. Add carrot and celery; simmer, uncovered, for 5 minutes or until vegetables are tender. Add to milk mixture and stir until blended. Reduce heat; add cheeses. Cook and stir until cheese is melted (do not boil). Garnish with chives if desired. **Yield: 4 servings.**

Lentil Barley Soup

Soups are one of my favorite things to prepare—they're so easy, and nothing is better on a chilly evening with some homemade bread or biscuits.
—Anita Warner, Mt. Crawford, Virginia

- 1 medium onion, chopped
- 1/2 cup chopped green pepper
- 3 garlic cloves, minced
- 1 tablespoon butter
- 1 can (49-1/2 ounces) chicken broth
- 3 medium carrots, chopped
- 1/2 cup dried lentils
- 1-1/2 teaspoons Italian seasoning
- 1 teaspoon salt
- 1/4 teaspoon pepper
- 1 cup cubed cooked chicken *or* turkey
- 1/2 cup quick-cooking barley
- 2 medium fresh mushrooms, chopped
- 1 can (28 ounces) crushed tomatoes, undrained

In a Dutch oven, saute the onion, green pepper and garlic in butter until tender. Add the broth, carrots, lentils, Italian seasoning, salt and pepper; bring to a boil. Reduce heat; cover and simmer for 25 minutes.

Add the chicken, barley and mushrooms; return to a boil. Reduce heat; cover and simmer for 10-15 minutes or until the lentils, barley and carrots are tender. Add tomatoes; heat through. **Yield: 8-10 servings (about 2-1/2 quarts).**

Navy Bean Squash Soup

On a cool day, what could be more comforting than a pot of this made-from-scratch soup simmering on the stove? The mix of ham, beans and squash is such a hearty combination, you'll savor every steamy spoonful.
—Linda Eggers, Albany, California

Navy Bean Squash Soup

- 1 pound dried navy beans
- 2 cans (14-1/2 ounces *each*) chicken broth
- 2 cups water
- 1 meaty ham bone
- 2 to 2-1/2 pounds butternut squash, peeled, seeded and cubed (about 5 cups)
- 1 large onion, chopped
- 1/2 teaspoon salt
- 1/2 teaspoon pepper

Place beans in a large saucepan or Dutch oven; add water to cover by 2 in. Bring to a boil; boil for 2 minutes. Remove from the heat; cover and let stand for 1-4 hours or until beans are softened. Drain and rinse beans, discarding liquid.

Return beans to pan. Add the broth, water, ham bone, squash, onion, salt and pepper. Bring to a boil. Reduce heat; cover and simmer for 1-1/2 to 1-3/4 hours or until beans are tender.

Remove ham bone. Mash the soup mixture, leaving some chunks if desired. Remove ham from bone; cut into chunks. Discard bone and fat. Return meat to the soup; heat through. **Yield: 12-14 servings (about 3 quarts).**

White Bean and Pasta Soup

White Bean and Pasta Soup

My husband and I savor every spoonful of this hearty soup. It makes a real stick-to-your-ribs meal when served with crusty, oven-fresh bread.
—Michelle Harbour, Lebanon, Tennessee

- 1-1/2 cups dried great northern beans
- 3/4 pound Italian sausage links, casings removed
- 1 large onion, chopped
- 1 large carrot, chopped
- 3 garlic cloves, minced
- 6 cups chicken broth
- 3 cups water
- 2 tablespoons dried currants
- 1 teaspoon dried basil
- 1 can (14-1/2 ounces) diced tomatoes, undrained
- 1 cup uncooked small shell pasta

Grated Parmesan cheese

Place beans in a Dutch oven; add water to cover by 2 in. Bring to a boil; boil for 2 minutes. Remove from the heat; cover and let stand for 1-4 hours or until beans are softened. Drain and rinse beans, discarding liquid.

In the same pan, cook the sausage, onion, carrot and garlic over medium heat until the meat is no longer pink; drain. Add the broth, water, currants, basil and beans. Bring to a boil. Reduce heat; cover and simmer for 1-1/2 to 2 hours or until the beans are tender, stirring occasionally.

Add tomatoes and pasta; bring to a boil. Reduce heat; cover and simmer for 15 minutes or until pasta is tender. Serve with Parmesan cheese. **Yield: 12 servings (3 quarts).**

Split Pea Sausage Soup

When my husband and I eat out and enjoy a dish, I go home and try to duplicate it. That's how I came up with this recipe.
—Donna Mae Young, Menomonie, Wisconsin

- 1 pound smoked kielbasa *or* Polish sausage
- 1 pound dried split peas
- 6 cups water
- 1 cup chopped carrots
- 1 cup chopped onion
- 1 cup chopped celery
- 1 tablespoon minced fresh parsley
- 1 teaspoon salt
- 1/2 teaspoon coarse black pepper
- 2 bay leaves

Cut sausage in half lengthwise; cut into 1/4-in. pieces. Place in a Dutch oven; add the remaining ingredients. Bring to a boil. Reduce heat; cover and simmer for 1-1/4 to 1-1/2 hours or until peas are tender. Discard bay leaves. **Yield: 8 servings (2 quarts).**

Baked Chili

This main dish is wonderful the first day and also makes outstanding leftovers. As a student living on my own, I love savory one-pot suppers like this.
—Michelle Gal, Toronto, Ontario

- 1 pound ground beef
- 1 large onion, chopped
- 1 large green pepper, chopped
- 1 can (16 ounces) kidney beans, rinsed and drained

- 1 can (15-1/4 ounces) whole kernel corn, drained
- 1 can (15 ounces) tomato sauce
- 1 can (14-1/2 ounces) diced tomatoes, undrained
- 1 can (4 ounces) chopped green chilies
- 2 teaspoons chili powder
- 1 teaspoon salt
- 1 teaspoon ground cumin
- 1/2 teaspoon sugar
- 1/2 teaspoon garlic powder

CORN BREAD BISCUITS:

- 1 cup all-purpose flour
- 1 cup cornmeal
- 2 teaspoons baking powder
- 1/8 teaspoon salt
- 1 egg
- 1/2 cup milk
- 1/2 cup sour cream

In a Dutch oven, cook the beef, onion and green pepper over medium heat until meat is no longer pink; drain. Add the remaining ingredients; bring to a boil, stirring occasionally. Reduce heat; cover and simmer for 10 minutes.

Meanwhile, combine the flour, cornmeal, baking powder and salt in a bowl. Beat the egg, milk and sour cream until smooth; stir into dry ingredients just until moistened.

Transfer chili to an ungreased 13-in. x 9-in. x 2-in. baking dish. Drop batter by heaping teaspoonfuls onto hot chili. Bake, uncovered, at 400° for 15-17 minutes or until biscuits are lightly browned. **Yield: 8 servings.**

Split Pea Sausage Soup

Baked Chili

Ground Beef Chili

Ground Beef Chili

Everyone who tastes my chili comments that it is restaurant-quality. It's especially good with homemade corn bread. I have always loved to cook, and I enjoy developing original recipes like this one.
—Shannon Wright, Erie, Pennsylvania

- 3 pounds ground beef
- 1 large onion, chopped
- 1 medium green pepper, chopped
- 2 celery ribs, chopped
- 2 cans (16 ounces *each*) kidney beans, rinsed and drained
- 1 can (29 ounces) tomato puree
- 1 jar (16 ounces) salsa
- 1 can (14-1/2 ounces) diced tomatoes, undrained
- 1 can (10-1/2 ounces) condensed beef broth, undiluted
- 1 to 2 cups water
- 1/4 cup chili powder
- 2 tablespoons Worcestershire sauce
- 1 tablespoon dried basil
- 2 teaspoons ground cumin
- 2 teaspoons steak sauce
- 1 teaspoon garlic powder
- 1 teaspoon salt
- 1 teaspoon coarsely ground pepper
- 1-1/2 teaspoons browning sauce, optional
- Additional chopped onion, optional

In a Dutch oven, cook the beef, onion, green pepper and celery over medium heat until meat is no longer pink and vegetables are tender; drain.

Stir in the beans, tomato puree, salsa, tomatoes, broth, water, seasonings and browning sauce if desired. Bring to a boil. Reduce heat; simmer, uncovered, for 30 minutes or until chili reaches desired thickness. Garnish with chopped onion if desired. **Yield: 16 servings.**

Cowpoke Chili

Many friends and relatives have requested my chili recipe, which I've been using for nearly 30 years. It actually won first place in a local contest, chosen from among 10 other entries. It always comes out delicious.
—Ramona Nelson, Fairbanks, Alaska

- 1 pound ground beef
- 1 small onion, chopped
- 1 garlic clove, minced
- 1 can (10-1/2 ounces) condensed beef broth, undiluted
- 1 can (8 ounces) tomato sauce
- 1 can (6 ounces) tomato paste
- 1 can (15-1/2 ounces) hot chili beans
- 1 can (15 ounces) black beans, rinsed and drained
- 2 tablespoons sugar
- 1 tablespoon butter
- 1 teaspoon chili powder
- 1/4 teaspoon salt
- 1/4 teaspoon dried oregano
- 1/8 teaspoon ground cumin
- 1/8 teaspoon crushed red pepper flakes
- Dash cayenne pepper
- 2 cups frozen lima beans, thawed
- Cherry tomatoes, fresh oregano and small chili peppers, optional

In a large saucepan, cook the beef, onion and garlic over medium heat until meat is no longer pink; drain. Stir in the broth, tomato sauce and paste until blended. Add the next 10 ingredient. Bring to a boil. Reduce heat; cover and simmer for 30 minutes.

Add lima beans; cook 5-10 minutes longer or until beans are tender. Garnish with the tomatoes, oregano and peppers if desired. **Yield: 7 servings.**

Cowpoke Chili

California Pepper Chili

Pepperoni Pizza Chili

California Pepper Chili

In my opinion, this is the world's best chili! It features three meats in a peppery, eye-opening broth.
—Robyn Thompson, Los Angeles, California

- 1/2 pound bacon, diced
- 2-1/2 pounds beef stew meat, cut into 3/4-inch cubes
- 1-1/2 pounds pork stew meat, cut into 3/4-inch cubes
- 2 medium onions, chopped
- 6 to 8 garlic cloves, minced
- 1 to 2 tablespoons chopped seeded fresh serrano chili peppers
- 1 to 2 tablespoons chopped seeded fresh poblano chili peppers
- 1 to 2 tablespoons chopped seeded fresh jalapeno peppers
- 2 to 3 teaspoons cayenne pepper
- 1-1/2 teaspoons dried oregano
- 1 teaspoon salt
- 1 teaspoon ground cumin
- 1 can (15 ounces) tomato puree
- 1 can (14-1/2 ounces) beef broth
- 7 plum tomatoes, chopped
- Shredded cheddar cheese, optional

In a large saucepan, cook bacon over medium heat until crisp. Using a slotted spoon, remove to paper towels; drain, reserving 3 tablespoons drippings.

In the drippings, cook the beef, pork and onions until meat is browned; drain. Add the garlic, peppers and seasonings; cook and stir for 1-2 minutes.

Stir in the tomato puree, broth and tomatoes. Bring to a boil. Reduce heat; cover and simmer for 1 to 1-1/2 hours or until meat is tender. Garnish with reserved bacon and cheese if desired. **Yield: 8 servings.**

Editor's Note: When cutting or seeding hot peppers, use rubber or plastic gloves to protect your hands. Avoid touching your face.

Pepperoni Pizza Chili 1st prize

I first made this recipe one day when I decided I didn't enjoy making pizza crust—I just put the pizza in a bowl instead! —Marilouise Wyatt, Cowen, West Virginia

- 1 pound ground beef
- 1 can (16 ounces) kidney beans, rinsed and drained
- 1 can (15 ounces) pizza sauce
- 1 can (14-1/2 ounces) Italian stewed tomatoes
- 1 can (8 ounces) tomato sauce
- 1-1/2 cups water
- 1 package (3-1/2 ounces) sliced pepperoni
- 1/2 cup chopped green pepper
- 1 teaspoon pizza seasoning *or* Italian seasoning
- 1 teaspoon salt
- Shredded part-skim mozzarella cheese, optional

In a large saucepan, cook beef over medium heat until no longer pink; drain. Stir in the beans, pizza sauce, tomatoes, tomato sauce, water, pepperoni, green pepper, pizza seasoning and salt. Bring to a boil. Reduce heat; simmer, uncovered, for 30 minutes or until chili reaches desired thickness. Garnish with cheese if desired. **Yield: 8 servings.**

Bold Bean and Pork Chili

This tempting chili is big on flavor and really very simple to prepare. Sometimes on a Sunday, I'll get a good start on it—up to where it's time to add the beans. Then the next day, I'll take it out of the fridge and finish it off in just a few minutes.
—Natercia Yailaian, Somerville, Massachusetts

- 1 pork shoulder *or* butt roast (4 to 5 pounds), trimmed and cut into 3/4-inch cubes

Bold Bean and Pork Chili

- 3 tablespoons olive oil
- 2 large onions, chopped
- 8 garlic cloves, minced
- 4 cans (14-1/2 ounces *each*) chicken broth
- 1 can (28 ounces) crushed tomatoes
- 1/2 to 2/3 cup chili powder
- 3 tablespoons dried oregano
- 2 to 3 tablespoons ground cumin
- 4-1/2 teaspoons salt
- 2 teaspoons cayenne pepper
- 4 cans (15 ounces *each*) black beans, rinsed and drained
- Minced fresh cilantro, optional

In a Dutch oven, saute pork in oil until no longer pink; drain. Add onions; cook and stir for 3 minutes. Add garlic; cook 2 minutes longer. Stir in the broth, tomatoes and seasonings. Bring to a boil. Reduce heat; simmer, uncovered, for 1 hour, stirring several times.

Skim fat; stir in beans. Simmer 15-30 minutes longer or until chili reaches desired thickness. Garnish with cilantro if desired. **Yield: 15 servings.**

Slow-Cooked Chunky Chili

Slow-Cooked Chunky Chili

Pork sausage, ground beef and plenty of beans make this chili a hearty meal-starter. I keep the versatile mixture in serving-size containers in my freezer at all times. I can quickly warm up bowls of it on cold days—or use it to fix chili dogs, tacos and more.
—Margie Shaw, Greenbrier, Arkansas

- 1 pound ground beef
- 1 pound bulk pork sausage
- 4 cans (16 ounces *each*) kidney beans, rinsed and drained
- 2 cans (14-1/2 ounces *each*) diced tomatoes, undrained
- 2 cans (10 ounces *each*) diced tomatoes and green chilies, undrained
- 1 large onion, chopped
- 1 medium green pepper, chopped
- 1 envelope taco seasoning
- 1/2 teaspoon salt
- 1/4 teaspoon pepper

In a skillet, cook beef and sausage over medium heat until meat is no longer pink; drain. Transfer to a 5-qt. slow cooker. Stir in the remaining ingredients. Cover and cook on high for 4-5 hours or until vegetables are tender. Serve desired amount. Cool the remaining chili; transfer to freezer bags or containers. Freeze for up to 3 months.

To use frozen chili: Thaw in the refrigerator; place in saucepan and heat through. Add water if desired. **Yield: 10-12 servings (3 quarts).**

Zippy Pork Chili

In addition to eating this chili, with a spoon, my family likes to scoop bites onto tortilla chips. The leftovers are great rolled in tortillas and reheated, too.
—Michelle Beran, Claflin, Kansas

- 1 boneless pork roast (3 to 4 pounds), cut into 1-inch cubes
- 1 medium onion, chopped
- 1 garlic clove, minced
- 2 tablespoons vegetable oil
- 2 cans (15-1/2 ounces *each*) chili beans
- 2 cans (10 ounces *each*) diced tomatoes with mild green chilies, undrained
- 1 can (14-1/2 ounces) diced tomatoes, undrained
- 1 cup water
- 1 teaspoon beef bouillon granules

Chili powder, pepper and cayenne pepper to taste

Sour cream, tortilla chips and shredded cheddar cheese, optional

In a Dutch oven, cook pork, onion and garlic in oil over medium heat until meat is browned. Add the beans, tomatoes, water, bouillon and seasonings. Bring to a boil. Reduce heat; cover and simmer for 2 hours or until meat is tender. If desired, serve with sour cream, tortilla chips and cheese. **Yield: 10 servings.**

Zippy Pork Chili

Creamy White Chili

I received this wonderful recipe from my sister-in-law, who made a big batch and served a crowd one night. It was a hit. In all my years of 4-H cooking, I've never had another dish get so many compliments.
—Laura Brewer, Lafayette, Indiana

- 1 pound boneless skinless chicken breasts, cut into 1/2-inch cubes
- 1 medium onion, chopped
- 1-1/2 teaspoons garlic powder
- 1 tablespoon vegetable oil
- 2 cans (15-1/2 ounces *each*) great northern beans, rinsed and drained
- 1 can (14-1/2 ounces) chicken broth
- 2 cans (4 ounces *each*) chopped green chilies
- 1 teaspoon salt
- 1 teaspoon ground cumin
- 1 teaspoon dried oregano
- 1/2 teaspoon pepper
- 1/4 teaspoon cayenne pepper
- 1 cup (8 ounces) sour cream
- 1/2 cup heavy whipping cream

In a large saucepan, saute the chicken, onion and garlic powder in oil until chicken is no longer pink. Add the beans, broth, chilies and seasonings. Bring to a boil. Reduce heat; simmer, uncovered, for 30 minutes. Remove from the heat; stir in sour cream and cream. Serve immediately. **Yield: 7 servings.**

Creamy White Chili

Spicy White Chili

Spicy White Chili

My son can't get enough spice, so I added green chilies and other seasonings until I created a quick and easy chili he's wild about.

—Carlene Bailey, Bradenton, Florida

- 2 medium onions, chopped
- 1 tablespoon vegetable oil
- 4 garlic cloves, minced
- 2 cans (4 ounces *each*) chopped green chilies
- 2 teaspoons ground cumin
- 1 teaspoon dried oregano
- 1/4 teaspoon cayenne pepper
- 1/4 teaspoon ground cloves
- 2 cans (14-1/2 ounces *each*) chicken broth
- 4 cups cubed cooked chicken
- 3 cans (15-1/2 ounces *each*) great northern beans, rinsed and drained
- 2 cups (8 ounces) shredded Monterey Jack cheese

Sour cream and sliced jalapeno peppers, optional

In a large saucepan, saute onions in oil until tender. Stir in the garlic, chilies, cumin, oregano, cayenne and cloves; cook and stir 2-3 minutes longer. Add the broth, chicken and beans. Bring to a boil. Reduce heat; simmer, uncovered, for 15 minutes.

Remove from the heat. Add cheese, stirring until melted. Garnish with sour cream and jalapeno peppers if desired. **Yield: 6-8 servings (2-1/4 quarts).**

Garden Harvest Chili

Any time you're looking for a way to use up your zucchini and squash, give this recipe a try. It's delicious!

—Debbie Cosford, Bayfield, Ontario

- 1 medium sweet red pepper, chopped
- 1 medium onion, chopped
- 4 garlic cloves, minced
- 2 tablespoons vegetable oil
- 1 tablespoon chili powder
- 1 teaspoon ground cumin
- 1 teaspoon dried oregano
- 2 cups cubed peeled butternut squash
- 1 can (28 ounces) diced tomatoes, undrained
- 2 cups diced zucchini
- 1 can (15 ounces) black beans, rinsed and drained
- 1 can (8-3/4 ounces) whole kernel corn, drained
- 1/4 cup minced fresh parsley

In a 3-qt. saucepan, saute the red pepper, onion and garlic in oil until tender. Stir in the chili powder, cumin, oregano, butternut squash and tomatoes; bring to a boil.

Reduce heat; cover and simmer for 10-15 minutes or until squash is almost tender. Stir in remaining ingredients; cover and simmer 10 minutes longer. **Yield: 7 servings (1-3/4 quarts).**

Garden Harvest Chili

SANDWICHES

LAYERED DELI LOAF, pg. 117

Sandwiches

Roast Beef Sandwich Roll

I'm a teacher and am always looking for quick and delicious recipes. I like how easily this sandwich roll comes together. —Shonda Haught, Wichita, Kansas

- 2 loaves (1 pound *each*) frozen bread dough, thawed
- 3/4 cup chopped sweet red pepper
- 1/2 cup chopped red onion
- 1 teaspoon garlic salt
- 1 teaspoon Italian seasoning
- 8 to 10 ounces thinly sliced deli roast beef, julienned
- 2 cups (8 ounces) finely shredded cheddar cheese
- 1 egg white
- 1 tablespoon water

Combine loaves of dough and shape into one ball. Place in a greased bowl, turning once to grease top. Cover and let rise in a warm place for 90 minutes.

In a microwave-safe bowl, combine the red pepper, onion, garlic salt and Italian seasoning. Cover and microwave on high for 1 minute or until vegetables are tender.

Punch dough down. On a lightly floured surface, roll into a 15-in. x 12-in. rectangle. Combine the beef, cheese and red pepper mixture; spread over the dough to within 1/2 in. of edges. Roll up jelly-roll style, starting with a long edge; pinch seams and ends to seal. Place seam side down on a lightly greased baking sheet.

In a small bowl, beat egg white and water; brush over dough. Cut a slit with a sharp knife in top of dough. Bake at 400° for 30-35 minutes or until golden brown. Let stand for 10 minutes before slicing. **Yield: 8 servings.**

Roast Beef Sandwich Roll

Mushroom Steak Hoagies

Mushroom Steak Hoagies

My Aunt Diane perfected the recipe for these hearty hoagies. We often double or triple it for family gatherings since they're such a hit. I begin marinating the beef the night before so the sandwiches can be put together in less than 30 minutes on a hectic evening.
—Jennifer Walker, Logan, Utah

- 1 cup water
- 1/3 cup soy sauce
- 1-1/2 teaspoons garlic powder
- 1-1/2 teaspoons pepper
- 1 pound boneless beef round steak, cut into 1/4-inch strips
- 1 medium onion, chopped
- 1 medium green pepper, julienned
- 1 can (4 ounces) mushroom stems and pieces, drained
- 2 cups (8 ounces) shredded part-skim mozzarella cheese
- 6 hoagie buns, split and toasted
- Sliced tomatoes

In a large resealable plastic bag, combine the water, soy sauce, garlic powder and pepper; add steak. Seal bag and turn to coat; refrigerate for 6-8 hours or overnight.

Drain and discard marinade. In a large skillet, brown steak over medium heat. Add the onion, green pepper and mushrooms; stir-fry until tender. Reduce heat. Sprinkle with cheese. Remove from the heat; stir until cheese is melted and meat is coated. Spoon onto buns; top with tomatoes. **Yield: 6 servings.**

Barbecued Beef Sandwiches

The great thing about this recipe—especially for noncabbage lovers!—is that you can't taste the cabbage in the meat. Yet, at the same time, it adds a nice heartiness and moistness to it. I credit my mother for my love for cooking. My grandmother, too—I remember how she made barbecued beef on weekends when grandkids visited.
—Denise Marshall, Bagley, Wisconsin

- 2 pounds beef stew meat
- 2 cups water
- 4 cups shredded cabbage
- 1/2 cup bottled barbecue sauce
- 1/2 cup ketchup
- 1/3 cup Worcestershire sauce
- 1 tablespoon prepared horseradish
- 1 tablespoon prepared mustard
- 10 hamburger *or* other sandwich buns, split

In a Dutch oven or large saucepan, bring beef and water to a boil. Reduce heat; cover and simmer for 1-1/2 hours or until tender. Drain cooking liquid, reserving 3/4 cup.

Cool beef; shred with two forks and return to the Dutch oven. Add the cabbage, barbecue sauce, ketchup, Worcestershire sauce, horseradish, mustard and the reserved cooking liquid. Cover and simmer for 1 hour. Serve warm in buns. **Yield: 10 servings.**

Layered Deli Loaf

This recipe is special to me because it was handed down from my grandma. A tangy sauce, flavored with horseradish and Dijon mustard, sparks a hearty assortment of meats and cheeses. It feeds a crowd, so it's perfect for a party or a potluck. My husband says it's the best sub sandwich he's ever had.

—Sarah Kraemer, Rockford, Illinois

- 1/4 cup mayonnaise
- 2 tablespoons prepared horseradish, drained
- 1 tablespoon Dijon mustard
- 1 round loaf (1 pound) unsliced bread
- 2 tablespoons butter, softened
- 1/3 pound thinly sliced deli ham
- 1/3 pound sliced Monterey Jack cheese
- 1/3 pound thinly sliced deli turkey
- 1/3 pound sliced cheddar cheese
- 1/3 pound thinly sliced deli roast beef
- 1 medium tomato, sliced
- 1 large dill pickle, sliced lengthwise
- 1 small red onion, thinly sliced

Lettuce leaves

In a small bowl, combine the mayonnaise, horseradish and mustard. Cut bread in half. Carefully hollow out bottom and top of loaf, leaving 3/4-in. shell (discard removed bread or save for another use). Spread butter on cut sides of bread.

In the shell, layer ham, a third of the mayonnaise mixture, Monterey Jack cheese, turkey, a third of the mayonnaise mixture, cheddar cheese, roast beef, remaining mayonnaise mixture, tomato, pickle, onion and lettuce.

Replace top. Wrap tightly in plastic wrap; cover and refrigerate for at least 1 hour. Unwrap and cut into wedges. **Yield: 8 servings.**

Barbecued Beef Sandwiches

Layered Deli Loaf

Cajun Burgers

Super Sloppy Joes

Cajun Burgers

I found the original recipe for these burgers in a cookbook, then added and subtracted ingredients until they suited our taste. They're always on the menu for our cookouts.
—Julie Culbertson, Bansalem, Pennsylvania

CAJUN SEASONING BLEND:

- 3 tablespoons ground cumin
- 3 tablespoons dried oregano
- 1 tablespoon garlic powder
- 1 tablespoon paprika
- 2 teaspoons salt
- 1 teaspoon cayenne pepper

BURGERS:

- 1 pound ground beef
- 1/4 cup finely chopped onion
- 1 teaspoon salt
- 1 teaspoon Cajun Seasoning Blend (recipe above)
- 1/2 to 1 teaspoon hot pepper sauce
- 1/2 teaspoon dried thyme

1/4 teaspoon dried basil
1 garlic clove, minced
4 hamburger buns
Sauteed onions, optional

Combine the first six ingredients in a small bowl or resealable plastic bag. In a bowl, combine the first eight burger ingredients; shape into four patties. Cook in a skillet or grill over medium-hot heat for 4-5 minutes on each side or until burgers are no longer pink and a thermometer reads 160°.

Serve on buns; top with sauteed onions if desired. Store remaining seasoning blend in an airtight container for up to 3 months. **Yield: 4 servings.**

Super Sloppy Joes

Mother made these fresh-tasting sloppy joes many times when I was growing up. She passed the recipe on to me when I got married. My brother-in-law says they're the best sandwiches he's ever tasted. He ought to know, because his name is Joe!
—Ellen Stringer, Bourbonnais, Illinois

2 pounds ground beef
1/2 cup chopped onion
2 celery ribs with leaves, chopped
1/4 cup chopped green pepper
1-2/3 cups canned crushed tomatoes
1/4 cup ketchup
2 tablespoons brown sugar
1 tablespoon cider vinegar
1 tablespoon Worcestershire sauce
1 tablespoon steak sauce
1/2 teaspoon garlic salt
1/4 teaspoon ground mustard
1/4 teaspoon paprika
8 to 10 hamburger buns, split

In a Dutch oven, cook the beef, onion, celery and green pepper over medium heat until the meat is no longer pink and the vegetables are tender; drain. Add the next nine ingredients; mix well.

Simmer, uncovered, for 35-40 minutes, stirring occasionally. Spoon 1/2 cup meat mixture onto each bun. **Yield: 8-10 servings.**

Apple-Ham Grilled Cheese

Apple-Ham Grilled Cheese

After finding this recipe years ago, I altered it to fit our tastes by adding the apples. Our whole family loves it! *—Shirley Brazel, Rocklin, California*

1 cup chopped tart apples
1/3 cup mayonnaise
1/4 cup finely chopped walnuts
8 slices process American cheese
8 slices sourdough bread
4 slices fully cooked ham
1/4 cup butter, softened

In a bowl, combine the apples, mayonnaise and walnuts. Place a slice of cheese on four slices of bread. Layer each with 1/3 cup of the apple mixture, a slice of ham and another slice of cheese; cover with remaining bread.

Butter the outsides of the sandwiches. In a large skillet over medium heat, toast sandwiches until bread is lightly browned on both sides and cheese is melted. **Yield: 4 servings.**

Sourdough Cheeseburgers

Sourdough Cheeseburgers

Here's a mouth-watering cheeseburger that's easy and quick. I came up with it one night when I realized I'd run out of hamburger buns. My husband loved the tang and toasty crunch of the sourdough bread.
—Michelle Dommel, Quakertown, Pennsylvania

- 3 tablespoons mayonnaise
- 1 tablespoon ketchup
- 1 tablespoon sweet pickle relish
- 1/2 pound ground beef
- Salt and pepper to taste
- 1 small onion, sliced and separated into rings
- 4 tablespoons butter, *divided*
- 4 slices sourdough bread
- 4 slices Swiss cheese

In a small bowl, combine the mayonnaise, ketchup and relish; cover and refrigerate. Shape beef into two oval patties. In a large skillet, cook burgers over medium heat for 4-5 minutes on each side or until a meat thermometer reads 160°. Season with salt and pepper; remove and keep warm. In the same skillet, saute onion in 1 tablespoon butter until tender. Remove and keep warm.

Using 2 tablespoons butter, butter one side of each slice of bread. Melt remaining butter in the skillet. Place bread buttered side up in the skillet; cook for 2-3 minutes or until golden brown. Turn; top two of the bread slices with the cheese. Cook 2 minutes longer or until cheese is melted.

To serve, place toast cheese side up on a plate. Top with a burger, relish mixture, onion and remaining toast. **Yield: 2 servings.**

Meatball Lover's Sandwich

You'll find that these hearty sandwiches will satisfy even the healthiest appetites. I like the fact that the recipe makes a big batch of meatballs with tangy sauce. *—Kelly Gerhardt, Council Bluffs, Iowa*

- 2 eggs
- 1/3 cup milk
- 2 cups soft bread crumbs
- 1/2 cup finely chopped onion
- 1-1/2 teaspoons salt
- 2 pounds ground beef
- 2 garlic cloves, minced
- 1 teaspoon butter
- 1 cup ketchup
- 2/3 cup chili sauce
- 1/4 cup packed brown sugar
- 2 tablespoons Worcestershire sauce
- 2 tablespoons prepared mustard
- 2 teaspoons celery seed
- 1/2 teaspoon salt
- 1/4 teaspoon hot pepper sauce
- 8 hoagie buns *or* submarine rolls, split
- 1 large onion, sliced

In a bowl, beat eggs and milk. Stir in the bread crumbs, chopped onion and salt. Crumble beef over mixture and mix well. Shape into 1-in. balls. Place in a lightly greased 15-in. x 10-in. x 1-in. baking pan. Bake, uncovered, at 375° for 15-20 minutes or until meat is no longer pink.

In a saucepan, saute garlic in butter. Add the ketchup, chili sauce, brown sugar, Worcestershire sauce, mustard, celery seed, salt and hot pepper sauce. Bring to a boil; add meatballs. Reduce heat; cover and simmer for 20 minutes or until heated through, stirring occasionally.

Carefully hollow out buns, leaving a 1/2-in. shell. Spoon meatball mixture into buns; top with sliced onion. **Yield: 8 servings.**

Greek Pork Wraps

If you like gyros, you'll love these strips of grilled pork wrapped in tortillas. It's a popular summer dish in my home.

—Christine London, Kansas City, Missouri

- 1/4 cup lemon juice
- 2 tablespoons olive oil
- 1 tablespoon prepared mustard
- 1-3/4 teaspoons minced garlic, *divided*
- 1 teaspoon dried oregano
- 1 pork tenderloin (1 pound)
- 1 cup chopped peeled cucumber
- 1 cup reduced-fat plain yogurt
- 1/4 teaspoon salt
- 1/4 teaspoon dill weed
- 8 flour tortillas (6 inches)
- 1/2 cup chopped green onions

In a large resealable plastic bag, combine the lemon juice, oil, mustard, 1-1/4 teaspoons garlic and oregano; add the pork. Seal bag and turn to coat; refrigerate for 2 hours.

In a bowl, combine cucumber, yogurt, salt, dill and remaining garlic; cover and refrigerate until serving.

Drain and discard marinade. Coat grill rack with nonstick cooking spray before starting the grill for indirect medium-hot heat. Grill tenderloin, uncovered, over direct-heated area for 5 minutes, turning once. Move to indirect-heated area; cover and cook 10-15 minutes longer or until a meat thermometer reads 160°. Let stand for 5 minutes.

Meanwhile, wrap tortillas in foil; place on grill for 2-3 minutes or until warmed, turning once. Slice tenderloin into strips; place on tortillas. Top each with 3 tablespoons yogurt sauce and 1 tablespoon green onions. **Yield: 4 servings.**

Meatball Lover's Sandwich

Greek Pork Wraps

Grilled Ham and Egg Salad Sandwiches

Cheesy Sausage Stromboli

Grilled Ham and Egg Salad Sandwiches 1st prize

An aunt shared this recipe with me years ago when I was looking for some low-budget meals. The ham and toasted bread make it a deliciously different kind of egg salad sandwich.

—Beverly Stiger, Helena, Montana

- 6 hard-cooked eggs, chopped
- 1 cup diced fully cooked ham
- 1/2 cup finely chopped celery
- 1 tablespoon minced onion
- 1/2 cup mayonnaise
- 2 teaspoons prepared mustard
- 1/2 teaspoon salt
- 1/4 teaspoon pepper
- 12 slices whole wheat *or* white bread

BATTER:

- 1/2 cup cornmeal
- 1/2 cup all-purpose flour
- 1 teaspoon baking powder
- 1 teaspoon salt
- 2 cups milk
- 2 eggs, lightly beaten

Vegetable oil

Combine eggs, ham, celery, onion, mayonnaise, mustard, salt and pepper; spread on six slices of bread. Top with remaining bread and set aside. In a bowl, whisk together the first six batter ingredients until well blended.

Heat about 1/2 in. of oil in a large deep skillet. Dip sandwiches into batter. Fry in hot oil for 3 minutes on each side or until golden brown. Drain on paper towels. **Yield: 6 servings.**

Cheesy Sausage Stromboli

I've had a hundred requests for this recipe over the years. Perfect for brunch or as an evening snack, this sausage-filled bread is not tricky to make, and I never have to worry about storing leftovers!
—Vada McRoberts, Silver Lake, Kansas

- 5 cups all-purpose flour
- 2 tablespoons sugar
- 2 teaspoons salt
- 2 packages (1/4 ounce *each*) active dry yeast
- 1-1/2 cups warm water (120° to 130°)
- 1/2 cup warm milk (120° to 130°)
- 2 tablespoons butter, melted
- 2 pounds bulk pork sausage
- 4 cups (16 ounces) shredded part-skim mozzarella cheese
- 3 eggs
- 1 teaspoon minced fresh basil *or* 1/4 teaspoon dried basil
- 2 tablespoons grated Parmesan cheese

In a mixing bowl, combine the flour, sugar, salt and yeast. Add the water, milk and butter; beat on low until well combined.

Turn onto a well-floured surface; knead until smooth and elastic, about 6-8 minutes. Place in a greased bowl, turning once to grease top. Cover and let rise in a warm place until doubled, about 1 hour.

Meanwhile, in a skillet, cook sausage over medium heat until no longer pink; drain and cool. Stir in the mozzarella, 2 eggs and basil; set aside.

Punch dough down; divide in half. Roll one portion into a 15-in. x 10-in. rectangle on a greased baking sheet. Spoon half of the sausage mixture lengthwise down one side of rectangle to within 1 in. of edges. Fold dough over filling; pinch edges to seal. Cut four diagonal slits on top of stromboli. Repeat with remaining dough and filling.

Beat remaining egg; brush over loaves. Sprinkle with Parmesan. Cover and let rise until doubled, about 45 minutes. Bake at 375° for 20-25 minutes or until golden brown. Slice; serve warm. **Yield: 2 loaves.**

Bacon-Tomato Bagel Melts

Bacon-Tomato Bagel Melts

My husband introduced me to this open-faced sandwich shortly after we got married, and it quickly became an all-time favorite. It's good made with either plain or onion bagels.
—Lindsay Orwig, Grand Terrace, California

- 2 bagels, split and toasted
- 8 tomato slices
- 8 bacon strips, cooked
- 1 cup (4 ounces) shredded part-skim mozzarella cheese

Prepared ranch salad dressing

Place bagel halves cut side up on a baking sheet. Top each with two tomato slices and two bacon strips. Sprinkle with cheese.

Broil 5 in. from the heat for 1-2 minutes or until cheese is melted. Serve with ranch dressing. **Yield: 4 sandwiches.**

Barbecued Hot Dogs

Barbecued Hot Dogs

I grew up in a family of eight kids, and we never complained if Mom made these terrific hot dogs often!
—Joyce Koehler, Watertown, Wisconsin

- 3/4 cup chopped onion
- 3 tablespoons butter
- 1-1/2 cups chopped celery
- 1-1/2 cups ketchup
- 3/4 cup water
- 1/3 cup lemon juice
- 3 tablespoons brown sugar
- 3 tablespoons cider vinegar
- 1 tablespoon Worcestershire sauce
- 1 tablespoon yellow mustard
- 2 packages (1 pound *each*) hot dogs
- 20 hot dog buns, split

In a saucepan, saute onion in butter until tender. Add the celery, ketchup, water, lemon juice, sugar, vinegar, Worcestershire sauce and mustard; bring to a boil. Reduce heat; cover and simmer for 30 minutes.

Cut three 1/4-in.-deep slits on each side of the hot dogs; place in a 2-1/2-qt. baking dish. Pour the sauce over the hot dogs. Cover and bake at 350° for 40-45 minutes or until heated through. Serve on buns. **Yield: 20 servings.**

Hot Italian Patties

I've been making these spicy and satisfying sandwiches for more than a dozen years. On occasion, I substitute country sausage for the Italian sausage, and they taste just as good. Served with a zesty sauce for dipping, they're my family's favorite.
—Brenda Jackson, Garden City, Kansas

- 1 can (8 ounces) tomato sauce
- 1/4 teaspoon dried basil
- 1/4 teaspoon crushed red pepper flakes
- 1/8 teaspoon garlic powder
- 1 pound bulk Italian sausage
- 1 medium onion, thinly sliced and separated into rings
- 8 slices part-skim mozzarella cheese (about 6 ounces)
- 8 slices French bread (3/4 inch thick)
- 1/4 to 1/2 cup butter, softened

In a saucepan, combine the tomato sauce, basil, pepper flakes and garlic powder. Bring to a boil over medium heat. Reduce heat; simmer, uncovered, for 15 minutes.

Meanwhile, shape sausage into four thin oval patties. In a skillet, cook patties over medium heat until no longer pink; remove and keep warm.

In the drippings, saute onion until tender. Place a slice of cheese on four slices of bread; top each with a sausage patty, onion and remaining cheese. Top with remaining bread. Butter the outsides of sandwiches.

Cook on a griddle or in a large skillet over medium heat until both sides are golden brown and cheese is melted. Serve with herbed tomato sauce for dipping. **Yield: 4 servings.**

Ham and Cheese Calzones

This sort of inside-out pizza is something I concocted one evening when I had leftover baked ham and needed to fix something quick and simple. My husband loved it—so did all his friends when he took some to work for lunch.
—Shelby Marino, Neptune Beach, Florida

- 2 tubes (10 ounces *each*) refrigerated pizza crust
- 1 cup ricotta cheese
- 4 to 6 ounces sliced pepperoni
- 2 cups diced fully cooked ham
- 2 cups (8 ounces) shredded part-skim mozzarella cheese

Shredded Parmesan cheese, optional
Dried basil, optional
Meatless spaghetti sauce, warmed

Unroll one pizza crust, stretching gently to make a 14-in. x 11-in. rectangle. Spread half of the ricotta on half of the dough lengthwise, to within 1 in. of the edges. Sprinkle with half of the pepperoni, ham and mozzarella. Fold unfilled side of dough over filled half and press edges together firmly to seal. Transfer to a greased baking sheet.

Repeat with remaining crust and filling ingredients. Bake at 400° for 20-25 minutes or until golden brown. Sprinkle with Parmesan and basil if desired. Slice into serving-size pieces. Serve with spaghetti sauce. **Yield: 8 servings.**

Hot Italian Patties

Ham and Cheese Calzones

Hearty Chicken Club

Apple-Walnut Turkey Sandwiches

Hearty Chicken Club

I discovered the recipe for this sizable sandwich a while back and modified it to suit my family's tastes. We love it. The only problem is trying to open our mouths wide enough to take a bite!

—Debbie Johanesen, Missoula, Montana

- 1/4 cup mayonnaise
- 2 tablespoons salsa
- 4 slices seven-grain sandwich bread
- 2 lettuce leaves
- 4 slices tomato
- 1/2 pound sliced cooked chicken *or* turkey
- 4 bacon strips, cooked
- 4 slices cheddar cheese
- 1 ripe avocado, sliced

Combine mayonnaise and salsa; spread on two slices of bread. Layer with the lettuce, tomato, chicken or turkey, bacon, cheese and avocado. Top with remaining bread. **Yield: 2 servings.**

Apple-Walnut Turkey Sandwiches

When you live where temperatures easily climb to 100° or more in the summer, you look for recipes that get you in and out of the kitchen in minutes. This luscious sandwich, with its cool Waldorf salad filling, is a breeze to prepare.

—Cathy Dobbins, Rio Rancho, New Mexico

- 3/4 cup mayonnaise
- 1/4 cup chopped celery
- 1/4 cup raisins
- 1/4 cup chopped walnuts, toasted
- 1 medium tart apple, chopped
- 3/4 pound sliced deli turkey
- 8 slices sourdough bread

Lettuce leaves

In a bowl, combine the mayonnaise, celery, raisins and walnuts. Stir in apple; set aside. Place turkey on four slices of bread. Top with apple mixture, lettuce and remaining bread. **Yield: 4 servings.**

Fajita Pitas

I was late coming home one evening and forgot to pick up tortillas for the fajitas we planned for dinner. So we used pita bread that I had in the freezer instead. The warm chicken-filled pockets, garnished with a homemade sauce and other tasty toppings, are often requested when we're hungry for something in a hurry.

—Diana Jones, Springtown, Texas

- 6 boneless skinless chicken breast halves (4 ounces *each*)
- 1 large onion, sliced
- 1 large green pepper, thinly sliced
- 1 tablespoon vegetable oil

Fajita Pitas

- 2 cups (8 ounces) shredded Mexican cheese blend *or* cheddar cheese
- 8 pita breads (6 inches), halved

SAUCE:

- 1 medium onion, finely chopped
- 1 medium tomato, finely chopped
- 1/2 jalapeno pepper, finely chopped
- 1 tablespoon minced fresh cilantro
- 1 tablespoon vegetable oil

Guacamole and sour cream, optional

Grill chicken, covered, over medium heat for 8-10 minutes on each side or until juices run clear. Cut into strips. In a skillet, saute onion and green pepper in oil. Add chicken and cheese. Stuff into pita halves; place on an ungreased baking sheet. Bake at 325° for 10 minutes or until cheese is melted.

Meanwhile, for sauce, combine the onion, tomato, jalapeno, cilantro and oil in a bowl. Serve the sauce, guacamole and sour cream if desired with pitas. **Yield: 8 servings.**

Editor's Note: When cutting or seeding hot peppers, use rubber or plastic gloves to protect your hands. Avoid touching your face.

Dilly Turkey Melt

Dilly Turkey Melt

This is a hearty grilled sandwich with a distinctive and delicious combination of ingredients. The pickle slices add a bit of fun, and the barbecue sauce provides a hint of sweetness.

—Henry Mujica, North Riverside, Illinois

- **2 medium onions, sliced**
- **4 tablespoons butter, *divided***
- **4 tablespoons barbecue sauce**
- **8 slices sourdough bread**
- **8 slices Monterey Jack cheese**
- **8 slices Canadian bacon**
- **8 slices deli turkey**
- **Dill pickle slices**

In a large skillet, saute onions in 1 tablespoon of butter until tender; remove and set aside. Spread barbecue sauce on four slices of bread. Layer each with one slice of cheese, bacon, turkey, pickles, onions and another slice of cheese. Cover with remaining slices of bread.

In the same skillet over medium-low heat, melt remaining butter. Cook sandwiches on both sides until golden brown and cheese is melted (skillet may be covered the last few minutes to help melt cheese if necessary). **Yield: 4 servings.**

Cheesy Chicken Subs

I've been part of the Food Services staff at Appalachian State University for over 30 years. One summer we created this flavorful sandwich that combines seasoned grilled chicken, Swiss cheese and sauteed mushrooms and onions. Thousands of students have enjoyed this wonderful sub since then.

—Jane Hollar, Vilas, North Carolina

- **12 ounces boneless skinless chicken breasts, cut into strips**
- **1 envelope Parmesan Italian *or* Caesar salad dressing mix**
- **1 cup sliced fresh mushrooms**
- **1/2 cup sliced red onion**
- **1/4 cup olive oil**
- **4 submarine buns, split and toasted**
- **4 slices Swiss cheese**

Place chicken in a bowl; sprinkle with salad dressing mix. In a skillet, saute mushrooms and onion in oil for 3 minutes. Add the chicken; saute for 6 minutes or until chicken juices run clear.

Spoon mixture onto roll bottoms; top with cheese. Broil 4 in. from the heat for 4 minutes or until cheese is melted. Replace tops. **Yield: 4 servings.**

Barbecued Turkey Sandwiches

I have an excellent source for turkey recipes, since many of our neighbors are poultry farmers! These satisfying sandwiches, with their mildly tangy sauce, are a great way to use up leftover turkey from the holidays. *—Pamela Siegrist, Fort Recovery, Ohio*

- **2 celery ribs, chopped**
- **1/2 cup chopped onion**
- **1/4 cup chopped green pepper**
- **1/3 cup butter**

Cheesy Chicken Subs

- 1/2 cup ketchup
- 1/4 cup packed brown sugar
- 3 tablespoons Worcestershire sauce
- 1-1/2 teaspoons chili powder
- 1 teaspoon salt
- 1/8 teaspoon pepper
- 1/8 teaspoon hot pepper sauce
- 4 cups shredded cooked turkey
- 8 hamburger buns, split, toasted and buttered

In a saucepan, saute the celery, onion and green pepper in butter until tender. Add the next seven ingredients. Bring to a boil. Reduce heat; cover and simmer for 5 minutes. Add turkey; heat through. Serve on buns. **Yield: 8 servings.**

Barbecued Turkey Sandwiches

Salmon Salad Sandwiches

Crabby Bagels

Salmon Salad Sandwiches

These are perfect to pack in your kids' lunch boxes. We love the salmon, cream cheese and dill tucked inside a crusty roll. The carrots and celery add a nice crunch. —*Yvonne Shust, Shoal Lake, Manitoba*

- 1 package (3 ounces) cream cheese, softened
- 1 tablespoon mayonnaise
- 1 tablespoon lemon juice
- 1 teaspoon dill weed
- 1/4 to 1/2 teaspoon salt
- 1/8 teaspoon pepper
- 1 can (6 ounces) pink salmon, drained, bones and skin removed
- 1/2 cup shredded carrot
- 1/2 cup chopped celery
- Lettuce leaves
- 2 whole wheat buns, split

In a mixing bowl, beat cream cheese, mayonnaise, lemon juice, dill, salt and pepper until smooth. Add the salmon, carrot and celery; mix well. Place a lettuce leaf and about 1/2 cup salmon salad on each bun. **Yield: 2 servings.**

Crabby Bagels

When my husband and I get tired of the peanut butter and jelly our daughter favors, we make this grown-up sandwich shared by a dear lady at church.
—Connie Faulkner, Moxee, Washington

- 1 can (6 ounces) crabmeat, drained, flaked and cartilage removed
- 1/2 cup shredded cheddar cheese
- 1/4 cup finely chopped celery
- 1/4 cup sour cream
- 3/4 teaspoon Worcestershire sauce
- 1/4 teaspoon salt
- 4 onion bagels, split
- 1 package (3 ounces) cream cheese, softened
- 4 lettuce leaves

In a bowl, combine the first six ingredients. Toast bagels; spread with cream cheese. On the bottom of each bagel, place a lettuce leaf and 1/4 cup of crab mixture. Replace tops. **Yield: 4 servings.**

Shrimp Patty Sandwiches

Quite often when we eat at a restaurant, my husband will try something and tell me that I could make it better at home. That was the case with this shrimp patty. I made some improvements, and now it's one of my husband's favorite sandwiches.
—Tina Jacobs, Hurlock, Maryland

- 4 eggs
- 4 cans (6 ounces *each*) shrimp, rinsed and drained *or* 2 cups medium cooked shrimp, peeled and deveined
- 1/2 pound haddock, cooked and flaked
- 1 cup plus 3 tablespoons pancake mix
- 2 tablespoons cornmeal
- 1/2 teaspoon dried parsley flakes
- 1/2 teaspoon celery salt

Shrimp Patty Sandwiches

- 1/4 teaspoon ground mustard
- 1/4 teaspoon paprika
- 1/2 cup dry bread crumbs
- 3 to 4 tablespoons vegetable oil
- 8 hamburger buns

Lettuce leaves, tomato slices and onion slices, optional

In a large bowl, beat the eggs. Add the shrimp, haddock, pancake mix, cornmeal, parsley, celery salt, mustard and paprika; mix well. Shape into eight patties. Coat with bread crumbs.

In a large skillet, cook patties in oil over medium-high heat for 2 minutes on each side or until golden brown. Serve on buns with lettuce, tomato and onion if desired. **Yield: 8 servings.**

The Ultimate Grilled Cheese

The Ultimate Grilled Cheese 1st prize

These gooey grilled cheese sandwiches, subtly seasoned with garlic, taste great for lunch with sliced apples. And they're really fast to whip up, too. To save seconds, I soften the cream cheese in the microwave, then blend it with the rest of the ingredients in the same bowl. That makes cleanup a breeze. —*Kathy Norris, Streator, Illinois*

- 1 package (3 ounces) cream cheese, softened
- 3/4 cup mayonnaise
- 1 cup (4 ounces) shredded cheddar cheese
- 1 cup (4 ounces) shredded part-skim mozzarella cheese
- 1/2 teaspoon garlic powder
- 1/8 teaspoon seasoned salt
- 10 slices Italian bread (1/2 inch thick)
- 2 tablespoons butter, softened

In a mixing bowl, beat cream cheese and mayonnaise until smooth. Stir in the cheeses, garlic powder and seasoned salt. Spread five slices of bread with the cheese mixture, about 1/3 cup on each. Top with remaining bread.

Butter the outsides of sandwiches; cook in a large skillet over medium heat until golden brown on both sides. **Yield: 5 servings.**

Egg Salad Pitas

I came up with this recipe purely by accident. I was making egg salad and just kept adding different seasonings. When my friend tried it, she raved about it. —*Ricquel Stinson, Mt. Orab, Ohio*

- 2/3 cup mayonnaise
- 2 tablespoons sweet pickle relish
- 1 teaspoon prepared mustard
- 1/4 teaspoon pepper
- 1/4 teaspoon celery salt
- 1/4 teaspoon paprika
- 1/4 teaspoon dried basil
- 1/4 teaspoon salt
- 6 hard-cooked eggs, coarsely chopped
- 1/2 cup shredded cheddar cheese
- 1 small onion, finely chopped
- 1 large carrot, grated
- 2 bacon strips, cooked and crumbled
- 3 pita breads (6 inches), halved

Lettuce leaves and sliced tomatoes, optional

In a bowl, combine the first eight ingredients. Stir in the eggs, cheese, onion, carrot and bacon. Spoon about 1/2 cup into each pita half. Add lettuce and tomatoes if desired. **Yield: 3-6 servings.**

Egg Salad Pitas

BREAKFAST & BRUNCH

ROCCOLI HAM QUICHE, pg. 145

Breakfast & Brunch

Morning Mix-Up

Here's a filling egg dish that's super to serve for breakfast or supper. It's one of my family's favorites—even our daughter eats a hearty helping.
—Kim Scholting, Springfield, Nebraska

- 2 cups frozen shredded hash brown potatoes
- 1 cup chopped fully cooked ham
- 1/2 cup chopped onion
- 2 tablespoons vegetable oil
- 6 eggs

Salt and pepper to taste

- 1 cup (4 ounces) shredded cheddar cheese

Minced fresh chives

In a skillet, saute potatoes, ham and onion in oil for 10 minutes or until potatoes are tender. In a small bowl, beat the eggs, salt and pepper.

Add to the skillet; cook and stir over medium heat until eggs are completely set. Remove from the heat and gently stir in cheese. Spoon onto a serving platter; sprinkle with chives. **Yield: 4 servings.**

Morning Mix-Up

Cheesy O'Brien Egg Scramble

Cheesy O'Brien Egg Scramble

This breakfast bake is a snap to prepare. It's perfect for a brunch buffet or when out-of-town guests stay the night. Full of bacon, cheese, hash browns and eggs, the all-in-one dish is a hearty crowd-pleaser.
—Margaret Edmondson, Red Oak, Iowa

- 1 package (28 ounces) frozen O'Brien hash brown potatoes
- 1/2 teaspoon garlic salt
- 1/4 teaspoon pepper
- 1 can (10-3/4 ounces) condensed cheddar cheese soup, undiluted
- 1 pound sliced bacon, cooked and crumbled, *divided*
- 12 eggs, lightly beaten
- 2 tablespoons butter
- 2 cups (8 ounces) shredded cheddar cheese

In a skillet, prepare hash browns according to package directions. Sprinkle with garlic salt and pepper. Transfer to a greased 2-1/2-qt. baking dish. Top with soup. Set aside 1/2 cup of bacon; sprinkle remaining bacon over soup.

In a bowl, whisk the eggs. In another large skillet, heat butter until hot. Add eggs; cook and stir over medium heat until eggs are nearly set. Spoon over bacon. Sprinkle with cheese and reserved bacon. Bake, uncovered, at 350° for 20-25 minutes or until cheese is melted. **Yield: 12 servings.**

Wild Rice Mushroom Omelet

Since wild rice is plentiful here, I love to create recipes starring that crunchy staple. Pork sausage helps spice up the mild rice flavor in this hearty omelet, which is draped with a silky-smooth cheese sauce. You can easily serve it to guests with little last-minute fuss.

—Bonne Bourdeau, Akeley, Minnesota

- **1/2 pound bulk pork sausage**
- **1 medium onion, chopped**
- **1 celery rib, finely chopped**
- **2 tablespoons butter**
- **1 can (4 ounces) mushroom stems and pieces, drained**
- **1-1/2 cups cooked wild rice**
- **1 teaspoon dried parsley flakes**
- **14 eggs**
- **1/2 cup water**
- **1/4 teaspoon salt**
- **1/8 teaspoon pepper**

CHEESE SAUCE:

- **2 tablespoons butter**
- **1 teaspoon chicken bouillon granules**
- **2 tablespoons all-purpose flour**
- **1 cup milk**
- **1/4 cup cubed process cheese (Velveeta)**

Minced fresh parsley, optional

In a skillet, cook sausage over medium heat until no longer pink; drain. Remove and set aside. In the same skillet, saute onion and celery in butter until tender. Add mushrooms; heat through. Stir in sausage, rice and parsley.

In a bowl, whisk the eggs, water, salt and pepper. Heat an 8-in. nonstick skillet coated with nonstick cooking spray over medium heat. Add 1/2 cup egg mixture. As eggs set, lift edges, letting uncooked portion flow underneath. When nearly set, spoon 1/2 cup of

Wild Rice Mushroom Omelet

sausage-rice mixture over one side of eggs; fold in half and press down lightly for about 30 seconds. Remove and keep warm. Repeat to make six more omelets.

For cheese sauce, melt butter in a saucepan over medium heat. Stir in the bouillon until dissolved. Stir in flour until smooth; gradually add milk. Bring to a boil; cook and stir for 2 minutes or until thickened. Reduce heat to low; add cheese, stirring until cheese is melted. Drizzle over omelets. Sprinkle with parsley if desired. **Yield: 7 omelets.**

Open-Faced Omelet

This tasty breakfast dish is a snap to make with convenient frozen hash browns. It gets its colorful look and fresh flavor from broccoli, red pepper and green onions. *—Cynthia Hinkle, Front Royal, Virginia*

- **1 cup fresh broccoli florets**
- **1/2 cup chopped sweet red pepper**
- **1/4 cup thinly sliced green onions**
- **1-1/2 cups cubed fully cooked ham**
- **1 cup frozen shredded hash brown potatoes, thawed**
- **2-1/2 cups egg substitute**
- **1/4 teaspoon pepper**
- **1/2 cup shredded reduced-fat cheddar cheese**

In a 9-in. or 10-in. skillet coated with nonstick cooking spray, saute the broccoli, red pepper and onions until crisp-tender. Add ham and hash browns. Cook for 2 minutes, stirring frequently.

In a bowl, whisk together the egg substitute and pepper. Pour over vegetable mixture. Reduce heat; cover and cook for 10-12 minutes or until set.

Remove from the heat. Sprinkle with cheese; cover and let stand for 5 minutes or until cheese is melted. Cut into wedges. **Yield: 6 servings.**

Open-Faced Omelet

Sheepherder's Breakfast

My sister-in-law always made this delicious breakfast dish when we were camping. Served with toast, juice and milk or coffee, it's a sure hit with the breakfast crowd! One-dish casseroles like this were a big help while I was raising my nine children. Now I've passed this recipe on to them.

—Pauletta Bushnell, Albany, Oregon

- 1 pound sliced bacon, diced
- 1 medium onion, chopped
- 32 ounces frozen shredded hash brown potatoes, thawed
- 10 eggs
- Salt and pepper to taste
- 2 cups (8 ounces) shredded cheddar cheese, optional
- Chopped fresh parsley

In a large skillet, cook bacon and onion over medium heat until the bacon is crisp. Drain, reserving 1/2 cup drippings. Add hash browns to skillet; mix well.

Cook over medium heat for 10 minutes, turning when browned. Make 10 "wells" evenly spaced in hash browns. Place one egg in each well. Sprinkle with salt and pepper. Sprinkle with cheese if desired.

Cover and cook over low heat for about 10 minutes or until whites are completely set and yolks begin to thicken (but are not hard). Garnish with parsley; serve immediately. **Yield: 10 servings.**

Sheepherder's Breakfast

Cajun Corned Beef Hash

Maple Toast and Eggs

Cajun Corned Beef Hash

Neither the flavor nor the texture is "mushy" when you whip up a skillet of this tongue-tingling hash. This is an all-time favorite of mine. I created it after eating a similar variation in Texas.
—Del Mason, Martensville, Saskatchewan

- 6 cups frozen shredded hash brown potatoes, thawed
- 1/4 cup butter
- 1/2 cup *each* finely chopped green onions, sweet red pepper and green pepper
- 1 teaspoon seasoned salt
- 3/4 teaspoon Cajun seasoning
- 3/4 teaspoon chili powder
- 1/2 teaspoon pepper
- 1-1/2 cups chopped cooked corned beef
- 1 tablespoon white vinegar
- 8 eggs
- Additional Cajun seasoning and hot pepper sauce, optional

In a large skillet, cook hash browns in butter until almost tender. Stir in the onions, peppers and seasonings. Cook until hash browns are lightly browned and peppers are tender. Add corned beef; heat through.

Meanwhile, in a skillet with high sides, bring 2-3 in. of water and vinegar to a boil. Reduce heat; simmer gently. For each egg, break cold egg into a custard cup or saucer, then hold the cup close to the surface of the water and slip the egg into simmering water. Cook 4 eggs at a time, uncovered, until whites are completely set and yolks begin to thicken, about 3-5 minutes. With a slotted spoon, remove each egg. Repeat with remaining eggs.

Serve over the hash mixture. Sprinkle with additional Cajun seasoning and serve with hot pepper sauce if desired. **Yield: 4 servings.**

Editor's Note: If poaching eggs using a metal poaching insert, increase poaching time to 6-7 minutes.

Maple Toast and Eggs

My home's in the country, right next door to my sister and brother-in-law's. They and their two children all love this dish each time I serve it as a special evening meal. But it can also be made for breakfast or lunch.
—Susan Buttel, Plattsburgh, New York

- 12 bacon strips, diced
- 1/2 cup maple syrup
- 1/4 cup butter
- 12 slices firm-textured white bread
- 12 eggs

Salt and pepper to taste

In a large skillet, cook bacon over medium heat until crisp. Using a slotted spoon, remove to paper towels to drain.

In a small saucepan, heat syrup and butter until butter is melted; set aside. Trim crust from bread; flatten slices with a rolling pin. Brush one side generously with the syrup mixture; press each slice into an ungreased muffin cup with syrup side down.

Divide bacon among muffin cups. Carefully break one egg into each cup. Sprinkle with salt and pepper. Cover with foil. Bake at 400° for 18-20 minutes or until the eggs reach desired doneness. Serve immediately. **Yield: 12 cups.**

Three Cheese Souffles

No matter when I've made these—for breakfast, brunch or lunch—they have never failed. I have not had them fall once. I often get asked for the recipe.
—Jean Ference, Sherwood Park, Alberta

- 1/3 cup butter
- 1/3 cup all-purpose flour
- 2 cups milk
- 1 teaspoon Dijon mustard
- 1/4 teaspoon salt

Dash hot pepper sauce

- 1-1/2 cups (6 ounces) shredded Swiss cheese

Three Cheese Souffles

- 1 cup (4 ounces) shredded cheddar cheese
- 1/4 cup shredded Parmesan cheese
- 6 eggs, *separated*
- 1/2 teaspoon cream of tartar

Melt butter in a medium saucepan. Stir in flour until smooth; gradually add the milk, mustard, salt and hot pepper sauce. Bring to a boil; cook and stir for 2 minutes or until thickened. Reduce heat; add cheeses, stirring until cheese is melted. Remove from the heat and set aside.

In a small mixing bowl, beat egg yolks until thick and lemon-colored, about 5 minutes. Add 1/3 cup cheese mixture and mix well. Return all to the saucepan; return to the heat and cook for 1-2 minutes. Cool completely, about 30-40 minutes.

In another mixing bowl, beat egg whites and cream of tartar until stiff peaks form. Fold into cheese mixture. Pour into ungreased 1-cup souffle dishes or custard cups.

Place in a shallow pan; add 1 in. of hot water to larger pan. Bake, uncovered, at 325° for 40-45 minutes or until tops are golden brown. Serve immediately. **Yield: 8 servings.**

Editor's Note: Souffles can be made ahead and frozen. Cover each dish or cup with foil and freeze. To bake, remove foil and place unthawed souffles in a shallow pan; add warm water to a depth of 1 in. Bake at 325° for 60-65 minutes or until tops are golden brown.

Egg and Corn Quesadilla

Egg and Corn Quesadilla

For a deliciously different breakfast or brunch, try this excellent quesadilla. It's also great for a light lunch or supper. Corn is a natural in Southwestern cooking and a tasty addition to this zippy egg dish.
—Stacy Joura, Stoneboro, Pennsylvania

- 1 medium onion, chopped
- 1 medium green pepper, chopped
- 1 garlic clove, minced
- 2 tablespoons olive oil
- 3 cups fresh *or* frozen corn
- 1 teaspoon minced chives
- 1/2 teaspoon dried cilantro flakes
- 1/2 teaspoon salt
- 1/4 teaspoon pepper
- 4 eggs, beaten
- 4 flour tortillas (10 inches)
- 1/2 cup salsa
- 1 cup (8 ounces) sour cream
- 1 cup (4 ounces) shredded cheddar cheese
- 1 cup (4 ounces) shredded part-skim mozzarella cheese

Additional salsa and sour cream, optional

In a skillet, saute the onion, green pepper and garlic in oil until tender. Add the corn, chives, cilantro, salt and pepper. Cook until heated through, about 3 minutes. Stir in eggs; cook until completely set, stirring occasionally. Remove from the heat.

Place one tortilla on a lightly greased baking sheet or pizza pan; top with a third each of the corn mixture, salsa and sour cream. Sprinkle with a fourth of each cheese. Repeat layers twice. Top with remaining tortilla and cheeses.

Bake at 350° for 10 minutes or until cheese is melted. Cut into wedges. Serve with salsa and sour cream if desired. **Yield: 6-8 servings.**

BLT Egg Bake

BLTs are a favorite at my house, so I created this recipe to combine those flavors in a dressier dish. It was such a hit with my family.
—Priscilla Detrick, Catoosa, Oklahoma

- 1/4 cup mayonnaise
- 5 slices bread, toasted
- 4 slices process American cheese
- 12 bacon strips, cooked and crumbled
- 1 to 2 tablespoons butter
- 4 eggs
- 1 medium tomato, halved and sliced

SAUCE:

- 2 tablespoons butter
- 2 tablespoons all-purpose flour
- 1/4 teaspoon salt
- 1/8 teaspoon pepper
- 1 cup milk
- 1/2 cup shredded cheddar cheese
- 2 green onions, thinly sliced

Shredded lettuce

Spread mayonnaise on one side of each slice of toast and cut into small pieces. Arrange the toast mayonnaise side up in a greased 8-in. square baking dish. Top with the cheese slices and bacon.

In a large skillet, heat butter until hot. Add eggs; reduce heat to low. Fry until white is completely set and yolks begin to thicken but are not hard. Place over bacon and top with tomato slices; set aside.

In a saucepan, melt butter. Stir in the flour,

salt and pepper until smooth. Gradually add milk. Bring to a boil; cook and stir for 2 minutes or until thickened. Pour over tomato. Sprinkle with cheddar cheese and onions.

Bake, uncovered, at 325° for 10 minutes. Cut in squares; serve with lettuce. **Yield: 4 servings.**

BLT Egg Bake

Ham 'n' Cheese Omelet Roll

This brunch dish has wonderful ingredients and an impressive look all rolled into one! A platter of these pretty swirled slices always disappears in no time.
—Nancy Daugherty, Cortland, Ohio

- 4 ounces cream cheese, softened
- 3/4 cup milk
- 2 tablespoons all-purpose flour
- 1/4 teaspoon salt
- 12 eggs
- 2 tablespoons Dijon mustard
- 2-1/4 cups shredded cheddar cheese, *divided*
- 2 cups finely chopped fully cooked ham
- 1/2 cup thinly sliced green onions

Line the bottom and sides of a greased 15-in. x 10-in. x 1-in. baking pan with parchment paper; grease the paper and set aside.

In a small mixing bowl, beat cream cheese and milk until smooth. Add flour and salt; mix until combined. In a large mixing bowl, beat the eggs until blended. Add cream cheese mixture; mix well. Pour into prepared pan.

Bake at 375° for 30-35 minutes or until eggs are puffed and set. Remove from the oven. Immediately spread with the mustard and sprinkle with 1 cup cheese. Sprinkle with the ham, onions and 1 cup cheese.

Roll up from a short side, peeling the parchment paper away while rolling. Sprinkle top of roll with the remaining cheese; bake 3-4 minutes longer or until cheese is melted. **Yield: 12 servings.**

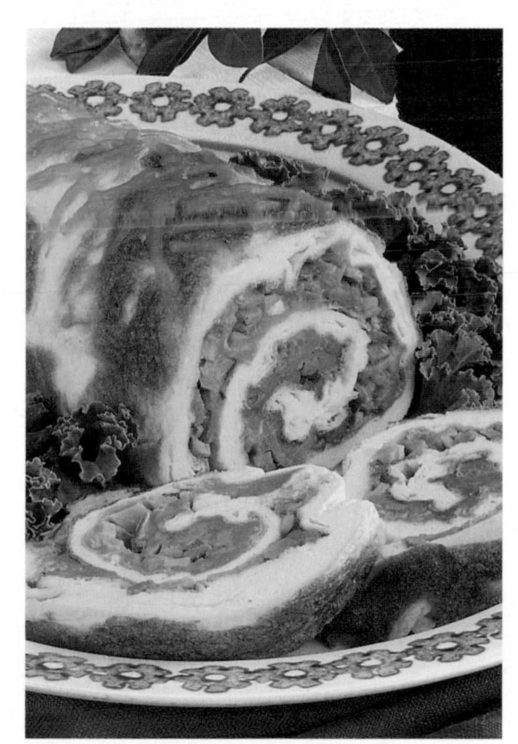

Ham 'n' Cheese Omelet Roll

Baked Breakfast Burritos

Bacon 'n' Egg Lasagna

Baked Breakfast Burritos

Every week, I try a minimum of three new recipes. This is one I clipped from the paper. When I served it to my five grown children, not a morsel was left!
—Carol Towey, Pasadena, California

- **6 to 8 bacon strips**
- **8 fresh mushrooms, sliced**
- **6 green onions, sliced**
- **1/3 cup chopped green pepper**
- **1 garlic clove, minced**
- **8 eggs**
- **1/4 cup sour cream**
- **3/4 cup shredded cheddar cheese, *divided***
- **3 tablespoons enchilada sauce**
- **1 tablespoon butter**
- **4 flour tortillas (10 inches)**

Sour cream and additional enchilada sauce, optional

In a skillet, cook bacon over medium heat until crisp. Remove to paper towels; drain, reserving 1 tablespoon of drippings. Saute the mushrooms, onions, green pepper and garlic in drippings until tender; set aside and keep warm.

In a bowl, beat eggs and sour cream. Stir in 1/4 cup cheese and enchilada sauce.

In a skillet, melt butter; add egg mixture. Cook over low heat, stirring occasionally, until eggs are set. Remove from the heat. Crumble bacon; add to eggs with mushroom mixture. Spoon down center of tortillas; roll up.

Place seam side down in an 11-in. x 7-in. x 2-in. baking dish. Sprinkle with remaining cheese. Bake at 350° for 5 minutes or until cheese is melted. Serve with sour cream and enchilada sauce if desired. **Yield: 4 servings.**

Ham 'n' Egg Pizza

Ham 'n' Egg Pizza

I like to fix this fun dish when we invite our children and grandchildren for brunch. There's never a slice left! The recipe is quick and easy to prepare, using refrigerated crescent rolls to form the crust. The ham makes it hearty.
—Margaret Smith, Superior, Wisconsin

- 1 tube (8 ounces) refrigerated crescent rolls
- 3 eggs
- 2 tablespoons milk
- 1/8 teaspoon pepper
- 2 cups finely chopped fully cooked ham
- 1 cup frozen shredded hash brown potatoes
- 1 cup (4 ounces) shredded cheddar cheese
- 1/2 cup shredded Parmesan cheese

Unroll crescent roll dough and place on an ungreased 12-in. pizza pan. Press onto the bottom and 1/4 in. up the sides, sealing seams and perforations. Bake at 375° for 5 minutes.

Meanwhile, in a bowl, beat the eggs, milk and pepper. Sprinkle the ham, hash browns and cheddar cheese over crust. Carefully pour egg mixture over the cheese. Sprinkle with Parmesan. Bake for 25-30 minutes or until eggs are completely set. **Yield: 6 servings.**

Bacon 'n' Egg Lasagna

My sister-in-law served this special dish for Easter breakfast one year, and our whole family loved the mix of bacon, eggs, noodles and cheese.
—Dianne Meyer, Graniteville, Vermont

- 1 pound sliced bacon, diced
- 1 large onion, chopped
- 1/3 cup all-purpose flour
- 1/2 to 1 teaspoon salt
- 1/4 teaspoon pepper
- 4 cups milk
- 12 lasagna noodles, cooked and drained
- 12 hard-cooked eggs, sliced
- 2 cups (8 ounces) shredded Swiss cheese
- 1/3 cup grated Parmesan cheese
- 2 tablespoons minced fresh parsley

In a skillet, cook bacon over medium heat until crisp. Using a slotted spoon, remove to paper towels; drain, reserving 1/3 cup drippings. In the same skillet, saute onion in drippings until tender. Stir in the flour, salt and pepper until blended. Gradually stir in milk. Bring to a boil; cook and stir for 2 minutes. Remove from the heat.

Spread 1/2 cup sauce in a greased 13-in. x 9-in. x 2-in. baking dish. Layer with four noodles, a third of the eggs and bacon, Swiss cheese and white sauce. Repeat layers twice. Sprinkle with Parmesan cheese.

Bake, uncovered, at 350° for 35-40 minutes or until bubbly. Sprinkle with parsley. Let stand for 15 minutes before cutting. **Yield: 12 servings.**

Breakfast Bake

Breakfast Bake

This light, fluffy egg casserole, sprinkled with tasty bacon, retains its fresh flavor after freezing. While it's great for breakfast, it's an easy-to-reheat meal for lunch or dinner, too. The recipe makes two casseroles, so you can serve one right away and freeze the second one for later. —Kim Weaver, Olathe, Kansas

- **4-1/2 cups seasoned croutons**
- **2 cups (8 ounces) shredded cheddar cheese**
- **1 medium onion, chopped**
- **1/4 cup chopped sweet red pepper**
- **1/4 cup chopped green pepper**
- **1 jar (4-1/2 ounces) sliced mushrooms, drained**
- **8 eggs**
- **4 cups milk**
- **1 teaspoon salt**
- **1 teaspoon ground mustard**
- **1/8 teaspoon pepper**
- **8 bacon strips, cooked and crumbled**

Sprinkle the croutons, cheese, onion, sweet peppers and mushrooms into two greased 8-in. square baking dishes. In a bowl, combine the eggs, milk, salt, mustard and pepper. Slowly pour over vegetables. Sprinkle with bacon.

Cover and freeze one casserole for up to 3 months. Bake the other casserole, uncovered, at 350° for 45-50 minutes or until a knife inserted near the center comes out clean.

To use frozen casserole: Completely thaw in the refrigerator for 24-36 hours. Remove from refrigerator 30 minutes before baking. Bake, uncovered, at 350° for 50-60 minutes or until a knife inserted near the center comes out clean. **Yield: 2 casseroles (6-8 servings each).**

Crustless Swiss Quiche

I received this recipe from my mother-in-law, an all-around great cook. Everyone raves about her rich quiche when she serves it at card parties and other occasions. —Marlene Kole, Highland Heights, Ohio

- **1/2 cup butter**
- **1/2 cup all-purpose flour**
- **1-1/2 cups milk**
- **2-1/2 cups cottage cheese**
- **1 teaspoon baking powder**
- **1 teaspoon salt**
- **1 teaspoon Dijon mustard**
- **9 eggs**
- **2 packages (one 8 ounces, one 3 ounces) cream cheese, softened**
- **3 cups (12 ounces) shredded Swiss cheese**
- **1/3 cup grated Parmesan cheese**

Melt butter in a medium saucepan. Stir in flour until smooth; gradually add milk. Bring to a boil over medium heat; cook and stir for 2 minutes or until thickened. Remove from the heat; cool, about 15-20 minutes.

Meanwhile, combine the cottage cheese, baking powder, salt and mustard; set aside. In a large mixing bowl, beat the eggs. Slowly add cream cheese, cottage cheese mixture and cream sauce. Fold in Swiss and Parmesan cheeses. Pour into two greased 10-in. pie plates. Bake at 350° for 40 minutes or until puffed and lightly browned. Serve immediately. **Yield: 16-20 servings.**

Broccoli Ham Quiche

This quiche recipe is featured in a family cookbook I compiled. It's attractive enough to serve for a company brunch, and it tastes terrific. My husband is proof that quiche can satisfy even a man-sized appetite!
—Marilyn Day, North Fort Myers, Florida

- 1 unbaked deep-dish pastry shell (9 inches)
- 1 cup water
- 1/2 cup chopped fresh broccoli
- 1 cup (4 ounces) shredded Swiss cheese
- 1 cup (4 ounces) shredded part-skim mozzarella cheese
- 2 tablespoons all-purpose flour
- 4 eggs
- 1-1/2 cups milk
- 2 tablespoons chopped green onion
- 1/4 teaspoon salt
- 1/8 teaspoon pepper
- 1/8 teaspoon dried thyme
- 1/8 teaspoon dried rosemary, crushed
- 1/2 cup diced fully cooked ham

Line unpricked pastry shell with a double thickness of heavy-duty foil. Bake at 450° for 8 minutes. Remove foil; bake 5 minutes longer. Cool on a wire rack.

Meanwhile, in a saucepan, bring water to a boil. Add broccoli; cover and cook for 2 minutes. Drain and immediately place the broccoli in ice water. Drain and pat dry with paper towels.

Toss cheeses with flour; set aside. In a bowl, beat the eggs. Add the milk, onion and seasonings; mix well. Stir in the ham, broccoli and cheese mixture. Pour into prepared crust.

Bake at 350° for 40-45 minutes or until a knife inserted near the center comes out clean. Let stand for 10 minutes before cutting. **Yield: 6-8 servings.**

Crustless Swiss Quiche

Broccoli Ham Quiche

Best-of-Show Tomato Quiche

Hash Brown Ham Quiche

Best-of-Show Tomato Quiche 1st prize

I knew this delicious recipe was a keeper when I first tried it as a new bride—it impressed my in-laws when I made it for them!
—Dorothy Swanson, Affton, Missouri

- 3/4 cup all-purpose flour
- 1/2 cup cornmeal
- 1/2 teaspoon salt
- 1/8 teaspoon pepper
- 1/3 cup shortening
- 4 to 5 tablespoons cold water

FILLING:

- 2 cups chopped plum tomatoes
- 1 teaspoon salt
- 1/2 teaspoon dried basil
- 1/8 teaspoon pepper
- 1/2 cup chopped green onions
- 1/2 cup shredded cheddar cheese
- 1/2 cup shredded Swiss cheese
- 2 tablespoons all-purpose flour
- 1 cup evaporated milk
- 2 eggs

In a bowl, combine the first four ingredients. Cut in shortening until crumbly. Add water, tossing with a fork until dough forms a ball. Refrigerate for 30 minutes.

On a lightly floured surface, roll out dough to fit a 9-in. pie plate; transfer pastry to plate. Trim to 1/2 in. beyond edge of plate; flute the edges. Bake at 375° for 10 minutes. Cool completely on a wire rack.

Place tomatoes in the crust; sprinkle with the salt, basil, pepper, onions and cheese. In a bowl, whisk the flour, milk and eggs until smooth. Pour over filling. Bake at 375° for 40-45 minutes or until a knife inserted near the center comes out clean. Let stand for 10 minutes before cutting. **Yield: 6-8 servings.**

Garden Frittata

Garden Frittata

I created this dish one day to use up some fresh yellow squash, zucchini and tomato. It's so easy to make because you don't have to fuss with a crust like with quiches. Give it different twist by trying it with whatever veggies you have on hand.
—Catherine Michel, O'Fallon, Missouri

- 1 small yellow summer squash, thinly sliced
- 1 small zucchini, thinly sliced
- 1 small onion, chopped
- 1 cup (4 ounces) shredded part-skim mozzarella cheese
- 1 medium tomato, sliced
- 1/4 cup crumbled feta cheese
- 4 eggs
- 1 cup fat-free milk
- 2 tablespoons minced fresh basil
- 1 garlic clove, minced
- 1/2 teaspoon salt
- 1/4 teaspoon pepper
- 1/4 cup shredded Parmesan cheese

In a microwave-safe bowl, combine the squash, zucchini and onion. Cover and microwave on high for 7-9 minutes or until the vegetables are tender; drain well. Transfer to a 9-in. pie plate coated with nonstick cooking spray. Top with the mozzarella, tomato and feta cheese.

In a bowl, whisk the eggs, milk, basil, garlic, salt and pepper; pour over the cheese and tomato layer. Sprinkle with Parmesan cheese. Bake, uncovered, at 375° for 45-50 minutes or until a knife inserted near the center comes out clean. Let stand for 10 minutes before cutting. **Yield: 8 servings.**

Hash Brown Ham Quiche

My family loves this cheesy ham quiche on Sunday morning after church. I'm a registered nurse, and I got this recipe from the mother of one of my patients. It's delicious for brunch and not hard to prepare.
—Sara Bowen, Upland, California

- 3 cups frozen shredded hash brown potatoes, thawed
- 1/4 cup butter, melted, *divided*
- 1 cup (4 ounces) shredded pepper Jack cheese
- 1 cup (4 ounces) shredded Swiss cheese
- 1 cup diced fully cooked ham
- 2 eggs
- 1/2 cup heavy whipping cream
- 1/4 teaspoon seasoned salt

Press hash browns between paper towels to remove excess moisture. Grease a 9-in. pie plate with 2 teaspoons butter. Press the hash browns onto the bottom and up the sides of plate. Drizzle with remaining butter. Bake, uncovered, at 425° for 20-25 minutes or until edges are browned.

Combine cheeses and ham; spoon into the crust. In a bowl, beat the eggs, cream and seasoned salt; pour over ham.

Reduce heat to 350°. Bake, uncovered, for 20-25 minutes or until a knife inserted near the center comes out clean. Let stand for 10 minutes before cutting. **Yield: 6 servings.**

Creamed Ham in Toast Cups

Creamed Ham In Toast Cups

My grandmother taught me many of her recipes in show-and-cook sessions. Usually, we had this dish on Mondays, following a Sunday lunch of ham, peas and corn. These buttery cups are one of my favorite ways to use leftover ingredients.
—Catherine Crandall, Amity, Oregon

- 8 slices bread
- 1/2 cup butter, softened, *divided*
- 1/4 cup all-purpose flour
- 1/8 teaspoon white pepper
- 1 cup milk
- 1 cup heavy whipping cream
- 2 cups chopped fully cooked ham
- 1 cup frozen green peas, thawed
- 1 cup whole kernel corn
- Paprika

Remove and discard crusts from bread; using a rolling pin, flatten to 1/8-in. thickness. Butter both sides of each slice, using 1/4 cup of butter.

Press into eight greased muffin cups or 6-oz. custard cups. Bake at 350° for 15-18 minutes or until golden brown.

Meanwhile, in a saucepan, melt the remaining butter. Stir in flour and pepper until smooth; gradually stir in milk and cream. Bring to a boil; cook and stir for 2 minutes or until thickened. Reduce heat. Stir in the ham, peas and corn. Cook and stir for 5 minutes or until heated through. Pour into warm toast cups; sprinkle with paprika. **Yield: 4 servings.**

Editor's Note: This recipe is best made with a soft-textured bread such as Wonder Bread.

Brunch Berry Pizza

This beautiful berry-topped pizza tastes as good as it looks! It's impossible to resist the pecan shortbread crust, rich cream cheese layer, glossy berry topping and sprinkling of luscious fresh berries. It's so convenient to make the night before and serve the next morning. —Maria Schuster, Wolf Point, Montana

- 1 cup all-purpose flour
- 1/4 cup confectioners' sugar
- 1/2 cup cold butter
- 1/2 cup chopped pecans
- 1 package (8 ounces) cream cheese, softened
- 1 egg
- 1/3 cup sugar

TOPPING:

- 1-3/4 cups frozen mixed berries, thawed
- 1/2 cup sugar
- 2 tablespoons cornstarch
- 1/4 cup water
- 2-1/2 cups fresh strawberries, sliced
- 2 cups fresh blackberries
- 2 cups fresh raspberries
- 1 cup fresh blueberries

In a bowl, combine flour and confectioners' sugar. Cut in butter until crumbly. Stir in pecans. Press into an ungreased 12-in. pizza pan. Bake at 350° for 12-14 minutes or until crust is set and edges are lightly browned.

Meanwhile, in a mixing bowl, beat cream

cheese, egg and sugar until smooth. Spread over crust. Bake 8-10 minutes longer or until set. Cool to room temperature.

For topping, place mixed berries and sugar in a blender or food processor; cover and process until blended. In a saucepan, combine cornstarch and water until smooth. Add mixed berry mixture. Bring to a boil; cook and stir for 2 minutes or until thickened. Set saucepan in ice water for 15 minutes, stirring several times.

Spread berry mixture over the cream cheese layer. Arrange fresh fruit on top. Refrigerate for at least 2 hours before slicing. **Yield: 10-12 servings.**

Garlic Cheese Grits

Garlic Cheese Grits

My dad prepared this family favorite every Christmas morning. Grits are a true Southern specialty. The garlic and cheese add a tasty touch.

—Bobbie Jo Yokley, Franklin, Kentucky

- 1 cup quick-cooking grits
- 1 cup (4 ounces) shredded process American cheese
- 1/2 cup butter
- 1 teaspoon garlic salt
- 1 egg
- 1/4 to 1/3 cup milk
- Additional cheese, optional

Cook grits according to package directions. Add the cheese, butter and garlic salt; stir until cheese and butter are melted. In a measuring cup, beat egg; add milk to measure 1/2 cup. Stir into grits.

Pour into a greased 1-1/2-qt. baking dish. Bake, uncovered, at 350° for 20-25 minutes or until bubbly around the edges. Sprinkle with additional cheese if desired. **Yield: 4-6 servings.**

Brunch Berry Pizza

Blueberry Sour Cream Pancakes

Broccoli-Ham Puff Pancake

Blueberry Sour Cream Pancakes

Serve these delicious pancakes as is with blueberries inside and out. Or prepare them as simple, classic pancakes without the blueberries and serve them with butter and warm maple syrup.

—Paula Hadley, Forest Hill, Louisiana

- 1/2 cup sugar
- 2 tablespoons cornstarch
- 1 cup cold water
- 4 cups fresh *or* frozen blueberries

PANCAKES:

- 2 cups all-purpose flour
- 1/4 cup sugar
- 4 teaspoons baking powder
- 1/2 teaspoon salt
- 2 eggs
- 1-1/2 cups milk
- 1 cup (8 ounces) sour cream
- 1/3 cup butter, melted
- 1 cup fresh *or* frozen blueberries

In a large saucepan, combine the sugar and cornstarch. Stir in water until smooth. Add blueberries. Bring to a boil over medium heat; cook and stir for 2 minutes or until thickened. Remove from the heat; cover and keep warm.

For pancakes, in a large bowl, combine the flour, sugar, baking powder and salt. Combine the eggs, milk, sour cream and butter. Stir into flour mixture just until moistened. Fold in blueberries.

Pour batter by 1/4 cupfuls onto a greased hot griddle. Turn when bubbles form on top; cook until the second side is golden brown. Serve with blueberry topping. **Yield: about 20 pancakes (3-1/2 cups topping).**

Editor's Note: If using frozen blueberries, do not thaw before adding to batter.

Broccoli-Ham Puff Pancake 1st prize

You won't have to pay a pretty penny to prepare this special-looking Sunday supper. The golden brown puff pancake makes a tasty main dish for brunch, lunch or dinner when filled with a creamy ham and broccoli mixture.—Edna Hoffman, Hebron, Indiana

- 1/4 cup butter
- 1 cup all-purpose flour
- 4 eggs
- 1 cup milk

FILLING:

- 3 tablespoons butter
- 3 tablespoons all-purpose flour
- 1 cup plus 2 tablespoons milk
- 1 package (16 ounces) frozen chopped broccoli, thawed
- 1-1/2 cups cubed fully cooked ham
- 1/3 cup sour cream
- 1-1/2 teaspoons lemon juice
- 1/8 teaspoon hot pepper sauce

Place butter in a 10-in. ovenproof skillet; place in a 425° oven for 3-4 minutes or until melted. In a small mixing bowl, beat the flour, eggs and milk until smooth. Pour into prepared skillet. Bake at 425° for 22-25 minutes or until puffed and golden brown.

Meanwhile, in a saucepan, melt butter. Stir in flour until smooth; gradually add milk. Bring to a boil; cook and stir for 2 minutes or until thickened. Reduce heat; add the remaining filling ingredients. Cook for 10 minutes or until heated through. Spoon into center of puff pancake. Cut into wedges; serve immediately. **Yield: 6 servings.**

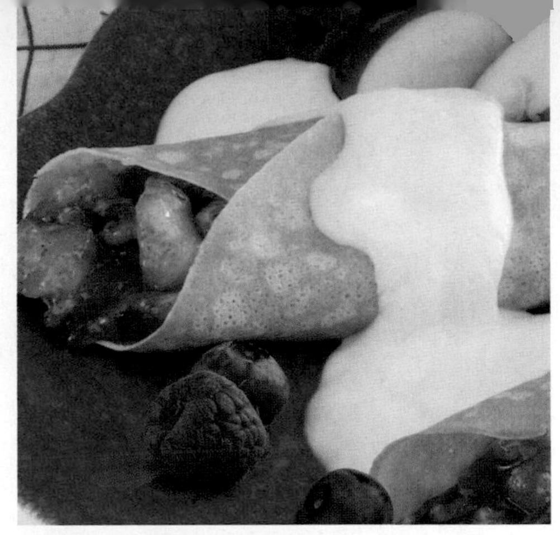

Apple Pecan Crepes

Apple Pecan Crepes

This is a very easy, quick and delicious brunch item. When they taste the nutty apple pie filling tucked inside and the vanilla sauce draped over the tender crepes, everyone oohs and aahs between bites. Prepare a big batch—people tend to go back for seconds and even thirds! —Carolyn Hayes, Marion, Illinois

- 1 can (21 ounces) apple pie filling
- 1/2 cup coarsely chopped pecans
- 1/2 teaspoon ground cinnamon
- 12 prepared crepes (7 inches *each*)
- 1 egg, beaten
- 3/4 cup half-and-half cream
- 2 tablespoons sugar
- 1/2 teaspoon vanilla extract
- 1/4 teaspoon almond extract

In a bowl, combine pie filling, pecans and cinnamon. Spread 2 rounded tablespoonfuls down the center of each crepe; roll up tightly. Place in a greased 13-in. x 9-in. x 2-in. baking dish. Bake, uncovered, at 375° for 10-14 minutes or until heated through.

Meanwhile, in a microwave-safe bowl, combine the egg, cream, sugar and extracts. Cover and microwave at 50% power for 5-6 minutes or until thickened, stirring every 2 minutes. Cool. Serve over crepes. **Yield: 6 servings.**

Editor's Note: This recipe was tested in an 850-watt microwave.

True Belgian Waffles

True Belgian Waffles

When I served the waffles to my husband's Belgian-born grandmother, she said they tasted just like home. The grandkids love these waffles with about any kind of topping—blueberries, strawberries, raspberries, fried apples, powdered sugar or whipped topping.
—Rose Delemeester, St. Charles, Michigan

- 2 cups all-purpose flour
- 3/4 cup sugar
- 3-1/2 teaspoons baking powder
- 2 eggs, *separated*
- 1-1/2 cups milk
- 1 cup butter, melted
- 1 teaspoon vanilla extract
- Sliced fresh strawberries *or* syrup

In a bowl, combine the flour, sugar and baking powder. In another bowl, lightly beat egg yolks. Add the milk, butter and vanilla; mix well. Stir into dry ingredients just until combined. Beat egg whites until stiff peaks form; fold into batter.

Bake in a preheated waffle iron according to manufacturer's directions until golden brown. Serve with strawberries or syrup. **Yield: 10 waffles (about 4-1/2 inches).**

Amish Baked Oatmeal

The first time I had this treat was at a bed-and-breakfast in Lancaster, Pennsylvania. To me, it tasted just like a big warm-from-the-oven oatmeal cookie!
—Colleen Butler, Inwood, West Virginia

- 1-1/2 cups quick-cooking oats
- 1/2 cup sugar
- 1/2 cup milk
- 1/4 cup butter, melted
- 1 egg
- 1 teaspoon baking powder
- 3/4 teaspoon salt
- 1 teaspoon vanilla extract
- Warm milk
- Fresh fruit *and/or* brown sugar, optional

Combine the first eight ingredients; mix well. Spread evenly in a greased 13-in. x 9-in. x 2-in. baking pan. Bake at 350° for 25-30 minutes or until edges are golden brown. Immediately spoon into bowls; add milk. Top with fruit and/or brown sugar if desired. **Yield: 6 servings.**

Amish Baked Oatmeal

Cherry Almond Granola

Skim milk turns this crunchy snack into a healthy breakfast cereal, while a dollop of low-fat yogurt makes it a delicious dessert. Try adding a little baking cocoa to the brown sugar for a flavor twist.

—Deborah Purdue, Freeland, Michigan

- 1 cup packed brown sugar
- 1/2 cup nonfat dry milk powder
- 1/2 cup honey
- 1/3 cup unsweetened apple juice concentrate
- 2 tablespoons canola oil
- 3 teaspoons almond extract
- 6 cups old-fashioned oats
- 1-1/2 cups dried cherries *or* cranberries
- 1 cup slivered almonds

Fat-free vanilla yogurt, optional

In a saucepan, combine the brown sugar, milk powder, honey, apple juice concentrate and oil. Cook and stir over medium heat until sugar is dissolved; stir in extract. In a large bowl, combine the oats, cherries and almonds. Drizzle with sugar mixture and mix well.

Spread in a thin layer in two 15-in. x 10-in. x 1-in. baking pans coated with nonstick cooking spray. Bake at 375° for 15-20 minutes or until golden brown, stirring occasionally. Cool completely. Serve with yogurt if desired. Store in an airtight container. **Yield: 3 quarts.**

Cherry Almond Granola

Morning Orange Drink

Morning Orange Drink

Although it requires only a few basic ingredients and little preparation, this drink always draws raves from overnight guests about its wake-up taste.

—Joyce Mummau, Mt. Airy, Maryland

- 1 can (6 ounces) frozen orange juice concentrate
- 1 cup cold water
- 1 cup milk
- 1/3 cup sugar
- 1 teaspoon vanilla extract
- 10 ice cubes

Combine the first five ingredients in a blender; cover and process at high speed. Add ice cubes, a few at a time, blending until smooth. Pour into glasses; serve immediately. **Yield: 4-6 servings.**

Breakfast Wassail

Breakfast Wassail

This fruity beverage is great all year-round and tasty hot or chilled. I got the recipe from a co-worker and made it one Christmas for a family gathering. Now whenever we get together for the holidays, I'm always the designated wassail-maker.

—Amy Holtsclaw, Carbondale, Illinois

- 1 can (64 ounces) cranberry juice
- 1 can (32 ounces) apple juice
- 1 can (12 ounces) frozen pineapple juice concentrate, undiluted
- 1 can (12 ounces) frozen lemonade concentrate, undiluted
- 3 to 4 cinnamon sticks (3 inches *each*)
- 1 quart water, optional

In a large saucepan or Dutch oven, combine the juices, lemonade and cinnamon sticks. Bring to a boil. Reduce heat; cover and simmer for 1 hour. Add water if desired. Serve hot or cold. **Yield: about 4 quarts.**

BEEF

TOVETOP POT ROAST, pg. 157

Beef

Stovetop Pot Roast 1st prize

I make this hearty stovetop favorite at least twice a month—my husband, Jim, loves it!
—Mary Lou Chernik, Taos, New Mexico

- 1 boneless beef chuck roast (3 to 4 pounds)
- 2 to 3 garlic cloves, halved lengthwise
- 2 tablespoons olive oil
- 1 large onion, cut into 1/2-inch slices
- 3 celery ribs, cut into 1/2-inch slices
- 2 medium turnips, peeled and cut into chunks
- 4 cups water
- 2 beef bouillon cubes
- 4 medium potatoes, peeled and quartered
- 1 pound carrots, cut into chunks
- 1/2 pound fresh *or* frozen green beans, partially thawed
- 1/2 pound fresh mushrooms, sliced
- 3 tablespoons cornstarch
- 1/4 cup cold water

Salt and pepper to taste

Cut slits in roast; insert garlic slivers. In a large deep skillet, brown roast on all sides in oil over medium heat. Remove roast. Add the onion, celery and turnips to skillet. Place roast over vegetables; add water and bouillon. Bring to a boil. Reduce heat; cover and simmer for 2 hours.

Add the potatoes, carrots and beans; cover and cook for 45 minutes. Add mushrooms; cover and cook 15 minutes longer or until meat and vegetables are tender. Remove to a serving platter and keep warm.

Stovetop Pot Roast

Skim fat from pan juices. Combine cornstarch and cold water until smooth; stir into pan juices. Bring to a boil; cook and stir for 2 minutes or until thickened. Season with salt and pepper. Slice roast; serve with vegetables and gravy. **Yield: 8-10 servings.**

Herb-Crusted Chuck Roast

This recipe turns an inexpensive cut of beef into a delicious main dish. I got the recipe from a family member several years ago and have made it often.
—Rita Drewes, Craig, Missouri

- 1/4 cup dry bread crumbs
- 2 tablespoons olive oil
- 1 garlic clove, minced
- 1 teaspoon ground mustard
- 1 teaspoon dried savory
- 1 teaspoon pepper
- 1/2 teaspoon dried rosemary, crushed
- 1 boneless beef chuck eye *or* top blade roast (about 3 pounds)

SAUCE:

- 1 cup (8 ounces) sour cream
- 3 tablespoons prepared horseradish
- 1 teaspoon lemon juice
- 1/4 teaspoon salt

In a bowl, combine the first seven ingredients. Rub over entire roast. Place on a rack in a shallow roasting pan. Bake, uncovered, at 325° for 1-1/2 to 2 hours or until meat is tender and reaches desired doneness (for medium-rare, a meat thermometer should read 145°; medium, 160°; well-done, 170°). Let stand for 10 minutes before carving.

Meanwhile, in a bowl, combine the sauce ingredients. Serve with the roast. **Yield: 8 servings.**

Tangy Beef Brisket 1st prize

We like the sauce for this brisket over elk, moose and venison, too. We also use it to spice hamburgers and hot dogs we sizzle on the grill.
—Jacque Watkins, Green River, Wyoming

Herb-Crusted Chuck Roast

- 1 large onion, diced
- 1/2 cup butter
- 1 bottle (28 ounces) ketchup
- 1-1/2 cups packed brown sugar
- 1/2 cup Worcestershire sauce
- 1/3 cup lemon juice
- 2 tablespoons chili powder
- 1-1/2 teaspoons hot pepper sauce
- 1 teaspoon prepared horseradish
- 1 teaspoon salt
- 1/2 teaspoon garlic powder
- 1 boneless beef brisket (6 pounds)

In a saucepan, saute onion in butter until tender. Add the next nine ingredients; bring to a boil. Reduce heat; simmer, uncovered, for 30-40 minutes.

Place brisket in a roasting pan. Add 3 cups of sauce. Cover and bake at 350° for 4 hours, basting occasionally. Skim fat. Remove brisket; thinly slice the beef and return to pan. Add remaining sauce if desired. **Yield: 12-14 servings (6 cups sauce).**

Editor's Note: This is a fresh beef brisket, not corned beef. The meat comes from the first cut of the brisket.

Tenderloin with Creamy Garlic Sauce

This is the main course at my family's annual Christmas gathering. Everyone always comments on its tenderness and flavor. Since garlic goes well with everything, the sauce would be good with pork or poultry, too. —Beth Taylor, Chapin, South Carolina

- 1 jar (8 ounces) Dijon mustard, *divided*
- 10 garlic cloves, peeled, *divided*
- 2 tablespoons whole black peppercorns, coarsely crushed, *divided*
- 3 tablespoons vegetable oil, *divided*
- 1 beef tenderloin (4 to 5 pounds), halved
- 2 cups heavy whipping cream
- 1 cup (8 ounces) sour cream

In a blender, combine half of the mustard, eight garlic cloves and 1 tablespoon peppercorns; cover and process for 1 minute, scraping sides occasionally. Add 1 tablespoon oil; process until a paste forms. Spread over beef.

In a large skillet, heat the remaining oil over medium-high heat. Brown beef, one piece at a time, on all sides. Place in a shallow roasting pan coated with nonstick cooking spray. Bake, uncovered, at 400° for 25-45 minutes or until meat reaches desired doneness (for medium-rare, a meat thermometer should read 145°; medium, 160°; well done, 170°). Let stand for 10-15 minutes before slicing.

Meanwhile, mince remaining garlic. In a saucepan, combine the garlic, whipping cream, sour cream and remaining mustard and peppercorns. Cook and stir over low heat until heated through. Slice beef; serve with the sauce. **Yield: 12 servings.**

Tangy Beef Brisket

Tenderloin with Creamy Garlic Sauce

Pot Roast with Cranberry Sauce

Slow-Cooked Rump Roast

Pot Roast with Cranberry Sauce

My friends rave about the different taste the cranberry sauce gives to this roast, and I couldn't agree more. I've made the sauce ahead of time and froze it, which saves preparation time on a busy schedule.
—Elinor Muller, Vineyard Haven, Massachusetts

- 1/2 cup all-purpose flour
- 1 garlic clove, minced
- 1 teaspoon salt
- 1/2 teaspoon pepper
- 1 boneless beef rump *or* chuck roast (about 3-1/2 pounds)
- 3 tablespoons vegetable oil
- 2 cups beef broth
- 1 medium onion, grated
- Dash ground cinnamon
- Dash ground cloves

CRANBERRY SAUCE:

- 2 cups fresh *or* frozen cranberries
- 1 small navel orange, peeled and diced
- 1/2 cup sugar
- 1 tablespoon red wine vinegar

Combine the flour, garlic, salt and pepper; rub over the roast. In a Dutch oven, brown roast in oil over medium heat. Add the broth, onion, cinnamon and cloves. Cover and simmer for 2-1/2 hours or until the meat is tender.

Meanwhile, combine the cranberries, orange and sugar in a saucepan. Cover and cook over low heat for 5 minutes. Uncover; simmer until the berries burst and the mixture is thickened, about 20 minutes.

Remove roast and keep warm. Skim fat from pan juices, reserving 2 cups. Stir vinegar and reserved pan juices into the cranberry sauce. Slice roast; serve with the cranberry sauce. **Yield: 8 servings.**

Marinated Beef Tenderloin

Slow-Cooked Rump Roast

I enjoy a good pot roast, but I was tired of the same old thing, so I started experimenting. Cooking the beef in horseradish sauce gives it a tangy flavor.
—Mimi Walker, Palmyra, Pennsylvania

- 1 boneless beef rump roast (3 to 3-1/2 pounds)
- 2 tablespoons vegetable oil
- 4 medium carrots, halved lengthwise and cut into 2-inch pieces
- 3 medium potatoes, peeled and cut into chunks
- 2 small onions, sliced
- 1/2 cup water
- 6 to 8 tablespoons horseradish sauce
- 1/4 cup red wine vinegar
- 1/4 cup Worcestershire sauce
- 2 garlic cloves, minced
- 1-1/2 to 2 teaspoons celery salt
- 3 tablespoons cornstarch
- 1/3 cup cold water

Cut roast in half. In a large skillet, brown meat on all sides in oil over medium-high heat; drain. Place carrots and potatoes in a 5-qt. slow cooker. Top with meat and onions. Combine the water, horseradish sauce, vinegar, Worcestershire sauce, garlic and celery salt. Pour over meat. Cover and cook on low for 10-12 hours or until meat and vegetables are tender.

Combine cornstarch and cold water until smooth; stir into slow cooker. Cover and cook on high for 30 minutes or until gravy is thickened. **Yield: 6-8 servings.**

Marinated Beef Tenderloin

My three grown children and grandkids enjoy this tempting tenderloin. Leftovers make wonderful sandwiches with fresh bread and Dijon mustard. I sometimes substitute a marinated eye of round roast...and it turns out fine.
—Connie Scheffer, Salina, Kansas

- 1 cup soy sauce
- 3/4 cup beef broth
- 1/2 cup olive oil
- 2 tablespoons red wine vinegar
- 4 to 5 garlic cloves, minced
- 1 teaspoon coarsely ground pepper
- 1 teaspoon dried thyme
- 1/2 teaspoon salt
- 1/2 teaspoon hot pepper sauce
- 1 bay leaf
- 1 whole beef tenderloin (3-1/2 to 4 pounds)

In a bowl, combine the first nine ingredients. Cover and refrigerate 1 cup for basting. Pour remaining marinade into a large resealable plastic bag; add bay leaf and tenderloin. Seal bag and turn to coat; refrigerate overnight.

Drain and discard marinade and bay leaf. Place tenderloin on a rack in a shallow roasting pan. Bake, uncovered, at 425° for 55-60 minutes or until meat reaches desired doneness (for medium-rare, a meat thermometer should read 145°; medium, 160°; well-done, 170°), basting often with reserved marinade. Let stand for 15 minutes before slicing. **Yield: 6-8 servings.**

Sweet 'n' Sour Pot Roast

Sweet 'n' Sour Pot Roast

Just a whiff of this pot roast reminds me of my grandmother. She's been making this family favorite for over 45 years. For variety, try the recipe with a whole chicken instead, or add potatoes, carrots and onions or Chinese vegetables to the pot.
—Taryn Daniels, Maple City, Michigan

- 1 teaspoon garlic salt
- 1/2 teaspoon ground mustard
- 1/4 teaspoon pepper
- 1 boneless beef chuck roast (4-1/2 to 5 pounds)
- 2 tablespoons vegetable oil
- 2 cups water
- 1/2 cup soy sauce
- 2 tablespoons white vinegar
- 2 tablespoons honey
- 1 tablespoon celery seed
- 2 tablespoons minced fresh gingerroot
- 6 tablespoons cornstarch
- 1/2 cup cold water
- Hot cooked brown rice, optional

Combine garlic salt, mustard and pepper; rub over entire roast. In a Dutch oven, brown roast on all sides in oil over medium-high heat; drain. Combine the water, soy sauce, vinegar, honey, celery seed and ginger; pour over roast. Bring to a boil. Reduce heat; cover and simmer for 3 to 3-1/2 hours or until meat is tender.

Remove roast from pan and keep warm. Pour pan drippings and loosened brown bits into a measuring cup. Skim fat, reserving drippings. Add enough water, if needed, to measure 5 cups. Return to Dutch oven. Combine cornstarch and cold water until smooth; gradually add to drippings. Bring to a boil; cook and stir for 2 minutes or until thickened. Slice roast; serve with gravy and brown rice if desired. **Yield: 12-16 servings.**

Beef Stew Pie

This tastes just like beef stew in a pie crust! The pie is especially good made the day before so the flavors can blend. *—Karol Sprague, Gables, Michigan*

- 6 tablespoons all-purpose flour, *divided*
- 1-1/2 teaspoons salt
- 1/2 teaspoon pepper
- 1 pound boneless beef round steak, cut into 1-inch pieces
- 2 tablespoons vegetable oil
- 1/2 cup chopped onion
- 2 garlic cloves, minced
- 2-1/4 cups water, *divided*
- 1 tablespoon tomato paste
- 1/2 teaspoon Italian seasoning
- 1/2 teaspoon dried basil
- 1 bay leaf
- 2 cups cubed cooked potatoes
- 1-1/2 cups sliced cooked carrots
- 2 tablespoons minced fresh parsley
- Pastry for single-crust pie (9 inches)

In a large resealable plastic bag, combine 3 tablespoons flour, salt and pepper. Add beef in batches; shake to coat. In a large skillet, brown beef in oil over medium heat. Add onion and garlic; cook and stir until onion is tender. Add 1/4 cup water, stirring to scrape browned bits.

Combine 1-1/2 cups water, tomato paste, Italian seasoning and basil; stir into skillet. Add bay leaf. Bring to a boil. Reduce heat; cover and simmer for 1-1/4 to 1-1/2 hours or until meat is tender.

Combine the remaining flour and water

until smooth; gradually stir into skillet. Bring to a boil; cook and stir for 2 minutes or until thickened. Discard bay leaf. Stir in the potatoes, carrots and parsley. Transfer to a greased 2-qt. baking dish.

On a floured surface, roll out pastry to fit dish. Place over filling; flute edges. Cut slits in top. Bake at 425° for 25-30 minutes or until golden brown. Let stand for 10 minutes. **Yield: 4-6 servings.**

Zucchini con Carne

Living in the land of green chilies and hot peppers, my family has grown to love the flavors of the Southwest, as in this dish. —Sharon Secrest, Tucson, Arizona

- 1-1/2 pounds beef stew meat, cut into 1-inch cubes
- 1/4 cup all-purpose flour
- 2 tablespoons vegetable oil
- 1-1/2 cups water
- 2 garlic cloves, minced
- 1 teaspoon salt
- 1/2 teaspoon pepper
- 4 large zucchini, cut into chunks
- 2 cups whole kernel corn
- 1 medium onion, cut into wedges
- 2 cans (4 ounces *each*) chopped green chilies, undrained
- Shredded Monterey Jack cheese
- Warmed flour tortillas, optional

Toss beef with flour to coat. In a Dutch oven, brown beef in oil over medium heat. Add the water, garlic, salt and pepper; bring to a boil. Reduce heat; cover and simmer for 1 hour and 15 minutes or until the meat is tender.

Add zucchini, corn, onion and chilies; bring to a boil. Reduce heat; cover and simmer for 20-30 minutes or until the vegetables are tender. Sprinkle with cheese and serve with tortillas if desired. **Yield: 8-10 servings.**

Zucchini con Carne

Beef Stew Pie

Stew with Confetti Dumplings

Apple Beef Stew

Stew with Confetti Dumplings

If you want a stew that will warm you to the bone, try this one. My family really likes the dumplings.
—Lucile Cline, Wichita, Kansas

- 2 pounds boneless beef chuck roast, cut into 1-inch cubes
- 2 tablespoons vegetable oil
- 1/2 pound fresh mushrooms, halved
- 1 large onion, thinly sliced
- 1 garlic clove, minced
- 2 cans (14-1/2 ounces *each*) beef broth
- 1 teaspoon Italian seasoning
- 1 teaspoon salt
- 1/4 teaspoon pepper
- 1 bay leaf
- 1/3 cup all-purpose flour
- 1/2 cup water
- 1 package (10 ounces) frozen peas

DUMPLINGS:

- 1-1/2 cups biscuit/baking mix
- 2 tablespoons diced pimientos, drained
- 1 tablespoon minced chives
- 1/2 cup milk

In a Dutch oven, brown meat in oil over medium heat. Add the mushrooms, onion and garlic; cook until onion is tender, stirring occasionally. Stir in the broth, Italian seasoning, salt, pepper and bay leaf; bring to a boil. Cover and simmer for 1-1/2 hours.

Discard bay leaf. Combine the flour and water until smooth; stir into stew. Bring to a boil; cook and stir for 2 minutes or until thickened. Reduce heat. Stir in peas.

For dumplings, combine the biscuit mix, pimientos and chives in a bowl. Stir in enough milk to form a soft dough. Drop by tablespoonfuls onto the simmering stew. Cover and simmer for 10-12 minutes or until a toothpick inserted in a dumpling comes out clean (do not lift lid while simmering). Serve immediately. **Yield: 10-12 servings (about 3 quarts).**

Apple Beef Stew

Just about everyone has a recipe they know by heart. Well, this is mine. It's easy because all the ingredients (except the salt) are in measurements of two.
—Paula Pelis, Lenhartsville, Pennsylvania

- 2 pounds boneless beef chuck roast, cut into 1-1/2-inch cubes
- 2 tablespoons butter
- 2 medium onions, cut into wedges
- 2 tablespoons all-purpose flour
- 1/8 teaspoon salt
- 2 cups water
- 2 tablespoons apple juice
- 2 bay leaves
- 2 whole allspice
- 2 whole cloves
- 2 medium carrots, sliced
- 2 medium apples, peeled and cut into wedges

In a large skillet or Dutch oven, brown beef in butter over medium heat. Add onions; cook until lightly browned. Sprinkle with flour and salt. Gradually add water and apple juice. Bring to a boil; cook and stir for 2 minutes or until thickened.

Place the bay leaves, allspice and cloves in a double thickness of cheesecloth; bring up corners of cloth and tie with string to form a bag. Add to pan.

Reduce heat; cover and simmer for 1-1/2 hours or until meat is almost tender. Add carrots and apples; cover and simmer 15 minutes longer or until meat, carrots and apples are tender. Discard spice bag. Thicken if desired. **Yield: 4 servings.**

Salsa Beef Skillet

Salsa Beef Skillet

Here's a main dish that's delicious, attractive and economical. It's great with a guacamole salad.
—Jeanne Bennett, North Richland Hills, Texas

- 1 boneless beef chuck roast (2 to 2-1/2 pounds), cut into 3/4-inch cubes
- 2 tablespoons vegetable oil
- 1 jar (16 ounces) chunky salsa
- 1 can (8 ounces) tomato sauce
- 2 garlic cloves, minced
- 2 tablespoons brown sugar
- 1 tablespoon soy sauce
- 2 tablespoons minced fresh cilantro
- 2 tablespoons lime juice

Hot cooked rice

In a large skillet, cook beef over medium heat in oil until no longer pink; drain. Add the salsa, tomato sauce, garlic, brown sugar and soy sauce. Bring to a boil. Reduce heat; cover and simmer for 2 hours or until meat is tender. Stir in cilantro and lime juice; heat through. Serve over rice. **Yield: 4-6 servings.**

Old-Fashioned Swiss Steak

Our ladies' group held monthly dinners at our church to raise money, and this is one of the dishes we served. We never had to advertise these dinners—word about the good food got around quickly.
—Elaine De Witt, Lake City, Minnesota

- 2 pounds beef round steak
- 1/2 cup all-purpose flour
- 1/2 teaspoon salt
- 1/2 teaspoon pepper, *divided*
- 2 tablespoons vegetable oil
- 1 cup chopped onion
- 1/2 cup chopped green pepper
- 1/4 cup soy sauce
- 1/2 teaspoon garlic salt

Hot cooked noodles, optional

Cut steak into serving-size pieces. Combine the flour, salt and 1/4 teaspoon pepper; sprinkle over steak and pound into both sides. In a skillet, brown steak in oil on both sides over medium heat.

Transfer to a greased 13-in. x 9-in. x 2-in. baking dish; top with onion and green pepper. Drizzle with soy sauce; sprinkle with garlic salt and remaining pepper. Cover and bake at 325° for 1-1/2 hours or until meat is tender. Serve over noodles if desired. **Yield: 6-8 servings.**

Old-Fashioned Swiss Steak

Marinated Flank Steak

I first grilled this appetizing flank steak for my father on a special occasion. We loved it so much that I now make it this way all the time. The steak marinates overnight, so there's little last-minute preparation to worry about.
—Ann Fox, Austin, Texas

- 2/3 cup olive oil
- 1/4 cup lemon juice
- 2 tablespoons red wine vinegar
- 1 tablespoon Worcestershire sauce
- 1 tablespoon soy sauce
- 1 tablespoon Dijon mustard
- 1 teaspoon dried basil
- 1/2 teaspoon dried oregano
- 1/4 teaspoon dried thyme
- 1 beef flank steak (about 1-1/2 pounds)

In a large resealable plastic bag, combine the first nine ingredients; add steak. Seal bag and turn to coat; refrigerate for 8 hours or overnight, turning occasionally.

Drain and discard marinade. Grill steak, covered, over medium-hot heat for 6-10 minutes on each side or until meat reaches desired doneness (for medium-rare, a meat thermometer should read 145°; medium, 160°; well-done, 170°). **Yield: 4-6 servings.**

Cajun Pepper Steak

Cajun recipes have become popular across the country, but they've always been loved here. See if this recipe doesn't become a family favorite at your house!
—Martha Sue Kinnaird, Ruston, Louisiana

- 1-1/2 pounds boneless beef round steak, cut into cubes
- 2 tablespoons vegetable oil
- 1 can (14-1/2 ounces) beef broth
- 1 can (14-1/2 ounces) diced tomatoes, undrained
- 1 cup chopped green pepper
- 1/2 cup chopped onion
- 3 garlic cloves, minced
- 2 teaspoons Worcestershire sauce
- 1 bay leaf
- 1/2 teaspoon dried basil
- 1/4 to 1/2 teaspoon Cajun seasoning
- 1/8 teaspoon salt
- 1/8 teaspoon pepper
- 2 tablespoons cornstarch
- 2 tablespoons cold water
- Hot cooked rice *or* noodles

In a large skillet, cook beef in oil over medium heat until browned; drain. Stir in the broth, tomatoes, green pepper, onion, garlic, Worcestershire sauce and seasonings. Bring to a boil. Reduce heat; cover and simmer for 1 hour or until meat is tender.

Discard bay leaf. Combine cornstarch and water until smooth; stir into meat mixture. Bring to a boil; cook and stir for 2 minutes or until thickened. Serve over rice or noodles. **Yield: 4-6 servings.**

Marinated Flank Steak

Cajun Pepper Steak

Steak with Citrus Salsa

Stir-Fried Steak and Veggies

Steak with Citrus Salsa

A lime juice marinade really perks up grilled steaks, and the snappy, light citrus salsa is a super change from the usual heavy steak sauce.
—Kathleen Smith, Pittsburgh, Pennsylvania

- 1/2 cup soy sauce
- 1/4 cup chopped green onions
- 3 tablespoons lime juice
- 2 tablespoons brown sugar
- 1/8 teaspoon hot pepper sauce
- 1 garlic clove, minced
- 1-1/2 pounds boneless beef sirloin steak (about 1 inch thick)

SALSA:

- 2 navel oranges, peeled, sectioned and chopped
- 1/4 cup chopped green onions
- 2 tablespoons orange juice
- 2 tablespoons red wine vinegar
- 2 tablespoons chopped lemon
- 1 tablespoon chopped lime
- 1 tablespoon sugar
- 1 tablespoon minced fresh cilantro
- 1 teaspoon minced jalapeno pepper
- 1/2 teaspoon grated lemon peel
- 1/2 teaspoon grated lime peel
- 1/8 teaspoon salt

In a large resealable plastic bag, combine the first six ingredients; add beef. Seal bag and turn to coat; refrigerate for 2 hours or overnight, turning occasionally.

Drain and discard marinade. Broil or grill steak, uncovered, over medium heat for 4-6 minutes on each side or until meat reaches desired doneness (for medium-rare, a meat thermometer should read 145°; medium, 160°; well-done, 170°).

Steak on a Stick

Combine salsa ingredients in a bowl. Cut steak across the grain into thin slices. Serve with salsa. **Yield: 4-6 servings.**

Editor's Note: When cutting or seeding hot peppers, use rubber or plastic gloves to protect your hands. Avoid touching your face.

Stir-Fried Steak And Veggies

There's just enough ginger, chili powder and garlic powder in the sauce to spark the taste of this enjoyable steak specialty. For variety, you can substitute chicken or pork for the sirloin.

—Inez Glover, Wainwright, Alberta

- 1 tablespoon cornstarch
- 1 tablespoon brown sugar
- 3/4 teaspoon ground ginger
- 1/2 teaspoon chili powder
- 1/4 teaspoon garlic powder
- 1/4 teaspoon pepper
- 1/2 cup cold water
- 1/4 cup soy sauce
- 1 pound boneless beef sirloin steak, cut into thin strips
- 2 tablespoons vegetable oil
- 2 cups broccoli florets
- 2 cups cauliflowerets
- 1 large onion, chopped
- 1 cup sliced carrots

Hot cooked rice

In a small bowl, whisk together the first eight ingredients until smooth; set aside. In a skillet or wok, stir-fry steak in oil for 3-5 minutes. Add the broccoli, cauliflower, onion, carrots and soy sauce mixture; cover and cook for 8 minutes or until vegetables are crisp-tender, stirring occasionally. Serve over rice. **Yield: 4 servings.**

Steak on a Stick

I combine molasses, mustard and soy sauce to make these the most robust kabobs you've ever tasted. You'll never miss the oil in this hearty marinade.

—Jennifer Schwerin, Rockford, Illinois

- 1 beef flank steak (1-1/2 pounds)
- 1/2 cup reduced-sodium soy sauce
- 1/4 cup water
- 2 tablespoons molasses
- 2 teaspoons ground mustard
- 1 teaspoon ground ginger
- 1/2 teaspoon garlic powder

Freeze steak for 1-1/2 hours. Cut diagonally into 1/4-in. slices. In a bowl, combine the remaining ingredients. Pour 1/4 cup into a small bowl for basting; cover and refrigerate. Pour remaining marinade into a large resealable plastic bag; add the beef. Seal bag and turn to coat; refrigerate for at least 4 hours.

Coat grill rack with nonstick cooking spray before starting the grill. Drain and discard marinade. Thread beef ribbon-style on 12 metal or soaked wooden skewers. Grill, uncovered, over medium heat for 3-4 minutes on each side or until meat reaches desired doneness, basting frequently with reserved marinade. **Yield: 6 servings.**

Bacon Cheeseburger Pizza

Kids of all ages love pizza and cheeseburgers, and this recipe combines them both. My grandchildren usually request pizza for supper when they visit me. They like to help me assemble this version, and they especially enjoy eating it!

—Cherie Ackerman, Lakeland, Minnesota

- 1/2 pound ground beef
- 1 small onion, chopped
- 1 prebaked Italian bread shell crust (1 pound)
- 1 can (8 ounces) pizza sauce
- 6 bacon strips, cooked and crumbled
- 20 dill pickle coin slices
- 2 cups (8 ounces) shredded part-skim mozzarella cheese
- 2 cups (8 ounces) shredded cheddar cheese
- 1 teaspoon pizza *or* Italian seasoning

In a skillet, cook beef and onion over medium heat until meat is no longer pink; drain and set aside.

Place crust on an ungreased 12-in. pizza pan. Spread with pizza sauce. Top with beef mixture, bacon, pickles and cheeses. Sprinkle with pizza seasoning. Bake at 450° for 8-10 minutes or until cheese is melted. **Yield: 8 slices.**

Bacon Cheeseburger Pizza

Creamy Beef Lasagna

The creamy Stroganoff-like filling in this distinctive lasagna makes it a stick-to-your-ribs entree. My family loves the delicious taste, and I appreciate that it's inexpensive to fix.

—Jane Frawley, Charles Town, West Virginia

- 1-1/2 pounds ground beef
- 2 cans (15 ounces *each*) tomato sauce
- 1/4 cup chopped onion
- 2 teaspoons sugar
- 2 teaspoons salt
- 2 teaspoons Worcestershire sauce
- 1/2 teaspoon garlic salt
- 2 packages (8 ounces *each*) cream cheese, softened
- 1 cup (8 ounces) sour cream
- 1/4 cup milk
- 18 lasagna noodles, cooked and drained
- 1 cup (4 ounces) shredded cheddar cheese

Minced fresh parsley, optional

In a skillet, cook beef over medium heat until no longer pink; drain. Stir in the tomato sauce, onion, sugar, salt, Worcestershire sauce and garlic salt. In a mixing bowl, beat cream cheese, sour cream and milk until smooth.

In a greased 13-in. x 9-in. x 2-in. baking dish, layer a fourth of the meat sauce, six noodles and a third of cream cheese mixture. Repeat layers twice. Top with remaining meat sauce.

Cover and bake at 350° for 40 minutes. Uncover; sprinkle with cheddar cheese. Bake 5 minutes longer or until cheese is melted. Let stand for 15 minutes before cutting. Sprinkle with parsley if desired. **Yield: 12 servings.**

Taco-Filled Pasta Shells 1st prize

I've been stuffing pasta shells with different fillings for years, but my family enjoys this version with taco-seasoned meat the most. The frozen shells are so convenient, because you can take out only the number you need for a single-serving lunch or family dinner.

—Marge Hodel, Roanoke, Illinois

Creamy Beef Lasagna

- 2 pounds ground beef
- 2 envelopes taco seasoning
- 1 package (8 ounces) cream cheese, cubed
- 24 uncooked jumbo pasta shells
- 1/4 cup butter, melted

ADDITIONAL INGREDIENTS (for *each* casserole):

- 1 cup salsa
- 1 cup taco sauce
- 1 cup (4 ounces) shredded cheddar cheese
- 1 cup (4 ounces) shredded Monterey Jack cheese
- 1-1/2 cups crushed tortilla chips
- 1 cup (8 ounces) sour cream
- 3 green onions, chopped

In a skillet, cook beef over medium heat until no longer pink; drain. Add taco seasoning; prepare according to package directions. Add cream cheese; cover and simmer for 5-10 minutes or until cheese is melted. Transfer to a bowl; cover and refrigerate for 1 hour. Cook pasta according to package directions; drain. Gently toss with butter. Fill each shell with about 3 tablespoons meat mixture.

Place 12 shells in a greased 9-in. square baking dish. Cover and freeze for up to 3 months. To prepare remaining shells, spoon salsa into a greased 9-in. square baking dish. Top with stuffed shells and taco sauce. Cover and bake at 350° for 30 minutes. Uncover; sprinkle with cheeses and chips. Bake 15 minutes longer or until heated through. Serve with sour cream and onions.

To use frozen shells: Thaw in the refrigerator for 24 hours (shells will be partially frozen). Remove from dish. Add salsa to dish; top with shells and taco sauce. Cover and bake at 350° for 40 minutes. Uncover and continue as above. **Yield: 2 casseroles (4 to 6 servings each).**

Taco-Filled Pasta Shells

Fiesta Meatballs

Meatball Shish Kabobs

Fiesta Meatballs

My rancher husband is crazy about rice, less so about zucchini. But when I serve this flavorful combination, he comes back for more.

—Patricia Archie, Geldo, Wyoming

- 1 egg
- 1-1/2 teaspoons Worcestershire sauce
- 1/4 cup finely chopped onion
- 1/4 cup finely chopped celery
- 2-1/2 teaspoons garlic salt, *divided*
- 1/4 teaspoon pepper
- 1 pound ground beef
- 1 cup soft bread crumbs
- 1 tablespoon cornstarch
- 1 cup beef broth
- 1 can (14-1/2 ounces) stewed tomatoes
- 2 cups sliced zucchini
- 1 teaspoon dried oregano
- 1/2 teaspoon sugar
- 1/2 teaspoon dried basil

In a large bowl, combine egg, Worcestershire sauce, onion, celery, 1-1/2 teaspoons garlic salt and pepper. Crumble beef over mixture and mix well. Sprinkle with bread crumbs; mix just until combined. Shape into 2-in. balls. Place in an ungreased 15-in. x 10-in. x 1-in. baking pan. Bake, uncovered, at 375° for 20 minutes or until meat is no longer pink.

Meanwhile, in a saucepan, combine the cornstarch and broth until smooth. Stir in the stewed tomatoes, zucchini, oregano, sugar, basil and remaining garlic salt. Bring to a boil; cook and stir for 2 minutes or until thickened.

Drain meatballs; top with the tomato mixture. Bake 10 minutes longer or until heated through. **Yield: 4 servings.**

Meatball Shish Kabobs

Convenience foods make this hearty entree a snap to prepare. Purchased meatballs are easy to thread onto skewers. And since they're precooked, you just need to grill the kabobs until the fresh veggies are tender. Basting with bottled barbecue sauce adds fast flavor.
—Shawn Solley, Lawton, Oklahoma

- 1 package (16 ounces) frozen fully cooked meatballs, thawed (about 30 meatballs)
- 2 medium zucchini, cut into 1/2-inch slices
- 2 medium yellow summer squash, cut into 1/2-inch slices
- 12 cherry tomatoes
- 12 pearl onions
- 1 cup barbecue sauce

Hot cooked rice

On metal or soaked bamboo skewers, thread the meatballs, zucchini, summer squash, tomatoes and onions. Grill, uncovered, over medium heat for 6 minutes, turning once.

Baste with barbecue sauce. Grill 8-10 minutes longer or until meatballs are heated through and vegetables are tender, turning and basting frequently. Serve over rice. **Yield: 6 servings.**

Meat Loaf Miniatures

I don't usually like meat loaf, but my family and I can't get enough of these little muffins topped with a sweet ketchup sauce. This recipe requires no chopping, so it's quick and easy to make a double batch and have extras for another day. They're great to give to new moms, too. —Joyce Wegmann, Burlington, Iowa

- 1 cup ketchup
- 3 to 4 tablespoons packed brown sugar

Meat Loaf Miniatures

- 1 teaspoon ground mustard
- 2 eggs, beaten
- 4 teaspoons Worcestershire sauce
- 3 cups Crispix cereal, crushed
- 3 teaspoons onion powder
- 1/2 to 1 teaspoon seasoned salt
- 1/2 teaspoon garlic powder
- 1/2 teaspoon pepper
- 3 pounds lean ground beef

In a large bowl, combine the ketchup, brown sugar and mustard. Remove 1/2 cup for topping; set aside. Add eggs, Worcestershire sauce, cereal and seasonings to remaining ketchup mixture; mix well. Let stand for 5 minutes. Crumble beef over cereal mixture and mix well.

Press meat mixture into 18 muffin cups (about 1/3 cup each). Bake at 375° for 18-20 minutes. Drizzle with reserved ketchup mixture; bake 10 minutes longer or until meat is no longer pink and a meat thermometer reads 160°. Serve desired number of meat loaves. Cool remaining loaves; freeze. Transfer to freezer bags; freeze for up to 3 months.

To use frozen meat loaves: Completely thaw in the refrigerator. Place loaves in a greased baking dish. Bake at 350° for 30 minutes or until heated through, or cover and microwave on high for 1 minute or until heated through. **Yield: 1-1/2 dozen.**

Tasty Meat Pie

Tasty Meat Pie

I work full-time as a nurse, so I like meals that are quick and easy. This comforting all-in-one pie is filled with ground beef and tender vegetables. At my sister's suggestion, I replaced the prepared gravy I had been using with canned soups for better flavor. Now my husband and teenage son ask for seconds and thirds. —Cheryl Cattane, Lapeer, Michigan

- 1 pound ground beef
- 1 small onion, chopped
- 1 can (11 ounces) condensed beef with vegetables and barley soup, undiluted
- 1 can (10-3/4 ounces) condensed golden mushroom soup, undiluted
- 3 medium uncooked potatoes, cut into 1/2-inch cubes
- 4 medium carrots, sliced 1/8 inch thick
- 1/4 teaspoon salt
- 1/8 teaspoon pepper

Pastry for double-crust pie (9 inches)

In a skillet, cook beef and onion over medium heat until meat is no longer pink; drain. Add the soups, potatoes, carrots, salt and pepper; mix well. Divide between two ungreased 9-in. pie plates.

On a floured surface, roll pastry to fit the top of each pie; place over filling. Seal and flute edges; cut slits in top. Bake at 350° for 45-50 minutes or until golden brown. Let stand on a wire rack for 15 minutes before serving. **Yield: 2 pies (6 servings each).**

Garlic Beef Enchiladas

I use flour tortillas in this saucy casserole that has irresistible home-cooked flavor and a subtle kick. —Jennifer Standridge, Dallas, Georgia

- 1 pound ground beef
- 1 medium onion, chopped
- 2 tablespoons all-purpose flour
- 1 tablespoon chili powder
- 1 teaspoon salt
- 1 teaspoon garlic powder
- 1/2 teaspoon ground cumin
- 1/4 teaspoon rubbed sage
- 1 can (14-1/2 ounces) stewed tomatoes

SAUCE:

- 4 to 6 garlic cloves, minced
- 1/3 cup butter
- 1/2 cup all-purpose flour
- 1 can (14-1/2 ounces) beef broth
- 1 can (15 ounces) tomato sauce
- 1 to 2 tablespoons chili powder
- 1 to 2 teaspoons ground cumin
- 1 to 2 teaspoons rubbed sage
- 1/2 teaspoon salt
- 10 flour tortillas (7 inches)
- 2 cups (8 ounces) shredded Colby-Monterey Jack cheese

In a saucepan, cook beef and onion over medium heat until meat is no longer pink; drain. Stir in the flour and seasoning until blended. Stir in tomatoes; bring to a boil. Reduce heat; cover and simmer for 15 minutes.

Meanwhile, in another saucepan, saute garlic in butter until tender. Stir in flour until blended; gradually stir in broth. Bring to a boil; cook and stir for 2 minutes or until thickened. Stir in tomato sauce and seasonings; heat through.

Pour about 1-1/2 cups sauce into an

ungreased 13-in. x 9-in. x 2-in. baking dish. Spread about 1/4 cup beef mixture down the center of each tortilla; top with 1-2 tablespoons cheese. Roll up tightly; place seam side down over sauce. Top with remaining sauce.

Cover and bake at 350° for 30-35 minutes. Sprinkle with remaining cheese. Bake, uncovered, 10-15 minutes longer or until the cheese is melted. **Yield: 4-6 servings.**

Garlic Beef Enchiladas

Meaty Mac 'n' Cheese

My husband is disabled and requires constant care. This doesn't leave me a lot of time to cook, so I came up with this tasty way to beef up a box of macaroni and cheese. The hearty mixture gets extra flavor from corn, ripe olives and zippy salsa.

—Charlotte Kremer, Pahrump, Nevada

- 1 package (7-1/4 ounces) macaroni and cheese dinner mix
- 1 pound ground beef
- 1/4 cup chopped onion
- 1-1/2 cups salsa
- 1/2 cup fresh *or* frozen corn
- 1 can (2-1/4 ounces) sliced ripe olives, drained
- 3 tablespoons diced pimientos
- Shredded cheddar cheese
- Chopped tomato

Set aside cheese sauce mix from macaroni and cheese; cook macaroni according to package directions. Meanwhile, in a large saucepan, cook beef and onion over medium heat until meat is no longer pink; drain. Add the salsa, corn, olives and pimientos; heat through.

Drain macaroni; add to beef mixture with contents of cheese sauce mix. Mix well; heat through. Garnish with cheese and tomato. **Yield: 4-6 servings.**

Editor's Note: The milk and butter listed on the macaroni and cheese package are not used in this recipe.

Meaty Mac 'n' Cheese

Where's the Squash Lasagna

Colorful Stuffed Peppers

Where's the Squash Lasagna

I devised this recipe to hide zucchini from my unsuspecting grandchildren and any others who think they don't like it. It's always at hit at our house.
—Norma Brinson, Greenville, North Carolina

- 1 pound ground beef
- 2 large zucchini (about 1 pound), shredded
- 3/4 cup chopped onion
- 2 garlic cloves, minced
- 1 can (14-1/2 ounces) stewed tomatoes
- 2 cups water
- 1 can (12 ounces) tomato paste
- 1 tablespoon minced fresh parsley
- 1-1/2 teaspoons salt
- 1 teaspoon sugar
- 1/2 teaspoon dried oregano
- 1/2 teaspoon pepper
- 9 lasagna noodles, cooked, rinsed and drained
- 1 carton (15 ounces) ricotta cheese
- 2 cups (8 ounces) shredded part-skim mozzarella cheese
- 1 cup grated Parmesan cheese

In a skillet, cook the beef, zucchini, onion and garlic over medium heat until meat is no longer pink; drain. Place tomatoes in a food processor or blender; cover and process until smooth. Stir into beef mixture. Add the water, tomato paste, parsley and seasonings. Bring to a boil. Reduce heat; simmer, uncovered, for 30 minutes, stirring occasionally.

Spread 1 cup meat sauce in a greased 13-in. x 9-in. x 2-in. baking dish. Arrange three noodles over sauce. Spread with a third of meat sauce; top with half of the ricotta. Sprinkle with a third of the mozzarella and Parmesan. Repeat. Top with the remaining noodles, meat sauce and cheeses.

Reuben Meatballs

Cover and bake at 350° for 45 minutes. Uncover; bake 15 minutes longer or until bubbly. Let stand for 15 minutes before cutting. **Yield: 12 servings.**

Colorful Stuffed Peppers

You're sure to enjoy this tasty twist on traditional stuffed peppers with south-of-the-border flavor.
—Angie Dierikx, State Center, Iowa

- 1 pound ground beef
- 2 cups salsa
- 1 cup frozen corn
- 1/4 cup water
- 3/4 teaspoon ground cumin
- 3/4 teaspoon dried oregano
- 1 teaspoon salt
- 1/2 teaspoon pepper
- 1/2 cup uncooked instant rice
- 1 cup (4 ounces) shredded cheddar cheese, *divided*
- 4 medium green peppers, halved lengthwise

Sliced canned jalapeno peppers, optional

Crumble beef into a 2-qt. microwave-safe dish. Cover and microwave on high for 2 minutes; stir. Cook on high 1-2 minutes or until the meat is no longer pink; drain. Stir in the next seven ingredients.

Cover and heat on high for 3 minutes or until bubbly around edges. Stir in rice and 1/2 cup cheese. Cover and let stand for 5 minutes; stir.

Spoon 1/2 cup into each pepper half. Place on a 12-in. round microwave-safe plate. Cover loosely and cook on high for 8-10 minutes or until peppers are tender, rotating a half turn once. Cover and let stand for 4 minutes. Sprinkle with remaining cheese; top with jalapenos if desired. **Yield: 4 servings.**

Editor's Note: This recipe was tested with an 850-watt microwave.

Reuben Meatballs

Those who like the taste of Reuben sandwiches and sauerkraut are sure to savor these distinctive meatballs.
—Irlana Waggoner, Hays, Kansas

- 1 egg
- 1 small onion, finely chopped
- 2/3 cup soft bread crumbs
- 1/4 cup minced fresh parsley
- 1/2 teaspoon salt
- 1/2 teaspoon pepper
- 1 cup cooked rice
- 1-1/2 pounds lean ground beef
- 2 cups sauerkraut, rinsed and well drained
- 1 to 2 teaspoons caraway seeds
- 1 can (10-3/4 ounces) condensed cream of mushroom soup, undiluted
- 1/2 cup Thousand Island salad dressing
- 1/4 cup shredded Swiss cheese

Rye bread, optional

In a bowl, mix the first seven ingredients. Crumble beef over the mixture; mix well. Shape into 15 balls. Place in an ungreased 13-in. x 9-in. x 2-in. baking dish. Bake, uncovered, at 350° for 15-20 minutes or until browned; drain.

Place the sauerkraut on top; sprinkle with caraway seeds. Combine soup and dressing; spread over top. Cover; bake 35-45 minutes or until meat is no longer pink. Uncover; sprinkle with cheese. Bake 10 minutes or until cheese is melted. Serve with rye bread if desired. **Yield: 5 servings.**

Chili Nacho Supper

Chili Nacho Supper

The recipe for this creamy, chili-like dish was passed down through our church years ago. It's so warm and filling that we often prepare it when we take skiing trips to Colorado. It can be served over corn chips and eaten with a fork, or kept warm in a slow cooker and served as a hearty dip at parties.

—Laurie Withers, Wildomar, California

- **2-1/2 pounds ground beef**
- **3 cans (15 ounces *each*) tomato sauce**
- **2 cans (16 ounces *each*) pinto beans, rinsed and drained**
- **1 can (10 ounces) diced tomatoes and green chilies, undrained**
- **2 envelopes chili seasoning**
- **2 pounds process American cheese, cubed**
- **1 cup heavy whipping cream**
- **2 packages (16 ounces *each*) corn chips**
- **Sour cream**

In a Dutch oven, cook the beef over medium heat until no longer pink; drain. Add the tomato sauce, beans, tomatoes and chili seasoning; heat through. Add cheese and cream; cook and stir until the cheese is melted. Serve over chips. Top with sour cream. **Yield: 14-16 servings.**

Spinach-Beef Spaghetti Pie

With its angel hair pasta crust, this cheesy ground beef, tomato and spinach pie is always a hit when I serve it. Each neat slice has layers of pasta, cream cheese filling and spinach topping.

—Carol Hicks, Pensacola, Florida

- **6 ounces uncooked angel hair pasta**
- **2 eggs, lightly beaten**
- **1/3 cup grated Parmesan cheese**
- **1 pound ground beef**
- **1/2 cup chopped onion**
- **1/4 cup chopped green pepper**
- **1 jar (14 ounces) meatless spaghetti sauce**
- **1 teaspoon Creole seasoning**
- **3/4 teaspoon garlic powder**
- **1/2 teaspoon dried basil**
- **1/2 teaspoon dried oregano**
- **1 package (8 ounces) cream cheese, softened**
- **1 package (10 ounces) frozen chopped spinach, thawed and squeezed dry**
- **1/2 cup shredded mozzarella cheese**

Cook pasta according to package directions; drain. Add eggs and Parmesan cheese. Press onto the bottom and up the sides of a greased 9-in. deep-dish pie plate. Bake at 350° for 10 minutes.

Meanwhile, in a skillet, cook the beef, onion and green pepper over medium heat until meat is no longer pink and vegetables are tender; drain. Stir in spaghetti sauce and seasonings. Bring to a boil. Reduce heat; cover and simmer for 10 minutes.

Between two pieces of waxed paper, roll out cream cheese into a 7-in. circle. Place in crust. Top with spinach and meat sauce. Sprinkle with mozzarella cheese. Bake at 350° for 20-30 minutes or until set. **Yield: 6-8 servings.**

Meaty Stuffed Onions

I won a prize for this recipe in a contest sponsored by our local newspaper. I got it from my mother-in-law, who's originally from Italy.
—Lorraine Grasso, Allentown, Pennsylvania

- 4 large sweet onions
- 1 pound ground beef
- 1/2 pound bulk pork sausage
- 1 package (10 ounces) frozen chopped spinach, thawed and drained
- 5 slices day-old bread, crumbled
- 1/2 to 2/3 cup beef broth
- 1/2 cup grated Parmesan cheese
- 1 egg, beaten
- 1 tablespoon minced fresh parsley
- 1/2 teaspoon salt
- 1/4 teaspoon pepper
- 1/8 teaspoon ground nutmeg

Peel onions and cut 1/2 in. off tops and bottoms. Place onions in a large saucepan. Cover with boiling water. Cook until tender, about 20 minutes; drain.

Cool slightly. Carefully remove inside layers of onion, separating into eight individual shells (refrigerate remaining onion for another use). Drain on paper towels.

In a skillet, cook beef and sausage over medium heat until no longer pink; drain. Add spinach; cook and stir for 2 minutes. Remove from the heat; stir in the remaining ingredients. Spoon into the onion shells.

Place in a greased 13-in. x 9-in. x 2-in. baking pan. Bake, uncovered, at 350° for 15-20 minutes or until heated through and lightly browned. **Yield: 8 servings.**

Spinach-Beef Spaghetti Pie

Meaty Stuffed Onions

Beef Stroganoff Meatballs

Blue Plate Beef Patties

Beef Stroganoff Meatballs

A rich sour cream and mushroom sauce gives this dish an elegant flavor. Yet it's so easy to prepare for a special occasion or for company.
—Christine Duncan, Ellensburg, Washington

- 1 egg
- 1/4 cup milk
- 1/4 cup finely chopped onion
- 2 teaspoons Worcestershire sauce
- 1-1/2 cups soft bread crumbs
- 1 teaspoon salt
- 1/4 teaspoon pepper
- 1-1/2 pounds ground beef

SAUCE:

- 1-1/2 cups sliced fresh mushrooms
- 1/2 cup chopped onion
- 1/4 cup butter
- 4 tablespoons all-purpose flour, *divided*
- 1/4 teaspoon salt
- 1-1/2 cups beef broth
- 1 cup (8 ounces) sour cream

Hot cooked noodles

Paprika, optional

In a bowl, combine the egg, milk, onion and Worcestershire sauce. Stir in bread crumbs, salt and pepper. Crumble beef over mixture and mix well. Shape into 1-1/4-in. balls. Place in a lightly greased 15-in. x 10-in. x 1-in. baking pan. Bake, uncovered, at 350° for 15-20 minutes or until meat is no longer pink.

In a saucepan, saute mushrooms and onion in butter until tender. Stir in 3 tablespoons flour and salt until blended. Gradually add broth. Bring to a boil over medium heat. Cook and stir for 2 minutes; reduce heat.

Combine sour cream and remaining flour until smooth; stir into mushroom mixture. Add meatballs. Simmer, uncovered, for 4-5

Corn Tortilla Pizzas

minutes or until heated through, stirring occasionally. Serve over noodles. Sprinkle with paprika if desired. **Yield: 6 servings.**

Blue Plate Beef Patties

A friend and I discovered this recipe together and both consider it a staple menu item. I fix the moist, mild-tasting patties often for family and friends.
—Phyllis Miller, Danville, Indiana

- 1 egg
- 2 green onions with tops, sliced
- 1/4 cup seasoned bread crumbs
- 1 tablespoon prepared mustard
- 1-1/2 pounds ground beef
- 1 jar (12 ounces) beef gravy
- 1/2 cup water
- 2 to 3 teaspoons prepared horseradish
- 1/2 pound fresh mushrooms, sliced

In a bowl, beat the egg; stir in tbe onions, bread crumbs and mustard. Crumble beef over mixture and mix well. Shape into four 1/2-in.-thick patties.

In an ungreased skillet, cook patties for 4-5 minutes on each side or until meat is no longer pink; drain.

In a small bowl, combine the gravy, water and horseradish; add mushrooms. Pour over patties. Cook, uncovered, for 5 minutes or until mushrooms are tender and heated through. **Yield: 4 servings.**

Corn Tortilla Pizzas

These tasty individual pizzas have the zippy flavor of tacos. When I created this recipe and served these pizzas to my husband and day-care kids, they made them disappear. The recipe produces a big batch of the meat mixture, but leftovers can be frozen for up to 3 months.
—Karen Housley-Raatz, Walworth, Wisconsin

- 1-1/4 pounds ground beef
- 1 small onion, chopped
- 1/2 cup chopped green pepper
- 3 cans (6 ounces *each*) tomato paste
- 1-1/4 cups water
- 1 cup salsa
- 2 cups fresh *or* frozen corn
- 1-1/2 cups chopped fresh tomatoes
- 3/4 cup chopped ripe olives
- 1 envelope taco seasoning
- 3 teaspoons garlic powder
- 1-1/2 teaspoons dried parsley flakes
- 1/2 teaspoon dried oregano
- 1/8 teaspoon salt
- 1/4 teaspoon pepper
- 32 corn *or* flour tortillas (6 inches)
- 8 cups (2 pounds) shredded part-skim mozzarella cheese

In a skillet, cook beef, onion and green pepper over medium heat until meat is no longer pink; drain. In a bowl, combine tomato paste and water until blended; add salsa. Stir into meat mixture. Stir in the corn, tomatoes, olives and seasonings.

Place tortillas on ungreased baking sheets. Spread each with 1/4 cup meat mixture to within 1/2 in. of edge and sprinkle with 1/4 cup of cheese. Bake at 375° for 5-7 minutes or until the cheese is melted. **Yield: 32 pizzas.**

Meatball Sub Casserole 1st prize

If you like meatball subs, you'll love this tangy casserole—it has all the rich flavor of the popular sandwiches with none of the mess.
—Gina Harris, Seneca, South Carolina

- **1/3 cup chopped green onions**
- **1/4 cup seasoned bread crumbs**
- **3 tablespoons grated Parmesan cheese**
- **1 pound ground beef**
- **1 loaf (1 pound) Italian bread, cut into 1-inch slices**
- **1 package (8 ounces) cream cheese, softened**
- **1/2 cup mayonnaise**
- **1 teaspoon Italian seasoning**
- **1/4 teaspoon pepper**
- **2 cups (8 ounces) shredded part-skim mozzarella cheese, *divided***
- **1 jar (28 ounces) spaghetti sauce**
- **1 cup water**
- **2 garlic cloves, minced**

In a bowl, combine onions, crumbs and Parmesan cheese. Crumble beef over mixture and mix well. Shape into 1-in. balls; place on a rack in a shallow baking pan. Bake at 400° for 15-20 minutes or until no longer pink.

Meanwhile, arrange bread in a single layer in an ungreased 13-in. x 9-in. x 2-in. baking dish (all of the bread might not be used). Combine the cream cheese, mayonnaise, Italian seasoning and pepper; spread over the bread. Sprinkle with 1/2 cup mozzarella.

Combine the sauce, water and garlic; add meatballs. Pour over cheese mixture; sprinkle with remaining mozzarella. Bake, uncovered, at 350° for 30 minutes or until heated through. **Yield: 6-8 servings.**

Editor's Note: Reduced-fat or fat-free mayonnaise is not recommended for this recipe.

Meatball Sub Casserole

Skillet Bow Tie Lasagna

This quick and easy to make recipe tastes just like lasagna, but you cook it on the stove. It's very tasty and is always a hit with my family.
—Arleta Schurle, Clay Center, Kansas

- **1 pound ground beef**
- **1 small onion, chopped**
- **1 garlic clove, minced**
- **1 can (14-1/2 ounces) diced tomatoes, undrained**
- **1-1/2 cups water**
- **1 can (6 ounces) tomato paste**
- **1 tablespoon dried parsley flakes**
- **2 teaspoons dried oregano**
- **1 teaspoon salt**
- **2-1/2 cups uncooked bow tie pasta**
- **3/4 cup small-curd cottage cheese**
- **1/4 cup grated Parmesan cheese**

In a large skillet, cook beef, onion and garlic over medium heat until meat is no longer pink; drain. Add the tomatoes, water, tomato paste, parsley, oregano and salt; mix well. Stir in pasta. Bring to a boil. Reduce heat; cover and simmer for 20-25 minutes or until pasta is tender, stirring once. Combine cheeses; drop by rounded tablespoonfuls onto pasta mixture. Cover and cook for 5 minutes. **Yield: 4 servings.**

Skillet Bow Tie Lasagna

Cool-Kitchen Meat Loaf

Juicy slices of this tender meat loaf are wonderful served with a homemade sweet-and-sour sauce. It's an easy way to fix supper.

—Susan Taul, Birmingham, Alabama

- 1 cup soft bread crumbs
- 1 medium onion, chopped
- 1/2 cup tomato sauce
- 1 egg
- 1-1/2 teaspoons salt
- 1/4 teaspoon pepper
- 1-1/2 pounds lean ground beef

SAUCE:

- 1/2 cup ketchup
- 3 tablespoons brown sugar
- 3 tablespoons Worcestershire sauce
- 2 tablespoons cider vinegar
- 2 tablespoons prepared mustard

In a bowl, combine the first six ingredients. Crumble beef over mixture and mix well. Shape into two loaves; place each loaf in a disposable foil 8-in. x 4-in. x 2-in. loaf pan. Cover with foil. Grill, covered, over indirect medium heat for 30 minutes or until the meat is no longer pink and a meat thermometer reads 160°.

Meanwhile, in a saucepan, combine the sauce ingredients. Cook and stir over low heat until sugar is dissolved. Spoon over meat loaves before serving. **Yield: 2 loaves (3 servings each).**

Cool-Kitchen Meat Loaf

Mashed Potato Beef Casserole

Traditional Lasagna

Mashed Potato Beef Casserole

This recipe came out of my mother's cookbook. The smudges and splatters on the page show that Mom used it extensively. Now I prepare it for our children and grandchildren.
—Helen McGeorge, Abbotsford, British Columbia

- 2 bacon strips, diced
- 1 pound ground beef
- 1 large onion, finely chopped
- 1/4 pound fresh mushrooms, sliced
- 1 large carrot, finely chopped
- 1 celery rib, finely chopped
- 3 tablespoons all-purpose flour
- 1 cup beef broth
- 1 tablespoon Worcestershire sauce
- 1 teaspoon dried tarragon
- 1/4 teaspoon pepper
- 3 cups hot mashed potatoes
- 3/4 cup shredded cheddar cheese, *divided*

Paprika

In a skillet, cook bacon over medium heat until crisp. Using a slotted spoon, remove to paper towels; drain, reserving 1 teaspoon drippings. Cook beef in drippings over medium heat until no longer pink; drain.

Toss the vegetables with the flour; add to skillet along with the broth, Worcestershire sauce, tarragon and pepper. Bring to a boil. Reduce the heat; simmer, uncovered, 15-20 minutes or until vegetables are tender.

Add bacon; transfer to a greased 2-qt. baking dish. Combine potatoes and 1/2 cup cheese; spread over beef mixture. Sprinkle with paprika and remaining cheese. Bake, uncovered, at 350° for 20-25 minutes or until heated through. Broil 4 in. from the heat for 5 minutes or until lightly browned. **Yield: 4-6 servings.**

Spanish Noodles 'n' Ground Beef

Traditional Lasagna 1st prize

My family first tasted this rich, classic lasagna at a friend's home on Christmas Eve. We were so impressed that it became our own holiday tradition as well.
—Lorri Foockle, Granville, Illinois

- 1 pound ground beef
- 3/4 pound bulk pork sausage
- 3 cans (8 ounces *each*) tomato sauce
- 2 cans (6 ounces *each*) tomato paste
- 2 garlic cloves, minced
- 2 teaspoons sugar
- 1 teaspoon Italian seasoning
- 1 teaspoon salt
- 1/2 teaspoon pepper
- 3 eggs
- 3 tablespoons minced fresh parsley
- 3 cups (24 ounces) small-curd cottage cheese
- 1 carton (8 ounces) ricotta cheese
- 1/2 cup grated Parmesan cheese
- 9 lasagna noodles, cooked and drained
- 6 slices provolone cheese
- 3 cups (12 ounces) shredded part-skim mozzarella cheese

In a large skillet, cook beef and sausage over medium heat until no longer pink; drain. Add the tomato sauce, tomato paste, garlic, sugar, seasoning, salt and pepper. Bring to a boil. Reduce heat; simmer, uncovered, for 1 hour, stirring occasionally.

In a large bowl, combine eggs and parsley. Stir in cottage cheese, ricotta and Parmesan.

Spread 1 cup of meat sauce in an ungreased 13-in. x 9-in. x 2-in. baking dish. Layer with three noodles, provolone cheese, 2 cups cottage cheese mixture, 1 cup mozzarella, three noodles, 2 cups meat sauce, remaining cottage cheese mixture and 1 cup mozzarella. Top with the remaining noodles, meat sauce and mozzarella (dish will be full).

Cover and bake at 375° for 50 minutes. Uncover; bake 20 minutes longer or until heated through. Let stand for 15 minutes before cutting. **Yield: 12 servings.**

Spanish Noodles 'n' Ground Beef

Bacon adds flavor to this comforting stovetop supper my mom frequently made when we were growing up. Now I prepare it for my own family.
—Kelli Jones, Peris, California

- 1 pound ground beef
- 1 small green pepper, chopped
- 1/3 cup chopped onion
- 3-1/4 cups uncooked medium egg noodles
- 1 can (14-1/2 ounces) diced tomatoes, undrained
- 1 cup water
- 1/4 cup chili sauce
- 1 teaspoon salt
- 1/8 teaspoon pepper
- 4 bacon strips, cooked and crumbled

In a large skillet, cook the beef, green pepper and onion over medium heat until meat is no longer pink and vegetables are tender; drain. Stir in the noodles, tomatoes, water, chili sauce, salt and pepper. Cover and cook over low heat for 15-20 minutes or until the noodles are tender, stirring frequently. Top with bacon. **Yield: 5 servings.**

Skillet Enchiladas

Skillet Enchiladas

This stovetop Mexican-style dish disappears fast when our two grown children and three grandchildren visit. —*Cathie Beard, Philomath, Oregon*

- **1 pound ground beef**
- **1 medium onion, chopped**
- **1 can (10-3/4 ounces) condensed cream of mushroom soup, undiluted**
- **1 can (10 ounces) enchilada sauce**
- **1/3 cup milk**
- **1 to 2 tablespoons canned chopped green chilies**
- **Vegetable oil**
- **8 corn tortillas**
- **2-1/2 cups (10 ounces) finely shredded cheddar cheese, *divided***
- **1/2 cup chopped ripe olives**

In a large skillet, cook beef and onion over medium heat until meat is no longer pink; drain. Stir in soup, enchilada sauce, milk and chilies. Bring to a boil. Reduce heat; cover and simmer for 20 minutes, stirring occasionally.

Meanwhile, in another skillet, heat 1/4 in. of oil. Dip each tortilla in hot oil for 3 seconds on each side or just until limp; drain on paper towels. Top each tortilla with 1/4 cup cheese and 1 tablespoon olives. Roll up and place over beef mixture, spooning some of mixture over the enchiladas. Cover and cook until heated through, about 5 minutes. Sprinkle with remaining cheese; cover and cook until cheese is melted. **Yield: 8 enchiladas.**

Mushroom Salisbury Steak

My family really looks forward to supper when these tasty beef patties are on the menu. I often bring it to covered-dish gatherings, and then hand out the recipe. —*Louise Miller, Westminster, Maryland*

- **1/4 cup cornstarch**
- **2 cans (10-1/2 ounces *each*) condensed beef consomme, undiluted**
- **1 jar (6 ounces) sliced mushrooms, drained**
- **4 teaspoons Worcestershire sauce**
- **1 teaspoon dried basil**
- **1 egg, beaten**
- **1/2 cup soft bread crumbs**
- **1 medium onion, finely chopped**
- **1/2 to 1 teaspoon seasoned salt**
- **1/4 teaspoon pepper, optional**
- **1-1/2 pounds ground beef**
- **Hot mashed potatoes *or* cooked noodles**

In a large bowl, combine the cornstarch and consomme until smooth. Stir in the mushrooms, Worcestershire sauce and basil; set aside.

In another bowl, combine the egg, bread crumbs, onion, seasoned salt and pepper if desired. Crumble beef over mixture and mix well. Shape into six oval patties; place in a shallow 1-1/2-qt. microwave-safe dish.

Cover and microwave on high for 6 minutes; drain. Turn patties, moving the ones in the center to the outside of dish. Pour consomme mixture over patties. Cover and microwave on high for 8-10 minutes or until meat is no longer pink. Let stand for 5 minutes. Serve with potatoes or noodles. **Yield: 6 servings.**

Editor's Note: This recipe was tested with an 850-watt microwave.

Taco Chili Pie

Ground beef, stewed tomatoes, beans and seasonings are tucked into a flaky golden crust to create this zesty pie. —Liza Taylor, Seattle, Washington

- 1 pound ground beef
- 2 cups sliced fresh mushrooms
- 1 cup chopped onion
- 4 cups torn fresh spinach
- 1 can (16 ounces) kidney beans, rinsed and drained
- 1 can (15 ounces) pinto beans, rinsed and drained
- 1 can (15 ounces) tomato sauce
- 1 can (14-1/2 ounces) stewed tomatoes, undrained
- 2 tablespoons taco seasoning
- 1 tablespoon sugar
- 1 tablespoon molasses

CRUST:

- 4-1/2 cups all-purpose flour
- 4 teaspoons sugar
- 2 teaspoons salt
- 2 cups cold butter
- 12 to 14 tablespoons cold water

In a skillet, cook beef, mushrooms and onion until meat is no longer pink; drain. Stir in next eight ingredients. Bring to a boil. Reduce heat; simmer, uncovered, for 20-30 minutes.

Meanwhile, combine flour, sugar and salt. Cut in butter until crumbly. Gradually add water, tossing with a fork until dough forms a ball. Divide into fourths; flatten each portion into a circle. Cover and chill for 30 minutes.

Line two 9-in. pie plates with pastry. Add beef mixture. Roll out remaining pastry; place over filling. Trim, seal and flute edges. Cut slits in top.

Bake at 400° for 20 minutes. Reduce heat to 375°; bake 30-35 minutes longer or until golden brown. Let stand 15 minutes before cutting. **Yield: 2 pies (6-8 servings each).**

Mushroom Salisbury Steak

Taco Chili Pie

Classic Cabbage Rolls

Sloppy Joe Under a Bun

Classic Cabbage Rolls

I've always enjoyed cabbage rolls but didn't make them since most methods were too complicated. This recipe is fairly simple and results in the best cabbage rolls. —*Beverly Zehner, McMinnville, Oregon*

- **1 medium head cabbage, cored**
- **1-1/2 cups chopped onion, *divided***
- **1 tablespoon butter**
- **2 cans (14-1/2 ounces *each*) Italian stewed tomatoes**
- **4 garlic cloves, minced**
- **2 tablespoons brown sugar**
- **1-1/2 teaspoons salt, *divided***
- **1 cup cooked rice**
- **1/4 cup ketchup**
- **2 tablespoons Worcestershire sauce**
- **1/4 teaspoon pepper**
- **1 pound lean ground beef**
- **1/4 pound bulk Italian sausage**
- **1/2 cup V8 juice, optional**

In a Dutch oven, cook cabbage in boiling water for 10 minutes or until outer leaves are tender; drain. Rinse in cold water; drain. Remove eight large outer leaves (refrigerate remaining cabbage for another use); set aside.

In a saucepan, saute 1 cup onion in butter until tender. Add the tomatoes, garlic, brown sugar and 1/2 teaspoon salt. Bring to a boil. Reduce heat; simmer, uncovered, for 15 minutes, stirring occasionally.

Meanwhile, in a bowl, combine the rice, ketchup, Worcestershire sauce, pepper and remaining onion and salt. Crumble beef and sausage over mixture; mix well. Cut out the thick vein from the bottom of each reserved leaf, making a V-shaped cut. Place about 1/2 cup meat mixture on each cabbage leaf; overlap cut ends of leaf. Fold in sides, beginning from the cut end. Roll up completely to enclose filling. Place seam side down in a skillet. Top with the sauce.

Cheeseburger Meat Loaf

Cover and cook over medium-low heat for 1 hour. Add V8 juice if desired. Reduce heat to low; cook 20 minutes longer or until rolls are heated through and meat is no longer pink. **Yield: 4 servings.**

Sloppy Joe Under a Bun 1st prize

A can of sloppy joe sauce is a must-have in our pantry, because our kids love the meaty mixture. But sometimes I don't have buns on hand. With this casserole, we can still enjoy the flavor they love in a flash. The bun-like top crust is made with biscuit mix.

—Trish Bloom, Ray, Michigan

1-1/2 pounds ground beef
1 can (15-1/2 ounces) sloppy joe sauce
2 cups (8 ounces) shredded cheddar cheese
2 cups biscuit/baking mix
2 eggs, beaten
1 cup milk
1 tablespoon sesame seeds

In a skillet, cook beef over medium heat until no longer pink; drain. Stir in sloppy joe sauce; mix well. Transfer to a lightly greased 13-in. x 9-in. x 2-in. baking dish; sprinkle with cheese.

In a bowl, combine the biscuit mix, eggs and milk just until blended. Pour over cheese; sprinkle with sesame seeds. Bake, uncovered, at 400° for 25 minutes or until golden brown. **Yield: 8 servings.**

Cheeseburger Meat Loaf

One day when I wanted to make cheeseburgers but it was too chilly to grill outside, I created this meat loaf to satisfy my cheeseburger craving. I've served it numerous times since then, and it never fails to get rave reviews. Even your most finicky eater will enjoy this oven-baked main dish.

—Paula Sullivan, Barker, New York

1/2 cup ketchup, *divided*
1 egg
1/4 cup dry bread crumbs
1 teaspoon onion powder
1 pound lean ground beef
2 teaspoons prepared mustard
2 teaspoons dill pickle relish
6 slices process American cheese

In a bowl, combine 1/4 cup ketchup, egg, bread crumbs and onion powder. Crumble beef over mixture and mix well. On a large piece of waxed paper, pat beef mixture into a 10-in. x 6-in. rectangle. Spread remaining ketchup over meat to within 1/2 in. of long sides and 1-1/2 in. of short sides. Top with mustard and relish.

Place four cheese slices on top; set remaining cheese aside. Roll up loaf jelly-roll style, starting with a short side and pulling away waxed paper while rolling. Seal seams and ends well. Place loaf seam side down in a greased 11-in. x 7-in. x 2-in. baking pan.

Bake at 350° for 45 minutes or until meat is no longer pink and a meat thermometer reads 160°. Cut the reserved cheese slices in half diagonally; place on top of loaf. Bake 5 minutes longer or until cheese is melted. Let stand for 10 minutes before slicing. **Yield: 6 servings.**

Spaghetti 'n' Meatballs

Spaghetti 'n' Meatballs

Always a favorite with my family and friends, these meatballs take little time to prepare, because they don't need to be browned before being added to the sauce.
—Ann Rath, Mankato, Minnesota

- 2 eggs, lightly beaten
- 1/2 cup dry bread crumbs
- 1 garlic clove, minced
- 2 teaspoons dried parsley flakes
- 1 pound lean ground beef
- 1 cup grated Parmesan cheese
- 1 cup chopped onion
- 1 tablespoon vegetable oil
- 1 can (28 ounces) stewed tomatoes
- 2 cans (6 ounces *each*) tomato paste
- 1 tablespoon sugar
- 1 teaspoon salt
- 1/2 teaspoon dried basil
- 1/4 teaspoon dried oregano
- 1/8 teaspoon dried marjoram
- 1/8 teaspoon paprika
- Dash pepper
- Hot cooked spaghetti

In a large bowl, combine the eggs, bread crumbs, garlic and parsley. Crumble beef over mixture, then sprinkle with cheese and mix well. Shape into 1-1/2-in. balls and set aside.

In a Dutch oven, saute the onion in oil until tender. Stir in the tomatoes, tomato paste, sugar and seasonings.

Bring to a boil. Carefully add reserved meatballs to sauce. Reduce heat; cover and simmer for 30 minutes or until meat is no longer pink. Serve meatballs and sauce over spaghetti. **Yield: 4 servings.**

Pizza Tot Casserole

You'll need just seven basic ingredients to make this effortless upside-down pizza casserole. Since I cook for two, I often divide it into two smaller casserole dishes—one for dinner and one to freeze.
—Chris Stukel, Des Plaines, Illinois

- 1 pound ground beef
- 1 medium green pepper, chopped
- 1 medium onion, chopped
- 1 can (11-1/8 ounces) condensed Italian tomato soup, undiluted
- 1 jar (4-1/2 ounces) sliced mushrooms, drained
- 2 cups (8 ounces) shredded part-skim mozzarella cheese
- 1 package (32 ounces) frozen Tater Tots

In a skillet, cook the beef, pepper and onion over medium heat until meat is no longer pink and vegetables are tender; drain. Add soup and mushrooms.

Transfer to a greased 13-in. x 9-in. x 2-in. baking dish. Top with cheese and potatoes. Bake, uncovered, at 400° for 30-35 minutes or until golden brown. **Yield: 6-8 servings.**

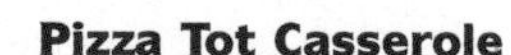

Pizza Tot Casserole

PORK

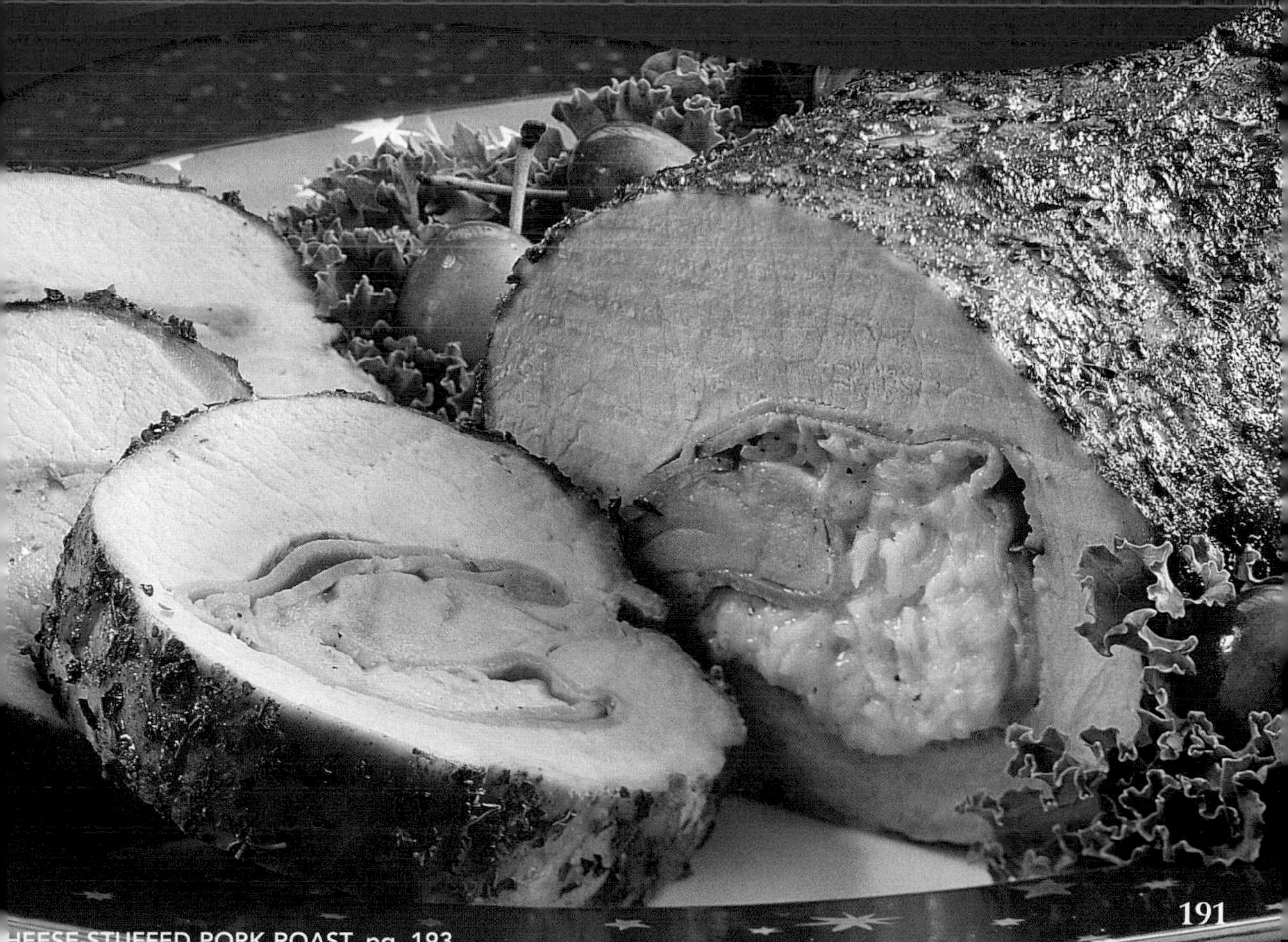

HEESE-STUFFED PORK ROAST, pg. 193

Pork

Cheese-Stuffed Pork Roast

Cheese-Stuffed Pork Roast

I first served this roast for a Christmas dinner. My family raved about it, so I make it often.
—Kara Holtkamp, West Point, Iowa

- 1 tablespoon all-purpose flour
- 1/4 teaspoon lemon-pepper seasoning
- 2 tablespoons butter, melted
- 2 tablespoons heavy whipping cream
- 1 cup (4 ounces) shredded Swiss cheese
- 1 boneless pork loin roast (2 to 2-1/2 pounds), trimmed
- 6 ounces thinly sliced deli ham
- 1 teaspoon paprika
- 1/2 teaspoon *each* dried marjoram, oregano and basil

CREAM SAUCE:

- 1 small onion, finely chopped
- 1 tablespoon butter
- 1 tablespoon cornstarch
- 1 cup heavy whipping cream
- 1/4 cup chicken broth
- 1 teaspoon sour cream

Salt to taste

In a bowl, combine the flour, lemon-pepper, butter and cream until smooth. Stir in the cheese; set aside. Cut a lengthwise slit down the center of the roast to within 1/2 in. of the bottom. Open roast so it lies flat; cover with plastic wrap. Flatten to 3/4-in. thickness.

Remove plastic; place ham slices over roast. Spread cheese mixture lengthwise down the center of one side of roast to within 1-1/2 in. of ends. Roll up jelly-roll style, starting with the long side with the cheese filling. Tie several times with kitchen string; secure ends with toothpicks.

Combine the paprika, marjoram, oregano and basil; rub over roast. Place on a rack in a shallow roasting pan. Bake, uncovered, at 325° for 1-1/4 to 1-1/2 hours or until a meat thermometer reads 160°. Let stand for 10 minutes.

Meanwhile, in a skillet, saute onion in butter until tender. Stir in the cornstarch until blended. Whisk in cream and broth. Bring to a boil; cook and stir for 2 minutes or until thickened. Remove from the heat; stir in sour cream and salt. Slice roast; serve with cream sauce. **Yield: 8-10 servings.**

Roast Pork with Raspberry Sauce

Roast Pork with Raspberry Sauce

Want to treat your guests to a spectacular meal? Plan this pork as the centerpiece of your menu. The fruity sauce enhances the meat's flavor and looks so pretty!
—Carolyn Zimmerman, Fairbury, Illinois

- 1 teaspoon salt
- 1 teaspoon rubbed sage
- 1 teaspoon pepper
- 1 boneless rolled pork loin roast (3-1/2 to 4 pounds)

SAUCE:

- 1 package (10 ounces) frozen sweetened raspberries, thawed
- 1-1/2 cups sugar
- 1/4 cup white vinegar
- 1/4 teaspoon *each* ground ginger, nutmeg and cloves
- 1/4 cup cornstarch
- 1 tablespoon butter, melted
- 1 tablespoon lemon juice
- 3 to 4 drops red food coloring, optional

Combine the salt, sage and pepper; rub over entire roast. Place roast fat side up on a rack in a shallow roasting pan. Bake, uncovered, at 350° for 70-80 minutes or until a meat thermometer reads 160°.

For the sauce, drain raspberries, reserving liquid. Set berries aside. Add enough water to juice to measure 3/4 cup. In a saucepan, combine the sugar, vinegar, spices and 1/2 cup raspberry juice. Bring to a boil. Reduce heat; simmer, uncovered, for 10 minutes.

Combine cornstarch and remaining raspberry juice until smooth; stir into the saucepan. Bring to a boil; cook and stir for 2 minutes or until thickened. Remove from the heat. Stir in the butter, lemon juice, food coloring if desired and reserved raspberries. Let roast stand for 10-15 minutes before slicing. Serve with the raspberry sauce. **Yield: 10 servings.**

Pork Loin with Spinach Stuffing

I can't say whether leftovers from this eye-catching roast are good, because we never have any! I've been making this flavorful main dish for years and have never been disappointed.

—Lois Kinneberg, Phoenix, Arizona

- 1 package (10 ounces) frozen chopped spinach, thawed and squeezed dry
- 1/2 cup chopped onion
- 1 garlic clove, minced
- 3 tablespoons butter
- 1 cup soft bread crumbs
- 1/2 teaspoon salt
- 1 boneless rolled pork loin roast (3-1/2 pounds)
- 1/4 cup orange juice
- 2 tablespoons soy sauce
- 1 tablespoon ketchup
- 1 cup (8 ounces) sour cream
- 2 tablespoons prepared horseradish
- 1 teaspoon Dijon mustard
- 1/2 teaspoon seasoned salt
- 1/4 teaspoon dill weed

Set aside 1/2 cup spinach for sauce. In a skillet, saute the onion, garlic and remaining spinach in butter until tender. Remove from the heat; stir in bread crumbs and salt.

Separate roast into two pieces; spoon spinach mixture onto one piece of meat. Top with second piece; tie with kitchen string. Place in a shallow roasting pan.

Combine the orange juice, soy sauce and ketchup; pour half over roast. Bake, uncovered, at 350° for 45 minutes. Baste with remaining orange juice mixture. Cover and bake 30-45 minutes longer or until a meat thermometer reads 160°. Let stand for 10 minutes before slicing.

In a saucepan, combine the sour cream, horseradish, mustard, seasoned salt, dill and reserved spinach. Cook over medium heat just until heated through (do not boil). Serve warm with pork. **Yield: 10-12 servings.**

Pork Loin with Spinach Stuffing

Apricot-Filled Pork Tenderloin

Pear-Stuffed Tenderloin

Apricot-Filled Pork Tenderloin

This flavorful main course is a great company offering. The tenderloin tastes wonderful and looks so pretty when it's sliced to reveal a golden apricot center. In the 15 years I've been using this recipe, it has never failed me. —*Jo Ann Hettel, Bushnell, Florida*

- 2 pork tenderloins (1 pound *each*)
- 1 package (6 ounces) dried apricots

MARINADE:

- 1/3 cup sweet-and-sour salad dressing
- 1/4 cup packed brown sugar
- 3 tablespoons teriyaki sauce
- 2 tablespoons ketchup
- 1 teaspoon Dijon mustard
- 1 onion slice, separated into rings
- 1 garlic clove, minced
- 2 teaspoons minced fresh gingerroot
- 1/4 teaspoon pepper
- 1/8 teaspoon pumpkin pie spice

Make a lengthwise cut three-quarters of the way through each tenderloin; open and flatten to 1/4-in. thickness. Set aside three apricots for marinade. Place remaining apricots over tenderloins to within 1/2 in. of ends. Roll up from a long side; tuck in ends. Secure with toothpicks or kitchen string.

In a blender, combine the remaining ingredients and reserved apricots. Cover and process until smooth; set aside 1/3 cup. Pour remaining marinade into a large resealable bag; add tenderloins. Seal bag and turn to coat; chill for at least 2 hours, turning often.

Drain and discard marinade from meat. Place pork in a greased 13-in. x 9-in. x 2-in. baking dish. Drizzle with reserved marinade. Bake, uncovered, at 400° for 30-35 minutes or until a meat thermometer reads 160°. Let stand for 10 minutes before slicing. **Yield: 6 servings.**

Glazed Country Ribs

Pear-Stuffed Tenderloin

You'll be proud to serve your family this succulent entree. There's very little fuss to making this main dish, and the meat always turns out extremely tender.
—Aloma Hawkins, Bixby, Missouri

- 1 cup chopped peeled ripe pears
- 1/4 cup hazelnuts, toasted
- 1/4 cup soft bread crumbs
- 1/4 cup finely shredded carrot
- 2 tablespoons chopped onion
- 1/8 teaspoon ground ginger
- 1/4 teaspoon salt
- 1/4 teaspoon pepper
- 1 pork tenderloin (3/4 to 1 pound)

Vegetable oil

- 2 tablespoons orange marmalade

In a bowl, combine the first eight ingredients; set aside. Make a lengthwise cut three-quarters of the way through the tenderloin; open and flatten to 1/4-in. thickness. Spread pear mixture over tenderloin. Roll up from a long side; tuck in ends. Secure with toothpicks or kitchen string.

Place tenderloin on a rack in a shallow roasting pan. Brush lightly with oil. Bake, uncovered, at 425° for 20-25 minutes or until a meat thermometer inserted into pork reads 155°. Brush with marmalade. Bake 5-10 minutes longer or until thermometer reads 160°. Let stand for 5 minutes. Discard toothpicks and slice. **Yield: 2-3 servings.**

Glazed Country Ribs

When I take these mouth-watering ribs to our frequent potlucks at work, they're a hit. I like them basted only with the mildly sweet glaze, but you can serve your favorite barbecue sauce on the side, too. They taste as good reheated as they do right off the grill. *—Tamrah Bird, Gaines, Michigan*

- 3 pounds boneless country-style pork ribs
- 3/4 cup pineapple juice
- 1/2 cup vegetable oil
- 1/2 cup white wine
- 1/4 cup packed brown sugar
- 1 tablespoon Worcestershire sauce
- 6 garlic cloves, minced
- 1 teaspoon salt
- 1 teaspoon pepper
- 1 teaspoon dried rosemary, crushed

Place ribs in a large shallow glass container. Pierce several times with a fork. In a bowl, combine the remaining ingredients; set aside 1/2 cup for basting. Pour the remaining marinade over ribs. Cover and refrigerate for 8 hours or overnight, turning once. Cover and refrigerate reserved marinade.

Drain and discard marinade from meat. Grill ribs, covered, over indirect medium heat for 10 minutes on each side. Baste with some of the reserved marinade. Grill 20-25 minutes longer or until juices run clear and meat is tender, turning and basting occasionally. **Yield: 6 servings.**

Calgary Stampede Ribs

Calgary Stampede Ribs

"More, please!" is what I hear when I serve these zippy, finger-licking ribs to family or guests. The recipe has its roots in the Calgary Stampede, an annual Western and agricultural fair and exhibition in our province.

—Marian Misik, Sherwood Park, Alberta

- 4 pounds pork back ribs, cut into serving-size pieces
- 3 garlic cloves, minced
- 1 tablespoon sugar
- 1 tablespoon paprika
- 2 teaspoons *each* salt, pepper, chili powder and ground cumin

BARBECUE SAUCE:

- 1 small onion, finely chopped
- 2 tablespoons butter
- 1 cup ketchup
- 1/4 cup packed brown sugar
- 3 tablespoons lemon juice
- 3 tablespoons Worcestershire sauce
- 2 tablespoons cider vinegar
- 1-1/2 teaspoons ground mustard
- 1 teaspoon celery seed
- 1/8 teaspoon cayenne pepper

Rub ribs with garlic; place in a shallow roasting pan. Cover and bake at 325° for 2 hours. Cool slightly. Combine the seasonings and rub over ribs. Cover and refrigerate for 8 hours or overnight.

In a saucepan, saute onion in butter until tender. Stir in remaining sauce ingredients. Bring to a boil. Reduce heat; cook and stir until thickened, about 10 minutes. Remove from the heat; set aside 3/4 cup. Brush ribs with some of the remaining sauce.

Grill, covered, over medium heat for 12 minutes, turning and basting with sauce. Serve with reserved sauce. **Yield: 4 servings.**

Sweet 'n' Sour Ribs 

If you're looking for a change from typical barbecued ribs, you'll enjoy this recipe my mom always prepared on birthdays and special occasions. The tender ribs have a slight sweet-and-sour taste that my family loves. I usually serve them with garlic mashed potatoes and a salad or coleslaw.

—Dorothy Voelz, Champaign, Illinois

- 3 to 4 pounds boneless country-style pork ribs
- 1 can (20 ounces) pineapple tidbits, undrained
- 2 cans (8 ounces *each*) tomato sauce
- 1/2 cup thinly sliced onion
- 1/2 cup thinly sliced green pepper
- 1/2 cup packed brown sugar
- 1/4 cup cider vinegar
- 1/4 cup tomato paste
- 2 tablespoons Worcestershire sauce
- 1 garlic clove, minced

Salt and pepper to taste

Place ribs in an ungreased 5-qt. slow cooker. In a bowl, combine the remaining ingredients; pour over the ribs. Cover and cook on low for 8-10 hours or until meat is tender. Thicken the sauce if desired. **Yield: 8 servings.**

Chops with Mushroom Gravy

These comforting pork chops come out great every time. We love the rich gravy over the chops and mashed potatoes.

—Loraine Van Broeck, Geneva, Illinois

- 1/2 cup all-purpose flour
- 1 to 2 teaspoons paprika
- 1-1/2 teaspoons salt
- 1/4 teaspoon pepper
- 6 to 8 boneless pork loin chops (1 inch thick)
- 1/4 cup butter
- 1 medium onion, chopped
- 1/2 cup chopped green pepper
- 1 can (4 ounces) mushroom stems and pieces, drained
- 2 cups milk
- 2 tablespoons lemon juice
- Hot mashed potatoes

In a large resealable plastic bag, combine the first four ingredients; reserve 3 tablespoons flour mixture. Add pork chops, one at a time; shake to coat.

In a large skillet, saute chops in butter until golden brown; transfer to a greased 13-in. x 9-in. x 2-in. baking dish. In the same skillet, saute the onion, green pepper and mushrooms until tender. Stir in reserved flour mixture until blended; gradually add milk. Bring to a boil; cook and stir for 2 minutes or until thickened. Remove from heat; stir in lemon juice. Pour over chops.

Cover and bake at 350° for 50-60 minutes or until the meat is no longer pink. Serve with potatoes. **Yield: 6-8 servings.**

Sweet 'n' Sour Ribs

Chops with Mushroom Gravy

Corn-Stuffed Butterfly Chops

Pork Chops with Apples and Stuffing

Corn-Stuffed Butterfly Chops

Corn stuffing is a delicious twist in this old family recipe from an aunt. I fix these chops for special meals with scalloped potatoes, coleslaw and pickled beets.
—Marie Dragwa, Simpson, Pennsylvania

- 1-1/2 cups frozen corn, thawed
- 1-1/2 cups soft bread crumbs
- 1 tablespoon minced fresh parsley
- 1 tablespoon finely chopped onion
- 3/4 teaspoon rubbed sage
- 3/4 teaspoon salt
- 1/4 teaspoon pepper
- 1 egg
- 3 tablespoons milk
- 4 bone-in pork loin chops (1-1/2 inches thick)
- 2 tablespoons vegetable oil
- 1/4 cup water

In a bowl, combine the first seven ingredients. In another bowl, lightly beat the egg and milk; stir into the corn mixture. Cut a pocket in each chop almost to the bone. Stuff about 1/4 cupful corn mixture into each chop; secure with toothpicks.

In a large skillet, cook chops in oil until browned on both sides. Transfer to a greased 13-in. x 9-in. x 2-in. baking dish; add water. Cover and bake at 350° for 1 hour or until a thermometer inserted into stuffing reads 160°. Discard toothpicks. **Yield: 4 servings.**

Pork Chops over Rice

Pork Chops with Apples And Stuffing 1st prize

The heartwarming taste of cinnamon and apples is the perfect accompaniment to these tender pork chops.
—Joan Hamilton, Worcester, Massachusetts

- 6 boneless pork loin chops (1 inch thick)
- 1 tablespoon vegetable oil
- 1 package (6 ounces) crushed stuffing mix
- 1 can (21 ounces) apple pie filling with cinnamon

In a large skillet, brown pork chops in oil over medium-high heat. Meanwhile, prepare stuffing according to package directions. Spread pie filling into a greased 13-in. x 9-in. x 2-in. baking dish. Place the pork chops on top; spoon stuffing over chops.

Cover and bake at 350° for 35 minutes. Uncover; bake 10 minutes longer or until a meat thermometer reads 160°. **Yield: 6 servings.**

Pork Chops over Rice

If you asked my husband to name his favorite foods, he'd likely mention these chops. I've also served this appealing skillet supper to company.
—Nancy Christenberry, Ortonville, Michigan

- 8 boneless pork chops (3/4 inch thick)
- 1 tablespoon vegetable oil
- 1 cup uncooked long grain rice
- 1 can (14-1/2 ounces) chicken broth
- 1/2 cup water
- 1 small onion, chopped
- 1 package (10 ounces) frozen peas
- 1/2 teaspoon salt
- 1/2 teaspoon dried thyme

In a large skillet over medium heat, brown pork chops in oil; remove. Drain. Add the remaining ingredients to skillet. Place pork chops over the rice mixture. Bring to a boil. Reduce heat; cover and simmer for 20-25 minutes or until rice is tender. **Yield: 8 servings.**

Maple-Glazed Pork Chops

Everyone cleaned their plates when my mother made these succulent sweet pork chops when I was growing up. Now, I get the same results when I serve them to my family alongside applesauce and au gratin potatoes. —*Cheryl Miller, Fort Collins, Colorado*

- 1/2 cup all-purpose flour
- Salt and pepper to taste
- 4 bone-in pork loin chops (1 inch thick)
- 2 tablespoons butter
- 1/4 cup cider vinegar
- 1/3 cup maple syrup
- 1 tablespoon cornstarch
- 3 tablespoons water
- 2/3 cup packed brown sugar

In a large resealable plastic bag, combine flour, salt and pepper. Add pork chops and shake to coat. In a skillet, brown chops on both sides in butter. Place in an ungreased 13-in. x 9-in. x 2-in. baking pan. Bake, uncovered, at 450° for 20-25 minutes or until juices run clear.

Meanwhile, in a skillet, bring the vinegar to a boil. Reduce heat; add maple syrup. Cover and cook for 10 minutes. Combine cornstarch and water until smooth; add to the maple mixture. Bring to a boil; cook and stir for 2 minutes or until thickened.

Place chops on a broiler pan; sprinkle with brown sugar. Broil 4 in. from the heat for 2-3 minutes or until sugar is melted. Drizzle with maple glaze. **Yield: 4 servings.**

Orange-Ginger Pork Chops

Basting chops with this Asian-inspired sauce makes them extremely tender and savory. My family requests this dish because they like its terrific taste. —*Lynette Randleman, Buffalo, Wyoming*

Maple-Glazed Pork Chops

- 4 teaspoons minced fresh gingerroot
- 1 garlic clove, minced
- 1 tablespoon canola oil
- 1/2 cup sherry *or* chicken broth
- 1/4 cup honey
- 1/4 cup reduced-sodium soy sauce
- 1 tablespoon sesame seeds
- 1 tablespoon grated orange peel
- 3/4 teaspoon hot pepper sauce
- 4 bone-in pork loin chop (6 ounces *each*)
- 1 teaspoon cornstarch
- 2 tablespoons water

In a saucepan, cook ginger and garlic in oil for 1 minute; remove from the heat. Stir in the sherry or broth, honey, soy sauce, sesame seeds, orange peel and hot pepper sauce; mix well. Pour 1/2 cup into a small bowl; set aside. Pour the remaining marinade into a large resealable plastic bag; add pork chops. Seal bag and turn to coat; refrigerate for at least 1 hour.

Meanwhile, in a saucepan, combine cornstarch and water until smooth; add reserved marinade. Bring to a boil; cook and stir for 1 minute or until thickened.

Coat grill rack with nonstick cooking spray before starting the grill. Drain and discard marinade from the pork. Grill chops, covered, over medium heat for 4 minutes. Turn; baste with sauce. Grill 15-20 minutes longer or until juices run clear, basting occasionally. Serve with any remaining sauce. **Yield: 4 servings.**

Pork Veggie Stir-Fry

A colorful combination of vegetables, juicy pork strips, flavorful seasonings and crunchy peanuts makes this main dish appealing even to kids.
—Laurel Reisinger, Saskatoon, Saskatchewan

- 3 cups sliced cauliflower
- 3 tablespoons vegetable oil, *divided*
- 2 medium carrots, julienned
- 1 can (15 ounces) whole baby corn, rinsed and drained
- 1/2 cup frozen peas, thawed
- 1 pound boneless pork, cut into thin strips
- 2 green onions, thinly sliced
- 2 garlic cloves, minced
- 1 tablespoon minced fresh gingerroot
- 1/2 to 1 teaspoon chili powder
- 1 cup water
- 1/4 cup soy sauce
- 4 teaspoons honey
- 2 teaspoons chicken bouillon granules
- 4 teaspoons cornstarch
- 2 tablespoons cold water
- 1/4 cup salted peanuts
- Hot cooked rice

In a skillet or wok, stir-fry cauliflower in 2 tablespoons oil for 3 minutes. Add carrots; stir-fry for 2 minutes. Add corn and peas; stir-fry until vegetables are crisp-tender. Remove; keep warm. Stir-fry pork in remaining oil for 2 minutes. Add onions, garlic, ginger and chili powder; stir-fry until pork is no longer pink. Remove; keep warm.

Combine the water, soy sauce, honey and bouillon in same pan. Combine cornstarch and cold water until smooth; gradually add to pan. Bring to a boil; cook and stir for 2 minutes or until thickened. Return vegetables and pork mixture to pan; heat through. Stir in peanuts. Serve over rice. **Yield: 6 servings.**

Orange-Ginger Pork Chops

Pork Veggie Stir-Fry

Peanutty Pork Kabobs

Pork and Apple Supper

Peanutty Pork Kabobs

Cubes of pork tenderloin and green pepper chunks get a spicy treatment from a combination of peanut butter, brown sugar, ginger and red pepper flakes.
—Ellen Koch, St. Martinville, Louisiana

- 1/2 cup soy sauce
- 1/4 cup lime juice
- 1/4 cup peanut butter
- 2 tablespoons brown sugar
- 2 garlic cloves, minced
- 1 teaspoon crushed red pepper flakes
- 1/4 teaspoon ground ginger
- 1 pork tenderloin (about 1 pound), cut into 1-inch cubes
- 2 medium green peppers, cut into 1-inch pieces

In a large bowl, combine the first seven ingredients. Set aside 1/2 cup for basting; cover and refrigerate. Pour remaining marinade into a large resealable plastic bag; add pork. Seal bag and turn to coat; refrigerate for 2-3 hours, turning occasionally.

Drain and discard the marinade from pork. On metal or soaked bamboo skewers, alternate pork and green peppers. Grill, uncovered, over medium heat for 6 minutes, turning once. Baste with reserved marinade. Grill 8-10 minutes longer or until meat juices run clear, turning and basting frequently. **Yield: 4 servings.**

Pork and Apple Supper

Our part of upstate New York was settled by the Dutch, and this recipe originated there. This is also apple country.
—Sharon Root, Wynantskill, New York

- 1-1/2 pounds boneless pork, cubed
- 1 tablespoon vegetable oil
- 4 cups water
- 1 tablespoon chicken bouillon granules

Green Chili Pork Stew

1 teaspoon dried thyme
1/4 teaspoon pepper
1 bay leaf
10 to 12 small red potatoes (about 2 pounds), quartered
4 medium tart apples, peeled and cut into wedges
2 tablespoons cornstarch
2 tablespoons cold water

In a Dutch oven, brown pork in oil. Add the water, bouillon, thyme, pepper and bay leaf; bring to a boil. Reduce heat; cover and simmer for 1-1/2 to 2 hours or until pork is almost tender.

Add potatoes; cover and cook for 15 minutes. Add apples; cover and cook for 10-12 minutes or until crisp-tender. Discard bay leaf.

Combine cornstarch and cold water until smooth; stir into pork mixture. Bring to a boil; cook and stir for 2 minutes or until thickened. **Yield: 6-8 servings.**

Green Chili Pork Stew

Green chilies are a big favorite here in the Southwest—my family likes anything with them in it, especially this stew.

—Pat Henderson, Deer Park, Texas

2 pounds lean boneless pork, cut into 1-1/2-inch cubes
1 tablespoon vegetable oil
4 cups chicken broth, *divided*
3 cans (11 ounces *each*) whole kernel corn, drained
2 celery ribs, diced
2 medium potatoes, peeled and diced
2 medium tomatoes, diced
3 cans (4 ounces *each*) chopped green chilies
2 teaspoons ground cumin
1 teaspoon dried oregano
1 teaspoon salt, optional
3 tablespoons all-purpose flour
Cornbread *or* warmed flour tortillas, optional

In a 5-qt. Dutch oven, brown pork in oil over medium-high heat. Add 3-1/2 cups broth, corn, celery, potatoes, tomatoes, chilies, cumin, oregano and salt if desired; bring to a boil. Reduce heat; cover and simmer for 1 hour or until meat and vegetables are tender.

Combine flour and remaining broth until smooth; stir into stew. Bring to a boil; cook and stir for 2 minutes or until thickened. Serve with corn bread or tortillas if desired. **Yield: 8 servings.**

Cider-Baked Country Ham

This is the best ham I've ever made. I serve it often to family and friends, and each time I get requests for the recipe. —*Marion Lowery, Medford, Oregon*

- 1/2 bone-in fully cooked ham (5 to 7 pounds)
- 2 quarts apple cider *or* apple juice
- 1-1/2 teaspoons whole peppercorns
- 1 bay leaf
- Whole cloves
- 1 cup applesauce
- 1 tablespoon prepared horseradish
- 2 teaspoons ground mustard

Place ham in a Dutch oven or large kettle. Add the cider, peppercorns and bay leaf. Add enough water just to cover; bring to a boil. Reduce heat; cover and simmer for 1 hour.

Drain, reserving 3 cups cooking liquid; discard peppercorns and bay leaf. Remove skin from ham if desired; score the surface with shallow cuts, making diamond shapes. Insert whole cloves in the center of each diamond. Combine the applesauce, horseradish and mustard; rub over ham.

Place ham on a rack in shallow roasting pan; pour reserved liquid into pan. Bake, uncovered, at 350° for 1 hour or until a meat thermometer reads 140°. Let stand, covered with foil, for 10-15 minutes before slicing. **Yield: 16-20 servings.**

Cider-Baked Country Ham

Horseradish Honey Ham

When my husband and I first tasted this delicious ham, we were surprised to learn that the sauce included horseradish. That secret ingredient definitely is the key to its tangy taste. I serve it for Easter and Christmas. —*Beverly Loomis, Ithaca, Michigan*

- 1 boneless fully cooked ham (5 to 7 pounds)
- 1/4 cup honey, warmed
- 1/8 teaspoon ground cloves
- 1 cup packed brown sugar
- 1/2 cup prepared horseradish
- 1/4 cup lemon juice

Cut ham into 1/4-in. slices and tie with kitchen string. Place ham on a rack in a shallow roasting pan. Combine honey and cloves; drizzle over ham. Bake, uncovered, at 325° for 1-1/2 to 2 hours or until a meat thermometer reads 140° and ham is heated through, basting often with drippings.

Meanwhile, combine the brown sugar, horseradish and lemon juice. Increase oven temperature to 400°. Baste ham with brown sugar sauce, allowing sauce to drip down between the slices. Bake, uncovered, for 15-20 minutes. **Yield: 16 servings.**

Sliced Ham with Roasted Vegetables 1st prize

To prepare this colorful, zesty oven meal, I shop in my backyard for the fresh garden vegetables and oranges (we have our own tree!) that spark the ham's hearty flavor. It's my family's favorite main dish. —*Margaret Pache, Mesa, Arizona*

- 6 medium potatoes, peeled and cubed
- 5 medium carrots, julienned
- 1 medium turnip, peeled and cubed

- 1 large onion, cut into thin wedges
- 6 slices (4 to 6 ounces *each*) fully cooked ham, halved
- 1/4 cup orange juice concentrate
- 2 tablespoons brown sugar
- 1 teaspoon prepared horseradish
- 1 teaspoon grated orange peel

Line two 15-in. x 10-in. x 1-in. baking pans with foil and coat with nonstick cooking spray. Add the potatoes, carrots, turnip and onion; generously coat with nonstick cooking spray. Bake, uncovered, at 425° for 25-30 minutes or until tender.

Arrange ham slices over the vegetables. In a bowl, combine remaining ingredients. Spoon over ham and vegetables. Cover and bake 10 minutes longer or until the ham is heated through. **Yield: 6 servings.**

Sliced Ham with Roasted Vegetables

Horseradish Honey Ham

Curried Ham and Fruit

Broccoli Ham Stroganoff

Curried Ham and Fruit

This dish tastes as good as it looks! The different fruits add such pretty color and complement the ham nicely. I like to serve this over rice.

—Brenda DenHollander
Chilliwack, British Columbia

- 4 slices fully cooked ham (1/2 inch thick and 4 to 6 ounces *each*)
- 1 can (5-1/2 ounces) peach-orange nectar
- 1 can (20 ounces) pineapple tidbits, drained
- 1 can (15-1/4 ounces) sliced peaches, drained and halved
- 1 can (15-1/4 ounces) sliced pears, drained and halved
- 10 maraschino cherries
- 1/4 cup butter, melted
- 3/4 cup packed brown sugar
- 4 teaspoons curry powder

Place ham in a single layer in an ungreased 13-in. x 9-in. x 2-in. baking dish. Top with nectar. Bake, uncovered, at 350° for 20 minutes, basting once.

Combine fruits; spoon over ham. In a small bowl, combine the butter, brown sugar and curry powder. Drop by spoonfuls over fruit. Bake 15-20 minutes longer, basting once. **Yield: 4 servings.**

Broccoli Ham Stroganoff

Microwave cooking makes this tasty main dish in just minutes and also quickly goes together! It's a great way to use up extra ham. It works equally well with leftover chicken or turkey. The smooth white sauce gets its added creaminess from sour cream.

—Amanda Denton, Barre, Vermont

- 2 cups frozen chopped broccoli
- 1 tablespoon water
- 1 tablespoon butter

1/4 cup chopped onion
3 tablespoons all-purpose flour
1 can (10-1/2 ounces) chicken broth
2 cups cubed fully cooked ham
1 cup (8 ounces) sour cream
1 jar (4-1/2 ounces) sliced mushrooms, drained

Hot cooked noodles

Place broccoli and water in a 1-qt. microwave-safe bowl. Cover and microwave on high for 3-5 minutes or until the broccoli is tender, stirring once. Drain; set aside and keep warm.

In another microwave-safe bowl, heat butter, uncovered, on high for 20 seconds or until melted. Add onion; cover and microwave on high for 2 minutes or until tender. Stir in flour until blended; gradually stir in broth. Microwave, uncovered, on high for 4-6 minutes or until thickened and bubbly, stirring once.

Add the ham, sour cream, mushrooms and reserved broccoli; mix well. Cook, uncovered, on high for 3-5 minutes or until heated through, stirring once. Serve over noodles. **Yield: 4 servings.**

Editor's Note: This recipe was tested with an 850-watt microwave.

Pineapple Ham Loaf

My cousin served this tender ham loaf at a family get-together, and I eagerly asked for the recipe. Since then, I've often taken it to church functions and served it when friends come to dinner.

—Aleatha Smith, Billings, Montana

2 eggs
1/2 cup milk
1 teaspoon Worcestershire sauce
3/4 cup dry bread crumbs
1-1/2 teaspoons ground mustard, *divided*
1/4 teaspoon salt
1/4 teaspoon pepper

Pineapple Ham Loaf

1 pound fully cooked ham, ground (4 cups)
1 pound ground pork
1 can (20 ounces) sliced pineapple
1/2 cup packed brown sugar

In a bowl, combine the eggs, milk, Worcestershire sauce, bread crumbs, 1 teaspoon mustard, salt and pepper. Add ham and pork; mix well. Shape into eight oval patties; set aside.

Drain pineapple, reserving 1/2 cup juice. Place a pineapple slice between each ham patty. (Refrigerate remaining pineapple and juice for another use.) Carefully place in an ungreased 9-in. x 5-in. x 3-in. loaf pan. Pat patties around pineapple to form a loaf.

Combine the brown sugar, remaining mustard and reserved juice; pour a small amount over loaf. Bake, uncovered, at 350° for 1-1/4 hours or until lightly browned and a meat thermometer reads 160°, basting occasionally with remaining juice mixture. **Yield: 8 servings.**

Deluxe Ham Balls 1st prize

Whenever I serve these saucy baked ham balls to guests, they ask me for the recipe. It's one I've had for many years and is a great use for leftover ham. I love to entertain, and know I can count on these ham balls to be a hit. —*Joan Settle, Oceanside, California*

- 2 eggs
- 1/2 cup milk
- 3/4 cup dry bread crumbs
- 1/4 cup finely chopped onion
- 1 pound ground fully cooked ham
- 1/2 pound ground pork
- 1 can (8 ounces) crushed pineapple
- 1/2 cup packed brown sugar
- 1/3 cup white vinegar
- 1/3 cup ketchup
- 2 tablespoons soy sauce
- 1 teaspoon ground ginger

Hot cooked rice

In a bowl, combine the eggs, milk, bread crumbs and onion. Crumble ham and pork over mixture; mix well. Shape into 1-1/4-in. balls. Place in a greased 13-in. x 9-in. x 2-in. baking dish.

In a saucepan, combine the pineapple, brown sugar, vinegar, ketchup, soy sauce and ginger. Cook and stir until sugar is dissolved. Pour over ham balls.

Bake, uncovered, at 350° for 40-45 minutes or until a meat thermometer reads 160°. Serve over rice. **Yield: 6 servings.**

Ham a la King

My mom and I used to have a catering business, and this recipe was a popular choice from our menu. It looks elegant on the plate and always gets rave reviews. Being able to make the sauce a day ahead is a big plus. —*Jean Grubb, Austin, Texas*

Deluxe Ham Balls

- 1 package (10 ounces) frozen puff pastry shells
- 1/4 cup butter
- 1/4 cup all-purpose flour
- 1 teaspoon chicken bouillon granules
- 1/2 cup hot water
- 1-1/2 cups milk
- 3 slices process American cheese
- 1 teaspoon Worcestershire sauce
- 1 teaspoon prepared mustard
- 2 cups cubed fully cooked ham
- 1/2 cup frozen peas, thawed, optional
- 1 can (2-1/4 ounces) sliced ripe olives, drained
- 2 tablespoons diced pimientos
- 2 tablespoons minced fresh parsley

Bake the pastry shells according to package directions. Meanwhile, in a saucepan, melt butter; stir in flour until smooth. Dissolve bouillon in water. Gradually add milk and bouillon to the saucepan. Bring to a boil; cook and stir for 2 minutes or until thickened.

Reduce heat; add the cheese, Worcestershire and mustard; stir until the cheese is melted. Add the ham, peas if desired, olives, pimientos and parsley; heat through. Serve in pastry shells. **Yield: 6 servings.**

Farmer's Market Sausage Pie

Our son named this savory pie for the Saturday morning farmer's market that's held near our state capitol. Most of the fresh ingredients called for in the recipe can be found there and baked into this deliciously different entree.
—Teri Schuman, Oregon, Wisconsin

- 4 Italian sausage links, casings removed, halved and cut into 1/2-inch pieces
- 1 medium tomato, cut into chunks
- 1 small yellow tomato, cut into chunks
- 1 cup thinly sliced zucchini
- 1 cup thinly sliced yellow summer squash
- 1/2 cup julienned green pepper
- 1/2 cup julienned sweet red pepper
- 1 tablespoon Italian salad dressing mix
- 1/2 teaspoon garlic powder
- 1/4 to 1/2 teaspoon fennel seed, crushed
- Pastry for double-crust pie (9 inches)
- 1 cup (4 ounces) shredded cheddar cheese
- 1 cup (4 ounces) shredded part-skim mozzarella cheese

In a large skillet, cook sausage over medium heat until no longer pink; drain. Stir in the tomatoes, squash, peppers, salad dressing mix, garlic powder and fennel seed. Cook and stir for 10 minutes; drain. Cool for 10 minutes.

Line a 9-in. pie plate with bottom pastry; trim even with edge. Fill with the sausage mixture. Sprinkle with cheeses. Roll out remaining pastry to fit top of pie; place over filling. Trim, seal and flute edges. Cut slits in top.

Bake at 375° for 35-40 minutes or until filling is bubbly and crust is golden brown. Let stand for 10 minutes before cutting. **Yield: 8 servings.**

Ham a la King

Farmer's Market Sausage Pie

Spaghetti 'n' Meatballs

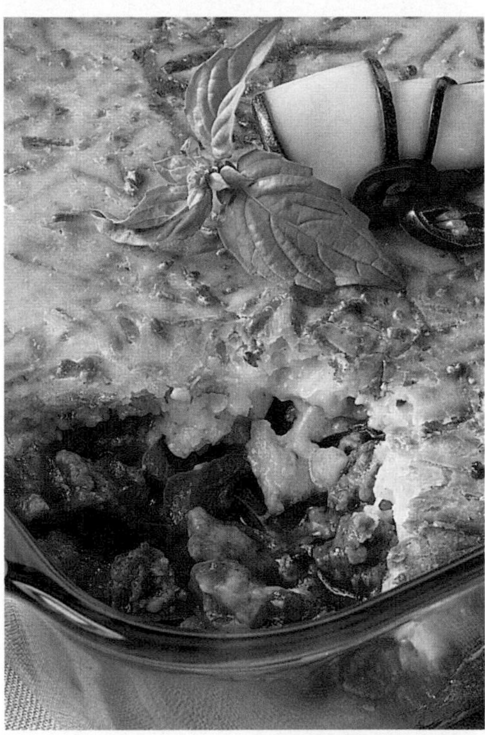
Upside-Down Pizza

Spaghetti 'n' Sausage Meatballs 1st prize

My mom's Italian friend taught her the secret to this saucy spaghetti dish. Our whole family is grateful!
—Marilou Krumm, Stanhope, Iowa

- 2 eggs
- 1 cup dry bread crumbs
- 1/2 cup grated Parmesan cheese
- 1/2 cup tomato juice, milk *or* beef broth
- 1/4 cup finely chopped green pepper
- 1/4 cup finely chopped onion
- 1 teaspoon Italian seasoning
- 1/2 teaspoon *each* salt, poultry seasoning and garlic powder
- 2 pounds bulk pork sausage

SAUCE:

- 4 cups water
- 2 cans (11-1/2 ounces *each*) tomato juice
- 3 cans (6 ounces *each*) tomato paste
- 1 jar (1/2 ounce) dried celery flakes
- 1 bay leaf
- 1 teaspoon Italian seasoning
- 1 teaspoon salt
- 1/2 teaspoon pepper
- 1/2 cup finely chopped green pepper
- 1/2 cup finely chopped onion
- 2 garlic cloves, minced

Hot cooked spaghetti

In a large bowl, combine the eggs, bread crumbs, Parmesan cheese, tomato juice, green pepper, onion and seasonings. Crumble sausage over mixture and mix well. Shape into 1-in. balls. In a skillet, brown meatballs over medium heat; drain.

In a large saucepan, combine the first eight sauce ingredients. Add the green pepper, onion and garlic. Bring to a boil. Reduce heat;

Au Gratin Sausage Skillet

simmer, uncovered, for 30-45 minutes or until thickened, stirring occasionally. Discard bay leaf.

Add meatballs to sauce; simmer for 1 hour or until meat is no longer pink. Serve over spaghetti. **Yield: 10 servings.**

Upside-Down Pizza

If you like pizza, I think you'll enjoy this recipe. I like making this better than regular pizza because I don't have to make a crust.
—Debra Derstine, Mapleton, Pennsylvania

- 1 pound bulk Italian sausage
- 1 medium onion, chopped
- 1/4 cup chopped green pepper
- 2 tablespoons plus 1 cup all-purpose flour, *divided*
- 1/2 teaspoon dried basil
- 1/2 teaspoon fennel seed, crushed
- 1 can (15 ounces) tomato sauce
- 2 cups (8 ounces) shredded part-skim mozzarella cheese
- 2 eggs
- 1 cup milk
- 1 tablespoon vegetable oil
- 1/2 teaspoon salt
- 2 tablespoons grated Parmesan cheese, optional

In a saucepan, cook the sausage, onion and green pepper over medium heat until meat is no longer pink; drain. Stir in 2 tablespoons flour, basil and fennel; mix well. Add tomato sauce. Bring to a boil; cook and stir for 2 minutes or until thickened.

Transfer to an ungreased 13-in. x 9-in. x 2-in. baking dish. Sprinkle with mozzarella cheese. Place the remaining flour in a mixing bowl. Beat in the eggs, milk, oil and salt until smooth; stir in Parmesan cheese if desired. Pour over casserole. Bake, uncovered, at 425° for 25-30 minutes or until browned. **Yield: 8 servings.**

Au Gratin Sausage Skillet

Using frozen vegetables and a package of au gratin potatoes, I can get this satisfying stovetop supper on the table in no time. Even our oldest daughter, who can be a picky eater, loves it—and it is an excellent way of getting her to eat her vegetables.
—Penny Greene, Lancaster, Ohio

- 1 pound smoked kielbasa *or* Polish sausage, halved and sliced 1/2 inch thick
- 2 tablespoons vegetable oil
- 1 package (5-1/4 ounces) au gratin potatoes
- 2-1/2 cups water
- 1 package (8 ounces) frozen California-blend vegetables
- 1 to 2 cups (4 to 8 ounces) shredded cheddar cheese

In a skillet, cook sausage in oil until lightly browned; drain. Add the potatoes with contents of sauce mix and water. Cover and cook over medium heat for 18-20 minutes or until the potatoes are almost tender, stirring occasionally.

Add vegetables; cover and cook for 8-10 minutes or until potatoes and vegetables are tender. Sprinkle with cheese. Remove from the heat; cover and let stand for 2 minutes or until the cheese is melted. **Yield: 4 servings.**

Creamy Sausage Stew 1st prize

Depending on the time of year, I serve my stew with bread or sweet corn muffins and fresh butter, and with salad or fruit.
—Rosemary Jesse, Cabool, Missouri

- **8 to 10 medium red potatoes, cut into 1-1/2-inch pieces**
- **2 large white onions, quartered**
- **1 large green pepper, cut into 1-inch pieces**
- **1 large sweet red pepper, cut into 1-inch pieces**
- **2 pounds smoked Polish sausage, cut into 1-inch slices**
- **1/3 cup vegetable oil**
- **1 tablespoon dried basil**
- **2 teaspoons salt**
- **1 teaspoon pepper**
- **2 cups heavy whipping cream**
- **3 tablespoons cornstarch**
- **3 tablespoons water**

Place potatoes in a large Dutch oven. Add the onions, peppers and sausage; toss gently. Combine the oil, basil, salt and pepper. Pour over the vegetable mixture; toss well. Cover and bake at 350° for 45 minutes; stir. Add the cream; cover and bake 30-40 minutes longer or until potatoes are tender.

Combine cornstarch and water until smooth; stir into stew. Place on stovetop and bring to a boil, stirring constantly until thickened. **Yield: 10-12 servings.**

Pepperoni Lasagna

I've made this satisfying lasagna for years—when our children were small, they preferred it more than a steak dinner! —Barbara McIntosh, Midland, Texas

Creamy Sausage Stew

- **1-1/2 pounds ground beef**
- **1 small onion, chopped**
- **2-1/2 cups water**
- **1 can (8 ounces) tomato sauce**
- **1 can (6 ounces) tomato paste**
- **1 teaspoon beef bouillon granules**
- **1 tablespoon dried parsley flakes**
- **2 teaspoons Italian seasoning**
- **1 teaspoon salt**
- **1/4 teaspoon garlic salt**
- **2 eggs**
- **1 carton (12 ounces) small-curd cottage cheese**
- **1/2 cup sour cream**
- **8 lasagna noodles, cooked and drained**
- **1 package (3-1/2 ounces) sliced pepperoni**
- **2 cups (8 ounces) shredded part-skim mozzarella cheese**
- **1/2 cup grated Parmesan cheese**

In a skillet, cook beef and onion over medium heat until meat is no longer pink; drain. Add the water, tomato sauce, tomato paste, bouillon and seasonings. Bring to a boil. Reduce heat; simmer, uncovered, for 30 minutes.

In a bowl, combine the eggs, cottage cheese and sour cream. Spread 1/2 cup meat sauce into a greased 13-in. x 9-in. x 2-in. baking dish. Layer with four noodles, the cottage cheese mixture and pepperoni. Top with remaining noodles and meat sauce. Sprinkle with mozzarella and Parmesan cheeses.

Cover and bake at 350° for 35 minutes. Uncover; bake 10 minutes longer or until heated through. Let stand for 15 minutes before cutting. **Yield: 12 servings.**

Sausage Spinach Turnovers

One Christmas, I gave these tasty meat pies to our neighbors as gifts instead of sweets—they loved them! I freeze any leftovers and reheat them later in the microwave when I need a quick meal.

—Vicky Henry, Aurora, Colorado

- **1 pound bulk pork sausage**
- **1/3 cup chopped onion**
- **1 package (10 ounces) frozen chopped spinach, thawed and squeezed dry**
- **1-1/2 cups (6 ounces) shredded sharp cheddar cheese**
- **2 teaspoons prepared mustard**
- **1 teaspoon dried marjoram**
- **Salt and pepper to taste**
- **1 loaf (16 ounces) frozen bread dough, thawed**
- **1 egg white, beaten**

In a skillet, cook sausage and onion over medium heat until meat is no longer pink; drain. Stir in the spinach, cheese, mustard, marjoram, salt and pepper. Cook and stir until cheese is melted. Remove from the heat; cool slightly.

Divide dough into eight portions; roll each into a 6-in. circle. Spoon about 1/2 cup meat mixture on half of each circle. Brush edges with egg white; fold dough over filling and press edges with a fork to seal. Place on greased baking sheets. Cover and let rise in a warm place for 20 minutes.

Brush tops with egg white; cut slits in the top of each. Bake at 350° for 20 minutes or until golden brown. **Yield: 8 turnovers.**

Pepperoni Lasagna

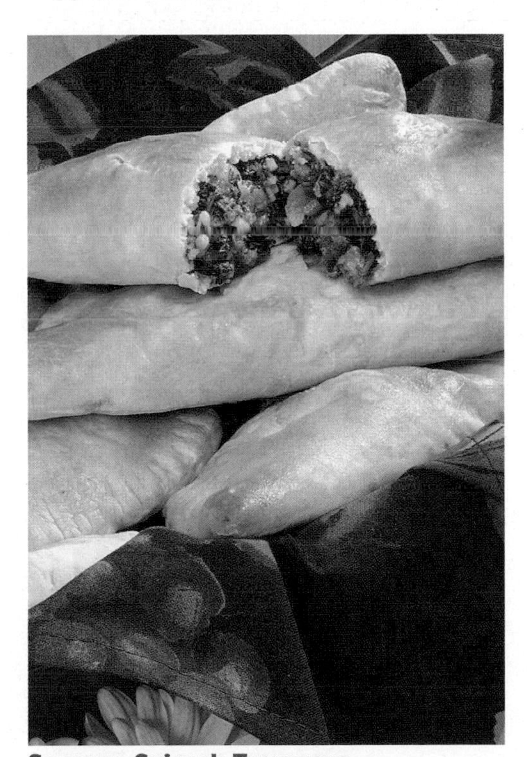

Sausage Spinach Turnovers

Italian Sausage Stew

Bavarian Bratwurst Supper

Italian Sausage Stew 1st prize

One day when I was preparing Italian sausages, I decided to do something different. After browning them, I added other ingredients, ending up with this stew that my husband and I like very much.
—Ann Erney, Middlebury Center, Pennsylvania

- 1-1/2 pounds Italian sausage links, cut into 1-inch pieces
- 3 cups water
- 4 medium potatoes, peeled and cut into chunks
- 2 medium carrots, cut into chunks
- 2 celery ribs, cut into chunks
- 2 small onions, cut into wedges
- 1/4 cup Worcestershire sauce
- 1 teaspoon dried oregano
- 1/2 teaspoon *each* dried basil, thyme and rosemary, crushed
- 1 bay leaf
- Salt and pepper to taste
- 3/4 cup ketchup
- 1/2 large green *or* sweet red pepper, cut into chunks
- 1 tablespoon minced fresh parsley
- 1 tablespoon cornstarch
- 1 tablespoon cold water

In a Dutch oven, cook sausage over medium heat until no longer pink; drain. Add the water, potatoes, carrots, celery, onions, Worcestershire sauce and seasonings. Bring to a boil. Reduce heat; cover and cook over low heat for 1 hour or until sausage is no longer pink and vegetables are tender.

Add the ketchup, green pepper and parsley; cook 12-15 minutes longer or until pepper is tender. Discard bay leaf. Combine cornstarch and cold water until smooth; stir into stew. Bring to a boil; cook and stir for 2 minutes or until thickened. **Yield: 6 servings.**

Bavarian Bratwurst Supper

My family enjoys the flavors of hot German potato salad and bratwurst, especially during the cooler months. This original skillet recipe is truly a one-dish meal, combining meat, potatoes, apple and sauerkraut. —*Jill Cook, Perry, Iowa*

- 4 bacon strips, diced
- 4 fresh bratwurst, cut into 2-inch pieces
- 1 medium tart apple, chopped
- 1 medium onion, chopped
- 1/2 cup cider vinegar
- 3 tablespoons brown sugar
- 1 tablespoon spicy brown mustard
- 1/2 teaspoon salt
- 1/8 teaspoon pepper
- 4 cups frozen cubed hash brown potatoes, thawed
- 1 can (14 ounces) Bavarian-style sauerkraut, drained

In a skillet, cook bacon over medium heat until crisp. Using a slotted spoon, remove to paper towels. In the drippings, cook and stir bratwurst for 10-12 minutes. Remove with a slotted spoon. Drain, reserving 2 tablespoons of drippings. Saute apple and onion in drippings until lightly browned.

Add the vinegar, brown sugar, mustard, salt, pepper and bratwurst. Cover and cook for 12 minutes, stirring frequently. Add potatoes and sauerkraut; cook and stir 12 minutes longer or until heated through and a meat thermometer inserted in bratwurst reads 160°. Sprinkle with bacon. **Yield: 4 servings.**

Pizza with Stuffed Crust

Cheese baked into the edge of the crust makes this extra-special pizza our favorite. It tastes like a restaurant-style pizza with mild ingredients. —*Sandra McKenzie, Braham, Minnesota*

Pizza with Stuffed Crust

- 2 teaspoons cornmeal
- 2 tubes (10 ounces *each*) refrigerated pizza crust
- 8 ounces string cheese
- 1 tablespoon butter, melted
- 1-1/2 teaspoons minced fresh basil *or* 1/2 teaspoon dried basil
- 1 can (8 ounces) pizza sauce
- 1 package (3-1/2 ounces) sliced pepperoni
- 1 can (4 ounces) mushroom stems and pieces, drained
- 1 can (2-1/4 ounces) sliced ripe olives, drained
- 2 cups (8 ounces) shredded part-skim mozzarella cheese

Sprinkle cornmeal evenly over a greased 15-in. x 10-in. x 1-in. baking pan. Unroll pizza dough and place on pan, letting dough drape 1 in. over the edges. Pinch center seam to seal. Place pieces of string cheese around edges of pan. Fold dough over cheese; pinch to seal. Brush the crust with butter; sprinkle with basil.

Bake at 425° for 5 minutes. Spread sauce over crust. Place two-thirds of the pepperoni in a single layer over sauce. Sprinkle with the mushrooms, olives and cheese. Top with remaining pepperoni. Bake for 10-12 minutes or until crust and cheese is melted. **Yield: 8-10 slices.**

Editor's Note: 8 ounces of bulk mozzarella cheese, cut into 4-in. sticks, may be substituted for the string cheese.

Sausage Bean Burritos

Sausage Bean Burritos

Like my mother and grandmother, I'm a frugal cook. I purchase meats in bulk, including sausage. This is one creative way I've found to use sausage in an evening entree. Our children often request these zippy burritos. —*Eleanor Chlan, Ellicott City, Maryland*

- 3/4 pound bulk pork sausage
- 1/2 cup chopped green pepper
- 1/3 cup chopped onion
- 1 can (15 ounces) black beans, rinsed and drained
- 1-1/2 cups cooked long grain rice
- 1-1/2 cups salsa, *divided*
- 10 flour tortillas (7 inches)
- 1 cup (4 ounces) shredded cheddar cheese, *divided*

In a large saucepan, cook sausage, green pepper and onion over medium heat until meat is no longer pink; drain. Stir in the beans, rice and 1 cup salsa; mix well.

Spread about 1/2 cup sausage mixture down the center of each tortilla; sprinkle each with 1 tablespoon cheese. Roll up and place seam side down in a greased 13-in. x 9-in. x 2-in. baking dish. Top with remaining salsa.

Cover and bake at 350° for 30 minutes. Uncover; sprinkle with remaining cheese. Bake 5-10 minutes longer or until cheese is melted. **Yield: 10 burritos.**

Polish Kraut and Apples

My family loves this hearty, heartwarming meal on cold winter nights. The tender apples, brown sugar and smoked sausage give this dish fantastic flavor. I like making it because the prep time is so very short.
—*Caren Markee, Cary, Illinois*

- 1 can (14 ounces) sauerkraut, rinsed and well drained
- 1 package (16 ounces) smoked Polish sausage
- 3 medium tart apples, peeled and cut into eighths
- 1/2 cup packed brown sugar
- 1/2 teaspoon caraway seeds, optional
- 1/8 teaspoon pepper
- 3/4 cup apple juice

Place half of the sauerkraut in an ungreased 3-qt. slow cooker. Top with sausage, apples, brown sugar, caraway seeds if desired and pepper. Top with remaining sauerkraut. Pour apple juice over all. Cover and cook on low for 4-5 hours or until apples are tender. **Yield: 4 servings.**

Polish Kraut and Apples

POULTRY

ERB-ROASTED TURKEY, pg. 240

Poultry

Zesty Mustard Chicken

Whether you're grilling a broiler chicken or chicken breasts, consider this lip-smacking glaze. There are only four ingredients in the honey-mustard sauce, so you can whip it up in minutes.
—Michael Everidge, Morristown, Tennessee

- **1/2 cup prepared mustard**
- **1/2 cup honey**
- **1 tablespoon salt-free seasoning blend**
- **1 tablespoon Worcestershire sauce**
- **1 broiler/fryer chicken (3 pounds), cut in half**

In a bowl, combine the first four ingredients. Carefully loosen the skin of the chicken; spoon some of the mustard sauce under the skin.

Coat grill rack with nonstick cooking spray before starting the grill. Place chicken skin side up on grill rack. Grill, covered, over indirect medium heat for 20 minutes. Turn; grill 20-30 minutes longer or until juices run clear, basting occasionally with remaining mustard sauce. Remove chicken skin if desired; cut into serving-size pieces. **Yield: 6 servings.**

Zesty Mustard Chicken

Herbed Chicken and Shrimp

Herbed Chicken And Shrimp

Tender chicken and shrimp make a flavorful combination that's easy to prepare, yet elegant enough to serve at a dinner party. While I clean the house, this dish practically cooks itself. I serve it over hot cooked rice with crusty bread and a green salad.
—Diana Knight, Reno, Nevada

- **1 teaspoon salt**
- **1 teaspoon pepper**
- **1 broiler/fryer chicken (3 to 4 pounds), cut up and skin removed**
- **1/4 cup butter**
- **1 large onion, chopped**
- **1 can (8 ounces) tomato sauce**
- **1/2 cup white wine *or* chicken broth**
- **1 garlic clove, minced**
- **1 teaspoon dried basil**
- **1 pound uncooked medium shrimp, peeled and deveined**

Combine salt and pepper; rub over the chicken pieces. In a skillet, brown chicken on all sides in butter. Transfer to an ungreased 5-qt. slow cooker. In a bowl, combine the onion, tomato sauce, wine or broth, garlic and basil; pour over chicken.

Cover and cook on low for 4-5 hours or until chicken juices run clear. Stir in the shrimp. Cover and cook on high for 20-30 minutes or until shrimp turn pink. **Yield: 4 servings.**

Baked Chicken and Acorn Squash

Barbecue Chicken Casserole

Baked Chicken And Acorn Squash 1st prize

This eye-pleasing main dish is ideal for harvest time with its colorful acorn squash and sweet peaches. The fragrance of rosemary-seasoned chicken baking is heavenly. My family says it's every bit as delicious as it smells. —*Connie Svoboda, Elko, Minnesota*

- 2 small acorn squash (1-1/4 pounds)
- 2 to 4 garlic cloves, minced
- 2 tablespoons vegetable oil, *divided*
- 4 chicken drumsticks (4 ounces *each*)
- 4 chicken thighs (4 ounces *each*)
- 1/4 cup packed brown sugar
- 1 teaspoon salt
- 1 tablespoon minced fresh rosemary *or* 1 teaspoon dried rosemary, crushed
- 1 can (15-1/4 ounces) sliced peaches, undrained

Cut squash in half lengthwise; discard seeds. Cut each half widthwise into 1/2-in. slices; discard ends. Place slices in an ungreased 13-in. x 9-in. x 2-in. baking dish. Sprinkle with garlic and drizzle with 1 tablespoon oil.

In a large skillet, brown chicken in remaining oil. Arrange chicken over squash. Combine the sugar, salt and rosemary; sprinkle over chicken. Bake, uncovered, at 350° for 45 minutes, basting with pan juices twice.

Pour peaches over chicken and squash. Bake, uncovered, 15 minutes longer or until chicken juices run clear and peaches are heated through. **Yield: 4 servings.**

Oven-Fried Chicken

My family tells me they'd like me to fix chicken with this coating mix all of the time. I've had the recipe for years. —*Dawn Supina, Edmonton, Alberta*

Oven-Fried Chicken

- 2 cups all-purpose flour
- 2 tablespoons salt
- 2 tablespoons pepper
- 1 tablespoon dried thyme
- 1 tablespoon dried tarragon
- 1 tablespoon ground ginger
- 1 tablespoon ground mustard
- 1 teaspoon garlic salt
- 1 teaspoon dried oregano
- 2 eggs
- 1/2 cup milk
- 1 broiler/fryer chicken (2-1/2 to 3-1/2 pounds), cut up

Oil for frying

Combine the first nine ingredients; store in an airtight container. In a shallow bowl, beat eggs and milk. Place 3/4 cup coating mix in a large resealable plastic bag. Store remaining mix in an airtight container for another use. Dip chicken into egg mixture, then add to the bag, a few pieces at a time; shake to coat.

Heat 1/4 in. of oil in a skillet over medium-high heat. Brown chicken on all sides; transfer to an ungreased 15-in. x 10-in. x 1-in. baking pan. Bake, uncovered, at 350° for 45-55 minutes or until juices run clear. **Yield: 2-1/2 cups coating mix (enough for 3 batches of chicken, 4-6 servings per batch).**

Barbecue Chicken Casserole

I am a minister's wife and have cooked for countless fellowships, funeral dinners and other church activities. This is a recipe I've used often for those occasions. —Gail Rector, Belle, Missouri

- 1 cup all-purpose flour
- 1 broiler/fryer chicken (3 to 4 pounds), cut up
- 2 tablespoons vegetable oil
- 1 cup chopped onion
- 1 cup chopped green pepper
- 1 cup thinly sliced celery
- 1 cup ketchup
- 1/2 cup water
- 3 tablespoons brown sugar
- 3 tablespoons Worcestershire sauce
- 1/2 teaspoon salt
- 1/4 teaspoon pepper
- 1 package (16 ounces) frozen corn, thawed

Place flour in a large resealable plastic bag. Add chicken, a few pieces at a time, and shake to coat. In a large skillet, brown the chicken on all sides in oil; transfer to an ungreased 13-in. x 9-in. x 2-in. baking dish.

Drain skillet, reserving 2 tablespoons drippings. In the drippings, saute the onion, green pepper and celery until tender. In a bowl, combine the ketchup, water, brown sugar, Worcestershire sauce, salt and pepper; add to vegetables. Bring to a boil. Pour over the chicken.

Cover and bake at 350° for 30 minutes. Sprinkle with corn. Cover and bake 18-20 minutes longer or until chicken juices run clear and corn is tender. **Yield: 4-6 servings.**

Mom's Chicken 'n' Buttermilk Dumplings

Mom's Chicken 'n' Buttermilk Dumplings

I serve this with a tossed or cucumber salad to friends dining with us or on visits by our two sons and their families. —*Ellen Proefrock, Brodhead, Wisconsin*

- 1 stewing chicken (about 5 pounds), cut up
- 10 cups water
- 1 large onion, chopped
- 2 medium carrots, sliced
- 3 celery ribs, chopped
- 4 garlic cloves, minced
- 1 teaspoon salt
- 1/4 cup butter
- 6 tablespoons all-purpose flour
- 1/8 teaspoon paprika
- 1/8 teaspoon pepper
- 1/2 cup half-and-half cream

DUMPLINGS:

- 2 cups all-purpose flour
- 4 teaspoons baking powder
- 4 teaspoons sugar
- 1 teaspoon salt
- 2 eggs
- 1/2 cup buttermilk
- 1/4 cup butter, melted

In a Dutch oven, combine the first seven ingredients. Slowly bring to a boil; skim foam from broth. Reduce heat; cover and simmer for 1-1/2 hours or until chicken is tender. Remove chicken. When cool enough to handle, remove meat from bones; discard bones. Cut meat into bite-size piece; set aside. Strain broth, reserving broth and vegetables.

In the same Dutch oven, melt butter. Stir in flour, paprika and pepper until smooth; gradually stir in 6 cups reserved broth (save remaining broth for another use). Bring to a boil; cook and stir for 2 minutes or until thickened. Reduce heat; stir in the cream, reserved vegetables and chicken. Cover and bring to a boil; reduce the heat to simmer.

For dumplings, combine the flour, baking powder, sugar and salt in a bowl. Combine the eggs, buttermilk and butter; stir into dry ingredients to form a stiff batter. Drop by tablespoonfuls onto simmering mixture. Cover and simmer for 20 minutes or until a toothpick inserted in a dumpling comes out clean (do not lift cover while simmering). Serve immediately. **Yield: 6-8 servings.**

Southern Chicken Roll-Ups

This is one of my favorite ways to cook chicken because it tastes so good and it doesn't take long to prepare. I like to serve it with rice.
—*Catherine Darr, Charlotte, Arkansas*

- 6 boneless skinless chicken breast halves (1-1/2 pounds)
- 6 slices Swiss cheese
- 3 tablespoons all-purpose flour
- 1/2 teaspoon pepper
- 2 tablespoons butter
- 3/4 cup chicken broth
- 1/2 teaspoon dried oregano

Flatten chicken to 1/4-in. thickness. Place a cheese slice on each; roll up jelly-roll style. In a shallow bowl, combine flour and pepper; add chicken and roll to coat.

In a skillet, cook chicken in butter for 10 minutes over medium heat until browned, turning frequently. Add broth and oregano; bring to boil. Reduce heat; simmer for 12-14 minutes or until chicken juices run clear. **Yield: 6 servings.**

Southern Chicken Roll-Ups

Chicken Sausage Skillet

My sister Mary, an excellent cook, shared this wonderful recipe—I've always loved its tantalizing blend of ingredients.

—Connie Dowell, Orlando, Florida

- 1 medium onion, thinly sliced
- 1 medium green pepper, thinly sliced
- 1 cup sliced fresh mushrooms
- 1 cup sliced zucchini
- 2 tablespoons olive oil
- 1/2 to 3/4 pound boneless skinless chicken breasts, thinly sliced
- 1/2 to 3/4 pound Italian sausage links, cut into 1/2-inch pieces
- 2 cans (14-1/2 ounces *each*) diced tomatoes, undrained
- 1 garlic clove, minced
- 3/4 teaspoon dried basil
- 3/4 teaspoon dried oregano
- Hot cooked rice

In a large skillet, saute the onion, green pepper, mushrooms and zucchini in oil until tender. Remove vegetables with a slotted spoon; set aside.

Add chicken and sausage to skillet; cook until no longer pink. Drain. Stir in the tomatoes, garlic, basil and oregano. Return vegetables to pan. Bring to a boil. Reduce heat; cover and simmer for 10 minutes or until heated through. Serve over rice. **Yield: 6-8 servings.**

Chicken Sausage Skillet

Orange Walnut Chicken

Italian Chicken Roll-Ups

Orange Walnut Chicken 1st prize

For an impressive main dish that's not tricky to prepare, try this mouth-watering chicken. With orange juice concentrate, orange juice, lemon juice and marmalade, the pretty sauce has a zesty taste.
—T. Moore, Haddon Township, New Jersey

- 3 tablespoons orange juice concentrate
- 3 tablespoons vegetable oil, *divided*
- 1 tablespoon soy sauce
- 1 garlic clove, minced
- 4 boneless skinless chicken breast halves
- 1/2 cup coarsely chopped walnuts
- 1 tablespoon butter
- 4 green onions, thinly sliced, *divided*
- 1/2 cup orange marmalade
- 1/2 cup orange juice
- 1/4 cup lemon juice
- 2 tablespoons honey
- 1 to 2 tablespoons grated orange peel
- 2 to 3 teaspoons grated lemon peel
- 1/2 teaspoon salt
- 1/8 teaspoon pepper
- Hot cooked rice

In a large resealable plastic bag, combine the orange juice concentrate, 2 tablespoons oil, soy sauce and garlic; add chicken. Seal bag and turn to coat; refrigerate for 2-3 hours.

Remove chicken; reserve marinade. In a skillet, cook chicken in remaining oil until juices run clear.

Meanwhile, in a saucepan, saute walnuts in butter until lightly browned; remove and set aside. Set aside 1/4 cup green onions for garnish. Add remaining onions to saucepan; saute until tender. Add reserved marinade and the next eight ingredients. Bring to a rolling boil; boil for 2 minutes.

Creamy Mushroom Chicken

Reduce heat; simmer, uncovered, for 5-10 minutes or until sauce reaches desired consistency. Serve chicken over rice; top with sauce and reserved walnuts and onions. **Yield: 4 servings.**

Italian Chicken Roll-Ups

I like to keep a batch of these tender chicken rolls in the freezer. Coated with golden crumbs, they seem fancy enough for company. I've used mozzarella cheese for the provolone and pastrami for the ham with equally delicious results.

—Barbara Wobser, Sandusky, Ohio

- 8 boneless skinless chicken breast halves (2 pounds)
- 8 thin slices (4 ounces) deli ham
- 4 slices provolone cheese, halved
- 2/3 cup seasoned bread crumbs
- 1/2 cup grated Romano *or* Parmesan cheese
- 1/4 cup minced fresh parsley
- 1/2 cup milk

Flatten chicken to 1/4-in. thickness. Place a slice of ham and half slice of cheese on each piece of chicken. Roll up from a short side and tuck in ends; secure with a toothpick. In a shallow bowl, combine the crumbs, grated cheese and parsley. Pour milk into another bowl. Dip chicken rolls in milk, then in crumb mixture.

If desired, wrap and freeze four chicken roll-ups for up to 2 months. Place the remaining roll-ups seam side down on a greased baking sheet. Spray chicken with nonstick cooking spray. Bake, uncovered, at 425° for 25 minutes or until juices run clear. Remove toothpicks.

To use frozen chicken: Completely thaw in the refrigerator. Unwrap roll-ups and place on a greased baking sheet. Spray with nonstick cooking spray. Bake, uncovered, at 425° for 30 minutes or until juices run clear. **Yield: 8 servings.**

Creamy Mushroom Chicken

I call this one-skillet meal the easy chicken fixin, and love it that the leftovers are equally delicious heated up in the microwave the next day.

—Sharon McMillen, Park City, Montana

- 6 boneless skinless chicken breast halves
- 1/4 teaspoon pepper
- 2 tablespoons vegetable oil
- 1 cup sliced fresh mushrooms
- 1/4 cup butter
- 4-1/2 teaspoons all-purpose flour
- 1 cup milk
- 3/4 cup grated Parmesan cheese, *divided*
- Minced fresh parsley
- Hot cooked pasta

Sprinkle the chicken with pepper. In a large skillet, brown chicken in oil over medium heat until juices run clear. Remove to a serving platter and keep warm.

In the same skillet, saute mushrooms in butter until tender. Sprinkle with flour and stir until blended; gradually add milk. Bring to a boil; cook and stir for 2 minutes or until thickened.

Remove from the heat; stir in 1/2 cup Parmesan cheese. Pour over chicken. Sprinkle with parsley and remaining cheese. Serve with pasta. **Yield: 6 servings.**

Quick Chicken Cordon Bleu

Quick Chicken Cordon Bleu

I used this speedy microwave recipe the first time I made chicken cordon bleu. Although I've since tried other recipes that bake in the oven, this remains the quickest and the best.

—Shirley Jackson, Elkton, Virginia

- 4 boneless skinless chicken breast halves
- 2 teaspoons Dijon mustard
- 1/2 teaspoon paprika
- 4 thin slices deli ham
- 1 cup soft bread crumbs
- 1/4 cup grated Parmesan cheese
- 1/4 teaspoon pepper
- 3 to 4 tablespoons mayonnaise

SAUCE:

- 1 tablespoon butter
- 1 tablespoon all-purpose flour
- 1 cup milk
- 1/4 teaspoon salt
- 1/2 cup shredded Swiss cheese
- 2 tablespoons white wine

Flatten the chicken to 1/2-in. thickness. Spread mustard on one side; sprinkle with paprika. Top each with a ham slice. Roll up tightly; secure with toothpicks. In a bowl, combine the bread crumbs, Parmesan cheese and pepper. Brush chicken with mayonnaise; roll in crumb mixture.

Place in a shallow 2-qt. microwave-safe dish; cover loosely. Microwave on high for 7 minutes; turn chicken. Cook 5-1/2 minutes longer or until juices run clear; keep warm.

In a 1-qt. microwave-safe dish, heat butter on high for 20 seconds; stir in flour until smooth. Cook, uncovered, on high for 20 seconds. Gradually add milk and salt. Cook 2-3 minutes longer or until thickened. Stir in cheese until smooth. Add wine. Discard toothpicks from chicken; top with sauce. **Yield: 4 servings.**

Editor's Note: This recipe was tested in a 1,100-watt microwave.

Honey-Dijon Chicken

These tender chicken breasts are nicely browned, then covered in a sauce that gets its sweetness from honey and pineapple juice.

—Barbara Leventhal, Hauppauge, New York

- 12 boneless skinless chicken breast halves (3 pounds)
- 4 garlic cloves, minced
- 2 teaspoons dried thyme
- Salt and pepper to taste
- 1 tablespoon vegetable oil
- 2 tablespoons cornstarch
- 1-1/2 cups pineapple juice
- 1/2 cup water
- 1/2 cup Dijon mustard
- 1/3 cup honey
- Hot cooked rice *or* noodles

Rub chicken with garlic and thyme. Sprinkle with salt and pepper. In a skillet, cook chicken in oil on both sides until no longer pink. In a bowl, combine the cornstarch, pineapple juice and water until smooth. Stir in mustard and honey. Add to the skillet. Bring to a boil; cook and stir for 2 minutes or until thickened.

Spoon half of the chicken and sauce into a greased 11-in. x 7-in. x 2-in. baking dish; cool.

Cover and freeze for up to 3 months. Serve remaining chicken and sauce over rice or noodles.

To use frozen chicken: Completely thaw in the refrigerator. Remove from the refrigerator 30 minutes before baking. Cover and bake at 350° for 35 minutes or until heated through. **Yield: 2 casseroles (6 servings each).**

Chicken in Basil Cream 1st prize

When I first read this recipe, I thought it looked difficult. But because I had all the ingredients on hand, I gave it a try. Am I glad I did. Turned out, it's simple to prepare! —*Judy Baker, Craig, Colorado*

- 1/4 cup milk
- 1/4 cup dry bread crumbs
- 4 boneless skinless chicken breast halves (4 ounces *each*)
- 3 tablespoons butter
- 1/2 cup chicken broth
- 1 cup heavy whipping cream
- 1 jar (4 ounces) sliced pimientos, drained
- 1/2 cup grated Parmesan cheese
- 1/4 cup minced fresh basil
- 1/8 teaspoon pepper

Place milk and bread crumbs in separate shallow bowls. Dip chicken in milk, then coat with crumbs. In a skillet over medium-high heat, cook chicken in butter on both sides until juices run clear, about 10 minutes. Remove and keep warm.

Add broth to the skillet. Bring to a boil over medium heat; stir to loosen browned bits. Stir in the cream and pimientos; boil and stir for 1 minute. Reduce heat. Add Parmesan cheese, basil and pepper; cook and stir until heated through. Pour over the chicken. **Yield: 4 servings.**

Honey-Dijon Chicken

Chicken in Basil Cream

Chicken Roll-Ups with Cherry Sauce

Honey Rosemary Chicken

Chicken Roll-Ups with Cherry Sauce

Since I grew up on a cherry farm, I have many recipes featuring that delightful fruit. This one is a delicious way to use chicken.
—Margaret Scott, Traverse City, Michigan

- 8 boneless skinless chicken breast halves
- 8 slices Swiss *or* Brie cheese
- 1 egg
- 1 tablespoon water
- 1 tablespoon Dijon mustard
- 3/4 cup dry bread crumbs
- 1/2 teaspoon dried thyme
- 1/4 teaspoon salt

Dash pepper

- 1/4 cup all-purpose flour
- 1/4 cup vegetable oil

CHERRY SAUCE:

- 2 cups canned pitted tart red cherries
- 3/4 cup sugar
- 2 tablespoons cornstarch
- 1 teaspoon lemon juice
- 1/4 teaspoon almond extract
- 3 drops red food coloring, optional

Flatten chicken breasts to 1/4-in. thickness. Place a slice of cheese on each; roll up and secure with toothpicks. In a shallow dish, beat the egg, water and mustard. In another shallow dish, combine bread crumbs, thyme, salt and pepper. Lightly coat chicken with flour, then dip in egg mixture and roll in bread crumb mixture.

In a large skillet, heat oil. Add roll-ups; cook until golden brown, turning often. Transfer to an ungreased 13-in. x 9-in. x 2-in. baking dish. Bake, uncovered, at 350° for 20-25 minutes or until chicken juices run clear.

Meanwhile, drain cherries, reserving juice.

Carrot-Chicken Fried Rice

Add enough water to juice to measure 1 cup. In a saucepan, combine sugar and cornstarch. Stir in cherry juice until smooth. Add cherries. Bring to a boil; cook and stir for 2 minutes or until thickened. Remove from the heat. Stir in the lemon juice, extract and food coloring if desired. Discard toothpicks from roll-ups; serve with cherry sauce. **Yield: 8 servings.**

Honey Rosemary Chicken 1st prize

I never get tired of finding new ways to cook with herbs! A rosemary marinade sweetened with honey gives this moist chicken wonderful flavor and a pretty golden sheen. —*Elsie Barton, Hoover, Alabama*

- 1/4 cup honey
- 1/4 cup balsamic vinegar
- 1/4 cup minced fresh rosemary
- 2 tablespoons olive oil *or* 2 tablespoons canola oil
- 6 bone-in skinless chicken breast halves (7 ounces *each*)
- 1 teaspoon salt
- 1/4 teaspoon pepper

In a bowl, combine the honey, vinegar, rosemary and oil. Pour half of the marinade into a large resealable plastic bag; add the chicken. Seal bag and turn to coat; refrigerate for 2 hours. Cover and refrigerate for 2 hours. Cover and refrigerate remaining marinade.

Drain and discard marinade from chicken. Place chicken bone side down in a 13-in. x 9-in. x 2-in. baking pan. Sprinkle with salt and pepper. Bake, uncovered, at 350° for 55-65 minutes or until juices run clear, basting occasionally with reserved marinade. **Yield: 6 servings.**

Carrot-Chicken Fried Rice

A dear friend shared this colorful stir-fry when my children were small. It quickly won over those picky eaters! To cut down on prep time, I make the rice ahead and often marinate the chicken beforehand. —*Peggy Spieckermann, Joplin, Missouri*

- 3/4 pound boneless skinless chicken breasts, cubed
- 4 tablespoons soy sauce, *divided*
- 2 garlic cloves, minced
- 1-1/2 cups chopped fresh broccoli
- 3 green onions, sliced
- 2 tablespoons vegetable oil, *divided*
- 3 large carrots, shredded
- 4 cups cold cooked rice
- 1/4 teaspoon pepper

In a bowl, combine the chicken, 1 tablespoon soy sauce and garlic; set aside. In a large skillet or wok, stir-fry the broccoli and green onions in 1 tablespoon oil for 5 minutes. Add carrots; stir-fry 4 minutes longer or until crisp-tender. Remove and set aside.

In the same skillet, stir-fry chicken in remaining oil until no longer pink and juices run clear. Add the rice, pepper, vegetables and remaining soy sauce. Stir-fry until heated through. **Yield: 4-6 servings.**

Sweet 'n' Spicy Chicken

Sweet 'n' Spicy Chicken 1st prize

My husband and three children love this tender chicken in a spicy sauce. Peach preserves add just a touch of sweetness, while taco seasoning and salsa give this dish some kick. This entree can be made even zippier yet by adding more taco seasoning and using spicier salsa. —*Sheri White, Higley, Arizona*

- 1 pound boneless skinless chicken breasts, cut into 1/2-inch cubes
- 3 tablespoons taco seasoning
- 1 to 2 tablespoons vegetable oil
- 1 jar (11 ounces) chunky salsa
- 1/2 cup peach preserves
- Hot cooked rice

Place the chicken in a large resealable plastic bag; add taco seasoning and toss to coat. In a skillet, brown chicken in oil. Combine salsa and preserves; stir into skillet. Bring to a boil. Reduce heat; cover and simmer for 2-3 minutes or until meat juices run clear. Serve over rice. **Yield: 4 servings.**

Chicken in Pear Sauce

Pairing poultry with pears brought applause from my husband and four growing children. Simple enough for everyday meals and ideal for company, this dish is a year-round standout.
—*Andrea Lunsford, Spokane, Washington*

- 4 boneless skinless chicken breast halves
- 1/2 teaspoon salt
- 1/8 teaspoon white pepper
- 2 tablespoons vegetable oil
- 5 thick-cut bacon strips, diced
- 1 can (14-1/2 ounces) chicken broth
- 2 to 3 medium ripe pears, peeled and diced
- 2 tablespoons cornstarch
- 2 tablespoons cold water
- 1/4 cup minced chives

Sprinkle chicken with salt and pepper. In a skillet over medium heat, cook chicken in oil on both sides for about 10 minutes or until juices run clear.

Meanwhile, in a saucepan, cook bacon over medium heat until crisp. Drain, reserving 1 tablespoon drippings; set bacon aside. Gradually stir broth into the drippings, scraping pan to loosen browned bits. Bring to a boil. Boil, uncovered, for 5 minutes. Add pears; return to a boil. Boil, uncovered, for 5 minutes or until pears are tender.

Combine cornstarch and water until smooth; add the chives. Gradually stir into pear sauce; bring to a boil. Cook and stir for 2 minutes or until thickened and bubbly. Stir in bacon. Serve over the chicken. **Yield: 4 servings.**

Chicken Stroganoff

I came up with this recipe, a variation on beef Stroganoff, as a way to use up roasted chicken, then I adjusted the recipe to use fresh chicken strips. It was a hit. I'm usually the only one in my family who enjoys noodles, but even our son will have more when they're topped with the creamy chicken.

—Laura Schimanski, Coaldale, Alberta

- 4 bacon strips, diced
- 1 pound boneless skinless chicken breasts, cut into 1/4-inch strips
- 1 medium onion, chopped
- 2 jars (4-1/2 ounces *each*) sliced mushrooms, drained
- 1-1/2 cups chicken broth
- 2 garlic cloves, minced
- 1/2 teaspoon salt
- 1/8 teaspoon paprika
- Pepper to taste
- 2 tablespoons all-purpose flour
- 1 cup (8 ounces) sour cream
- Hot cooked noodles
- Additional paprika, optional

In a skillet, cook bacon over medium heat until crisp. Using a slotted spoon, remove to paper towels. Drain, reserving 2 tablespoons drippings.

In the drippings, cook the chicken, onion and mushrooms until the chicken is no longer pink. Add broth, garlic, salt, paprika, pepper and bacon. Bring to a boil. Reduce heat; cover and simmer for 10 minutes.

Combine flour and sour cream until smooth; add to the skillet. Bring to a boil; cook and stir for 2 minutes or until thickened. Serve over noodles. Sprinkle with paprika if desired. **Yield: 4 servings.**

Chicken in Pear Sauce

Chicken Stroganoff

Special Chicken and Scallops

Teriyaki-Glazed Chicken

Special Chicken And Scallops

I make this main course when I want to wow company. It tastes heavenly, and guests always love it.
—Sheila Vail, Long Beach, California

- 1/2 cup all-purpose flour
- 1/2 teaspoon salt
- 1/2 teaspoon pepper
- 6 boneless skinless chicken breast halves
- 1/2 pound bay scallops
- 1/4 cup olive oil
- 1-1/2 cups sliced fresh mushrooms
- 1 medium onion, chopped
- 1/4 cup white wine *or* chicken broth
- 2 teaspoons cornstarch
- 1/2 cup heavy whipping cream
- 1 teaspoon dried tarragon
- 1/2 cup shredded Swiss cheese

In a large resealable plastic bag, combine the flour, salt and pepper. Add chicken and scallops in batches; shake to coat. In a large skillet, saute chicken and scallops in oil until lightly browned. Transfer to a greased 13-in. x 9-in. x 2-in. baking dish.

In the pan drippings, saute mushrooms and onion. Add wine or broth. Bring to a boil; cook until liquid is reduced to 2 tablespoons. Combine the cornstarch, cream and tarragon until blended; add to skillet. Bring to a boil; cook and stir for 1 minute or until thickened. Spoon over chicken and scallops. Sprinkle with the cheese. Bake, uncovered, at 375° for 18-20 minutes or until chicken juices run clear. **Yield: 6 servings.**

Teriyaki-Glazed Chicken

Chicken with Pineapple Sauce

Here's a sweet, thick glaze that really dresses up plain chicken. We think it also tastes good over ham.
—Mary Ealey, Smithfield, Virginia

- 2 tablespoons brown sugar
- 1 tablespoon cornstarch
- 2 cans (8 ounces *each*) crushed pineapple, undrained
- 1/4 cup soy sauce
- 1/4 teaspoon garlic salt
- 1/4 teaspoon ground ginger
- 6 boneless skinless chicken breast halves
- Minced chives, optional

In a saucepan, combine brown sugar and cornstarch. Stir in the pineapple, soy sauce, garlic salt and ginger. Bring to a boil; cook and stir for 2 minutes or until thickened.

Place chicken in a greased 9-in. square baking dish. Pour half of the sauce over chicken. Bake, uncovered, at 350° for 15 minutes; baste. Bake 10 minutes longer or until chicken juices run clear, basting several times with the remaining sauce. Sprinkle with chives if desired. **Yield: 6 servings.**

Teriyaki-Glazed Chicken

I love to experiment with food. For this recipe, I took advantage of the sweet onions grown on Maui. My whole family raves about this main dish.
—Kelly Brenneman, Riverdale, California

- 4 boneless skinless chicken breast halves, cut into strips
- 3 tablespoons vegetable oil, *divided*
- 4 medium carrots, julienned
- 1 medium sweet onion, julienned
- 1/2 cup soy sauce
- 1/4 cup packed brown sugar
- Hot cooked rice
- Sesame seeds, toasted, optional
- Sliced green onions, optional

In a large skillet or wok, stir-fry chicken in 2 tablespoons oil for 6-8 minutes or until juices run clear. Remove chicken and set aside. In the same skillet, stir-fry carrots in remaining oil for 2 minutes. Add onion; stir-fry about 2-4 minutes longer or until vegetables are tender.

Combine soy sauce and brown sugar; add to skillet. Bring to a boil. Return chicken to skillet. Boil for 5 minutes or until sauce is slightly thickened. Serve over rice. Sprinkle with sesame seeds and green onions if desired. **Yield: 4 servings.**

Old-Fashioned Chicken Potpie

Old-Fashioned Chicken Potpie 1st prize

Although this recipe uses leftover chicken, I serve it sometimes as a special company dinner. My husband adores it! —*Marilyn Hockey, Lisle, Ontario*

- 1/3 cup butter
- 1/3 cup all-purpose flour
- 1 garlic clove, minced
- 1/2 teaspoon salt
- 1/4 teaspoon pepper
- 1-1/2 cups water
- 2/3 cup milk
- 2 teaspoons chicken bouillon granules
- 2 cups cubed cooked chicken
- 1 cup frozen mixed vegetables

PASTRY:

- 1-2/3 cups all-purpose flour
- 2 teaspoons celery seed
- 1 package (8 ounces) cream cheese, cubed
- 1/3 cup cold butter

In a saucepan, melt butter. Stir in flour, garlic, salt and pepper until blended. Gradually stir in the water, milk and bouillon. Bring to a boil; cook and stir for 2 minutes or until thickened. Remove from the heat. Stir in chicken and vegetables; set aside.

For pastry, combine flour and celery seed in a bowl. Cut in cream cheese and butter until crumbly. Work mixture by hand until dough forms a ball. On a lightly floured surface, roll two-thirds of dough into a 12-in. square. Transfer to an 8-in. square baking dish. Pour filling into crust. Roll remaining dough into 9-in. square; place over filling. Trim, seal and flute edges. Cut slits in pastry.

Bake at 425° for 30-35 minutes or until crust is golden brown and filling is bubbly. Let stand for 5 minutes before cutting. **Yield: 6 servings.**

Spicy Chicken Linguine

Our state is famous for its green chilies. Naturally, my husband and I included them in this linguine dish we invented. The sauce is also excellent with spaghetti or fettuccine noodles. All of our children love it.
—*Tracy Haroldson, Aztec, New Mexico*

- 1/4 cup butter
- 3 tablespoons all-purpose flour
- 2 teaspoons garlic powder
- 1 teaspoon pepper
- 2-1/2 cups milk
- 1 package (8 ounces) cream cheese, cubed
- 1 cup (4 ounces) shredded Parmesan cheese
- 12 ounces uncooked linguine
- 3 cups cubed cooked chicken
- 1 can (4 ounces) diced green chilies

In a saucepan, melt butter. Stir in the flour, garlic powder and pepper until smooth; gradually add milk. Bring to a boil; cook and stir for 2 minutes or until thickened. Reduce heat; add cream cheese and Parmesan cheese. Cook and stir for 8-10 minutes or until cheese is melted.

Meanwhile, cook linguine according to package directions. Add chicken and chilies to cheese sauce; cook 5 minutes longer or until heated through. Drain linguine; top with chicken mixture. **Yield: 6 servings.**

Creamy Chicken and Rice

When my mom asked me to prepare a speedy supper to feed our family, I used leftover chicken to create this casserole. Cheese and sour cream make the chicken and rice so creamy and tasty.
—Jennifer Biggs Cassel, Mediapolis, Iowa

- 4 cups cooked rice
- 1/2 cup butter, *divided*
- 1/4 cup all-purpose flour
- 2 cups milk
- 2 teaspoons chicken bouillon granules
- 1/2 to 1 teaspoon seasoned salt
- 1/2 teaspoon garlic powder
- 1/4 teaspoon pepper
- 4 to 5 cups cubed cooked chicken
- 12 ounces process American cheese, cubed
- 2 cups (16 ounces) sour cream
- 1-1/4 cups crushed butter-flavored crackers (about 32)

Spread rice into a greased shallow 3-qt. or 13-in. x 9-in. x 2-in. baking dish; set aside. In a saucepan, melt 1/4 cup butter. Stir in flour until smooth; gradually add the milk, bouillon, seasoned salt, garlic powder and pepper. Bring to a boil; cook and stir for 2 minutes or until thickened. Reduce heat; add the chicken, cheese and sour cream; stir until cheese is melted.

Pour over rice. Melt the remaining butter; toss the cracker crumbs. Sprinkle over casserole. Bake, uncovered, at 425° for 10-15 minutes or until heated through. **Yield: 6-8 servings.**

Spicy Chicken Linguine

Creamy Chicken and Rice

Chicken Chili Lasagna

Savory Chicken Vegetable Strudel

Chicken Chili Lasagna

I adapted a chicken enchilada recipe and created this saucy lasagna. My husband and I enjoy the mild blend of seasonings, cheeses and tender chicken.
—Cindee Rolston, St. Marys, West Virginia

- 2 packages (3 ounces *each*) cream cheese, softened
- 1 medium onion, chopped
- 8 green onions, chopped
- 2 cups (8 ounces) shredded Mexican cheese blend, *divided*
- 2 garlic cloves, minced
- 3/4 teaspoon ground cumin, *divided*
- 1/2 teaspoon minced fresh cilantro
- 3 cups cubed cooked chicken
- 1/4 cup butter
- 1/4 cup all-purpose flour
- 1-1/2 cups chicken broth
- 1 cup (4 ounces) shredded Monterey Jack cheese
- 1 cup (8 ounces) sour cream
- 1 can (4 ounces) chopped green chilies, drained
- 1/8 teaspoon dried thyme
- 1/8 teaspoon salt
- 1/8 teaspoon pepper
- 12 flour tortillas (6 inches), halved

In a mixing bowl, combine the cream cheese, onions, 1-1/2 cups Mexican cheese, garlic, 1/4 teaspoon cumin and cilantro. Stir in chicken; set aside.

In a saucepan, melt butter. Stir in flour until smooth; gradually add broth. Bring to a boil; cook and stir for 2 minutes or until thickened. Remove from the heat. Stir in the Monterey Jack cheese, sour cream, chilies, thyme, salt, pepper and remaining cumin.

Spread 1/2 cup of the cheese sauce in a greased 13-in. x 9-in. x 2-in. baking dish. Top with six tortilla halves, a third of the chicken

Ham 'n' Swiss Chicken

mixture and a fourth of the cheese sauce. Repeat tortilla, chicken and cheese sauce layers twice. Top with remaining tortillas, cheese sauce and Mexican cheese.

Cover and bake at 350° for 30 minutes. Uncover; bake 10 minutes longer or until heated through. Let stand for 5 minutes before cutting. **Yield: 12 servings.**

Savory Chicken Vegetable Strudel

If you're looking for a way to sneak vegetables into a dish, try this one that looks fancy without the fuss. Now that our two sons are grown, I make it for just my husband and me. It definitely is a recipe for company, too. —Michele Barneson, Washburn, Wisconsin

- 2 cups diced cooked chicken
- 1/2 cup shredded carrots
- 1/2 cup finely chopped fresh broccoli
- 1/3 cup finely chopped sweet red pepper
- 1 cup (4 ounces) shredded sharp cheddar cheese
- 1/2 cup mayonnaise
- 2 garlic cloves, minced
- 1/2 teaspoon dill weed
- 1/4 teaspoon salt
- 1/4 teaspoon pepper
- 2 tubes (8 ounces *each*) refrigerated crescent rolls
- 1 egg white, beaten
- 2 tablespoons slivered almonds

In a bowl, combine the first 10 ingredients. Unroll crescent dough and place in a greased 15-in. x 10-in. x 1-in. baking pan; press seams and perforations together, forming a 15-in. x 12-in. rectangle (dough will hang over edges of pan).

Spread filling lengthwise down the center of the dough. On each long side, cut 1-1/2-in.-wide strips 3-1/2-in. into center. Starting at one end, alternate strips, twisting twice and laying at an angle across filling. Seal ends. Brush dough with egg white; sprinkle with almonds. Bake at 375° for 30-35 minutes or until golden brown. Cut into slices; serve warm. **Yield: 12 servings.**

Ham 'n' Swiss Chicken

This saucy casserole allows you to enjoy all the rich flavor of traditional chicken cordon bleu with less effort. —Dorothy Witmer, Ephrata, Pennsylvania

- 2 eggs
- 2 cups milk, *divided*
- 1/2 cup butter, melted
- 1/2 cup chopped celery
- 1 teaspoon finely chopped onion
- 8 slices bread, cubed
- 12 thin slices deli ham, rolled up
- 2 cups (8 ounces) shredded Swiss chicken
- 2-1/2 cups cubed cooked chicken
- 1 can (10-3/4 ounces) condensed cream of chicken soup, undiluted

In a large bowl, beat the eggs and 1-1/2 cups milk. Add the butter, celery and onion. Stir in bread cubes. Place half of the mixture in a greased 3-qt. slow cooker; top with half of the rolled-up ham, cheese and chicken. Combine soup and remaining milk; pour half over the chicken. Repeat layers once. Cover and cook on low for 4-5 hours or until a thermometer inserted into bread mixture reads 160°. **Yield: 6 servings.**

Orange-Glazed Cornish Hens

Orange-Glazed Cornish Hens 1st prize

This is a wonderfully elegant entree to serve at a cozy dinner party for four. Your guests will think you spent hours in the kitchen preparing the tender hens and perfecting the full-flavored basting sauce.
—Laurie Bartley, Lake Hiawatha, New Jersey

- 4 Cornish game hen (22 ounces *each*)
- 1/4 cup butter, melted
- 1 teaspoon salt
- 1/2 teaspoon pepper
- 3/4 cup orange juice
- 1/2 cup packed brown sugar
- 1/2 cup Madeira wine, sherry *or* chicken broth
- 2 tablespoons lemon juice
- 1 teaspoon ground mustard
- 1/4 teaspoon ground allspice

Tie legs of each hen together; turn wing tips under backs. Place on a greased rack in a roasting pan. Brush with butter; sprinkle with salt and pepper. Bake, uncovered, at 350° for 1 hour.

In a saucepan, combine the remaining ingredients; bring to a boil. Reduce heat; simmer, uncovered, for 15 minutes. Spoon over hens. Bake 15 minutes longer or until a meat thermometer reads 180°. **Yield: 4 servings.**

Herb-Roasted Turkey 1st prize

Our guests always comment on how moist and flavorful this elegant entree is. Rubbed with fresh herbs, this turkey has such a wonderful aroma when roasting that it lures everyone into the kitchen!
—Becky Goldsmith, Eden Prairie, Minnesota

- 1 turkey (14 pounds)
- 1 tablespoon salt
- 1 teaspoon pepper
- 18 sprigs fresh thyme, *divided*
- 4 medium onions, sliced
- 4 celery ribs, sliced
- 2 medium carrots, sliced
- 3 bay leaves
- 1 tablespoon peppercorns
- 1/2 cup butter, melted
- 1 teaspoon minced fresh sage *or* 1/2 teaspoon rubbed sage
- 1 teaspoon minced fresh thyme *or* 1/2 teaspoon dried thyme
- 1 teaspoon minced chives

Rub the surface of the turkey and sprinkle cavity with salt and pepper. Place 12 sprigs of thyme in cavity. In a large heavy roasting pan, place the onions, celery, carrots, bay leaves, peppercorns and remaining thyme sprigs. Place the turkey breast side up over vegetables. Drizzle butter over turkey and sprinkle with minced herbs.

Cover loosely with foil. Bake at 325° for 2-1/2 hours. Remove foil; bake 1-1/2 to 2 hours longer or until a meat thermometer reads 180°, basting every 20 minutes.

Cover and let stand for 20 minutes before carving. Discard bay leaves and peppercorns; thicken pan drippings for gravy if desired. **Yield: 12-14 servings.**

Stuffed Duckling

I really do enjoy experimenting in the kitchen. I started with a basic bread stuffing, then began adding different things from my cupboard. This is the result I came up with. The stuffing disappears long before the bird is gone.

—Joanne Callahan, Far Hills, New Jersey

- 1/2 cup chopped onion
- 1 garlic clove, minced
- 1 tablespoon butter
- 2 cups cubed day-old bread
- 1 cup cooked rice
- 1 teaspoon dried basil
- 1 teaspoon dried rosemary, crushed
- 1 teaspoon rubbed sage
- 1 teaspoon dried parsley flakes
- 1 teaspoon salt, *divided*
- 1/8 teaspoon pepper
- 1/2 cup raisins
- 1/2 cup chopped pecans
- 1/4 to 1/3 cup chicken broth
- 1 domestic duckling (4 to 5 pounds)

In a large skillet, saute onion and garlic in butter until tender; transfer to a large bowl. Add the bread cubes, rice, basil, rosemary, sage, parsley flakes, 1/2 teaspoon salt and pepper. Add the raisins, pecans and enough broth to moisten; toss gently.

Sprinkle duck cavity with remaining salt. Lightly stuff bread mixture into duck. Place breast side up on a rack in shallow roasting pan. Prick skin well with a fork.

Bake, uncovered, at 350° for 1-3/4 to 2 hours or until a meat thermometer reads 180° for duck and 165° for stuffing. Drain fat as it accumulates during roasting. Cover duck with foil and let stand for 20 minutes before removing stuffing and carving. **Yield: 4 servings.**

Herb-Roasted Turkey

Stuffed Duckling

Turkey with Cherry Stuffing

Turkey Lime Kabobs

Turkey with Cherry Stuffing

This moist stuffing, with its fruity blend of raisins and tart cherries, is a sweet twist on a traditional version. It's a tasty complement to tender poultry slices. —*Virginia Sacchetta, Leesburg, Florida*

- 3/4 cup chopped celery
- 1/3 cup chopped onion
- 2 tablespoons butter
- 3/4 teaspoon dried thyme
- 1/4 teaspoon poultry seasoning
- 5 cups seasoned stuffing cubes
- 3/4 cup golden raisins
- 3/4 cup chicken broth
- 1 can (14-1/2 ounces) pitted tart cherries, drained
- 1 turkey (10 to 12 pounds)
- 2 tablespoons vegetable oil

In a saucepan, saute celery and onion in butter until tender. Stir in thyme and poultry seasoning. In a large bowl, combine the stuffing, raisins and celery mixture. Add broth and cherries; toss to mix.

Loosely stuff turkey just before baking. Skewer openings; tie drumsticks together. Place the turkey breast side up on a rack in a roasting pan. Brush with oil.

Bake, uncovered, at 325° for 4 to 4-1/2 hours or until a meat thermometer reads 180° for the turkey and 165° for the stuffing. Baste occasionally with pan drippings. Cover loosely with foil if turkey browns too quickly. Cover and let stand for 20 minutes before removing the stuffing and carving the turkey. If desired, thicken pan drippings for gravy. **Yield: 10-12 servings (6 cups stuffing).**

Editor's Note: The stuffing may be prepared as directed and baked separately in a greased 2-qt. baking dish. Cover and bake at 325° for 50-60 minutes. Uncover; bake 10 minutes longer or until lightly browned.

Turkey Scallopini

Turkey Lime Kabobs

My husband loves to grill these deliciously different turkey kabobs. The tongue-tingling combination of flavors makes this one dish that always draws compliments.—Shelly Johnston, Rochester, Minnesota

- 3 cans (6 ounces *each*) orange juice concentrate, thawed
- 1-1/4 cups lime juice
- 1 cup honey
- 4 to 5 jalapeno peppers, seeded and chopped
- 10 garlic cloves, minced
- 3 tablespoons ground cumin
- 2 tablespoons grated lime peel
- 1 teaspoon salt
- 2 pounds boneless turkey, chicken *or* pork, cut into 1-1/4-inch cubes
- 4 medium sweet red *or* green peppers, cut into 1-inch pieces
- 1 large red onion, cut into 1-inch pieces
- 3 small zucchini, cut into 3/4-inch slices
- 8 ounces fresh mushrooms
- 3 medium limes, cut into wedges

In a bowl, combine the first eight ingredients. Pour half of marinade into a large resealable plastic bag; add meat and turn to coat. Pour remaining marinade into another large resealable plastic bag. Add vegetables and turn to coat. Seal and refrigerate for 8 hours or overnight, turning occasionally.

Drain meat, discarding marinade. Drain vegetables, reserving marinade for basting. On metal or soaked wooden skewers, alternate meat, vegetables and lime wedges. Grill, uncovered, over medium heat for 4-5 minutes on each side. Baste with reserved marinade. Continue turning and basting for 10-12 minutes or until meat juices run clear and vegetables are tender. **Yield: 8 servings.**

Editor's Note: When cutting or seeding hot peppers, use rubber or plastic gloves to protect your hands. Avoid touching your face.

Turkey Scallopini

Quick-cooking turkey breast slices make it easy to prepare a satisfying meal in minutes.
—Karen Adams, Seymour, Indiana

- 6 turkey breast slices (about 1-1/2 pounds)
- 1/4 cup all-purpose flour
- 1/8 teaspoon salt
- 1/8 teaspoon pepper
- 1 egg
- 2 tablespoons water
- 1 cup soft bread crumbs
- 1/2 cup grated Parmesan cheese
- 1/4 cup butter

Minced fresh parsley

Pound turkey to 1/4-in. thickness. In a shallow bowl, combine the flour, salt and pepper. In another bowl, beat egg and water. On a plate, combine the bread crumbs and Parmesan cheese. Dredge turkey in flour mixture, then dip in egg mixture and coat with crumbs. Let stand for 5 minutes.

Melt butter in a skillet over medium-high heat; cook turkey for 2-3 minutes on each side or until meat juices run clear and coating is golden brown. Sprinkle with parsley. **Yield: 6 servings.**

Turkey Ravioli Lasagna

Turkey Ravioli Lasagna

I came up with this short-cut lasagna one day when the dinner hour was fast approaching and all I had in the freezer was some frozen ravioli. Now I make it often, and my husband and son devour it.

—Anne Plesmid, Sagamore Hills, Ohio

- 1 pound ground turkey
- 1/2 teaspoon garlic powder
- Salt and pepper to taste
- 1 cup grated carrots
- 1 cup sliced fresh mushrooms
- 1 tablespoon olive oil
- 1 jar (28 ounces) spaghetti sauce
- 1 package (25 ounces) frozen cheese ravioli, cooked and drained
- 3 cups (12 ounces) shredded part-skim mozzarella cheese
- 1/2 cup grated Parmesan cheese
- Minced fresh parsley, optional

In a skillet, cook turkey over medium heat until no longer pink; drain. Sprinkle with garlic powder, salt and pepper; set aside.

In a saucepan, cook the carrots and mushrooms in oil until tender. Stir in the spaghetti sauce. Spread 1/2 cup sauce in a greased 13-in. x 9-in. x 2-in. baking dish. Layer with half of the ravioli, spaghetti sauce mixture, turkey and cheeses. Repeat layers. Sprinkle with parsley if desired.

Cover and bake at 375° for 25-30 minutes or until bubbly. Uncover; bake 10 minutes longer. Let stand for 15 minutes before serving. **Yield: 12 servings.**

Garden Turkey Burgers 1st prize

These moist burgers get plenty of color and flavor from onion, zucchini and red pepper. I often make the mixture ahead of time and put it in the refrigerator. Later, after helping my husband with yard work, I can put the burgers on the grill while whipping up a salad or side dish.

—Sandy Kitzmiller, Unityville, Pennsylvania

- 1 cup old-fashioned oats
- 3/4 cup chopped onion
- 3/4 cup finely chopped sweet red *or* green pepper
- 1/2 cup shredded zucchini
- 1/4 cup ketchup
- 2 garlic cloves, minced
- 1/4 teaspoon salt
- 1 pound ground turkey
- 6 whole wheat hamburger buns, split and toasted

Coat grill rack with nonstick cooking spray before starting the grill. In a bowl, combine the first seven ingredients. Crumble turkey over mixture and mix well. Shape into six 1/2-in.-thick patties.

Grill, covered, over indirect medium heat for 6 minutes on each side or until a meat thermometer reads 165°. Serve on buns. **Yield: 6 servings.**

Turkey Dressing Pie

People tell me this pie is almost better than the original dinner! I fix turkey all year long, and I purposely make too much just so we can have this later on. It's a complete meal in itself.
—De De Boekelheide, Northville, South Dakota

- 3-1/2 to 4 cups leftover cooked turkey dressing
- 1/2 cup turkey *or* chicken broth
- 2 tablespoons butter, melted
- 1 egg, beaten
- 1/2 cup chopped onion
- 1 tablespoon vegetable oil
- 3 cups diced leftover cooked turkey
- 1 cup leftover turkey gravy
- 1 cup peas, optional
- 2 tablespoons dried parsley flakes
- 2 tablespoons diced pimientos
- 1 teaspoon Worcestershire sauce
- 1/2 teaspoon dried thyme
- 4 slices process American cheese, optional

In a large bowl, combine the dressing, broth, butter and egg. Press into the bottom and up the sides of an ungreased 10-in. pie plate; set aside.

In a large skillet, saute onion in oil until tender. Stir in the turkey, gravy, peas if desired, parsley, pimientos, Worcestershire sauce and thyme; heat through. Pour over crust.

Bake at 375° for 20 minutes or until golden. If desired, arrange cheese slices on top of pie and bake 5 minutes longer or until cheese is melted. **Yield: 6 servings.**

Garden Turkey Burgers

Turkey Dressing Pie

Turkey Potpie

Turkey Potpie

My family raves over this comforting dish with its flaky homemade crust and saucy meat and veggie filling. Sometimes, I cook a bird specifically with this potpie in mind—when we just can't wait for leftovers to make it!
—Marie Elaine Basinger, Connellsville, Pennsylvania

- 1 medium onion, chopped
- 1/3 cup butter
- 1/2 cup all-purpose flour
- 1 teaspoon salt
- 1/4 teaspoon pepper
- 1-3/4 cups chicken broth
- 2/3 cup milk
- 2 cups cubed cooked turkey
- 1 cup (4 ounces) shredded cheddar cheese
- 1 package (10 ounces) frozen peas and carrots, thawed

Pastry:

- 2 cups all-purpose flour
- 2 teaspoons celery seed
- 1 teaspoon salt
- 2/3 cup plus 2 tablespoons shortening
- 4 to 5 tablespoons cold water

Milk, optional

In a saucepan, saute onion in butter. Stir in the flour, salt and pepper until blended; gradually add broth and milk. Bring to a boil; cook and stir for 2 minutes or until thickened. Add the turkey, cheese and vegetables; cook until the cheese is melted. Set aside and keep warm.

For the crust, combine the flour, celery seed and salt in a bowl. Cut in shortening until mixture resembles coarse crumbs. Gradually add water, tossing with a fork until dough forms a ball.

Divide dough in half. Line a 9-in. pie plate with bottom pastry; trim even with edge of plate. Pour hot turkey filling into crust. Roll out remaining pastry to fit top of pie; place over the filling. Trim, seal and flute edges. Cut slits in pastry. Brush tops with milk if desired. Bake at 375° for 40-45 minutes or until crust is golden brown. **Yield: 6 servings.**

SEAFOOD

ROCCOLI FISH BUNDLES, pg. 251

Seafood

Gingered Honey Salmon

Ginger, garlic powder and green onion blend nicely in an easy marinade that gives a pleasant flavor to salmon. We also like to use this versatile mixture when grilling chicken.
—Dan Strumberger, Farmington, Minnesota

- **1/3 cup orange juice**
- **1/3 cup soy sauce**
- **1/4 cup honey**
- **1 green onion, chopped**
- **1 teaspoon ground ginger**
- **1 teaspoon garlic powder**
- **1 salmon fillet (1-1/2 pounds and 3/4 inch thick)**

In a bowl, combine the first six ingredients. Set aside 1/3 cup for basting; cover and refrigerate. Pour remaining marinade into a large resealable plastic bag; add salmon. Seal bag and turn to coat; refrigerate for 30 minutes, turning once or twice.

Coat grill rack with nonstick cooking spray before starting the grill. Drain and discard the marinade from the salmon. Place the salmon skin side down on grill. Grill, covered, over medium-hot heat for 5 minutes. Baste with reserved marinade. Grill 10-15 minutes longer or until fish flakes easily with a fork, basting frequently. **Yield: 4-6 servings.**

Gingered Honey Salmon

Caesar Salmon Fillets

Not only is this my husband's favorite meal, but it's a dish dinner guests enjoy as well. The delicate flavor is a wonderful reminder that it is as tasty as it is healthy.
—Joan Garneau, Ellenton, Florida

- **4 salmon fillets (6 ounces *each*)**
- **1/2 cup fat-free Caesar salad dressing**
- **1/4 cup reduced-sodium soy sauce**
- **1 garlic clove, minced**

Place salmon fillets in a large resealable plastic bag; add the salad dressing. Seal bag and turn to coat; refrigerate for at least 2 hours.

Coat grill rack with nonstick cooking spray before starting the grill. Drain and discard the marinade from the salmon. Place salmon skin side down on grill rack. Grill, covered, over medium heat for 5 minutes.

In a small bowl, combine soy sauce and garlic; brush over salmon. Grill 10-15 minutes longer or until fish flakes easily with a fork, basting occasionally. **Yield: 4 servings.**

Caesar Salmon Fillets

Marinated Catfish Fillets

Trout Baked in Cream

Marinated Catfish Fillets

When we hosted a group of people from Canada, we wanted to give them a taste of Southern cooking. They loved this recipe.
—Pauletta Boese, Macon, Mississippi

- 1 bottle (16 ounces) Italian salad dressing
- 6 catfish fillets (about 8 ounces *each*)
- 1 can (10-3/4 ounces) condensed tomato soup, undiluted
- 3/4 cup vegetable oil
- 3/4 cup sugar
- 1/3 cup cider vinegar
- 3/4 teaspoon celery seed
- 3/4 teaspoon salt
- 3/4 teaspoon pepper
- 3/4 teaspoon ground mustard
- 1/2 teaspoon garlic powder

Place salad dressing in a large resealable plastic bag; add fish. Seal bag and turn to coat; refrigerate for 1 hour, turning occasionally.

Combine remaining ingredients. Remove 1 cup for basting. (Refrigerate remaining sauce for another use.)

Drain and discard marinade from fish. Grill fillets, covered, over medium-hot heat for 3 minutes on each side. Brush with the basting sauce. Grill 6-8 minutes longer or until fish flakes easily with a fork, turning once and basting several times. **Yield: 6 servings.**

Trout Baked in Cream

Here's a quick and delicious way to serve trout. It's definitely one of our family's favorites.
—Ann Nace, Perkasie, Pennsylvania

- 6 trout fillets (about 3-1/2 ounces *each*)
- 2 tablespoons lemon juice
- 1 teaspoon dill weed

Broccoli Fish Bundles

1/2 teaspoon salt
1/8 teaspoon pepper
1 cup heavy whipping cream
2 tablespoons seasoned bread crumbs

Place trout in a greased 13-in. x 9-in. x 2-in. baking dish. Sprinkle with the lemon juice, dill, salt and pepper. Pour cream over all. Sprinkle with bread crumbs. Bake, uncovered, at 350° for 11-15 minutes or until fish flakes easily with a fork. **Yield: 4-6 servings.**

Broccoli Fish Bundles

These bundles take a little time to assemble, but they're worth it! They're always popular at a shower or buffet, and they're great for an everyday dinner, too. This flavorful dish goes nicely with rice pilaf or a saucy pasta.

—Frances Quinn, Farmingdale, New York

18 fresh broccoli spears (about 1-1/2 pounds)
6 Monterey Jack cheese cubes
6 sole *or* flounder fillets (about 2 pounds)
1/8 teaspoon lemon-pepper seasoning, optional
1/3 cup butter, melted
2 teaspoons lemon juice
1 garlic clove, minced
1/4 teaspoon salt
1/8 teaspoon pepper

Place 1 in. water in a saucepan; add broccoli. Bring to a boil. Reduce heat; cover and simmer for 2-3 minutes or until crisp-tender. Rinse in cold water; drain.

For each bundle, place a cheese cube on three spears. Wrap with a fish fillet and fasten with a toothpick if necessary. Place on a greased foil-lined baking sheet. Sprinkle with lemon-pepper if desired. Bake, uncovered, at 350° for 15-25 minutes or until fish flakes easily with a fork.

Meanwhile, combine the butter, lemon juice, garlic, salt and pepper. Transfer fish bundles to a serving platter; remove toothpicks. Drizzle with butter mixture. **Yield: 6 servings.**

Honey Walleye

Our state is known as the "Land of 10,000 Lakes," so fishing is a favorite recreation here. This recipe is a quick way to prepare all the fresh walleye that's hooked by the anglers in our family.
—Kitty McCue, St. Louis Park, Minnesota

- 1 egg
- 2 teaspoons honey
- 2 cups crushed butter-flavored crackers (about 45 to 50)
- 1/2 teaspoon salt
- 4 to 6 walleye fillets (1-1/2 to 2 pounds)
- 1/3 to 1/2 cup vegetable oil
- Lemon wedges, optional

In a shallow bowl, beat egg; add honey. In a plastic bag, combine crackers and salt. Dip fish in egg mixture, then place in bag and shake to coat.

In a skillet, cook fillets in oil for 3-5 minutes per side or until golden and fish flakes easily with a fork. Serve with lemon wedges if desired. **Yield: 4-6 servings.**

Saucy Skillet Fish

The main industry here on Kodiak Island is fishing, so I'm always on the lookout for new seafood recipes. This is my favorite way to fix halibut since it's quick and tasty. I often get recipe requests when I serve this to guests. *—Merle Powell, Kodiak, Alaska*

- 1/2 cup all-purpose flour
- 1-1/4 teaspoons salt
- 1 teaspoon paprika
- 1/8 teaspoon pepper
- 2 pounds halibut, haddock *or* salmon fillets *or* steaks
- 1 medium onion, sliced
- 1/3 cup butter
- 1-1/2 cups (12 ounces) sour cream

Honey Walleye

- 1 teaspoon dried basil
- 1 tablespoon minced fresh parsley

In a large resealable plastic bag, combine the flour, salt, paprika and pepper. Add fish and shake to coat (if using fillets, cut into serving-size pieces first).

In a skillet, saute onion in butter until tender; remove and set aside. Add fish to the skillet, cook over medium heat for 3-5 minutes on each side or until the fish flakes easily with a fork. Remove fish to a serving plate and keep warm.

Add the sour cream, basil and onion to the skillet; heat through (do not boil). Serve over fish. Garnish with parsley. **Yield: 6-8 servings.**

Lemon-Batter Fish

My husband ranks this recipe as one of his favorites. A lot of fishing takes place in our area, which makes this a good choice for a regional recipe.
—Jackie Hannahs, Muskegon, Michigan

- 1-1/2 cups all-purpose flour, *divided*
- 1 teaspoon baking powder
- 3/4 teaspoon salt
- 1/2 teaspoon sugar
- 1 egg, beaten
- 2/3 cup water

2/3 cup lemon juice, *divided*
2 pounds perch fillets *or* walleye fillets, cut into bite-size pieces

Oil for frying

Lemon wedges, optional

In a shallow bowl, combine 1 cup flour, baking powder, salt and sugar; set aside. Combine the egg, water and 1/3 cup lemon juice; stir into dry ingredients until smooth.

In separate shallow bowls, place remaining lemon juice and remaining flour. Dip fillets in lemon juice, then flour and coat with the batter.

Heat 1 in. of oil in a skillet. Fry fish, a few at a time, over medium-high heat for 2-3 minutes on each side or until the fish flakes easily with a fork. Drain on paper towels. Garnish with lemon if desired. **Yield: 5 servings.**

Saucy Skillet Fish

Lemon-Batter Fish

Mushroom Shrimp Creole

Shrimp Monterey

Mushroom Shrimp Creole

We especially enjoy this hearty main dish on chilly or stormy days. The tomatoes, mushrooms, onions, green peppers and shrimp are nicely spiced with seasonings.
—Shirlee Vader, Hensley, Arizona

- 6 bacon strips, diced
- 2 large onions, chopped
- 1-1/2 cups chopped green peppers
- 1 garlic clove, minced
- 1 can (29 ounces) diced tomatoes, undrained
- 1 can (6 ounces) tomato paste
- 4-1/2 teaspoons brown sugar
- 1 tablespoon Worcestershire sauce
- 1 teaspoon salt
- 1/2 teaspoon pepper
- 1/2 teaspoon dried basil
- 1 bay leaf
- 1-1/2 pounds cooked medium shrimp, peeled and deveined
- 1 jar (4-1/2 ounces) whole mushrooms, drained
- 2 tablespoons butter
- 1 tablespoon lemon juice
- 1/4 teaspoon dried savory
- Hot cooked rice

In a large skillet, cook bacon over medium heat until crisp. Using a slotted spoon, remove to paper towels to drain, reserving drippings.

In the drippings, saute the onions, green peppers and garlic. Add the tomatoes, tomato paste, brown sugar, Worcestershire sauce, salt, pepper, basil and bay leaf. Bring to a boil. Reduce heat; cover and simmer for 30-45 minutes.

Add the shrimp, mushrooms, butter, lemon juice and savory. Cook 5-10 minutes longer or until heated through. Discard bay leaf. Stir in bacon. Serve over rice. **Yield: 6-8 servings.**

Shrimp Monterey

For a special occasion or when company's coming, this delicious seafood dish makes a lasting impression. You'll be surprised at how fast you can prepare it. A mild, fresh-tasting sauce and the Monterey Jack cheese nicely complement the shrimp. I serve it over pasta or rice. —*Jane Birch, Edison, New Jersey*

- 2 garlic cloves, minced
- 2 tablespoons butter
- 2 pounds uncooked medium shrimp, peeled and deveined
- 1/2 cup white wine *or* chicken broth
- 2 cups (8 ounces) shredded Monterey Jack cheese
- 2 tablespoons minced fresh parsley

In a skillet over medium heat, saute garlic in butter for 1 minute. Add shrimp; cook for 4-5 minutes or until shrimp turn pink.

Using a slotted spoon, transfer shrimp to a greased 11-in. x 7-in. x 2-in. baking dish; set aside and keep warm. Add wine or broth to the skillet; bring to a boil. Cook and stir for 5 minutes or until sauce is reduced. Pour over shrimp; top with cheese and parsley. Bake, uncovered, at 350° for 10 minutes or until cheese is melted. **Yield: 6 servings.**

Broccoli Shrimp Alfredo 1st prize

After tasting fettuccine Alfredo at a restaurant, I tried to duplicate the recipe at home. You can't imagine how pleased I was when I came up with this delicious version. Not only does my family love the creamy dish, but my husband prefers it to the one at the restaurant. —*Rae Natoli, Kingston, New York*

- 1 package (16 ounces) fettuccine
- 1 pound uncooked medium shrimp, peeled and deveined
- 3 garlic cloves, minced
- 1/2 cup butter

Broccoli Shrimp Alfredo

- 1 package (8 ounces) cream cheese, cubed
- 1 cup milk
- 1/2 cup shredded Parmesan cheese
- 1 package (10 ounces) frozen broccoli florets
- 1/2 teaspoon salt
- Dash pepper

Cook fettuccine according to package directions. Meanwhile, in a large skillet, saute shrimp and garlic in butter until shrimp turn pink. Remove and keep warm. In the same skillet, combine the cream cheese, milk and Parmesan cheese; cook until cheeses are melted and smooth.

Place 1 in. of water in a saucepan; add broccoli. Bring to a boil. Reduce heat; cover and simmer for 6-8 minutes or until tender. Drain. Stir the broccoli, shrimp, salt and pepper into cheese sauce; heat through. Drain fettuccine; top with shrimp mixture. **Yield: 4 servings.**

Pasta Crab Casserole

When company is coming, I reach for this recipe. It can also be made ahead and frozen. A yummy combination of spiral pasta, crab and sauteed veggies is coated with a buttery sauce, then covered with cheddar cheese. All that's needed to complete the meal is warm garlic bread and a tossed green salad.
—Georgia Mountain, Tampa, Florida

- **8 ounces uncooked spiral pasta**
- **2 large onions, chopped**
- **1/2 pound fresh mushrooms, sliced**
- **1/2 cup chopped green pepper**
- **2 garlic cloves, minced**
- **1/2 cup butter**
- **2 packages (8 ounces *each*) imitation crabmeat, chopped**
- **1/2 cup sour cream**
- **2 teaspoons salt**
- **1-1/2 teaspoons dried basil**
- **1-1/2 cups (6 ounces) shredded cheddar cheese**

Cook pasta according to package directions. Meanwhile, in a skillet, saute the onions, mushrooms, green pepper and garlic in butter until crisp-tender. Remove from the heat. Drain pasta; add to vegetable mixture. Stir in the crab, sour cream, salt and basil.

Transfer to two greased 8-in. square baking dishes. Sprinkle with cheese. Cover and freeze one casserole for up to 1 month. Cover and bake the second casserole at 350° for 20 minutes. Uncover; bake 5 minutes longer.

To use frozen casserole: Thaw in the refrigerator for 24 hours. Remove from the refrigerator 30 minutes before baking. Cover and bake at 350° for 55-60 minutes or until heated through. **Yield: 2 casseroles (4-6 servings each).**

Pasta Crab Casserole

Maryland Crab Cakes

I've lived in Maryland for more than 50 years, so I know firsthand how much folks around here love crab cakes. I experimented with a number of recipes and came up with this one. My family really likes it.
—Catherine Tocha, Silver Spring, Maryland

- **1 egg**
- **1/4 cup milk**
- **3 tablespoons mayonnaise**
- **1 tablespoon all-purpose flour**
- **1 tablespoon Worcestershire sauce**
- **1 teaspoon prepared mustard**
- **1 teaspoon salt**
- **1/4 teaspoon pepper**
- **1 pound cooked crabmeat *or* 3 cans (6 ounces *each*) crabmeat, drained, flaked and cartilage removed**
- **1/2 cup dry bread crumbs**
- **2 tablespoons butter**

In a large bowl, whisk together the first eight ingredients. Fold in crab. Place the bread crumbs in a shallow dish. Drop 1/3 cupful crab mixture into crumbs; shape into a 3/4-in.-thick patty. Carefully turn to coat. Repeat with remaining crab mixture.

In a skillet, cook patties in butter for 3 minutes on each side or until golden brown. **Yield: 6 patties.**

New Haven Clam Pizza

This appetizer is the perfect start to any meal. It's always a big hit with our family and friends.
—Susan Seymour, Valatie, New York

- 1 package (1/4 ounce) active dry yeast
- 1 cup warm water (110° to 115°)
- 1 teaspoon sugar
- 2-1/2 cups all-purpose flour
- 1 teaspoon salt
- 2 tablespoons vegetable oil
- 2 cans (6-1/2 ounces *each*) chopped clams, drained
- 4 bacon strips, cooked and crumbled
- 3 garlic cloves, minced
- 2 tablespoons grated Parmesan cheese
- 1 teaspoon dried oregano
- 1 cup (4 ounces) shredded part-skim mozzarella cheese

In a mixing bowl, dissolve yeast in warm water. Add sugar; let stand for 5 minutes. Add the flour, salt and oil; beat until smooth. Cover and let rise in a warm place until doubled, about 15-20 minutes.

Punch dough down. Press onto the bottom and up the sides of a greased 14-in. pizza pan; build up edges slightly. Prick dough several times with a fork.

Bake at 425° for 6-8 minutes. Sprinkle remaining ingredients over crust in order listed. Bake 13-15 minutes longer or until crust is golden and cheese is melted. Cut into wedges. **Yield: 8 servings.**

Maryland Crab Cakes

New Haven Clam Pizza

Seafood Lasagna

Seafood Lasagna 1st prize

This comforting dish, is loaded with scallops, shrimp and crab. The creamy sauce helps make it the crown jewel in my repertoire of recipes.
—Elena Hansen, Ruidoso, New Mexico

- **1 green onion, finely chopped**
- **2 tablespoons vegetable oil**
- **2 tablespoons butter plus 1/2 cup butter, *divided***
- **1/2 cup chicken broth**
- **1 bottle (8 ounces) clam juice**
- **1 pound bay scallops**
- **1 pound uncooked small shrimp, peeled and deveined**
- **1 package (8 ounces) imitation crabmeat, chopped**
- **1/4 teaspoon white pepper, *divided***
- **1/2 cup all-purpose flour**
- **1-1/2 cups milk**
- **1/2 teaspoon salt**
- **1 cup heavy whipping cream**
- **1/2 cup shredded Parmesan cheese, *divided***
- **9 lasagna noodles, cooked and drained**

In a large skillet, saute onion in oil and 2 tablespoons butter until tender. Stir in broth and clam juice; bring to a boil. Add the scallops, shrimp, crab and 1/8 teaspoon pepper; return to a boil. Reduce heat; simmer, uncovered, for 4-5 minutes or until shrimp turn pink and scallops are firm and opaque, stirring gently. Drain, reserving cooking liquid; set seafood mixture aside.

In a saucepan, melt the remaining butter; stir in flour until smooth. Combine milk and reserved cooking liquid; gradually add to the saucepan. Add salt and remaining pepper. Bring to a boil; cook and stir for 2 minutes or until thickened. Remove from the heat; stir in cream and 1/4 cup Parmesan cheese. Stir 3/4 cup white sauce into the seafood mixture.

Spread 1/2 cup white sauce in a greased 13-in. x 9-in. x 2-in. baking dish. Top with three noodles; spread with half of the seafood mixture and 1-1/4 cups sauce. Repeat layers. Top with remaining noodles, sauce and Parmesan.

Bake, uncovered, at 350° for 35-40 minutes or until golden brown. Let stand for 15 minutes before cutting. **Yield: 12 servings.**

MEATLESS

ERY VEGGIE LASAGNA, pg. 264

Meatless

Roasted Veggie Pizza

A bold, flavorful garlic and basil pesto sauce is an awesome change of pace from traditional tomato-based pizza sauce. Roasted vegetables are a fantastic topping. Whenever I serve it alongside a standard meat pizza, this one's always the first to go!
—Cindy Elsbernd, Des Moines, Iowa

- **8 to 10 medium fresh mushrooms, sliced**
- **1 small onion, sliced**
- **1/2 cup sliced green pepper**
- **1/2 cup sliced sweet red pepper**
- **2 teaspoons olive oil**
- **2 garlic cloves, minced**
- **1/4 teaspoon *each* oregano, thyme and dried rosemary, crushed**

PESTO SAUCE:

- **1/2 cup coarsely chopped fresh basil**
- **1/4 cup olive oil**
- **1/4 cup grated Parmesan cheese**
- **4 garlic cloves, minced**
- **1 prebaked Italian bread shell crust (1 pound)**
- **1 large tomato, thinly sliced**
- **2 cups (8 ounces) shredded part-skim mozzarella cheese**

Place the mushrooms, onion and peppers in a roasting pan or baking pan lined with heavy-duty foil. Combine the oil, garlic, oregano, thyme and rosemary; drizzle over vegetables and toss to coat. Cover and bake at 400° for 20 minutes.

Roasted Veggie Pizza

Meanwhile, for sauce, combine the basil, oil, Parmesan cheese and garlic in a food processor or blender; cover and process until smooth, scraping sides often. Set aside.

Place the crust on an ungreased 12-in. pizza pan. Spread with sauce; top with the tomato slices. Sprinkle with mozzarella cheese. Top with roasted vegetables. Bake for 15 minutes or until cheese is melted and bubbly. **Yield: 8 slices.**

Four-Cheese Spinach Lasagna

Southwestern Veggie Bake

Four-Cheese Spinach Lasagna

This rich cheesy lasagna has become one of my specialties. It's packed with fresh-tasting vegetables like spinach, carrots, red pepper and broccoli.
—Kimberly Kneisly, Englewood, Ohio

- 2 cups chopped fresh broccoli
- 1-1/2 cups julienned carrots
- 1 cup sliced green onions
- 1/2 cup chopped sweet red pepper
- 3 garlic cloves, minced
- 2 teaspoons vegetable oil
- 1/2 cup all-purpose flour
- 3 cups milk
- 1/2 cup grated Parmesan cheese, *divided*
- 1/2 teaspoon salt
- 1/4 teaspoon pepper
- 1 package (10 ounces) frozen chopped spinach, thawed and squeezed dry
- 1-1/2 cups small-curd cottage cheese
- 1 cup (4 ounces) shredded part-skim mozzarella cheese
- 1/2 cup shredded Swiss cheese
- 12 lasagna noodles, cooked and drained

In a large skillet, saute the vegetables and garlic in oil until crisp-tender. Set aside.

In a heavy saucepan, whisk flour and milk until smooth. Bring to a boil; cook and stir for 2 minutes or until thickened. Reduce heat; stir in 1/4 cup Parmesan cheese, salt and pepper. Cook 1 minute longer or until cheese is melted. Remove from the heat; stir in spinach. Set 1 cup aside.

In a bowl, combine the cottage cheese, mozzarella and Swiss. Spread 1/2 cup spinach mixture in a greased 13-in. x 9-in. x 2-in. baking dish. Layer with four noodles, half of the cheese mixture and vegetables and 3/4 cup spinach mixture. Repeat layers. Top with remaining noodles, reserved spinach mixture and remaining Parmesan cheese.

Cover and bake at 375° for 35 minutes. Uncover; bake 15 minutes longer or until bubbly. Let stand for 15 minutes before cutting. **Yield: 12 servings.**

Southwestern Veggie Bake

Refrigerated corn bread twists create an appealing lattice top on this zippy main dish. I use beans and celery instead of the chicken the original version called for. *—Julie Zeager, Kent, Ohio*

- 3 medium carrots, sliced
- 2 celery ribs, chopped
- 1 small onion, chopped
- 2 to 3 teaspoons chili powder
- 1 teaspoon ground cumin
- 1/4 teaspoon cayenne pepper
- 2 tablespoons butter
- 3 tablespoons all-purpose flour
- 1/2 cup milk
- 1 can (16 ounces) kidney beans, rinsed and drained
- 1 can (15 ounces) black beans, rinsed and drained
- 1 can (15-1/4 ounces) whole kernel corn, drained
- 1 can (14-1/2 ounces) diced tomatoes, undrained
- 1 can (4 ounces) chopped green chilies
- 1 tube (11-1/2 ounces) refrigerated corn bread twists

In a large skillet, saute the carrots, celery, onion and seasonings in butter until vegetables are crisp-tender. Stir in flour until blended; gradually add the milk. Bring to a boil; cook and stir for 2 minutes or until thickened and bubbly.

Remove from the heat; add the beans, corn, tomatoes and chilies. Spoon into an ungreased 13-in. x 9-in. x 2-in. baking dish. Separate corn bread twists; weave a lattice crust over filling. Bake, uncovered, at 350° for 20-25 minutes or until corn bread is done. **Yield: 8 servings.**

Spinach Swiss Pie

Spinach Swiss Pie

This egg dish has a wonderful flavor from the nutmeg, which combines well with the Swiss cheese. *—Phoebe Martin, Hampstead, Maryland*

- 1 package (10 ounces) frozen chopped spinach
- 1 cup (4 ounces) shredded Swiss cheese
- 2 tablespoons chopped onion
- 1-1/2 cups milk
- 3 eggs
- 3/4 cup biscuit/baking mix
- 1 teaspoon salt
- 1/4 teaspoon pepper
- 1/4 teaspoon ground nutmeg

Cook spinach according to package directions; drain well. In a bowl, combine the cheese, onion and spinach. Transfer to a greased 9-in. pie plate.

In a blender, combine the milk, eggs, biscuit mix, salt, pepper and nutmeg; cover and process until smooth. Pour over spinach mixture.

Bake at 350° for 45-50 minutes or until a knife inserted near the center comes out clean. Let stand for 5 minutes before cutting. **Yield: 6-8 servings.**

Vegetarian Cabbage Rolls

This meatless entree comes from my grandmother, who cooks a lot with grains, particularly bulgur.
—Michelle Dougherty, Lewiston, Idaho

- 1-1/2 cups chopped fresh mushrooms
- 1 cup diced zucchini
- 3/4 cup chopped green pepper
- 3/4 cup chopped sweet red pepper
- 3/4 cup vegetable broth
- 1/2 cup bulgur
- 1 teaspoon dried basil
- 1/2 teaspoon dried marjoram
- 1/2 teaspoon dried thyme
- 1/4 teaspoon pepper
- 1 large head cabbage
- 6 tablespoons shredded Parmesan cheese, *divided*
- 2 teaspoons lemon juice
- 1 can (8 ounces) tomato sauce
- 1/8 teaspoon hot pepper sauce

In a large saucepan, combine the first 10 ingredients. Bring to a boil over medium heat. Reduce heat; cover and simmer for 5 minutes. Remove from the heat; let stand for 5 minutes.

Cook cabbage in boiling water just until leaves fall off head. Set aside eight large leaves for rolls (refrigerate remaining cabbage for another use). Cut out the thick vein from each leaf, making a V-shape cut. Overlap cut ends before filling. Stir 4 tablespoons cheese and lemon juice into vegetable mixture.

Place a heaping 1/3 cupful on each cabbage leaf; fold in sides. Roll up to enclose filling.

Combine tomato sauce and pepper sauce; pour 1/3 cup into a 2-qt. baking dish. Add cabbage rolls, then top with remaining sauce. Cover and bake at 400° for 15 minutes or until heated through. Sprinkle with remaining cheese. **Yield: 4 servings.**

Editor's Note: Look for bulgur in the cereal, rice or organic food aisle of your grocery store.

Vegetarian Cabbage Rolls

Very Veggie Lasagna

I concocted this quick and easy recipe to use up some of the abundant fresh produce from my garden. When I made a batch to share at a church potluck, I received lots of compliments.
—Bernice Baldwin, Glennie, Michigan

- 2 medium carrots, julienned
- 1 medium zucchini, cut into 1/4-inch slices
- 1 yellow summer squash, cut into 1/4-inch slices
- 1 medium onion, sliced
- 1 cup fresh broccoli florets
- 1/2 cup sliced celery
- 1/2 cup julienned sweet red pepper
- 1/2 cup julienned green pepper
- 2 garlic cloves, minced
- 1/2 to 1 teaspoon salt
- 2 tablespoons vegetable oil
- 1 jar (28 ounces) spaghetti sauce
- 14 lasagna noodles, cooked and drained
- 4 cups (16 ounces) shredded part-skim mozzarella cheese

In a large skillet, stir-fry the vegetables, garlic and salt in oil until crisp-tender. Spread 3/4 cup spaghetti sauce in the greased 13-in. x

9-in. x 2-in. baking dish. Arrange seven noodles over sauce, overlapping as needed. Layer with half of the vegetables, spaghetti sauce and cheese. Repeat layers.

Cover and bake at 350° for 60-65 minutes or until bubbly. Let stand for 15 minutes before cutting. **Yield: 12 servings.**

Very Veggie Lasagna

Bell Pepper Enchiladas

Peppers are probably the vegetable that gets used most frequently in my kitchen. My freezer's constantly stocked in case I discover a new recipe or want to whip up an old favorite. These zesty enchiladas are a standby that I make often for supper throughout the year. —*Melissa Cowser, Greenville, Texas*

- 2 medium green peppers, chopped
- 1/2 cup shredded cheddar cheese
- 1/2 cup shredded Monterey Jack cheese
- 1/2 cup diced process American cheese
- 4 flour tortillas (8 inches)
- 1 small jalapeno pepper, minced, optional
- 1 cup salsa, *divided*

Additional shredded cheese, optional

Sprinkle the green peppers and cheeses down the center of the tortillas; add jalapeno if desired. Roll up. Spread 1/2 cup salsa in a shallow baking dish. Place tortillas seam side down over salsa. Top with remaining salsa.

Bake, uncovered, at 350° for 20 minutes or until heated through. Sprinkle with additional cheese if desired. **Yield: 4 enchiladas.**

Editor's Note: When cutting or seeding hot peppers, use rubber or plastic gloves to protect your hands. Avoid touching your face.

Bell Pepper Enchiladas

Pleasing Potato Pizza

Pleasing Potato Pizza 1st prize

I first heard of this delicious and distinctive pizza when a friend tried it at a restaurant. It sounded great so I experimented to come up with my own recipe. The pizza disappears fast when I serve it.
—Barbara Zimmer, Wanless, Manitoba

- 3 large potatoes, peeled and cubed
- 1 tube (10 ounces) refrigerated pizza crust
- 1/4 cup milk
- 1/2 teaspoon salt
- 1 pound sliced bacon, diced
- 1 large onion, chopped
- 1/2 cup chopped sweet red pepper
- 1-1/2 cups (6 ounces) shredded cheddar cheese
- 1-1/2 cups (6 ounces) shredded part-skim mozzarella cheese

Sour cream, optional

Place potatoes in a saucepan and cover with water. Bring to a boil. Reduce heat; cover and cook for 20-25 minutes or until very tender.

Meanwhile, unroll the pizza crust onto an ungreased 14-in. pizza pan; flatten dough and build up edges slightly. Prick dough several times with a fork. Bake at 350° for 15 minutes or until lightly browned. Cool on a wire rack.

Drain potatoes and transfer to a mixing bowl. Mash with milk and salt until smooth. Spread over crust. In a skillet, cook bacon over medium heat until partially cooked but not crisp. Add onion and red pepper; cook until bacon is crisp and vegetables are tender. Drain well; sprinkle over potatoes. Top with cheeses.

Bake at 375° for 20 minutes or until cheese is melted. Serve with sour cream if desired. **Yield: 8 slices.**

SIDES

COLORFUL OVEN VEGETABLES, pg. 276

Sides

Apple-a-Day Casserole

This sweet-tart casserole is a fun change of pace from traditional vegetable side dishes. It's super-quick to prepare if you use a food processor to slice the apples and carrots.— Elizabeth Erwin, Syracuse, New York

- 6 medium tart apples, peeled and sliced
- 6 medium carrots, thinly sliced
- 1/2 cup orange juice
- 1/3 cup all-purpose flour
- 1/3 cup sugar
- 1/2 teaspoon ground nutmeg
- 2 tablespoons cold butter

Combine apples and carrots; place in a greased 2-qt. baking dish. Drizzle with orange juice. Cover and bake at 350° for 40-45 minutes or until carrots are crisp-tender.

In a bowl, combine the flour, sugar and nutmeg; cut in butter until crumbly. Sprinkle over apple mixture. Bake, uncovered, 10-15 minutes longer or until the carrots are tender. **Yield: 6-8 servings.**

Apple-a-Day Casserole

Scalloped Apples

Scalloped Apples

When I was a child, I loved eating at my grandma's house, especially when she baked this comforting apple dish. As a busy mother of seven, I'm often short on time, so I use the microwave to fix it quickly. My family enjoys its apple pie flavor with a meal or topped with ice cream for dessert.
—Sandy Daniels, Grandville, Michigan

- 10 cups sliced peeled tart apple (about 8 medium)
- 1/3 cup sugar
- 2 tablespoons cornstarch
- 1/2 to 1 teaspoon ground cinnamon
- 1/4 teaspoon ground nutmeg
- 2 tablespoons butter, cubed

Place apples in a 2-1/2-qt. microwave-safe bowl. Combine the sugar, cornstarch, cinnamon and nutmeg; sprinkle over apples and toss to coat. Dot with butter. Cover and microwave on high for 15 minutes or until apples are tender, stirring every 5 minutes. **Yield: 8 servings.**

Editor's Note: This recipe was tested with an 850-watt microwave.

Maple Apple Rings

Artichoke Spinach Casserole

Maple Apple Rings

I live in maple syrup country and got this recipe from a sugarhouse. These fried apple rings are wonderful served with baked beans.
—Alma Jacklin, New Durham, New Hampshire

- **3/4 cup all-purpose flour**
- **1 egg, beaten**
- **1/4 cup maple syrup**
- **1/4 cup buttermilk**
- **3 large apples, peeled, cored and cut into 1/4-inch rings**

Oil for deep-fat frying
Confectioners' sugar

In a shallow bowl, combine the flour, egg, syrup and buttermilk. Dip apple rings on both sides into batter.

In an electric skillet or deep-fat fryer, heat 2 in. of oil to 375°. Fry apple rings, a few at a time, for 2 minutes or until golden brown on each side. Drain on paper towels. Dust with confectioners' sugar. **Yield: 4 servings.**

Artichoke Spinach Casserole

Although he isn't a fan of spinach, my husband loves this dish. The combination of ingredients may sound unusual, but the flavors meld well. It's an excellent side vegetable for a formal dinner.
—Judy Johnson, Missoula, Montana

- **1 pound fresh mushrooms, sliced**
- **1/3 cup chicken broth**
- **1 tablespoon all-purpose flour**
- **1/2 cup evaporated milk**
- **4 packages (10 ounces *each*) frozen chopped spinach, thawed and squeezed dry**
- **2 cans (14-1/2 ounces *each*) diced tomatoes, drained**

2 cans (14 ounces *each*) water-packed artichoke hearts, rinsed, drained and thinly sliced
1 cup (8 ounces) sour cream
1/2 cup mayonnaise
3 tablespoons lemon juice
1/2 teaspoon garlic powder
1/4 teaspoon salt
1/4 teaspoon pepper
Paprika, optional

In a large skillet, cook mushrooms in broth over medium heat for 3 minutes or until tender. Remove mushrooms with a slotted spoon and set aside.

Combine flour and milk until smooth; add to skillet. Bring to a boil; cook and stir for 2 minutes. Remove from the heat; stir in spinach, tomatoes and mushrooms.

Place half of the artichoke in an ungreased 13-in. x 9-in. x 2-in. baking dish. Top with half of the spinach mixture. Repeat layers. Combine the sour cream, mayonnaise, lemon juice, garlic powder, salt and pepper; dollop over top. Sprinkle with paprika if desired. Bake, uncovered, at 350° for 25-30 minutes or until bubbly. **Yield: 12-14 servings.**

Artichokes Au Gratin

This makes a great side dish for Thanksgiving, Christmas or any dinner. My niece served this at a family gathering and shared the recipe with me.
—Marjorie Bowen, Colorado Springs, Colorado

2 cans (14 ounces *each*) water-packed artichoke hearts, rinsed, drained and quartered
1 garlic clove, minced
1/4 cup butter, *divided*
2 tablespoons all-purpose flour
1/2 teaspoon salt
1/4 teaspoon pepper
1-1/2 cups milk

Artichokes Au Gratin

1 egg, lightly beaten
1/2 cup shredded Swiss cheese, *divided*
1 tablespoon dry bread crumbs
1/8 teaspoon paprika

In a skillet, saute the artichokes and garlic in 2 tablespoons butter until tender. Transfer to a greased 1-qt. baking dish.

In a saucepan, melt the remaining butter. Stir in the flour, salt and pepper until smooth; gradually add milk. Bring to a boil; cook and stir for 2 minutes or until thickened. Remove from the heat. Stir a small amount of hot mixture into egg; return all to pan, stirring constantly. Add 1/4 cup cheese, stirring until melted.

Pour over artichokes; sprinkle with remaining cheese. Combine crumbs and paprika; sprinkle over top. Bake, uncovered, at 400° for 20-25 minutes or until heated through. **Yield: 4-6 servings.**

Asparagus Onion Casserole

Asparagus Onion Casserole

Just about any meal pairs well with this savory vegetable dish. I've prepared it ahead of time, then popped it in the oven so it's ready with the meal.
—Judy Fleetwood, Beulah, Michigan

- 1 pound fresh asparagus, cut into 1-inch pieces *or* 2 packages (10 ounces *each*) asparagus cuts, thawed
- 2 medium onions, sliced
- 5 tablespoons butter, *divided*
- 2 tablespoons all-purpose flour
- 1 cup milk
- 1 package (3 ounces) cream cheese, cubed
- 1 teaspoon salt
- 1/8 teaspoon pepper
- 1/2 cup shredded cheddar cheese
- 1 cup soft bread crumbs

In a skillet, saute the asparagus and onions in 1 tablespoon of butter until crisp-tender, about 8 minutes. Transfer to an ungreased 1-1/2-qt. baking dish.

In a saucepan, melt 2 tablespoons butter. Stir in flour until smooth; gradually add milk. Bring to a boil; cook and stir for 2 minutes or until thickened. Reduce heat. Add the cream cheese, salt and pepper; stir until cheese is melted.

Pour over the vegetables. Sprinkle with cheddar cheese. Melt remaining butter; toss with bread crumbs. Sprinkle over top. Bake, uncovered, at 350° for 35-40 minutes or until heated through. **Yield: 4-6 servings.**

Festive Green Bean Casserole

This recipe came from a cookbook my son gave to me over 20 years ago. It's a tasty dish that I make often for family get-togethers and potluck suppers.
—June Mullins, Livonia, Missouri

- 1 cup chopped sweet red pepper
- 1 small onion, finely chopped
- 1 tablespoon butter
- 1 can (10-3/4 ounces) condensed cream of celery soup, undiluted
- 1/2 cup milk
- 1 teaspoon Worcestershire sauce
- 1/8 teaspoon hot pepper sauce
- 2 packages (16 ounces *each*) frozen French-style green beans, thawed and drained
- 1 can (8 ounces) sliced water chestnuts, drained
- 1 cup (4 ounces) shredded cheddar cheese

In a skillet, saute red pepper and onion in butter until tender. Add the soup, milk, Worcestershire sauce and hot pepper sauce; stir until smooth. Stir in beans and water chestnuts.

Transfer to an ungreased 1-1/2-qt. baking dish. Sprinkle with cheese. Bake, uncovered, at 350° for 15 minutes or until heated through. **Yield: 6-8 servings.**

Festive Green Bean Casserole

Maple Baked Beans

I came up with this recipe in a pinch after running out of baked beans at our oldest daughter's birthday party. I dressed up canned beans with maple syrup and a few other ingredients to produce this sweet, saucy version that takes like homemade. They're so easy to fix that I rarely make baked beans from scratch anymore.

—Brenda Tetreault, Newport Center, Vermont

- 1 medium onion, chopped
- 1 to 2 tablespoons vegetable oil
- 3 cans (28 ounces *each*) baked beans
- 1-1/2 teaspoons ground mustard
- 1 teaspoon garlic salt
- 3/4 to 1 cup maple syrup

In a Dutch oven, cook onion in oil until tender. Add the beans, mustard and garlic salt. Cook over medium heat until bubbly, stirring occasionally. Add maple syrup; heat through, stirring occasionally. **Yield: 8-10 servings.**

Maple Baked Beans

Mandarin Glazed Beets

Crumb-Topped Broccoli Bake

Mandarin Glazed Beets

Mandarin oranges and a warm glaze transform canned beets into a super dish. Lemon juice provides a bit of tartness. If your family doesn't like the tart flavor, I suggest adding a little more sugar.
—Shirley Dehler, Columbus, Wisconsin

- **1/4 cup sugar**
- **2 teaspoons cornstarch**
- **1/4 cup lemon juice**
- **2 tablespoons butter**
- **2 cans (15 ounces *each*) sliced beets, drained**
- **1 can (11 ounces) mandarin oranges, drained**

In a large saucepan, combine the sugar and cornstarch. Add lemon juice and butter. Bring to a boil; cook and stir for 2 minutes or until thickened. Stir in the beats; heat through. Gently stir in oranges; heat through. **Yield: 4 servings.**

Crumb-Topped Broccoli Bake

Broccoli is one of the main crops grown in this area. This recipe has pleased just about everyone who has tried it, including some who said they didn't like broccoli. —Hope Huggins, Santa Cruz, California

- 1/4 cup chopped onion
- 2 tablespoons butter
- 2 tablespoons all-purpose flour
- 1/2 cup milk
- 1 jar (8 ounces) process cheese sauce
- 2 packages (10 ounces *each*) frozen broccoli cuts
- 3 eggs, beaten
- 1/2 cup crushed butter-flavored crackers (about 12 crackers), *divided*

Salt and pepper to taste

In a saucepan, saute onion in butter until tender. Stir in flour until blended; gradually add milk. Bring to a boil; cook and stir for 2 minutes or until thickened. Reduce heat; stir in cheese sauce until smooth. Remove from the heat.

Cook broccoli according to package directions; drain and place in a bowl. Add cheese sauce mixture, eggs, 1/4 cup cracker crumbs, salt and pepper.

Transfer to a greased 1-1/2-qt. baking dish; sprinkle with remaining cracker crumbs. Place dish in a larger baking pan. Fill pan with hot water to a depth of 1 in. Bake, uncovered, at 350° for 50 minutes or until golden brown. **Yield: 6 servings.**

Zesty Broccoli And Artichokes

We grow broccoli in our garden, so I've experimented with different ways to prepare it. Fixed this way, it tastes delicious plus it's good for you.
—Mildred Sherrer, Bay City, Texas

Zesty Broccoli and Artichokes

- 2 cups water
- 4 cups fresh broccoli florets
- 1 can (14 ounces) water-packed artichoke hearts, rinsed and drained
- 2 garlic cloves, minced
- 1 tablespoon olive oil
- 1/4 teaspoon salt
- 1/4 teaspoon pepper
- 1/8 teaspoon hot pepper sauce
- 1 tablespoon lemon juice
- 2 tablespoons grated Parmesan cheese

In a saucepan, bring water to a boil. Add broccoli; cook, uncovered, for 2 minutes. Drain and set aside..

In a skillet, saute garlic in oil until tender. Add the artichokes and saute for 2 minutes. Add the broccoli, salt, pepper and hot pepper sauce; saute 3 minutes longer or until broccoli is tender. Remove from the heat; sprinkle with lemon juice and Parmesan cheese. **Yield: 6 servings.**

Colorful Oven Vegetables

Colorful Oven Vegetables

As a party planner for a catering company, I often serve this attractive side dish with a steak dinner or at a brunch. Our two grown sons and their families request these fresh-tasting oven-roasted vegetables, too. —*Grace Ammann, Richfield, Minnesota*

- 1/3 cup butter
- 1/2 teaspoon dried thyme
- 1/4 to 1/2 teaspoon salt
- 1/4 teaspoon pepper
- 3 cups caulifloweretts
- 2 cups broccoli florets
- 6 medium carrots, julienned
- 3 small onions, quartered

Place butter in a shallow 3-qt. baking dish. Bake at 400° for 5 minutes or until melted. Stir in the thyme, salt and pepper. Add the vegetables and toss to coat.

Cover and bake for 25-30 minutes or until the vegetables are crisp-tender. **Yield: 10-12 servings.**

Editor's Note: 2 cups baby carrots may be substituted; cut into julienne strips.

Red Cabbage Casserole

With its color and eye appeal, this dish is a hit on special days like Christmas or Easter when I'm cooking for a crowd. It also makes a nice dish to take to a potluck or (cut the recipe in half) for a tasty addition to a weeknight meal. —*Julie Murray, Sunderland, Ontario*

- 1 tablespoon shortening
- 8 cups shredded red cabbage
- 1 medium onion, chopped
- 1 teaspoon lemon juice
- 1/4 cup sugar
- 1 teaspoon salt
- 1 to 2 medium apples, chopped
- 1/4 cup red currant jelly
- Lemon slices, optional

In a Dutch oven, melt shortening. Add the cabbage, onion, lemon juice, sugar and salt; mix well. Cover and cook over medium heat for 10-15 minutes or until cabbage is crisp-tender, stirring occasionally.

Add apples; cook 10-15 minutes longer or until cabbage and apples are tender. Stir in jelly until melted. Garnish with lemon slices if desired. **Yield: 8-10 servings.**

Cabbage-Tomato Pasta Toss

Here's an unusual combination of ingredients that blends very well together. I find that it makes a nice side dish for any beef entree. —*Alcy Thorne, Los Molinos, California*

- 2 medium tomatoes, peeled and diced
- 2 tablespoons red wine vinegar
- 1 teaspoon dried basil
- 1/2 cup minced fresh parsley
- 8 ounces uncooked bow tie pasta
- 2 cups shredded cabbage

Red Cabbage Casserole

- 1-1/2 cups soft bread crumbs
- 1/2 cup slivered almonds
- 2 to 3 garlic cloves, minced
- 1/4 cup olive oil
- 1/4 cup butter

In a bowl, combine the tomatoes, vinegar, basil and parsley; set aside. Cook pasta according to package directions, adding the cabbage during the last 2 minutes.

Meanwhile, in a skillet, saute bread crumbs, almonds and garlic in oil and butter for 6 minutes or until golden brown.

Drain pasta and cabbage; place in a large bowl. Add tomato and crumb mixtures; toss and serve immediately. **Yield: 6 servings.**

Cabbage-Tomato Pasta Toss

Confetti Carrot Fritters

Creamy Carrot Casserole

Confetti Carrot Fritters

Crispy, sweet and savory, these delicate fritters are a fun twist on the traditional fruit-filled variety. They're yummy served with a mustard dipping sauce, but our kids enjoy them with a drizzle of warm maple syrup, too. —Peggy Camp, Twain, California

- 6 cups water
- 2-1/2 cups finely chopped carrots
- 1/4 cup all-purpose flour
- 1/4 teaspoon salt
- 1/4 teaspoon pepper
- 2 eggs, *separated*
- 3 tablespoons milk
- 2 tablespoons finely chopped onion
- 2 tablespoons minced fresh parsley

Vegetable oil for deep-fat frying

MUSTARD SAUCE:

- 1 tablespoon minced fresh parsley
- 1 tablespoon red wine vinegar
- 1 tablespoon Dijon mustard
- 1 teaspoon finely chopped green onion
- 1/4 cup olive oil

In a saucepan, bring water to a boil. Add carrots; cover and boil for 3 minutes. Drain and immediately place carrots in ice water. Drain and pat dry.

In a large bowl, combine the flour, salt and pepper. Combine egg yolks and milk; stir into the flour mixture until smooth. Stir in the onion, parsley and carrots. In a mixing bowl, beat egg whites on high speed until stiff peaks form; fold into batter.

In an electric skillet, heat 1/4 in. of oil on medium heat. Drop batter by 1/3 cupfuls; press lightly to flatten. Fry until golden brown, about 2 minutes on each side. Remove to paper towels to drain.

For mustard sauce, in a small bowl, combine the parsley, vinegar, mustard and green onion. Slowly whisk in oil until blended. Serve with the fritters. **Yield: 9 servings.**

Orange Candied Carrots

At Thanksgiving, my son always asks for these carrot coins. The orange flavor in the sweet, mild sauce really comes through. This pleasant side dish is a great way to dress up a meal of holiday leftovers.
—Lori Lockrey, West Hill, Ontario

- 1 pound carrots, cut into 1/2 inch slices
- 1/4 pound butter, softened
- 1/4 cup jellied cranberry sauce
- 1 orange peel strip (1 to 3 inches)
- 2 tablespoons brown sugar
- 1/2 teaspoon salt

Place carrots in a skillet; add 1 in. of water. Bring to a boil. Reduce heat; cover and simmer for 15-20 minutes or until crisp-tender.

Meanwhile, in a blender, combine the butter, cranberry sauce, orange peel, brown sugar and salt. Cover and process until blended. Drain carrots; drizzle with cranberry mixture. **Yield: 3 servings.**

Orange Candied Carrots

Creamy Carrot Casserole

My mom and I developed this recipe to see if there was a carrot dish that even people who don't care for carrots would enjoy. So far, I haven't met anyone who hasn't liked our creation.
—Laurie Heward, Fillmore, Utah

- 1-1/2 pounds carrots, peeled and sliced *or* 1 bag (20 ounces) frozen sliced carrots, thawed
- 1 cup mayonnaise
- 1 tablespoon grated onion
- 1 tablespoon prepared horseradish
- 1/4 cup shredded cheddar cheese
- 2 tablespoons buttered bread crumbs

Place 1 in. of water in a large saucepan; add carrots. Bring to a boil. Reduce heat; cover and simmer for 7-9 minutes or until crisp-tender. Drain, reserving 1/4 cup cooking liquid.

Place carrots in a 1-1/2-qt. baking dish. Combine the mayonnaise, onion, horseradish and reserved cooking liquid; spread evenly over carrots. Sprinkle with cheese; top with bread crumbs. Bake, uncovered, at 350° for 30 minutes or until heated through. **Yield: 8-10 servings.**

Creamed Cauliflower

This is a Hungarian recipe from my mother. It's easy to make and flavorful. Even those who don't normally care for cauliflower can't pass it up prepared this way. —*Peggie De Chick, Auburn, New York*

- 1 medium head cauliflower, broken into florets (about 7 cups)
- 1-1/2 teaspoons salt, *divided*
- 1/2 cup dry bread crumbs, *divided*
- 1 cup half-and-half cream
- 1 tablespoon butter
- Minced fresh parsley, optional

Place cauliflower in a saucepan; add 1 in. of water and 1 teaspoon salt. Bring to a boil. Reduce heat. Cover and simmer for 6-7 minutes or until crisp-tender; drain.

Grease the bottom and sides of a 2-qt. baking dish; sprinkle with 2 tablespoons bread crumbs. Add cauliflower. Pour cream over top. Dot with butter; sprinkle with remaining salt and bread crumbs.

Bake, uncovered, at 350° for 25-30 minutes or until cauliflower is tender. Garnish with parsley if desired. **Yield: 6-8 servings.**

End of Summer Vegetable Bake

When my husband worked as a deputy agriculture commissioner, he'd bring me bushels of vegetables from area farms. This pretty side dish is the result—it's easy to fix but impressive enough for company. —*Judy Williams, Hayden, Idaho*

- 1 small head cauliflower, broken into small florets (about 5 cups)
- 1 medium bunch broccoli, cut into small florets (about 4 cups)
- 1 medium onion, chopped
- 2 garlic cloves, minced
- 1 tablespoon butter

Creamed Cauliflower

- 2 medium tomatoes, chopped
- 3/4 teaspoon dried basil
- 3/4 teaspoon dried oregano
- 3/4 teaspoon salt
- 1/4 teaspoon pepper
- 1/4 teaspoon hot pepper sauce
- 4 eggs
- 1/3 cup half-and-half cream
- 1-1/2 cups (6 ounces) shredded Swiss cheese, *divided*
- 1/4 cup shredded Parmesan cheese

Place the cauliflower and broccoli in a saucepan with a small amount of water. Bring to a boil. Reduce heat; cover and simmer for 5-10 minutes or until crisp-tender. Drain and set aside.

In a large skillet, saute onion and garlic in butter until tender. Stir in the tomatoes, seasonings, cauliflower and broccoli. Cook, uncovered, until heated through, about 4 minutes, stirring occasionally. Remove from the heat and set aside.

In a large bowl, beat eggs and cream; stir in 1 cup Swiss cheese, Parmesan cheese and the vegetable mixture. Transfer to a greased shallow 2-qt. baking dish. Sprinkle with remaining Swiss cheese.

Bake, uncovered, at 375° for 25-30 minutes or until a knife inserted near the center comes out clean. Let stand for 10 minutes before serving. **Yield: 12 servings.**

Mushroom Corn Casserole

Corn brightens up any meal with its sunny color and sweet crispness. I decided to create a casserole that combined corn, mushrooms and a rich, cheesy sauce. I succeeded with this recipe.
—Mary Jones, Cumberland, Maine

- 1/3 cup chopped green pepper
- 1/3 cup finely chopped onion
- 3 tablespoons butter, *divided*
- 1/4 cup all-purpose flour
- 1 can (14-3/4 ounces) cream-style corn
- 1/2 teaspoon salt
- 1/8 teaspoon pepper
- 1 package (3 ounces) cream cheese, cubed
- 1 can (15-1/4 ounces) whole kernel corn, drained
- 1 can (4 ounces) mushroom stems and pieces, drained
- 1/2 cup shredded Swiss cheese
- 1-1/2 cups soft bread crumbs

In a saucepan, saute green pepper and onion in 1 tablespoon butter until tender. Stir in the flour, cream corn, salt and pepper until blended. Add cream cheese; stir until melted. Stir in the whole kernel corn, mushrooms and Swiss cheese.

Transfer to a greased 1-1/2-qt. baking dish. Melt remaining butter; toss with bread crumbs. Sprinkle over the corn mixture. Bake, uncovered, at 400° for 20-25 minutes or until heated through. **Yield: 4-6 servings.**

End of Summer Vegetable Bake

Mushroom Corn Casserole

Salsa Corn Cakes

Texas Two-Step Corn Medley

Salsa Corn Cakes

This recipe is super with fresh or canned corn. I whip up these patties to serve alongside nachos or tacos on hot summer evenings. The salsa is subtle but adds flavor. —Lisa Boettcher, Rosebush, Michigan

- 1-1/2 cups all-purpose flour
- 1/2 cup cornmeal
- 1 teaspoon baking powder
- 1 teaspoon salt
- 2 packages (3 ounces *each*) cream cheese, softened
- 6 eggs
- 1 cup milk
- 1/4 cup butter, melted
- 1 can (15-1/4 ounces) whole kernel corn, drained
- 1/2 cup salsa, drained
- 1/4 cup minced green onions
- Sour cream and additional salsa

Combine the flour, cornmeal, baking powder and salt; set aside. In a mixing bowl, beat cream cheese and eggs; add milk and butter. Add the dry ingredients just until moistened. Fold in the corn, salsa and onions.

Pour batter by 1/4 cupfuls onto a greased hot griddle. Turn when bubbles form on top; cook until the second side is golden brown. Serve with sour cream and salsa. **Yield: 6-8 servings.**

Texas Two-Step Corn Medley

I came up with this pleasing pairing of corn and summer squash as a side dish for a Mexican buffet. Family and friends who have tried it are generous with their compliments and recipe requests. This delicious dish is a regular menu item when husband, Bob, and I entertain.

—Pauline Howard, Lago Vista, Texas

- 1 medium onion, chopped
- 1/4 cup butter
- 2 medium yellow summer squash, sliced
- 2 garlic cloves, minced
- 2 tablespoons canned chopped green chilies
- 1/4 teaspoon salt
- 1/8 teaspoon pepper
- 2 cans (11 ounces *each*) Mexicorn, drained
- 3/4 cup shredded Colby-Monterey Jack cheese

In a skillet, saute onion in butter until tender. Add the squash, garlic, chilies, salt and pepper. Saute until squash is crisp-tender, about 5 minutes. Add the corn; cook and stir for 2 minutes. Sprinkle with cheese; cover and let stand until cheese is melted. **Yield: 4 servings.**

Church Supper Potatoes

As a pastor's wife, I often cook for crowds. This dish is alway a hit. My own family thinks the hearty potatoes are a must served with London Broil or marinated grilled chicken breast.

—Michelle Grigsby, Beavercreek, Ohio

- 3 pounds russet potatoes (about 9 medium), peeled and cut into 1/2-inch cubes
- 2 garlic cloves, peeled
- 2 packages (3 ounces *each*) cream cheese, softened
- 2 tablespoons butter
- 1/2 cup sour cream
- 2 cups (8 ounces) shredded cheddar cheese, *divided*
- 1 teaspoon garlic salt
- 1 teaspoon onion salt
- 1 package (10 ounces) frozen chopped spinach, thawed and squeezed dry

Church Supper Potatoes

Place the potatoes and garlic in a large saucepan; cover with water. Bring to a boil. Reduce heat; cover and cook for 20-25 minutes or until very tender. Drain well.

In a mixing bowl, mash potatoes and garlic with the cream cheese and butter. Add the sour cream, 1 cup cheddar cheese, garlic salt, onion salt and spinach. Stir just until mixed. Spread into a greased 2-qt. baking dish.

Bake, uncovered, at 350° for 30-35 minutes or until heated through. Top with remaining cheese; bake 5 minutes longer or until the cheese is melted. **Yield: 10-12 servings.**

Two-Tone Baked Potatoes

Two-Tone Baked Potatoes

One potato, two potato, this recipe is doubly wonderful as far as spud lovers are concerned. I have a reputation at home and at work for trying out new recipes. Everyone is glad I took a chance on this one.
—Sherree Stahn, Central City, Nebraska

- 6 medium russet potatoes
- 6 medium sweet potatoes
- 2/3 cup sour cream, *divided*
- 1/3 cup milk
- 3/4 cup shredded cheddar cheese
- 4 tablespoons minced chives, *divided*
- 1-1/2 teaspoons salt, *divided*

Pierce russet and sweet potatoes with a fork. Bake at 400° for 60-70 minutes or until tender. Set sweet potatoes aside.

Cut a third off the top of each russet potato; scoop out pulp, leaving skins intact. Place pulp in a bowl; mash with 1/3 cup sour cream, milk, cheese, 2 tablespoons chives and 3/4 teaspoon salt. Set aside.

Cut off the top of each sweet potato; scoop out pulp, leaving skins intact. Mash pulp with the remaining sour cream, chives and salt. Stuff mixture into half of each potato skin; spoon russet potato filling into other half. Place on a baking sheet. Bake at 350° for 15-20 minutes or until heated through. **Yield: 12 servings.**

Grilled Potato Fans

If you're looking for a change from plain baked potatoes, try these tender and buttery potato fans seasoned with oregano, garlic powder, celery and onion. To cut down on grilling time, I sometimes microwave the potatoes for 5-6 minutes before slicing them. —Jennifer Black-Ortiz, San Jose, California

- 6 medium baking potatoes
- 2 medium onions, halved and thinly sliced
- 6 tablespoons butter, cubed
- 1/4 cup finely chopped celery
- 1 teaspoon salt
- 1 teaspoon dried oregano
- 1/4 teaspoon garlic powder
- 1/4 teaspoon pepper

With a sharp knife, make cuts 1/2 in. apart in each potato, leaving slices attached at bottom. Fan the potatoes slightly. Place each on a piece of heavy-duty foil (about 12 in. square).

Insert onions and butter between potato slices. Sprinkle with the celery, salt, oregano, garlic powder and pepper. Fold foil around potatoes and seal tightly. Grill, covered, over medium-hot heat for 40-45 minutes or until tender. **Yield: 6 servings.**

Au Gratin Peas and Potatoes

While this delicious potato skillet is a wonderful side dish, we find it satisfying enough to be a main course, too. The skillet preparation makes it quick, but it's still good old-fashioned comfort food at its best!
—Marie Peterson, Deforest, Wisconsin

Grilled Potato Fans

- 6 bacon strips, diced
- 1 medium onion, chopped
- 4 cups sliced peeled cooked potatoes
- 1/2 teaspoon salt
- 1 package (10 ounces) frozen peas, cooked and drained
- 2 cups (8 ounces) shredded sharp cheddar cheese, *divided*
- 1/2 cup mayonnaise
- 1/2 cup milk

In a skillet, cook bacon over medium heat until crisp. Using a slotted spoon, remove to paper towels. Drain, reserving 1 tablespoon drippings. In the drippings, saute onion until tender. Layer with the potatoes, salt, peas, 1 cup cheese and bacon. Reduce heat; cover and simmer for 10 minutes or until heated through.

Combine mayonnaise and milk until smooth; pour over bacon. Sprinkle with the remaining cheese. Remove from the heat; let stand for 5 minutes before serving. **Yield: 4 servings.**

Au Gratin Peas and Potatoes

Golden Mashed Potatoes

Herbed Garlic Potatoes

Golden Mashed Potatoes

When there's no gravy with the meat, this is great to serve in place of regular mashed potatoes. I make it often to take to picnics and church socials. My husband even made it for his family's reunion one year when I couldn't go!

—Cindy Stith, Wickliffe, Kentucky

- 9 large potatoes (about 4 pounds), peeled and cubed
- 1 pound carrots, cut into 1/2-inch chunks
- 8 green onions, thinly sliced
- 1/2 cup butter
- 1 cup (8 ounces) sour cream
- 1-1/2 teaspoons salt
- 1/8 teaspoon pepper
- 3/4 cup shredded cheddar cheese

In a soup kettle or Dutch oven, cook the potatoes and carrots in boiling salted water until tender; drain. Place in a mixing bowl; mash and set aside.

In a skillet, saute onions in butter until tender. Add to potato mixture. Add sour cream, salt and pepper; mix until blended.

Transfer to a greased 13-in. x 9-in. x 2-in. baking dish. Sprinkle with cheese. Bake, uncovered, at 350° for 30-40 minutes or until heated through. **Yield: 10-12 servings.**

Herbed Garlic Potatoes

My dad invented this dish. The potatoes fit any kind of meal—fancy or burgers—and everyone asks for the recipe. —*Sherry DesJardin, Fairbanks, Alaska*

- 15 small red potatoes (about 2 pounds)
- 1/3 cup butter
- 1/4 cup minced fresh parsley
- 2 tablespoons minced fresh *or* dried chives
- 1-1/2 teaspoons minced fresh tarragon *or* 1/2 teaspoon dried tarragon
- 2 to 3 garlic cloves, minced
- 3 bacon strips, cooked and crumbled
- 1/2 to 1 teaspoon salt
- 1/4 teaspoon pepper

Cut the potatoes in half and place in a saucepan; cover with water. Cover and bring to a boil; cook until tender, about 15 minutes. Drain well.

In a large skillet, melt butter. Add the parsley, chives, tarragon and garlic; cook and stir over low heat for 1-2 minutes. Add the potatoes, bacon, salt and pepper; toss to coat. Cook until heated through, about 5 minutes. **Yield: 6-8 servings.**

Loaded Mashed Potatoes

Loaded Mashed Potatoes

Tired of the same old mashed potatoes, I whipped up this new family favorite. We can't get enough of them at our house. Often, I'll prepare this dish ahead and refrigerate it. —*Dawn Reuter, Oxford, Wisconsin*

- 5 pounds potatoes, peeled and cubed
- 3/4 cup sour cream
- 1/2 cup milk
- 3 tablespoons butter
- Salt and pepper to taste
- 3 cups (12 ounces) shredded cheddar cheese, *divided*
- 1/2 pound sliced bacon, cooked and crumbled
- 3 green onions, sliced

Place potatoes in a Dutch oven and cover with water; bring to a boil. Reduce heat; cover and cook for 15-20 minutes or until tender. Drain and place in a mixing bowl. Add the sour cream, milk, butter, salt and pepper. Beat on medium-low speed until light and fluffy. Stir in 2 cups cheese, bacon and onions.

Transfer to a greased 3-qt. baking dish. Top with remaining cheese. Bake, uncovered, at 350° for 30 minutes or until heated through and cheese is melted. **Yield: 14 servings.**

Spinach Artichoke Pie

Spinach is an abundant vegetable grown here in our state. I make this side dish often when spinach is in season. —Lori Coleman, Glassboro, New Jersey

- 3 tablespoons vegetable oil, *divided*
- 1/4 cup dry bread crumbs
- 1/2 pound fresh mushrooms, sliced
- 1 pound fresh spinach, chopped and cooked
- 1 jar (6-1/2 ounces) marinated artichoke hearts, drained and quartered
- 1 cup day-old bread cubes
- 1-1/4 cups (5 ounces) shredded cheddar cheese, *divided*
- 1 jar (4 ounces) diced pimientos, drained
- 2 eggs, beaten
- 1/4 to 1/2 teaspoon garlic powder

Brush the bottom and sides of a 9-in. pie plate with 2 tablespoons oil; sprinkle with bread crumbs. Set aside.

In a skillet, saute mushrooms in remaining oil; drain. Remove from the heat. Squeeze spinach dry; add to mushrooms. Stir in the artichokes, bread cubes, 1 cup cheddar cheese, pimientos, eggs and garlic powder; stir well.

Spoon into the prepared pie plate. Bake, uncovered, at 350° for 30 minutes. Sprinkle with remaining cheese. Bake 5-10 minutes longer or until the cheese is melted. Let stand for 10 minutes before cutting. **Yield: 6-8 servings.**

Spinach Artichoke Pie

Cheesy Zucchini Saute

Although I no longer have a garden of my own, friends and neighbors keep me amply supplied with squash. As a thank-you, I tell them how to make this refreshing zucchini saute. It's quick, easy and oh, so tasty! —Doris Biggs, Felton, Delaware

- 1/2 cup chopped onion
- 1/4 cup butter, cubed
- 3 cups coarsely shredded zucchini
- 2 teaspoons minced fresh basil *or* 1/2 teaspoon dried basil
- 1/2 teaspoon salt
- 1/8 teaspoon garlic powder
- 1 cup (4 ounces) shredded cheddar cheese
- 1 cup diced fresh tomato
- 2 tablespoons sliced ripe olives

In a large skillet, saute onion in butter until crisp-tender. Stir in the zucchini, basil, salt and garlic powder. Cook and stir for 4-5 minutes or until zucchini is crisp-tender. Sprinkle with the cheese, tomato and olives. Cover and cook for 4-5 minutes or until cheese is melted. Serve immediately. **Yield: 6 servings.**

Special Squash Casserole

Squash has traditionally been a food our family passes up, but this luscious casserole is an exception to the rule. It's one of the first dishes to return empty.
—Kathleen Cox, Wyoming, Michigan

- **3 pounds butternut squash, peeled, seeded and cubed**
- **3/4 cup milk**
- **6 tablespoons butter, melted**
- **3 eggs, beaten**
- **1/2 teaspoon vanilla extract**
- **3/4 cup sugar**
- **3 tablespoons all-purpose flour**
- **1/2 teaspoon ground cinnamon**
- **1/8 teaspoon ground cloves**
- **1/8 teaspoon ground nutmeg**

TOPPING:

- **1/2 cup crushed vanilla wafers (about 15 wafers)**
- **1/4 cup packed brown sugar**
- **2 tablespoons butter, melted**

Place squash in a large saucepan or Dutch oven; cover with water. Bring to a boil; cover and cook for 25-30 minutes or until tender. Drain and place in a mixing bowl; beat just until smooth;.

Add the milk, butter, eggs and vanilla; mix well. Combine the dry ingredients; add to squash mixture and mix well. Transfer to a greased 2-qt. baking dish. Cover and bake at 350° for 45 minutes.

Meanwhile, in a small bowl, combine topping ingredients until crumbly; sprinkle over squash. Bake, uncovered, for 12-15 minute or until heated through. **Yield: 8-10 servings.**

Cheesy Zucchini Saute

Special Squash Casserole

Sweet Potatoes with Apples

Sweet Potato Bake

Sweet Potatoes With Apples

This satisfying dish is very welcome at any meal at our house, especially on holidays. The tart apple slices taste so good baked on top of the mild sweet potatoes.
—Jean Winfree, Merrill, Wisconsin

- **3 to 3-1/2 pounds sweet potatoes**
- **2 tart apples, peeled, cored and cut into 1/4-inch rings**
- **1/2 cup orange juice**
- **1/4 cup packed brown sugar**
- **1/4 teaspoon ground ginger**
- **1/4 teaspoon ground cinnamon**
- **2 tablespoons butter**

Place sweet potatoes in a large saucepan and cover with water. Bring to a boil. Reduce heat; cover and cook for 30 minutes or until just tender. Drain and cool slightly. Peel and cut into 1/4-in. slices.

In a greased 13-in. x 9-in. x 2-in. baking dish, alternately layer potatoes and apples. Pour orange juice over top. Combine the brown sugar, ginger and cinnamon; sprinkle over potatoes and apples. Dot with butter. Bake, uncovered, at 350° for 35-45 minutes or until apples are tender and heated through. **Yield: 8 servings.**

Sweet Potato Bake

This is an easy dish to prepare and is a perfect addition to that special holiday meal. The topping is flavorful and gives a nice contrast of textures.
—Pam Holloway, Marion, Louisiana

- 7 large sweet potatoes (about 6 pounds), peeled and cubed
- 1/4 cup butter
- 1/2 cup orange marmalade
- 1/4 cup orange juice
- 1/4 cup packed brown sugar
- 2 teaspoons salt
- 1 teaspoon ground ginger

TOPPING:

- 12 oatmeal cookies, crumbled
- 6 tablespoons butter, softened

Place sweet potatoes in a Dutch oven and cover with water; bring to a boil. Reduce heat; cover and cook just until tender, about 15 minutes. Drain well.

Mash potatoes with butter. Add the marmalade, orange juice, brown sugar, salt and ginger. Transfer to a greased 13-in. x 9-in. x 2-in. baking dish. Toss cookie crumbs with butter; sprinkle over the top. Bake, uncovered, at 400° for 20 minutes or until browned. Let stand for 15 minutes before serving. **Yield: 10-12 servings.**

Candied Sweet Potatoes

Candied Sweet Potatoes

My town is known as the Yam Capital of the United States. This is a simple recipe that goes well with baked ham or roasted turkey.
—Essie Nealey, Tabor City, North Carolina

- 3 pounds sweet potatoes
- 1/2 cup packed brown sugar
- 1 teaspoon ground cinnamon
- 1/4 cup butter, cubed
- 1/4 cup corn syrup

Place the sweet potatoes in a large Dutch oven and cover with water. Cover and bring to a boil. Reduce heat; cook, covered, for 30-45 minutes or until potatoes can be easily pierced with the tip of a sharp knife.

When cool enough to handle, peel potatoes and cut into wedges. Place in an ungreased 11-in. x 7-in. x 2-in. baking dish. Sprinkle with brown sugar and cinnamon. Dot with butter; drizzle with corn syrup.

Bake, uncovered, at 375° for 15-20 minutes or until bubbly, basting occasionally with sauce. **Yield: 8-10 servings.**

Green Tomatoes Parmesan

If you follow the recipe directions, you should end up with firm tomatoes. It's been a tried-and-true method for me. I started cooking as a teenager. My first meal was spaghetti, and it was so salty we couldn't eat it!
—Clara Mifflin, Creal Springs, Illinois

- 3 medium green tomatoes, sliced 1/4 inch thick

Salt

- 1/4 cup cornmeal
- 1/4 cup grated Parmesan cheese
- 2 tablespoons all-purpose flour
- 3/4 teaspoon garlic salt
- 1/2 teaspoon dried oregano
- 1/8 teaspoon pepper
- 1 egg, beaten
- 1/4 cup vegetable oil

Lightly sprinkle tomatoes with salt; drain on paper towels for 30-60 minutes. Meanwhile, combine the cornmeal, Parmesan, flour, garlic salt, oregano and pepper in a shallow plate. Dip each tomato slice into egg, then coat with the cornmeal mixture.

In a medium skillet, heat oil over medium-high heat. Fry tomatoes, a few at a time, for 2 minutes on each side or until golden brown. Drain on a paper towel-lined wire rack. Serve immediately. **Yield: 4-6 servings.**

Green Tomatoes Parmesan

Dutch Potato Poultry Stuffing

All of my ancestors were Pennsylvania Dutch. Add to that the fact my father was a potato farmer, and you see why we never had a holiday dinner without potato "filling" (Pennsylvania Dutch for stuffing)!
—Sarah Krout, Warrington, Pennsylvania

- 5 cups mashed potatoes (without added milk, butter *or* seasoning)
- 6 cups cubed crustless day-old white bread
- 2-1/2 cups chopped onion
- 1 cup chopped celery leaves
- 1 cup chopped fresh parsley
- 3 tablespoons butter, melted
- 1 teaspoon salt
- 3/4 teaspoon pepper
- 1 tablespoon all-purpose flour
- 3/4 cup egg substitute
- 1 cup milk
- 1 turkey (12 to 14 pounds)

In a large bowl, combine the potatoes, bread cubes, onion, celery leaves, parsley, butter, salt and pepper. In a small bowl, beat flour and egg substitute. Stir in milk; pour into the potato mixture and mix well. Add more milk if filling seams dry.

Just before baking, stuff the turkey. Skewer openings; tie drumsticks together. Place on a rack in a roasting pan.

Bake at 325° for 4-1/2 to 5 hours or until a meat thermometer reads 180° for the turkey and 165° for the stuffing. When turkey begins to brown, cover lightly with a tent of aluminum foil and baste if needed. Remove all the stuffing. **Yield: 10-12 servings.**

Three-Rice Pilaf

My family's favorite rice dish is this tempting medley of white, brown and wild rice. I prepare it as a side dish or a stuffing. In fall, I add chopped dried apricots, and for the holidays, I mix in dried cranberries. My guests always ask for seconds.
—Ricki Bingham, Ogden, Utah

- **1/2 cup uncooked brown rice**
- **1/2 cup finely chopped carrots**
- **1/2 cup chopped onion**
- **1/2 cup sliced fresh mushrooms**
- **2 tablespoons vegetable oil**
- **1/2 cup uncooked wild rice**
- **3 cups chicken broth**
- **1/4 teaspoon dried thyme**
- **1/4 teaspoon dried rosemary, crushed**
- **1/2 cup uncooked long grain rice**
- **1/3 cup chopped dried apricots**
- **2 tablespoons minced green onions**
- **1/4 teaspoon salt**
- **1/8 teaspoon pepper**
- **1/2 cup chopped pecans, toasted**

In a large saucepan, saute the brown rice, carrots, onion and mushrooms in oil for 10 minutes or until rice is golden.

Add the wild rice, broth, thyme and rosemary; bring to a boil. Reduce heat; cover and simmer for 25 minutes. Stir in long grain rice; cover and simmer for 25 minutes or until liquid is absorbed and wild rice is tender.

Remove from the heat; stir in apricots, green onions, salt and pepper. Cover and let stand for 5 minutes. Sprinkle with pecans just before serving. **Yield: 8-10 servings.**

Three-Rice Pilaf

Dutch Potato Poultry Stuffing

Mushroom Wild Rice

Cheesy Corn Spoon Bread

Mushroom Wild Rice

This colorful casserole is a standout from my mother's collection of family recipes. Excellent texture and taste guarantee it won't play second fiddle to the main dish! —*Charlene Baert, Winnipeg, Manitoba*

- 4 cups water
- 1 cup uncooked wild rice
- 1 teaspoon butter
- 1-1/2 teaspoons salt, *divided*
- 1/2 cup uncooked brown rice
- 8 bacon strips, diced
- 2 cups sliced fresh mushrooms
- 1 large onion, chopped
- 1 medium green pepper, chopped
- 1 medium sweet red pepper, chopped
- 1 celery rib, thinly sliced
- 1 can (14-1/2 ounces) beef broth
- 2 tablespoons cornstarch
- 1/4 cup cold water
- 1/2 cup slivered almonds

In a saucepan, bring water, wild rice, butter and 1/2 teaspoon salt to a boil. Reduce heat; cover and simmer for 40 minutes. Stir in brown rice. Cover and simmer for 25-30 minutes longer or until rice is tender.

Meanwhile, in a large skillet, cook bacon over medium heat until crisp. Using a slotted spoon, remove bacon to paper towels; drain, reserving 2 tablespoons drippings. In the drippings, saute the mushrooms, onion, peppers and celery until tender. Stir in broth and remaining salt. Bring to a boil.

Combine the cornstarch and cold water until smooth; stir into the mushroom mixture. Cook and stir for 2 minutes or until thickened; stir in almonds and bacon. Drain rice; add mushroom mixture.

Transfer to a greased 13-in. x 9-in. x 2-in. baking dish. Cover and bake at 350° for 25 minutes. Uncover; bake 5-10 minutes longer or until heated through. **Yield: 12 servings.**

Cheesy Corn Spoon Bread

Homey and comforting, this custard-like side dish is a requested recipe at potlucks and holiday dinners.
—Katherine Franklin, Carbondale, Illinois

- 1 medium onion, chopped
- 1/4 cup butter
- 2 eggs
- 2 cups (16 ounces) sour cream
- 1 can (15-1/4 ounces) whole kernel corn, drained
- 1 can (14-3/4 ounces) cream-style corn
- 1/4 teaspoon salt
- 1/4 teaspoon pepper
- 1 package (8-1/2 ounces) corn bread/muffin mix
- 1 medium jalapeno pepper, minced
- 2 cups (8 ounces) shredded cheddar cheese, *divided*

In a skillet, saute onion in butter until tender; set aside. In a bowl, beat the eggs; add sour cream, both cans of corn, salt and pepper. Stir in corn bread mix just until blended. Fold in the sauteed onion, jalapeno and 1-1/2 cups cheese. Transfer to a greased shallow 3-qt. baking dish. Sprinkle with remaining cheese.

Bake, uncovered, at 375° for 35-40 minutes or until a toothpick inserted near the center comes out clean; cool slightly. **Yield: 12-15 servings.**

Editor's Note: When cutting or seeding hot peppers, use rubber or plastic gloves to protect your hands. Avoid touching your face.

Rich 'n' Cheesy Macaroni 1st prize

This delicious dish puts a new twist on traditional macaroni and cheese. The three different cheese flavors blend together wonderfully. Plus, it's easy to prepare—I plan to make it often when my husband, Ken, and I start traveling.
—Gwen Miller, Rolling Hills, Alberta

Rich 'n' Cheesy Macaroni

- 2-1/2 cups uncooked elbow macaroni
- 6 tablespoons butter, *divided*
- 1/4 cup all-purpose flour
- 1 teaspoon salt
- 1 teaspoon sugar
- 2 cups milk
- 8 ounces process American cheese, cubed
- 1-1/3 cups small-curd cottage cheese
- 2/3 cup sour cream
- 2 cups (8 ounces) shredded sharp cheddar cheese
- 1-1/2 cups soft bread crumbs

Cook macaroni according to package directions; drain. Meanwhile, in a saucepan, melt 4 tablespoons butter. Stir in the flour, salt and sugar until smooth; gradually stir in milk. Bring to a boil; cook and stir for 2 minutes or until thickened.

Reduce heat; add American cheese, stirring until melted. Stir in cottage cheese and sour cream.

Drain pasta; place in a greased 2-1/2-qt. baking dish. Spoon cheese sauce over pasta; toss to coat. Sprinkle with cheddar cheese. Melt remaining butter and toss with bread crumbs; sprinkle over top. Bake, uncovered, at 350° for 30 minutes or until golden brown. **Yield: 6-8 servings.**

Tangy Barbecue Sauce

My mother-in-law created this recipe, and we just can't get enough of her delectable sauce! I always keep a little out of the basting dish prior to using it on the grill so we have some to serve at the table. It tastes terrific on any grilled meat.
—Mary Kaye Rackowitz, Marysville, Washington

- 1 cup ketchup
- 2 tablespoons lemon juice
- 2 tablespoons cider vinegar
- 1/4 cup packed brown sugar
- 2 teaspoons prepared mustard
- 1 teaspoon salt
- 1/2 to 1 teaspoon hot pepper sauce
- 1 bay leaf
- 1 garlic clove, minced
- 1/2 cup water
- 2 teaspoons Worcestershire sauce

Combine all the ingredients in a small saucepan; bring to a boil, stirring occasionally. Reduce heat; cover and simmer for 30 minutes. Discard bay leaf. Use as a basting sauce when grilling chicken, pork or beef. **Yield: 1-1/2 cups.**

Tangy Barbecue Sauce

Colorful Apricot Chutney 1st prize

This chutney is great served over a variety of meats. You can use it as an appetizer on crackers, or try mixing it with cream cheese into a spread. When the local Extension office held a Pepper Day, I entered it in the recipe contest. It ended up winning first prize.
—Lucile Cline, Wichita, Kansas

- 3 large sweet red peppers, diced
- 12 ounces dried apricots, diced
- 1 cup raisins
- 1 cup sugar
- 1 large onion, finely chopped
- 3/4 cup red wine vinegar
- 5 garlic cloves, minced
- 1-1/2 teaspoons salt
- 1-1/2 teaspoons crushed red pepper flakes
- 1/4 teaspoon ground ginger
- 1/4 teaspoon ground cumin
- 1/4 teaspoon ground mustard

In a large heavy saucepan, combine all the ingredients; bring to a boil. Reduce heat; simmer, uncovered, for 25-30 minutes or until thickened, stirring occasionally. Cover and refrigerate. Serve as an accompaniment to pork or chicken. Chutney may be stored in the refrigerator for up to 1 month. **Yield: 4 cups.**

Cherry Almond Ham Glaze

I came across this recipe looking for an alternative to traditional sauces for holiday meats. Mostly, I serve it with holiday ham, and it goes over well—probably because it is such a change of taste. But the glaze should be fine with almost any meat, and its cheery color would add a festive touch to the table!
—Julie Sterchi, Fairfield, Illinois

Colorful Apricot Chutney

- 1 jar (12 ounces) cherry preserves
- 1/4 cup cider vinegar
- 2 tablespoons corn syrup
- 1/4 teaspoon ground cinnamon
- 1/4 teaspoon ground cloves
- 1/4 teaspoon ground nutmeg
- 1/3 cup slivered almonds
- 3 tablespoons water

In a saucepan, combine the first six ingredients. Bring to a boil. Reduce heat; simmer, uncovered, for 2 minutes, stirring frequently. Stir in the almonds.

About 15 minutes before ham is done, spoon 1/4 to 1/3 cup glaze over ham. Repeat if desired. Stir water into remaining glaze; heat through and serve with ham. **Yield: about 1-1/2 cups glaze.**

Cherry Almond Ham Glaze

Cherry Almond Preserves

Cherry Almond Preserves 1st prize

This recipe came from my mother-in-law. It's very old-fashioned. In fact, the friend who gave it to her used to cook it up on an old wood stove. With all the cherry orchards here in Bitterroot Valley, I make two batches of these preserves each summer. My family likes them on fresh bread, muffins, pancakes and even ice cream—the consistency's similar to a topping. I have to be careful, though, and ration the jars out or they'd be the first thing to disappear from the root cellar! *—Connie Lawrence, Hamilton, Montana*

- 8 cups pitted sour cherries (about 4 pounds)
- 1-1/2 cups water
- 10 cups sugar
- 2 pouches (3 ounces *each*) liquid fruit pectin
- 1 teaspoon almond extract

In a large kettle, bring the cherries and water to a boil; boil for 15 minutes. Add sugar and bring to a full rolling boil, stirring constantly. Boil for 4 minutes. Stir in pectin; return to a full rolling boil. Boil for 1 minute, stirring constantly. Remove from the heat; stir in extract. Skim off foam.

Pour hot into hot sterilized jars, leaving 1/4-in. headspace. Adjust caps. Process 15 minutes in a boiling-water bath. **Yield: 11 half-pints.**

Lemon Butter Spread

My grandmother, who was a great cook, brought this recipe with her from England. I use it as a spread on toast, for filling in a cake or on top of ice cream.
—Gloria Costes, West Hills, California

- 1 cup butter
- 2 cups sugar
- 3 eggs, lightly beaten
- 1/2 cup lemon juice
- 1 tablespoon grated lemon peel

In the top of a double boiler over boiling water, melt butter. Stir in the sugar, eggs, lemon juice and peel. Cook over simmering water for 1 hour or until mixture is thickened and coats the back of a spoon.

Pour into containers. Store in the refrigerator. Use over cake or spread on toast or muffins. **Yield: 3 cups.**

Lemon Butter Spread

QUICK BREADS

VEET RASPBERRY MUFFINS, pg. 313

Peachy Sour Cream Coffee Cake

When I was a little girl, my grandma got up early every Saturday to make this coffee cake for our family breakfast. —*Alice Brandt, Marengo, Illinois*

STREUSEL:

- 2 cups chopped pecans
- 1/3 cup packed brown sugar
- 3 tablespoons sugar
- 1 teaspoon ground cinnamon

CAKE:

- 1/2 cup butter-flavored shortening
- 1 cup sugar
- 2 eggs
- 1 teaspoon vanilla extract
- 2 cups all-purpose flour
- 1/2 teaspoon baking powder
- 1/2 teaspoon baking soda
- 1/2 teaspoon salt
- 1 cup (8 ounces) sour cream
- 2 cups sliced peeled fresh peaches

Combine the streusel ingredients; set aside. In a large mixing bowl, cream shortening and sugar until fluffy. Beat in eggs and vanilla. Combine all dry ingredients; add to creamed mixture alternately with the sour cream. Beat until smooth.

Peachy Sour Cream Coffee Cake

Pour half the batter into a 9-in. springform pan. Sprinkle with 1 cup of the streusel. Top with remaining batter and 1/2 cup streusel.

Bake at 350° for 30 minutes. Arrange peaches over cake; sprinkle with remaining streusel. Bake 30-40 minutes longer or until a toothpick inserted near the center comes out clean. Cool for 10 minutes before removing sides of pan. Serve coffee cake warm or at room temperature. **Yield: 12 servings.**

Triple-Chocolate Quick Bread

Every year around Christmas time, I make this bread for my family. I've also given it as a gift wrapped in colored foil.—Karen Grimes, Stephens City, Virginia

- 1/2 cup butter, softened
- 2/3 cup packed brown sugar
- 2 eggs
- 1 cup (6 ounces) miniature semisweet chocolate chips, melted
- 1-1/2 cups applesauce
- 2 teaspoons vanilla extract
- 2-1/2 cups all-purpose flour
- 1 teaspoon baking powder
- 1 teaspoon baking soda
- 1 teaspoon salt
- 1/2 cup miniature semisweet chocolate chips

GLAZE:

- 1/2 cup miniature semisweet chocolate chips
- 1 tablespoon butter
- 2 to 3 tablespoons half-and-half cream
- 1/2 cup confectioners' sugar
- 1/4 teaspoon vanilla extract

Pinch salt

In a mixing bowl, cream butter and sugar. Add eggs and melted chocolate; mix well. Add applesauce and vanilla. Combine the flour, baking powder, baking soda and salt; add to creamed mixture and mix well. Stir in chocolate chips.

Spoon the batter into four greased 5-1/2-in. x 3-in. x 2-in. loaf pans. Bake at 350° for 35-40 minutes or until a toothpick inserted near the center comes out clean. Cool for 10 minutes before removing to wire racks to cool completely.

For glaze, in a saucepan, melt chocolate chips and butter; stir in cream. Remove from the heat; stir in sugar, vanilla and salt. Drizzle over warm bread. **Yield: 4 mini-loaves.**

Triple-Chocolate Quick Bread

Strawberries 'n' Cream Bread

Once strawberry-picking time arrives here each summer, my husband and I look forward to this bread. Since only fresh strawberries will do, I have been thinking of trying a different kind of berry, so we can enjoy it more often.

—Suzanne Randall, Dexter, Maine

- 1/2 cup butter, softened
- 3/4 cup sugar
- 2 eggs
- 1/2 cup sour cream
- 1 teaspoon vanilla extract
- 1-3/4 cups all-purpose flour
- 1/2 teaspoon baking powder
- 1/2 teaspoon baking soda
- 1/2 teaspoon salt
- 1/4 teaspoon ground cinnamon
- 3/4 cup chopped fresh strawberries
- 3/4 cup chopped walnuts, toasted, *divided*

In a large mixing bowl, cream butter and sugar until fluffy. Beat in eggs, one at a time, beating well after addition. Add sour cream and vanilla; mix well. Combine the flour, baking powder, baking soda, salt and cinnamon; stir into creamed mixture just until moistened. Fold in the strawberries and 1/2 cup walnuts.

Pour into a greased 8-in. x 4-in. x 2-in. loaf pan. Sprinkle with remaining nuts. Bake at 350° for 65-70 minutes or until a toothpick inserted near the center comes out clean. Cool for 10 minutes before removing from pan to a wire rack to cool completely. **Yield: 1 loaf.**

Aloha Quick Bread

The addition of coconut, orange peel, pineapple and nuts gives a new twist to a loaf of banana bread. It's so good I sometimes serve slices of it for dessert.
—Lanita Anderson, Chesapeake, Virginia

- 1/2 cup butter, softened
- 1 cup sugar
- 2 eggs
- 1 cup mashed ripe bananas (about 2 medium)
- 1/4 cup milk
- 1 tablespoon grated orange peel
- 1 teaspoon vanilla extract
- 1/2 teaspoon almond extract
- 2 cups all-purpose flour
- 1 teaspoon baking soda
- 1/2 teaspoon salt
- 1 cup flaked coconut
- 1/2 cup chopped nuts
- 1/2 cup crushed pineapple

In a mixing bowl, cream butter and sugar. Add the eggs, one at a time, beating well after each addition. Beat in the banana, milk, orange peel and extracts. Combine the flour, baking soda and salt; add to the creamed mixture just until moistened. Fold in the coconut, nuts and pineapple.

Transfer to a greased 9-in. x 5-in. x 3-in. loaf pan. Bake at 350° for 1 hour and 20 minutes or until a toothpick inserted near the center comes out clean. Cool for 10 minutes before removing from pan to a wire rack. **Yield: 1 loaf.**

Strawberries 'n' Cream Bread

Aloha Quick Bread

Raspberry Streusel Coffee Cake

Chocolate Chip Pumpkin Bread

Raspberry Streusel Coffee Cake 1st prize

One of my mother's friends used to bring this over at the holidays, and it never lasted long. With the tangy raspberry filling, tender cake and crunchy topping, it has become a favorite at our house.
—*Amy Mitchell, Sabetha, Kansas*

- 3-1/2 cups unsweetened raspberries
- 1 cup water
- 2 tablespoons lemon juice
- 1-1/4 cups sugar
- 1/3 cup cornstarch

BATTER:
- 3 cups all-purpose flour
- 1 cup sugar
- 1 teaspoon baking powder
- 1 teaspoon baking soda
- 1 cup cold butter
- 2 eggs, lightly beaten
- 1 cup (8 ounces) sour cream
- 1 teaspoon vanilla extract

TOPPING:
- 1/2 cup all-purpose flour
- 1/2 cup sugar
- 1/4 cup butter, softened
- 1/2 cup chopped pecans

GLAZE:
- 1/2 cup confectioners' sugar
- 2 teaspoons milk
- 1/2 teaspoon vanilla extract

In a large saucepan, cook raspberries and water over medium heat for 5 minutes. Add lemon juice. Combine sugar and cornstarch; stir into fruit mixture. Bring to a boil; cook and stir for 2 minutes or until thickened. Cool.

In a large bowl, combine the flour, sugar, baking powder and baking soda. Cut in butter until mixture resembles coarse crumbs. Stir in eggs, sour cream and vanilla (batter will be stiff). Spread half into a greased 13-in. x 9-in. x 2-in. baking dish. Spread raspberry filling over batter; spoon remaining batter over filling. Combine topping ingredients; sprinkle over top. Bake at 350° for 40-45 minutes or until golden brown. Combine the glaze ingredients; drizzle over warm cake. **Yield: 12-16 servings.**

Chocolate Chip Pumpkin Bread

A touch of cinnamon helps blend the chocolate and pumpkin flavors you'll find in this tender bread. And since the recipe makes two loaves, you can send one to a bake sale and keep one at home for your family to enjoy. —*Lora Stanley, Bennington, Kansas*

- 3 cups all-purpose flour
- 2 teaspoons ground cinnamon
- 1 teaspoon salt
- 1 teaspoon baking soda
- 4 eggs
- 2 cups sugar
- 2 cups canned pumpkin
- 1-1/2 cups vegetable oil
- 1-1/2 cups semisweet chocolate chips

In a large bowl, combine the flour, cinnamon, salt and baking soda. In another bowl, beat the eggs, sugar, pumpkin and oil. Stir into dry ingredients just until moistened. Fold in chocolate chips.

Pour into two greased 8-in. x 4-in. x 2-in. loaf pans. Bake at 350° for 60-70 minutes or until a toothpick inserted near the center comes out clean. Cool for 10 minutes before removing from pans to wire racks. **Yield: 2 loaves.**

Mango Nut Bread

Mango Nut Bread

We live on the slopes of Haleakala, where carrots, potatoes, cabbage, bananas, litchis and mangoes are grown. This is my favorite recipe using mangoes. —*Jo Sherley, Kahului, Hawaii*

- 2 cups all-purpose flour
- 1-1/2 cups sugar
- 1 teaspoon baking soda
- 1/2 teaspoon salt
- 1/2 teaspoon ground cinnamon
- 3 eggs
- 1/2 cup vegetable oil
- 1 teaspoon vanilla extract
- 2 cups chopped mangoes
- 1/2 cup chopped dates
- 1/2 cup chopped walnuts *or* macadamia nuts

In a bowl, combine the first five ingredients. In another bowl, beat the eggs, oil and vanilla. Stir into dry ingredients just until moistened. Fold in mangoes, dates and nuts (batter will be stiff).

Spoon into two greased 8-in. x 4-in. x 2-in. loaf pans. Bake at 350° for 50-55 minutes or until a toothpick inserted near the center comes out clean. Cool for 10 minutes before removing from pans to wire racks. **Yield: 2 loaves.**

Pineapple Zucchini Bread

Meals are even more memorable when I complement them with this light, garden-fresh bread. The zucchini makes it so moist and tender, and the pineapple lends a delicate tropical twist to every delicious slice.

—Shirley Boulet, Whitefield, New Hampshire

- 3 eggs
- 2 cups finely shredded zucchini
- 1 cup vegetable oil
- 1 can (8 ounces) crushed pineapple, drained
- 2 teaspoons vanilla extract
- 3 cups all-purpose flour
- 2 cups sugar
- 2 teaspoons baking soda
- 1-1/2 teaspoons ground cinnamon
- 1 teaspoon salt
- 3/4 teaspoon ground nutmeg
- 1/2 teaspoon baking powder
- 1 cup chopped nuts
- 1 cup raisins, optional

In a bowl, combine the eggs, zucchini, oil, pineapple and vanilla. Combine the dry ingredients; stir into egg mixture just until moistened. Fold in nuts and raisins if desired.

Pour into two greased 8-in. x 4-in. x 2-in. loaf pans. Bake at 350° for 50-60 minutes or until a toothpick inserted near the center comes out clean. Cool for 10 minutes before removing from pans to wire racks. **Yield: 2 loaves.**

Pineapple Zucchini Bread

Chocolate Chip Carrot Bread

My family likes sweet breads, and this loaf incorporates many of their favorite ingredients. I'm a former newspaper food columnist, and coming up with flavorful recipes that are a little out-of-the-ordinary is a favorite pastime of mine.

—Sharon Setzer, Philomath, Oregon

- 3 cups all-purpose flour
- 1 cup sugar
- 1 cup packed brown sugar
- 2 to 3 teaspoons ground cinnamon
- 2 teaspoons baking powder
- 1 teaspoon baking soda
- 1 teaspoon salt
- 1 teaspoon ground ginger
- 1/4 to 1/2 teaspoon ground cloves
- 3 eggs
- 3/4 cup orange juice
- 3/4 cup vegetable oil
- 1 teaspoon vanilla extract
- 2 cups grated carrots
- 1 cup (6 ounces) semisweet chocolate chips

In a large bowl, combine the first nine ingredients. In a small bowl, beat the eggs, orange juice, oil and vanilla. Stir into the dry ingredients just until moistened. Fold in the carrots and chocolate chips.

Transfer to two greased 8-in. x 4-in. x 2-in. loaf pans. Bake at 350° for 55-60 minutes or until a toothpick inserted near the center comes out clean. Cool for 10 minutes before removing from pans to wire racks. **Yield: 2 loaves.**

Broccoli Corn Bread

This recipe was inspired by my husband's love of corn bread. It's so good, he and folks who dine with us eat it plain. — *Lois Triplet, Springhill, Louisiana*

- 1 cup plus 1 tablespoon cornmeal, *divided*
- 1/3 cup all-purpose flour
- 1-1/2 teaspoons baking powder
- 3/4 teaspoon salt
- 1/4 teaspoon baking soda
- 5 eggs, beaten
- 1 package (10 ounces) frozen chopped broccoli, thawed and drained
- 1-1/2 cups (6 ounces) shredded cheddar cheese
- 1 carton (12 ounces) small-curd cottage cheese
- 1 medium onion, chopped
- 3/4 cup butter, melted

In a bowl, combine 1 cup of cornmeal, flour, baking powder, salt and baking soda. In another bowl, combine the eggs, broccoli, cheeses, onion and butter. Add to cornmeal mixture; mix just until moistened.

Sprinkle remaining cornmeal in a greased 13-in. x 9-in. x 2-in. baking pan. Pour batter into pan. Bake at 350° for 30-40 minutes or until a toothpick inserted near the center comes out clean. Serve warm. **Yield: 12-15 servings.**

Chocolate Chip Carrot Bread

Broccoli Corn Bread

Gingerbread Loaf

Citrus Streusel Quick Bread

Gingerbread Loaf

Enjoy the old-fashioned appeal of gingerbread in a loaf with this recipe originally from Holland. This moist, spicy bread smells delicious while it's baking, and slices are wonderful spread with cream cheese. This recipe makes two big loaves, so we have one to eat and one to freeze for later or to give away.

—Martina Biemond, Rosedale, British Columbia

- 4 cups all-purpose flour
- 2 cups sugar
- 4 teaspoons baking powder
- 2 teaspoons ground cinnamon
- 1-1/4 teaspoons ground cloves
- 1-1/4 teaspoons ground nutmeg
- 1 teaspoon baking soda
- 1 teaspoon ground ginger
- 2 eggs
- 2 cups milk
- 1 cup maple syrup
- 2 tablespoons vegetable oil

In a bowl, combine the first eight ingredients. In another bowl, combine the eggs, milk, syrup and oil. Stir into the dry ingredients just until moistened (batter will be thin).

Pour into two greased 9-in. x 5-in. x 3-in. loaf pans. Bake at 325° for 60-70 minutes or until a toothpick inserted near the center comes out clean. Cool for 10 minutes before removing from pans to wire racks. **Yield: 2 loaves.**

Citrus Streusel Quick Bread

As a minister's wife, I do a lot of baking and cooking for church. Often, I'll find myself copying down recipes to share. This one's generally in demand.

—Debra White, Williamson, West Virginia

- 1 package (18-1/4 ounces) lemon *or* orange cake mix, *divided*
- 2 tablespoons brown sugar

Southern Banana Nut Bread

- 1 teaspoon ground cinnamon
- 1 tablespoon cold butter
- 1/2 cup chopped pecans
- 1 package (3.4 ounces) instant vanilla pudding mix
- 4 eggs
- 1 cup (8 ounces) sour cream
- 1/3 cup vegetable oil

GLAZE:

- 1 cup confectioners' sugar
- 2 to 3 tablespoons milk

In a small bowl, combine 2 tablespoons cake mix, brown sugar and cinnamon; cut in butter until crumbly. Stir in pecans; set aside.

In a mixing bowl, combine the pudding mix, eggs, sour cream, oil and remaining cake mix; beat on medium speed for 2 minutes.

Pour into two greased 8-in. x 4-in. x 2-in. loaf pans. Sprinkle with pecan mixture. Bake at 350° for 45-50 minutes or until a toothpick inserted near the center comes out clean. Cool in pans for 10 minutes before removing to wire racks. Combine glaze ingredients; drizzle over warm bread. **Yield: 2 loaves.**

Southern Banana Nut Bread

I found this recipe in an old church cookbook. Pecans in the bread and topping make it unique.
—Viva Forman, Tallahassee, Florida

- 1/2 cup butter-flavored shortening
- 1-1/2 cups sugar
- 2 eggs
- 1 cup mashed ripe bananas (about 2 medium)
- 1 teaspoon vanilla extract
- 2 cups self-rising flour
- 1/2 cup buttermilk
- 3/4 cup chopped pecans

TOPPING:

- 1/4 to 1/3 cup mashed ripe bananas
- 1-1/4 cups confectioners' sugar
- 1 teaspoon lemon juice
- Additional chopped pecans

In a mixing bowl, cream shortening and sugar; beat in eggs. Blend in bananas and vanilla. Add flour to cream mixture alternately with buttermilk. Fold in pecans.

Pour into two greased 8-in. x 4-in. x 2-in. loaf pans. Bake at 350° for 45-55 minutes or until a toothpick inserted near the center comes out clean. Cool for 10 minutes before removing from pans to wire racks to cool completely.

For topping, combine the bananas, confectioners' sugar and lemon juice; spread over loaves. Sprinkle with pecans. Store in the refrigerator. **Yield: 2 loaves.**

Editor's Note: As a substitute for each cup of self-rising flour, place 1-1/2 teaspoons baking powder and 1/2 teaspoon salt in a measuring cup. Add all-purpose flour to measure 1 cup.

Cinnamon Rolls in a Snap

I turned biscuits into hot cinnamon rolls one morning because a friend was stopping by. She was so impressed with the results.
—Laura McDermott, Big Lake, Minnesota

- 4-1/2 cups biscuit/baking mix
- 1-1/3 cups milk
- 2 tablespoons butter, softened
- 1/4 cup sugar
- 1 teaspoon ground cinnamon
- 1/3 cup raisins, optional

ICING:

- 2 cups confectioners' sugar
- 2 tablespoons milk
- 2 tablespoons butter, melted
- 1 teaspoon vanilla extract

In a bowl, combine biscuit mix and milk. Turn onto a floured surface; knead 8-10 times. Roll dough into a 12-in. x 10-in. rectangle. Spread with butter. Combine the sugar, cinnamon and raisins if desired; sprinkle over butter.

Roll up jelly-roll style, starting with a long side; pinch seam to seal. Cut into 12 slices; place cut-side down on a greased baking sheet. Bake at 450° for 10-12 minutes or until golden brown. Combine the icing ingredients; spread over rolls. Serve warm. **Yield: 1 dozen.**

Cherry Almond Muffins

As a kid, I loved doughnuts filled with custard or jelly, so I decided to experiment with fillings in muffins. The result was this terrific recipe.
—John Montgomery, Fortuna, California

- 1-3/4 cups all-purpose flour
- 1/2 cup plus 1 tablespoon sugar
- 1/2 teaspoon baking powder
- 1/2 teaspoon baking soda
- 1/4 teaspoon salt

Cinnamon Rolls in a Snap

- 1/2 cup cold butter
- 1 egg
- 3/4 cup sour cream
- 1 teaspoon almond extract

TOPPING:

- 1/3 cup all-purpose flour
- 2 tablespoons sugar
- 2 tablespoons cold butter
- 1/3 cup chopped sliced almonds

FILLING:

- 1 package (8 ounces) cream cheese, softened
- 1 egg
- 1/4 cup sugar
- 1/2 teaspoon vanilla extract
- 3/4 cup cherry preserves, warmed

In a bowl, combine the flour, sugar, baking powder, baking soda and salt. Cut in butter until the mixture resembles coarse crumbs. Beat the egg, sour cream and extract until smooth; stir into dry ingredients just until moistened (batter will be thick).

For topping, in a small bowl, combine flour and sugar; cut in butter until crumbly. Stir in almonds; set aside. For filling, in a mixing bowl, beat cream cheese, egg, sugar and vanilla until smooth. In a saucepan over low heat, warm preserves.

Fill greased jumbo muffin cups half full with batter. Divide cream cheese filling and preserves evenly between muffin cups; swirl gently. Cover with remaining batter. Sprinkle with topping. Bake at 350° for 30-35 minutes or until a toothpick inserted in the muffin comes out clean. Cool for 5 minutes before removing from pans to wire racks. **Yield: 7 jumbo muffins or 14 regular muffins.**

Editor's Note: If using regular-size muffin cups, bake for 20-25 minutes.

Cherry Almond Muffins

Morning Maple Muffins

Maple combines with a subtle touch of cinnamon and nuts to give these muffins a hearty flavor.
—Elizabeth Talbot, Lexington, Kentucky

- 2 cups all-purpose flour
- 1/2 cup packed brown sugar
- 2 teaspoons baking powder
- 1/2 teaspoon salt
- 3/4 cup milk
- 1/2 cup butter, melted
- 1/2 cup maple syrup
- 1/4 cup sour cream
- 1 egg
- 1/2 teaspoon vanilla extract

TOPPING:

- 3 tablespoons all-purpose flour
- 3 tablespoons sugar
- 2 tablespoons chopped nuts
- 1/2 teaspoon ground cinnamon
- 2 tablespoons cold butter

In a bowl, combine the flour, brown sugar, baking powder and salt. In another bowl, combine the milk, butter, syrup, sour cream, egg and vanilla. Stir into the dry ingredients just until moistened. Fill greased or paper-lined muffin cups two-thirds full.

Combine flour, sugar, nuts and cinnamon; cut in butter until crumbly. Sprinkle over batter.

Bake at 400° for 16-20 minutes or until a toothpick inserted near the center comes out clean. Cool for 5 minutes before removing from pans to wire racks. **Yield: 16 muffins.**

Morning Maple Muffins

Lemon Tea Muffins

Apple Nut Muffins

Lemon Tea Muffins 1st prize

When it comes to baking, muffins are No. 1 to me. I bake a batch every day. These are great with your favorite tea. —*Terrie Cox, Honeyville, Utah*

- 2 eggs, *separated*
- 1/2 cup butter, softened
- 1/2 cup sugar
- 1 cup all-purpose flour
- 1 teaspoon baking powder
- 1/4 teaspoon salt
- 3 tablespoons lemon juice
- 1 teaspoon grated lemon peel

TOPPING:

- 1 tablespoon sugar
- 1/8 teaspoon ground cinnamon
- Dash ground nutmeg

In a small mixing bowl, beat egg yolks until light and lemon colored, about 3 minutes. In a large mixing bowl, cream butter and sugar. Fold in yolks. Combine the flour, baking powder and salt; add to the creamed mixture alternately with lemon juice and peel, stirring just until combined. Beat egg whites until stiff peaks form; fold into batter.

Fill greased or paper-lined muffin cups two-thirds full. Combine topping ingredients; sprinkle over muffins. Bake at 350° for 20-25 minutes or until toothpick inserted near the center comes out clean. Cool in pan 10 minutes before removing to a wire rack. **Yield: 8 muffins.**

Apple Nut Muffins

The inspiration for these muffins came from a favorite coffee cake. I wanted to put it in a form our four girls could munch while playing. For variety, I'll sometimes substitute prepared blueberry or lemon pie filling for the delectable from-scratch apple filling.
—*Hollie Gregory, Mt. Vision, New York*

2 tablespoons butter
1/3 cup packed brown sugar
1 tablespoon all-purpose flour
1/2 teaspoon ground cinnamon
1/8 to 1/4 teaspoon ground nutmeg
2 cups diced peeled apples
1/2 cup finely chopped nuts

MUFFINS:

3/4 cup butter, softened
1-1/2 cups sugar
3 eggs
1-1/2 teaspoons vanilla extract
3-1/2 cups all-purpose flour
1-1/2 teaspoons baking powder
1-1/2 teaspoons baking soda
3/4 teaspoon salt
1-1/2 cups (12 ounces) sour cream
Cinnamon-sugar

In a saucepan, melt butter. Stir in the brown sugar, flour, cinnamon and nutmeg until smooth. Add the apples; cook over medium-low heat for 10 minutes or until tender, stirring frequently. Remove from the heat; stir in nuts. Cool.

In a mixing bowl, cream butter and sugar. Add eggs, one at a time, beating well after each. Beat in vanilla. Combine dry ingredients; add to creamed mixture alternately with the sour cream.

Spoon 1/4 cupfuls of batter into greased jumbo muffin cups. Spoon apple mixture into the center of each (do not spread). Top with remaining batter. Sprinkle with cinnamon-sugar.

Bake at 350° for 25-27 minutes or until a toothpick inserted near the center comes out clean. Cool for 5 minutes before removing from pans to wire racks. **Yield: 1 dozen jumbo muffins or 2 dozen regular muffins.**

Editor's Note: If using regular-size muffin cups, fill cups half full with batter; add a rounded teaspoonful of apple mixture and remaining batter. Bake for 16-18 minutes.

Sweet Raspberry Muffins

Sweet Raspberry Muffins

I like to linger over a cup of coffee and a warm sweet treat on weekend mornings. These moist muffins are perfect because making them ties up so little time in the kitchen. —Teresa Raab, Tustin, Michigan

2 cups biscuit/baking mix
2 tablespoons sugar
1/4 cup cold butter
2/3 cup milk
1/4 cup raspberry jam

GLAZE:

1/2 cup confectioners' sugar
2 teaspoons warm water
1/4 teaspoon vanilla extract

In a bowl, combine biscuit mix and sugar. Cut in butter until the mixture resembles coarse crumbs. Stir in milk just until moistened (batter will be thick). Spoon about 1 tablespoon of batter into 12 paper-lined muffin cups. Top with 1 teaspoon jam. Spoon the remaining batter (about 1 tablespoon each) over jam.

Bake at 425° for 12-14 minutes or until lightly browned. Cool in pans for 5 minutes. Meanwhile, in a small bowl, combine glaze ingredients until smooth. Remove muffins to a wire rack. Drizzle with glaze. **Yield: 1 dozen.**

Spiced Pear Muffins

I got this outstanding recipe from the custodian at our church, who fixes these moist, fruity muffins and shares them with friends. The tasty combination of pears and spices is irresistible.
—Linda Jachimstal, Manitowoc, Wisconsin

- 2 cups all-purpose flour
- 1/2 cup packed brown sugar
- 2 teaspoons ground ginger
- 1 teaspoon baking soda
- 1 teaspoon ground cinnamon
- 1/2 teaspoon salt
- 1/8 teaspoon ground nutmeg
- 1/8 teaspoon ground cloves
- 1 egg
- 1 cup (8 ounces) plain yogurt
- 1/2 cup vegetable oil
- 3 tablespoons molasses
- 1-1/2 cups finely chopped peeled pears (about 2 medium)
- 1/2 cup raisins
- 1/3 cup chopped walnuts

In a large bowl, combine the first eight ingredients. In another bowl, beat the egg, yogurt, oil and molasses until smooth. Stir into dry ingredients just until moistened. Fold in pears, raisins and walnuts.

Fill greased or paper-lined miniature muffin cups two-thirds full. Bake at 400° for 10-12 minutes or until a toothpick inserted near the center comes out clean. Cool for 5 minutes before removing from pans to wire racks. Serve warm. **Yield: 2 dozen mini muffins or 16 regular muffins.**

Editor's Note: If using regular-size muffin cups, bake for 18-22 minutes.

Spiced Pear Muffins

Green Chili Corn Muffins

While visiting a local Mexican restaurant, I sampled a spicy corn muffin with a surprising sweetness. This recipe is a result of numerous attempts to re-create that treat using convenient mixes. These moist muffins are tasty with Mexican dishes, chili and soup.
—Melissa Cook, Chico, California

- 1 package (8-1/2 ounces) corn bread/muffin mix
- 1 package (9 ounces) yellow cake mix
- 2 eggs
- 1/2 cup milk
- 1/3 cup water
- 2 tablespoons vegetable oil
- 1 can (4 ounces) chopped green chilies, drained
- 1 cup (4 ounces) shredded cheddar cheese, *divided*

In a bowl, combine dry corn bread and cake mixes. In another bowl, combine the eggs, milk, water and oil. Stir into dry ingredients just until moistened. Add chilies and 3/4 cup cheese.

Fill greased or paper-lined muffin cups two-thirds full. Bake at 350° for 20-22 minutes or until a toothpick inserted near the center comes out clean. Immediately sprinkle with remaining cheese. Cool for 5 minutes before removing from pans to wire racks. Serve warm. **Yield: 16 servings.**

Dijon Ham Muffins

For a nice change from sweet muffins, try this delightful hearty variety. They're easy to fix and great for breakfast with scrambled eggs or on a brunch buffet. They're also super with soup for lunch.
—Karen Davis, Springfield, Missouri

- 1-2/3 cups all-purpose flour
- 1/3 cup cornmeal
- 1/4 cup sugar
- 1 teaspoon baking powder
- 1 to 2 teaspoons ground mustard
- 1/2 teaspoon salt
- 1/2 teaspoon baking soda
- 1/8 teaspoon ground cloves
- 2 eggs
- 1 cup buttermilk
- 1/3 cup vegetable oil
- 3 tablespoons Dijon mustard
- 1 cup finely chopped fully cooked ham

In a bowl, combine the first eight ingredients. Combine the eggs, buttermilk, oil and mustard; stir into the dry ingredients just until moistened. Fold in the ham.

Fill greased muffin cups three-fourths full. Bake at 375° for 20-25 minutes or until a toothpick inserted near the center comes out clean. Cool for 5 minutes before removing from pans to wire racks. Refrigerate leftovers. **Yield: 14 muffins.**

Green Chili Corn Muffins

Dijon Ham Muffins

Savory Italian Rounds

Whole Wheat Biscuits

Savory Italian Rounds 1st prize

A friend gave me the recipe for these cheesy, golden rounds years ago. She said her dad used to make them for her when she was little. Because they're a snap to put together, I frequently fix them for my family during the week and for company on the weekends.
—Donna Ebert, Jackson, Wisconsin

- 2/3 cup grated Parmesan cheese
- 1/2 cup mayonnaise
- 1/4 teaspoon dried basil
- 1/8 teaspoon garlic powder
- 1/8 teaspoon garlic salt
- 1/8 teaspoon dried oregano
- Dash onion salt
- 1 tube (12 ounces) refrigerated buttermilk biscuits

In a bowl, combine the first seven ingredients. Separate biscuits and place on two ungreased baking sheets. Let stand for 5 minutes. Flatten biscuits into 4-in. circles. Spread about 1 tablespoon mayonnaise mixture over each circle to within 1/2 in. of edge.

Bake at 400° for 10-13 minutes or until golden brown. Serve immediately. **Yield: 10 servings.**

Editor's Note: Reduced-fat or fat-free mayonnaise may not be substituted for regular mayonnaise in this recipe.

Whole Wheat Biscuits

This quick and easy recipe adds a special touch to everyday meals. You'll get a lot of compliments when you serve these biscuits fresh from the oven.
—Margie Thomason, Belvidere, Kansas

- 1-1/2 cups all-purpose flour
- 1/2 cup whole wheat flour
- 2 tablespoons sugar
- 1 tablespoon baking powder

1/2 teaspoon cream of tartar
1/4 teaspoon salt
1/2 cup shortening
1 egg
1/2 cup milk
1 tablespoon butter, melted

In a bowl, combine the flours, sugar, baking powder, cream of tartar and salt. Cut in shortening until mixture resembles coarse crumbs. Beat egg and milk; stir into dry ingredients until a ball forms.

Turn onto a floured surface; knead 5-6 times. Roll to 1/2-in. thickness; brush with butter. Cut with a 2-in. biscuit cutter. Place on an ungreased baking sheet. Bake at 450° for 10-12 minutes or until golden brown. Serve warm. **Yield: about 1 dozen.**

Orange Biscuits

These biscuits are a special treat with a ham dinner, but they're also delicious just by themselves. They're often requested by my five children and seven grandchildren. —*Winifred Brown, Wilmette, Illinois*

1/2 cup orange juice
3/4 cup sugar, *divided*
1/4 cup butter
2 teaspoons grated orange peel
2 cups all-purpose flour
1 tablespoon baking powder
1/2 teaspoon salt
1/4 cup shortening
3/4 cup milk
Melted butter
1/2 teaspoon ground cinnamon

In a saucepan, combine the orange juice, 1/2 cup sugar, butter and orange peel. Cook and stir over medium heat for 2 minutes. Divide among 12 muffin cups; set aside.

In a large bowl, combine the flour, baking

Orange Biscuits

powder and salt. Cut in shortening until mixture resembles coarse crumbs. With a fork, stir in milk until mixture forms a ball. On a lightly floured surface, knead the dough 1 minute. Roll into a 9-in. square, about 1/2 in. thick. Brush with melted butter.

Combine the cinnamon and remaining sugar; sprinkle over butter. Roll up. Cut into 12 slices, about 3/4 in. thick. Place slices cut side down over orange mixture in muffin cups. Bake at 450° for 12-16 minutes or until browned. Cool for 2-3 minutes; remove from pan. **Yield: 1 dozen.**

Apricot Scones

Besides farming and raising cattle, our family has a home bakery that serves area restaurants and health food stores. These golden scones are a hit.
—Linda Swanson, Riverside, Washington

- 1-1/2 cups all-purpose flour
- 1/2 cup quick-cooking oats
- 1/4 cup sugar
- 2-1/2 teaspoons baking powder
- 1/4 teaspoon salt
- 1/3 cup cold butter, cubed
- 2 eggs
- 1/4 cup sour cream
- 1 tablespoon milk
- 3/4 cup finely chopped dried apricots

FILLING:

- 3 tablespoons brown sugar
- 1 tablespoon quick-cooking oats
- 1 tablespoon butter, softened

Additional sugar

In a bowl, combine the dry ingredients; cut in butter until mixture resembles fine crumbs. In a small bowl, beat eggs; set aside 1 tablespoon for glaze. In another bowl, combine the sour cream, milk and remaining beaten eggs; add apricots. Stir into crumb mixture until the dough clings together.

Turn onto a lightly floured surface; knead 12-15 times. Divide dough in half. Pat one portion into a 7-in. circle on a greased baking sheet. Combine the brown sugar, oats and butter; sprinkle over dough. Roll out remaining dough into a 7-in. circle; place over filling. Brush with reserved egg; sprinkle with additional sugar. Cut into wedges but do not separate.

Bake at 400° for 15-20 minutes or until scones are golden brown. Cool slightly; cut again if necessary. Serve warm. **Yield: 6 servings.**

Apricot Scones

Cherry Chip Scones 1st prize

These buttery scones, dotted with dried cherries and vanilla chips, are so sweet and flaky that I even serve them for dessert.
—Pamela Brooks, South Berwick, Maine

- 3 cups all-purpose flour
- 1/2 cup sugar
- 2-1/2 teaspoons baking powder
- 1/2 teaspoon baking soda
- 6 tablespoons cold butter
- 1 cup (8 ounces) vanilla yogurt
- 1/4 cup plus 2 tablespoons milk, *divided*
- 1-1/3 cups dried cherries
- 2/3 cup vanilla *or* white chips

In a large bowl, combine the flour, sugar, baking powder and baking soda. Cut in butter until the mixture resembles coarse crumbs. Combine yogurt and 1/4 cup milk; stir into crumb mixture just until moistened. Knead in the cherries and chips.

On a greased baking sheet, pat the dough into a 9-in. circle. Cut into eight wedges; separate wedges. Brush with the remaining milk. Bake at 400° for 20-25 minutes or until biscuits are golden brown. Serve warm. **Yield: 8 servings.**

Cherry Chip Scones

Flaky Dill Biscuits

The dill weed in these lovely golden biscuits really comes through. My friends like them because they're fluffy, tender and delicious. I like them because they don't take as much time to make as yeast rolls.
—Audrey Lockau, Kitchener, Ontario

- 2 cups all-purpose flour
- 3 teaspoons baking powder
- 2 to 3 teaspoons dill weed
- 3/4 teaspoon salt
- 1/4 teaspoon pepper
- 1/2 cup cold butter
- 2 eggs, lightly beaten
- 1/2 cup plus 1 tablespoon half-and-half cream, *divided*

In a bowl, combine the flour, baking powder, dill, salt and pepper. Cut in butter until the mixture resembles coarse crumbs. With a fork, stir in eggs and 1/2 cup cream just until moistened.

Drop by 1/4 cupfuls onto an ungreased baking sheet. Brush tops with remaining cream. Bake at 450° for 10-12 minutes or until golden brown. **Yield: 9 servings.**

Flaky Dill Biscuits

Funnel Cakes

Funnel Cakes

These are much simpler to make than doughnuts but taste just as good. They have been a regular treat of ours since we came across them when we lived in the Ozarks. —*Mary Faith Yoder, Unity, Wisconsin*

- 2 eggs
- 1 cup milk
- 1 cup water
- 1/2 teaspoon vanilla extract
- 3 cups all-purpose flour
- 1/4 cup sugar
- 1 tablespoon baking powder
- 1/4 teaspoon salt
- Oil for deep-fat frying
- Confectioners' sugar

In a mixing bowl, beat eggs. Add the milk, water and vanilla; mix well. Combine the flour, sugar, baking powder and salt; beat into egg mixture until smooth.

In an electric skillet or deep-fat fryer, heat oil to 375°. Cover the bottom of a funnel spout with your finger; ladle 1/2 cup of batter into the funnel. Holding the funnel several inches above the skillet, release your finger and move the funnel in a spiral motion until all the batter is released (scraping with a rubber spatula if needed). Fry for 2 minutes on each side or until golden brown.

Drain on paper towels. Dust with confectioners' sugar and serve warm. **Yield: 8 cakes.**

Editor's Note: The batter can be poured from a liquid measuring cup instead of a funnel.

YEAST BREADS

UT SWIRL BREAD, pg. 326

Yeast Breads

Orange Swirl Coffee Cake

My family and I look forward to warm slices of this citrus-flavored coffee cake every Christmas and Easter morning. It's a tasty tradition we've been sharing for a number of years.
—Barbara Daniel, Ducor, California

- 1 package (1/4 ounce) active dry yeast
- 1/4 cup warm water (110° to 115°)
- 1 cup sugar, *divided*
- 2 eggs
- 1/2 cup sour cream
- 8 tablespoons butter, *divided*
- 1 teaspoon salt
- 3-1/4 to 3-1/2 cups all-purpose flour
- 3/4 cup flaked coconut, toasted
- 2 tablespoons grated orange peel

ORANGE GLAZE:

- 6 tablespoons sugar
- 1-1/2 teaspoons cornstarch
- 1/4 cup sour cream
- 2 tablespoons butter
- 1 tablespoon orange juice
- 1/4 cup flaked coconut, toasted

In a mixing bowl, dissolve yeast in warm water. Add 1/4 cup sugar, eggs, sour cream, 6 tablespoons butter and salt; mix well. Stir in enough flour to form a soft dough.

Turn onto a floured surface; knead until smooth and elastic, about 6-8 minutes. Place in a greased bowl, turning once to grease top. Cover and let rise in a warm place until doubled, about 1 hour.

Meanwhile, combine the coconut, orange peel and remaining sugar; set aside. Punch dough down. Turn onto a floured surface; roll into an 18-in. x 10-in. rectangle. Melt remaining butter; brush over dough. Spread coconut mixture over dough. Roll up jelly-roll style, starting with a long side; pinch seam to seal. Place seam side near the top and facing the center tube in a greased fluted 10-in. tube pan; pinch ends together. Cover and let rise until doubled, about 1 hour.

Orange Swirl Coffee Cake

Bake at 350° for 30 minutes or until golden brown. Cool for 10 minutes before removing from pan to a wire rack.

For glaze, combine the sugar, cornstarch, sour cream, butter and orange juice in a saucepan. Bring to a boil; boil and stir for 2 minutes. Spoon or brush over warm coffee cake. Sprinkle with coconut. **Yield: 16-20 servings.**

Pineapple Cheese Braid

Pineapple Cheese Braids 1st prize

Folks will be pleasantly surprised by this bread's pineapple filling. If your're in a hurry, you can use canned pie filling.
—Shirley Kensinger, Roaring Spring, Pennsylvania

- 2 packages (1/4 ounce *each*) active dry yeast
- 1 cup warm water (110° to 115°)
- 1/2 cup butter, softened
- 5 tablespoons sugar
- 2 eggs
- 1/4 teaspoon salt
- 4-1/4 to 4-1/2 cups all-purpose flour

PINEAPPLE FILLING:

- 1 can (8 ounces) crushed pineapple, undrained
- 1/2 cup sugar
- 3 tablespoons cornstarch

CREAM CHEESE FILLING:

- 2 packages (8 ounces *each*) cream cheese, softened
- 1/3 cup sugar
- 1 tablespoon lemon juice
- 1/2 teaspoon vanilla extract

ICING (optional):

- 1 cup confectioners' sugar
- 2 to 3 tablespoons milk

In a mixing bowl, dissolve yeast in warm water. Add the butter, sugar, eggs, salt and 2 cups flour; beat on low speed for 3 minutes. Stir in enough remaining flour to form a soft dough.

Turn onto a floured surface; knead until smooth and elastic, about 6-8 minutes. Place in a greased bowl, turning once to grease top. Cover and let rise in a warm place until doubled, about 45 minutes.

In a saucepan, combine the pineapple filling ingredients. Bring to a boil; reduce heat. Cook and stir until thickened. Cool. Combine the cream cheese filling ingredients.

Punch dough down. Turn onto a floured surface; divide dough in half. Roll each portion into a 15-in. x 9-in. rectangle. Place on greased baking sheets. Spread the cream cheese filling lengthwise down center third of each rectangle. Spread the pineapple filling on top. On each long side, cut 1-in.-wide strips 3 in. into center. Starting at one end, fold alternately strips at an angle across filling. Seal ends. Cover and let rise for 20 minutes.

Bake at 350° for 25-30 minutes or until golden brown. Cool. If desired, combine the icing ingredients and drizzle over the braids. Refrigerate leftovers. **Yield: 2 loaves.**

Sour Cream Lemon Bread

My family always requests this light, tender bread with a hint of lemon. This loaf is so scrumptious that it complements almost any meal. I serve slices with a creamy lemon spread for an early-morning treat or late-night snack that's simply dreamy.

—Barbara Strickler, Syracuse, Indiana

- 1/4 cup sour cream
- 2 tablespoons lemon juice
- 2 to 3 tablespoons warm milk (70° to 80°)
- 2 tablespoons butter, softened
- 1 egg
- 2 teaspoons grated lemon peel
- 2 tablespoons sugar
- 1 teaspoon salt
- 1/4 teaspoon baking soda
- 2 cups bread flour
- 1-1/2 teaspoons active dry yeast

LEMON SPREAD:

- 1 package (3 ounces) cream cheese, softened
- 1/4 cup confectioners' sugar
- 1 tablespoon lemon juice
- 1 teaspoon lemon peel

In a measuring cup, combine sour cream and lemon juice. Add enough milk to measure 1/2 cup.

In a bread machine pan, place the sour cream mixture, butter, egg, lemon peel, sugar, salt, baking soda, flour and yeast in order suggested by manufacturer. Select sweet bread setting. Choose crust color and loaf size if available.

Bake according to bread machine directions (check dough after 5 minutes of mixing; add 1 to 2 tablespoons of water or flour if needed).

In a mixing bowl, beat spread ingredients until smooth; serve with the bread. **Yield: 1 loaf (1 pound) and about 1/2 cup spread.**

Editor's Note: Use of the timer feature is not recommended for this recipe. If your bread machine does not have a sweet bread setting, follow the manufacturer's directions using the basic setting.

Sour Cream Lemon Bread

Cranberry Eggnog Braid

Cranberry Eggnog Braid 1st prize

Whether at Thanksgiving, Christmas or New Year's, this is good as a party bread. You can't beat it as a gift, either. —Mary Lindow, Florence, Wisconsin

- 3 to 3-1/2 cups all-purpose flour, *divided*
- 1/4 cup sugar
- 1/2 teaspoon salt
- 1 package (1/4 ounce) active dry yeast
- 1/2 teaspoon ground nutmeg
- 1-1/4 cups eggnog
- 1/4 cup butter
- 1/2 cup dried cranberries

GLAZE:

- 1 cup confectioners' sugar
- 1 to 2 tablespoons eggnog
- 1/4 teaspoon vanilla extract

Dash nutmeg

In a mixing bowl, combine 1-1/2 cups flour, sugar, salt, yeast and nutmeg; set aside. In a saucepan, heat eggnog and butter to 120°-130° (the butter does not need to melt); add to flour mixture. Beat on low until moistened; beat on medium for 3 minutes. Stir in cranberries and enough remaining flour to make a soft dough.

Turn onto a floured surface; knead until smooth and elastic, about 6-8 minutes. Place in a greased bowl, turning once to grease top. Cover and let rise in a warm place until doubled, about 1 hour.

Punch dough down; divide into thirds. Shape each third into a 16-in. rope. Braid ropes on a greased baking sheet; tuck ends under. Cover and let rise until nearly doubled, about 30 minutes.

Bake at 350° for 25-30 minute or until golden. Immediately remove from pan to a wire rack to cool completely. Combine the first three glaze ingredients; drizzle over braid. Dust with nutmeg. **Yield: 1 loaf.**

Editor's Note: This recipe was tested with commercially prepared eggnog.

Nut Swirl Bread 1st prize

The best way that I can describe these loaves is to say they taste like a celebration!
—Darlene Simmons, Newfield, New Jersey

- 2 packages (1/4 ounce *each*) active dry yeast
- 1/4 cup warm water (110° to 115°)
- 2 cups warm milk (110° to 115°)
- 1/2 cup sugar
- 1/2 cup butter, softened
- 2 eggs
- 2 teaspoons salt
- 7 to 7-1/2 cups all-purpose flour

FILLING:

- **5 egg whites**
- **1 cup sugar**
- **5 cups finely chopped walnuts *or* pecans (about 1-1/2 pounds)**
- **1 tablespoon butter, melted**

Additional melted butter

- **1 egg, beaten**

In a large mixing bowl, dissolve yeast in water. Add the milk, sugar, butter, eggs, salt and 3-1/2 cups of flour; beat until smooth. Stir in enough remaining flour to form a soft dough.

Turn onto a floured surface; knead until smooth and elastic, 6-8 minutes. Place in a greased bowl; turn once to grease top. Cover and let rise in a warm place until doubled, about 1 hour.

For filling, in a mixing bowl, beat egg whites on medium speed until foamy; gradually add sugar, 1 tablespoon at a time; beat well. Stir in nuts and butter; mix well. Punch dough down; divided into eight balls. Roll each into an 8-in. circle; brush with butter. Spread about 2/3 cup filling on each circle. Roll up tightly into loaves; seal ends. Place on greased baking sheets.

Cover and let rise until doubled, about 50 minutes. Brush with egg. Bake at 350° for 20-25 minutes or until golden brown. Cool on wire racks. **Yield: 8 loaves.**

Nut Swirl Bread

Caramel Pecan Roll

Caramel Pecan Rolls 1st prize

There's not a better Christmas morning treat than these outstanding rolls. I make them every year.
—Carolyn Buschkamp, Emmetsburg, Iowa

- 2 cups milk
- 1/2 cup water
- 1/2 cup sugar
- 1/2 cup butter
- 1/3 cup cornmeal
- 2 teaspoons salt
- 7 to 7-1/2 cups all-purpose flour
- 2 packages (1/4 ounce *each*) active dry yeast
- 2 eggs

TOPPING:

- 2 cups packed brown sugar
- 1/2 cup butter
- 1/2 cup milk
- 1/2 to 1 cup chopped pecans

FILLING:

- 1/4 cup butter, softened
- 1/2 cup sugar
- 2 teaspoons ground cinnamon

In a saucepan, combine the first six ingredients; bring to a boil, stirring frequently. Set aside to cool to 120°-130°. In a mixing bowl, combine 2 cups flour and yeast. Add cooled cornmeal mixture; beat on low until smooth. Add eggs and 1 cup of flour; mix for 1 minute. Stir in enough remaining flour to form a soft dough.

Turn onto a floured surface; knead until smooth and elastic, about 6-8 minutes. Place in a greased bowl, turning once to grease top. Cover and let rise in a warm place until doubled, about 1 hour.

Combine the first three topping ingredients in a saucepan; bring to a boil, stirring occasionally. Pour into two greased 13-in. x 9-in. x 2-in. baking pans. Sprinkle with pecans; set aside.

Punch dough down; divide in half. Roll each into a 12-in. x 15-in. rectangle; spread with butter. Combine sugar and cinnamon; sprinkle over butter. Roll up dough jelly-roll style, starting with a long side; pinch seams to seal and tuck ends under. Cut each roll into 12 slices. Place 12 rolls cut side down in each baking pan. Cover and let rise until nearly doubled, about 30 minutes.

Bake at 375° for 20-25 minutes or until golden brown. Cool for 1 minute before inverting onto a serving platter. Serve warm. **Yield: 2 dozen.**

Cranberry Biscuits

I like the texture of potato rolls and the taste of orange-cranberry bread, so I combined them in these yummy breakfast biscuits. Dotted with dried cranberries and drizzled with a sweet glaze, these tender treats are a family favorite.

—Debra Fulenwider, Colfax, California

- 1-2/3 cups warm milk (70° to 80°)
- 2 eggs
- 3 tablespoons butter, softened
- 3/4 cup mashed potato flakes
- 1/4 cup sugar
- 2 teaspoons salt
- 1-1/4 teaspoons ground cinnamon
- 1 teaspoon grated orange peel
- 4 cups bread flour
- 1 tablespoon active dry yeast
- 1 cup dried cranberries

ORANGE GLAZE:

- 1 cup confectioners' sugar
- 2 to 3 tablespoons orange juice
- 3 tablespoons chopped dried cranberries, optional

In bread machine pan, place the first 10 ingredients in order suggested by manufacturer. Select dough setting (check dough after 5 minutes of mixing; add 1 to 2 tablespoons of water or flour if needed). Just before final kneading (your machine may audibly signal this), add cranberries.

When cycle is completed, turn dough onto a lightly floured surface. Cover and let rest for 15 minutes. Roll or pat to 1/2-in. thickness. Cut with a 2-1/2-in. biscuit cutter. Place in a greased 15-in. x 10-in. x 1-in. baking pan. Cover and let rise in a warm place until almost doubled, about 40 minutes.

Bake at 375° for 10-15 minutes or until golden brown. Combine confectioners' sugar and enough orange juice to achieve a glaze consistency. Drizzle over warm biscuits. Sprinkle with chopped cranberries if desired. **Yield: about 1-1/2 dozen.**

Editor's Note: If your bread machine has a time-delay feature, we recommend you do not use it for this recipe.

Cranberry Biscuits

Almond-Filled Butterhorns

These are very light and flavorful rolls. The filling gives them a fantastic taste.
— Lillian Tripke, Janesville, Wisconsin

3-1/4 teaspoons active dry yeast
1 cup warm milk (110° to 115°)
1/2 cup sugar, *divided*
1 cup butter, softened
4 cups all-purpose flour
1/8 teaspoon salt
4 eggs

FILLING:
5 tablespoons butter, softened, *divided*
1 cup sugar
1 cup ground almonds
1 egg, lightly beaten
1 teaspoon almond extract
1/2 teaspoon grated lemon peel

GLAZE:
1 cup confectioners' sugar
2 tablespoons milk
1/4 teaspoon vanilla extract

In a small bowl, dissolve yeast in warm milk. Add 1/4 cup sugar and butter; mix well. In a large mixing bowl, combine the flour, salt and remaining sugar. Add the eggs, one at a time, beating well after each addition. Add yeast mixture; beat until smooth. Cover and refrigerate overnight.

Punch dough down; divide into thirds. On a lightly floured surface, roll each portion into a 12-in. circle. Melt 3 tablespoons butter; brush 1 tablespoon over each circle. In a bowl, combine the sugar, almonds, egg, extract, lemon peel and remaining butter; mix well. Spread a third over each circle of dough.

Cut each into 12 wedges. Roll up wedges from the wide end; place point side down 2 in. apart on greased baking sheets. Curve ends to form a crescent.

Cover and let rise in a warm place or until doubled, about 30 minutes. Bake at 375° for 10-12 minutes or until lightly browned. Remove from pan to wire racks. Combine glaze ingredients; brush over warm rolls. **Yield: 3 dozen.**

Almond-Filled Butterhorns

No-Fry Doughnuts 1st prize

We have four boys and these doughnuts never last long at our house. I like them because I don't have to clean up a greasy mess.
—Susie Baldwin, Columbia, Tennessee

2 packages (1/4 ounce *each*) active dry yeast
1/4 cup warm water (110° to 115°)
1-1/2 cups warm milk (110° to 115°)
1/3 cup shortening

1/2 cup sugar
2 eggs
1 teaspoon salt
1 teaspoon ground nutmeg
1/4 teaspoon ground cinnamon
4-1/2 to 5 cups all-purpose flour
1/4 cup butter, melted

GLAZE:
1/2 cup butter
2 cups confectioners' sugar
5 teaspoons water
2 teaspoons vanilla extract

In a mixing bowl, dissolve yeast in warm water. Add milk and shortening; stir for 1 minute. Add the sugar, eggs, salt, nutmeg, cinnamon and 2 cups flour; beat on low speed until smooth. Stir in enough remaining flour to form a soft dough. Do not knead.

Cover and let rise in a warm place until doubled, about 1 hour. Punch dough down. Turn onto a floured surface; roll out to 1/2-in. thickness. Cut with a 2-3/4-in. doughnut cutter; place 2 in. apart on greased baking sheets. Brush with butter. Cover and let rise in a warm place until doubled, about 30 minutes.

Bake at 350° for 20 minutes or until lightly browned. Meanwhile, in a saucepan, melt butter; stir in the sugar, water and vanilla. Stir over low heat until smooth (do not boil). Keep warm. Dip warm doughnuts, one at a time, into glaze and turn to coat. Drain on a wire rack. Serve immediately. **Yield: 2 dozen.**

No-Fry Doughnuts

Dill Seed Braid

Garlic Herb Bubble Loaf

Dill Seed Braid 1st prize

Its pretty braided shape and pleasant dill flavor distinguishes this golden-brown loaf from other yeast breads. My family loves to eat it alongside soup, roast beef or pot roast. I almost always make two loaves—one just isn't enough!

—Lori Jameson, Walla Walla, Washington

- 1 package (1/4 ounce) active dry yeast
- 1/4 cup warm water (110° to 115°)
- 1 cup plain yogurt
- 1 small onion, finely chopped
- 1/4 cup sugar
- 2 tablespoons butter, softened
- 1 egg
- 1 tablespoon dill seed
- 1 teaspoon salt
- 3 to 3-1/2 cups all-purpose flour

In a large mixing bowl, dissolve yeast in warm water. Add the yogurt, onion, sugar, butter, egg, dill seed, salt and 1 cup flour. Beat until smooth. Stir in enough remaining flour to form a soft dough.

Turn onto a floured surface; knead until smooth and elastic, about 6-8 minutes. Place in a greased bowl, turning once to grease top. Cover and let rise in a warm place until doubled, about 1 hour.

Punch dough down. Turn onto a lightly floured surface; divide into thirds. Shape each portion into a 20-in. rope. Place ropes on a large greased baking sheet and braid; pinch ends to seal and tuck under. Cover and let rise until doubled, about 30 minutes.

Bake at 350° for 35-40 minutes or until golden brown. Remove from pan to a wire rack to cool. **Yield: 1 loaf.**

Pumpernickel Caraway Bread

Garlic Herb Bubble Loaf

I adapted an old sour cream bread recipe for this deliciously different, pull-apart loaf that smells heavenly while baking. It has a light crust, tender interior and lots of herb and butter flavor.
—Katie Crill, Priest River, Idaho

- 1/2 cup water (70° to 80°)
- 1/2 cup sour cream
- 2 tablespoons butter, softened
- 3 tablespoons sugar
- 1-1/2 teaspoons salt
- 3 cups bread flour
- 2-1/4 teaspoons active dry yeast

GARLIC HERB BUTTER:

- 1/4 cup butter, melted
- 4 garlic cloves, minced
- 1/4 teaspoon *each* dried oregano, thyme and rosemary, crushed

In bread machine pan, place the first seven ingredients in order suggested by manufacturer. Select dough setting (check dough after 5 minutes of mixing; add 1 to 2 tablespoons of water or flour if needed).

When cycle is completed, turn dough onto a lightly floured surface; divide dough into 36 pieces. Shape each into a ball. In a bowl, combine the butter, garlic and herbs. Dip each ball in mixture; place in an ungreased 9-in. x 5-in. x 3-in. loaf pan. Cover and let rise in a warm place until doubled, about 45 minutes.

Bake at 375° for 35-40 minutes or until golden brown. Remove from pan to a wire rack. Serve warm. **Yield: 1 loaf (1-1/2 pounds, 16 slices).**

Pumpernickel Caraway Bread

This rich, dark bread has an old-fashioned, homemade taste that's oh-so-satisfying. Made with molasses and caraway seeds, it's moist and flavorful. My family prefers slices of it slathered with apple butter or cream cheese.
—Lorraine Darocha, Berkshire, Massachusetts

- 3/4 cup water (70° to 80°)
- 2 tablespoons molasses
- 4-1/2 teaspoons butter
- 1 teaspoon salt
- 1 cup bread flour
- 2/3 cup rye flour
- 1/3 cup whole wheat flour
- 2 tablespoons cornmeal
- 5 teaspoons baking cocoa
- 4-1/2 teaspoons sugar
- 3 teaspoons nonfat dry milk powder
- 1 teaspoon caraway seeds
- 1/4 teaspoon instant coffee granules
- 1-1/2 teaspoons active dry yeast

In bread machine pan, place all ingredients in order suggested by manufacturer. Select basic bread setting. Choose crust color and loaf size if available.

Bake according to bread machine directions (check dough after 5 minutes of mixing; add 1 to 2 tablespoons of water or flour if needed). **Yield: 1 loaf (1 pound).**

Swedish Rye Bread

Swedish Rye Bread

This recipe came from my mother, and it's long been a family favorite. You can make a meal of it with soup and a salad.
—Mary Ann Ross, Crown Point, Indiana

- **1 package (1/4 ounce) active dry yeast**
- **1-3/4 cups warm water (110° to 115°), *divided***
- **1/4 cup packed brown sugar**
- **1/4 cup molasses**
- **2 tablespoons shortening**
- **2 teaspoons salt**
- **2-1/2 cups rye flour**
- **3-3/4 to 4-1/4 cups all-purpose flour**
- **2 tablespoons butter, melted**

In a mixing bowl, dissolve yeast in 1/4 cup water. Add the sugar, molasses, shortening, salt and remaining water; stir well. Add rye flour; beat until smooth. Stir in all-purpose flour to form a soft dough.

Turn onto a floured surface; knead until smooth and elastic, about 6-8 minutes. Place in a greased bowl, turning once to grease top. Cover and let rise in a warm place until doubled, about 1-1/2 hours. Punch dough down.

Shape into four round loaves. Place on greased baking sheets. Cover and let rise until doubled, about 45-60 minutes. Bake at 350° for 30-35 minutes or until golden brown. Brush with butter. **Yield: 4 loaves.**

Sesame Wheat Braids

I was thrilled when the judges at our county fair gave these braids both a blue ribbon and best of show award! *—Nancy Montgomery, Hartville, Ohio*

- **2 packages (1/4 ounce *each*) active dry yeast**
- **2-1/4 cups warm water (110° to 115°)**
- **1/3 cup sugar**
- **1 tablespoon vegetable oil**
- **1 cup whole wheat flour**
- **2 eggs**
- **1 tablespoon water**
- **1 tablespoon salt**
- **5 to 6 cups all-purpose flour**
- **2 teaspoons sesame seeds**

In a large mixing bowl, dissolve yeast in water. Add sugar and oil; mix well. Stir in whole wheat flour; let stand until the mixture bubbles, about 5 minutes.

In a small bowl, beat eggs and water. Remove 2 tablespoons to a small bowl; cover and refrigerate. Add remaining egg mixture and salt to batter; mix until smooth. Add 4 cups all-purpose flour and beat until smooth. Stir in enough remaining flour to form a soft dough.

Turn onto a floured surface; knead until smooth and elastic, about 6-8 minutes. Place in a greased bowl, turning once to grease top. Cover and let rise in a warm place until doubled, about 1 hour. Punch dough down and divide in half. Divide each half into thirds.

Shape each into a rope about 15 in. long. Place three ropes on a greased baking sheet; braid. Pinch each end firmly and tuck under.

Brush with the reserved egg mixture; sprinkle with sesame seeds. Repeat, placing second braid on the same baking sheet. Let rise until doubled, about 45 minutes.

Bake at 350° for 20-25 minutes. Remove from baking sheet to cool on a wire rack. **Yield: 2 loaves.**

Focaccia Bread Squares

Focaccia bread is a big hit at our house. We use it as an alternative to garlic bread. The dough is easy to whip up in the bread machine, then season with rosemary, garlic salt and Parmesan cheese.
—Kay King, Dyersville, Iowa

- 3/4 cup plus 3 tablespoons water (70° to 80°)
- 3 tablespoons butter, softened
- 2 tablespoons nonfat dry milk powder
- 3 tablespoons sugar
- 1-1/2 teaspoons salt
- 3 cups bread flour
- 2-1/4 teaspoons active dry yeast

TOPPING:

- 2 tablespoons olive oil
- 3 tablespoons grated Parmesan cheese
- 2 teaspoons minced fresh rosemary *or* 3/4 teaspoon dried rosemary, crushed
- 1/2 teaspoon garlic salt

In bread machine pan, place the first seven ingredients in order suggested by manufacturer. Select dough setting (check dough after 5 minutes of mixing; add 1 to 2 tablespoons of water or flour if needed).

When cycle is completed, turn dough onto a lightly floured surface. Cover and let rest for 15 minutes. Knead for 1 minute. Press into a 15-in. x 10-in. x 1-in. baking pan. Press dough 1/4 in. up the sides of pan. Cover and let rise in a warm place for 20-30 minutes or until slightly risen.

With a wooden spoon handle, make indentations at 1-in. intervals. Brush dough with oil; sprinkle with Parmesan cheese, rosemary and garlic salt. Bake at 400° for 13-15 minutes or until lightly browned. Cool slightly. Cut into squares; serve warm. **Yield: 2 dozen.**

Sesame Wheat Braid

Focaccia Bread Squares

Rosemary Orange Bread

Multigrain Bread

Rosemary Orange Bread

Of all the herbs, rosemary is my favorite. This bread goes great with a roast, chicken or pasta with red sauce. —*Deidre Fallavollita, Vienna, Virginia*

- **1 package (1/4 ounce) active dry yeast**
- **3/4 cup warm water (110° to 115°)**
- **3/4 cup orange juice**
- **2 tablespoons honey**
- **1 tablespoon vegetable oil**
- **1 tablespoon minced fresh rosemary *or* 1 teaspoon dried rosemary, crushed**
- **2 teaspoons salt**
- **1 teaspoon grated orange peel**
- **3-3/4 to 4-1/2 cups all-purpose flour**
- **1 egg white**
- **Additional fresh rosemary and whole peppercorns, optional**

In a large mixing bowl, dissolve yeast in warm water. Add the orange juice, honey, oil, rosemary, salt, orange peel and 2 cups flour; beat until smooth. Stir in enough remaining flour to form a soft dough.

Turn onto a floured surface; knead until smooth and elastic, about 6-8 minutes. Place in a greased bowl, turning once to grease top. Cover and let rise in a warm place until doubled, about 1 hour.

Punch dough down. Roll into a 15-in. x 1-in. rectangle. Starting at the short end, roll up jelly-roll style. Pinch edges to seal and shape into an oval. Place with seam side down on a greased baking sheet. Cover and let rise until nearly doubled, about 30 minutes.

Bake at 375° for 20 minutes. Whisk egg white; brush over loaf. Place small sprigs of rosemary and peppercorns on top if desired. Bake 25 minutes longer or until brown. Cool on a wire rack. **Yield: 1 loaf.**

Multigrain Bread 1st prize

It's hard to get a good whole-grain bread where I live, so my bread machine comes in very handy when making this hearty loaf. I adapted it from an old recipe, and I've been enjoying it ever since. Cornmeal and wheat germ give it a wonderful texture and a nutty flavor I love.
—*Michele MacKinlay, Madoc, Ontario*

- 1 cup water (70° to 80°)
- 2 tablespoons vegetable oil
- 2 egg yolks
- 1/4 cup molasses
- 1 teaspoon salt
- 1-1/2 cups bread flour
- 1 cup whole wheat flour
- 1/2 cup rye flour
- 1/2 cup nonfat dry milk powder
- 1/4 cup quick-cooking oats
- 1/4 cup wheat germ
- 1/4 cup cornmeal
- 2-1/4 teaspoons active dry yeast

In bread machine pan, place all ingredients in order suggested by manufacturer. Select basic bread setting. Choose crust color and loaf size if available.

Bake according to bread machine directions (check dough after 5 minutes of mixing; add 1 to 2 tablespoons water or flour if needed). **Yield: 1 loaf (2 pounds).**

Editor's Note: If your bread machine has a time-delay feature, we recommend you do not use it for this recipe.

Pull-Apart Bacon Bread

I stumbled across this recipe while looking for something different to take to a brunch. Boy, am I glad I did! Everyone asked for the recipe and could not believe it called for only five ingredients. It's the perfect item to bake for an informal get-together.
—*Traci Collins, Cheyenne, Wyoming*

Pull-Apart Bacon Bread

- 12 bacon strips, diced
- 1 loaf (1 pound) frozen bread dough, thawed
- 2 tablespoons olive oil, *divided*
- 1 cup (4 ounces) shredded part-skim mozzarella cheese
- 1 envelope (1 ounce) ranch salad dressing mix

In a skillet, cook bacon over medium heat for 5 minutes or until partially cooked; drain on paper towels. Roll out dough to 1/2-in. thickness; brush with 1 tablespoon of oil. Cut into 1-in. pieces; place in a large bowl. Add the bacon, cheese, dressing mix and remaining oil; toss to coat.

Arrange pieces in a 9-in. x 5-in. oval on a greased baking sheet, layering as needed. Cover and let rise in a warm place until doubled, about 30 minutes.

Bake at 350° for 15 minutes. Cover with foil; bake 5-10 minutes longer or until golden brown. Remove to a wire rack. Serve warm. **Yield: 1 loaf.**

Poppy Seed Rolls

Poppy Seed Rolls

There's nothing like homemade rolls to top off a meal. I've made these often for Sunday dinner, and they are delicious! —*Dottie Miller, Jonesborough, Tennessee*

- 1 package (1/4 ounce) active dry yeast
- 1/4 cup warm water (110° to 115°)
- 1/4 cup plus 1 teaspoon sugar, *divided*
- 1 cup warm milk (110° to 115°)
- 1/2 cup shortening
- 1-1/2 teaspoons salt
- 1 egg, beaten
- 3-3/4 to 4 cups all-purpose flour
- Butter, melted
- Poppy seeds

In a mixing bowl, dissolve yeast in warm water. Add 1 teaspoon sugar; let stand for 5 minutes. Beat in the milk, shortening, salt, egg and remaining sugar. Stir in enough flour to form a soft dough.

Turn onto a floured surface; knead until smooth and elastic, about 6-8 minutes. Place in a greased bowl, turning once to grease top. Cover and let rise in a warm place until doubled, about 1 hour.

Punch the dough down. Divide into 18 portions; shape into balls. Place in greased muffin cups. Cover and let rise until doubled, about 30 minutes.

Brush tops with butter; sprinkle with poppy seeds. Bake at 375° for 11-13 minutes or until golden brown. Remove from pans to wire racks. **Yield: 1-1/2 dozen.**

Cheddar-Chili Bread Twists

Green chilies are prolific here in New Mexico, so I'm always looking for new ways to cook with them. These twists are often requested by my family.
—*Carol Whitfield, Mentmore, New Mexico*

- 1-1/4 cups buttermilk
- 2 cups (8 ounces) shredded cheddar cheese
- 1 package (1/4 ounce) active dry yeast
- 2 tablespoons sugar, *divided*
- 1/4 cup warm water (110° to 115°)
- 1/2 teaspoon salt
- 2 eggs
- 5-1/4 to 5-3/4 cups all-purpose flour

TOPPING:

- 1-1/2 cups (6 ounces) shredded cheddar cheese
- 1 can (4 ounces) chopped green chilies, drained
- Grated Parmesan cheese

In a saucepan, heat the buttermilk and cheese over low heat, stirring until cheese is melted (mixture will appear curdled). Cool to 110° to 115°. In a mixing bowl, dissolve yeast and 1 tablespoon sugar in warm water. Add the buttermilk mixture, salt, eggs, remaining sugar and 3 cups flour. Beat until smooth. Stir in enough remaining flour to form a soft dough.

Turn onto a floured surface; knead until smooth and elastic, about 6-8 minutes. Place in a greased bowl, turning once to grease top. Cover and let rise in a warm place until doubled, about 1 hour. Meanwhile, for topping, combine cheddar cheese and chilies; set aside.

Punch dough down; turn onto a lightly floured surface and divide in half. Roll each portion into an 18-in. x 12-in. rectangle. Spray one half with nonstick cooking spray. Top with cheese mixture and remaining dough.

Cut into twelve 1-1/2-in. strips. Cut each strip in half and twist. Place 1 in. apart on greased foil-lined baking sheets. Sprinkle with Parmesan cheese.

Bake at 375° for 15-20 minutes or until lightly browned. Remove to wire racks. Serve warm. Refrigerate any leftovers. **Yield: 2 dozen.**

Cheddar-Chili Bread Twists

Buttermilk Pan Rolls

These wonderful rolls can be made very quickly. Hot, fresh rolls make people eager to come to the table.
—Patricia Young, Bella Vista, Arkansas

- 2 packages (1/4 ounce *each*) active dry yeast
- 1/4 cup warm water (110° to 115°)
- 1-1/2 cups warm buttermilk (110° to 115°)
- 1/2 cup vegetable oil
- 3 tablespoons sugar
- 4-1/2 cups all-purpose flour
- 1 teaspoon baking soda
- 1/2 teaspoon salt

In a large mixing bowl, dissolve yeast in warm water. Add the buttermilk, oil and sugar. Combine the flour, baking soda and salt; add to yeast mixture and beat until smooth. Do not knead. Let stand for 10 minutes.

Turn dough onto a lightly floured surface; punch down. Shape into 24 balls and place in two greased 9-in. square baking pans. Cover and let rise in a warm place until doubled, about 30 minutes.

Bake at 400° for 20 minutes or until golden brown. Remove to wire racks. **Yield: 2 dozen.**

Editor's Note: Warmed buttermilk will appear curdled.

Buttermilk Pan Rolls

Sweet Potato Crescents

Mashed Potato Rolls

Sweet Potato Crescents

My family agrees that our Thanksgiving feast would not be complete without these light-as-air crescent rolls. They're a nice accompaniment to any menu. Baking them always puts me in the holiday spirit.
—Rebecca Bailey, Fairbury, Nebraska

- 2 packages (1/4 ounce *each*) active dry yeast
- 1 cup warm water (110° to 115°)
- 1 can (15 ounces) cut sweet potatoes, drained and mashed
- 1/2 cup sugar
- 1/2 cup shortening
- 1 egg
- 1-1/2 teaspoons salt
- 5 to 5-1/2 cups all-purpose flour
- 1/4 cup butter, melted

In a large mixing bowl, dissolve yeast in warm water. Beat in the sweet potatoes, sugar, shortening, egg, salt and 3 cups flour. Stir in enough remaining flour to form a stiff dough.

Turn onto a floured surface; knead until smooth and elastic, about 6-8 minutes. Place in a greased bowl, turning once to grease top. Cover and let rise in a warm place until doubled, about 1 hour.

Punch dough down; divide into thirds. Roll each portion into a 12-in. circle; cut each into 12 wedges. Brush with butter. Roll up from the wide end and place point side down 2 in. apart on greased baking sheets. Cover and let rise until doubled, about 40 minutes.

Bake at 375° for 13-15 minutes or until golden brown. Remove from pans to wire racks. **Yield: 3 dozen.**

Mashed Potato Rolls

Potatoes are synonymous with our state. My grandmother always made these rolls, which everyone loved. Because it makes such a large batch, this recipe is great for company. *—Glenda Suit, Boise, Idaho*

1 package (1/4 ounce) active dry yeast
1/4 cup warm water (110° to 115°)
1-3/4 cups warm milk (110° to 115°)
1/4 cup butter, softened
1/4 cup vegetable oil
6 tablespoons sugar
1 egg
1/2 cup warm mashed potatoes (prepared with milk and butter)
1-1/2 teaspoons salt
1 teaspoon baking powder
1/2 teaspoon baking soda
6 cups all-purpose flour
Melted butter, optional

In a mixing bowl, dissolve yeast in warm water. Add milk, butter, oil, sugar, egg and mashed potatoes; mix well. Stir in the salt, baking powder, baking soda and enough flour to form a soft dough.

Turn onto a floured surface; knead until smooth and elastic, about 6-8 minutes. Place in a greased bowl, turning once to grease top. Cover and let rise in a warm place until doubled, about 1-1/2 hours.

Punch dough down. Turn onto a lightly floured surface; divide in half. Cover one piece. Shape the other piece into 16 balls. Place 2 in. apart on greased baking sheets. Repeat with the remaining dough. Cover and let rise until doubled, about 30 minutes.

Bake at 375° for 15-18 minutes or until golden brown. Brush with butter if desired. **Yield: 32 rolls.**

Cinnamon-Raisin Soft Pretzels

I came up with this recipe after sampling pretzels at a Pennsylvania Dutch farmers market. They're a nice morning treat.

—Susie King, Quarryville, Pennsylvania

Cinnamon-Raisin Soft Pretzels

1 package (1/4 ounce) active dry yeast
1-1/2 cups warm water (110° to 115°)
2 tablespoons brown sugar
1 teaspoon salt
2 cups cake flour
2 to 2-1/4 cups all-purpose flour
3/4 cup raisins
2 tablespoons baking soda
2 cups hot water (120° to 130°)
3 tablespoons butter, melted
3/4 cup sugar
1 teaspoon ground cinnamon

In a large bowl, dissolve yeast in warm water. Stir in brown sugar and salt. Add cake flour; stir well. Stir in enough all-purpose flour to form a soft dough. Stir in raisins.

Turn onto a floured surface; knead until smooth and elastic, about 6-8 minutes. Place in a greased bowl, turning once to grease top. Cover and let rise in a warm place until dough has risen slightly, about 30 minutes.

Punch dough down; divide into 14 balls. Roll each ball into a 15-in. rope.

In a bowl, dissolve baking soda in hot water. Dip each rope in baking soda mixture; drain on paper towels. Form into pretzel shapes and place on greased baking sheets. Bake at 400° for 15 minutes or until golden brown.

Combine sugar and cinnamon in a small bowl. Brush pretzels with butter, then dip in cinnamon-sugar. Serve warm. **Yield: 14 pretzels.**

Garlic Parmesan Breadsticks

I receive lots of raves when I make these delicious breadsticks. I've passed the recipe on to a number of family members and friends.
—Barbara Gross, Warden, Washington

- 1 tablespoon active dry yeast
- 1-1/2 cups warm water (110° to 115°)
- 2 tablespoons sugar
- 3/4 cup butter, melted, *divided*
- 1/2 teaspoon salt
- 4-1/2 cups all-purpose flour
- Garlic salt
- Grated Parmesan cheese
- Marinara *or* spaghetti sauce, warmed, optional

In a mixing bowl, dissolve yeast in warm water. Add sugar; let stand for 5 minutes. Add 1/2 cup butter, salt and 2 cups flour; beat until smooth. Stir in enough remaining flour to form a soft dough.

Turn onto a floured surface; knead until smooth and elastic, about 6-8 minutes. Place in a greased bowl, turning once to grease top. Cover and let rise in a warm place until doubled, about 45 minutes.

Punch dough down. Turn onto a lightly floured surface; roll into a 24-in. x 10-in. rectangle. Cut dough in half lengthwise, then into 5-in. x 1-in. strips. Twist each strip and place 2 in. apart on greased baking sheets.

Brush strips with remaining butter; sprinkle with garlic salt and Parmesan cheese. Cover and let rise in a warm place until doubled, about 20 minutes.

Bake at 350° for 20 minutes or until golden brown. Remove from pans to wire racks. If desired, serve with marinara or spaghetti sauce for dipping. **Yield: 4 dozen.**

Garlic Parmesan Breadsticks

Caraway Cloverleaf Rolls

I've taken these rolls to numerous get-togethers and have received many compliments. Folks around here love to bake, so there's always good eating at our socials.
—Ruth Reid, Jackson, Minnesota

- 2 packages (1/4 ounce *each*) active dry yeast
- 1-1/2 cups warm water (110° to 115°)
- 1 cup whole wheat flour
- 1/2 cup sugar
- 1/2 cup vegetable oil
- 2 teaspoons caraway seeds
- 1-1/2 teaspoons salt
- 3-1/2 to 4 cups all-purpose flour

In a mixing bowl, dissolve yeast in warm water. Add the whole wheat flour, sugar, oil, caraway, salt and 2 cups all-purpose flour; beat until smooth. Stir in enough of the remaining all-purpose flour to form a soft dough.

Turn onto a floured surface; knead until smooth and elastic, about 6-8 minutes. Place in a greased bowl, turning once to grease top. Cover and let rise in a warm place until doubled, about 1 hour.

Punch dough down. Divide in half, then divide each half into 36 pieces. Shape into balls; place three balls each in greased muffin cups. Cover and let rise until doubled, about 30 minutes.

Bake at 375° for 15-18 minutes or until golden brown. Remove from pans to wire racks. **Yield: 2 dozen.**

Caraway Cloverleaf Rolls

Golden Honey Pan Rolls

A cousin in North Carolina gave me the recipe for these delicious honey-glazed rolls. Using my bread machine to make the dough saves me about 2 hours compared to the traditional method. I usually make two batches so I have enough!

—Sara Wing, Philadelphia, Pennsylvania

- 1 cup warm milk (70° to 80°)
- 1 egg
- 1 egg yolk
- 1/2 cup vegetable oil
- 2 tablespoons honey
- 1-1/2 teaspoons salt
- 3-1/2 cups bread flour
- 2-1/4 teaspoons active dry yeast

GLAZE:

- 1/3 cup sugar
- 2 tablespoons butter, melted
- 1 tablespoon honey
- 1 egg white

Additional honey, optional

In bread machine pan, place the first eight ingredients in order suggested by manufacturer. Select dough setting (check dough after 5 minutes of mixing; add 1 to 2 tablespoons of water or flour if needed.)

When cycle is completed, turn dough onto a lightly floured surface. Punch dough down; cover and let rest for 10 minutes. Divide into 24 pieces; shape each into a ball. Place 12 balls each in two greased 8-in. baking pans. Cover and let rise in a warm place until doubled, about 30 minutes.

For glaze, combine the sugar, butter, honey and egg white; drizzle over dough. Bake at 350° for 20-25 minutes or until golden brown. Brush with additional honey if desired. **Yield: 2 dozen.**

Editor's Note: If your bread machine has a time-delay feature, we recommend you do not use it for this recipe.

Golden Honey Pan Rolls

Freeze-and-Bake Rolls

Freeze-and-Bake Rolls 1st prize

Almost any occasion's right for these handy rolls, so I keep them in the freezer for Sunday meals and for company. —*Jayne Duce, Raymond, Alberta*

- 2 packages (1/4 ounce *each*) active dry yeast
- 1-1/2 cups warm water (110° to 115°)
- 2 teaspoons plus 1/2 cup sugar, *divided*
- 1-1/2 cups warm milk (110° to 115°)
- 1/4 cup vegetable oil
- 4 teaspoons salt
- 7-1/2 to 8-1/2 cups all-purpose flour
- Butter, melted

In a large mixing bowl, dissolve yeast and 2 teaspoons sugar in warm water; let stand for 5 minutes. Add the milk, oil, salt and remaining sugar. Stir in enough flour to form a stiff dough.

Turn out onto a floured surface; knead until smooth and elastic, about 6-8 minutes. Place in a greased bowl, turning once to grease top. Cover and let rise in a warm place until doubled, about 1-1/2 hours.

Punch dough down. Divide into four pieces. Cover three pieces with plastic wrap. Divide one piece into 12 balls. To form knots, roll each ball into a 10-in. rope; tie into a knot and pinch ends together. Repeat with remaining dough. Place rolls on greased baking sheets; brush with melted butter. Cover and let rise until doubled, about 20-30 minutes.

To serve immediately, bake at 375° for 15-18 minutes. To freeze for later use, partially bake at 300° for 15 minutes. Allow to cool; freeze. Reheat frozen rolls at 375° for 12-15 minutes or until browned. **Yield: 4 dozen.**

COOKIES & BARS

...TE CREAM CHEESE BROWNIES, pg. 37...

Cookies & Bars

S'more Sandwich Cookies 1st prize

Capture the taste of campfire s'mores in your kitchen. Graham cracker crumbs added to chocolate chip cookie dough bring out the flavor of the fireside favorite. Melting the cookies' marshmallow centers in the microwave makes them simple to assemble.

—Abby Metzger, Larchwood, Iowa

- 3/4 cup butter, softened
- 1/2 cup sugar
- 1/2 cup packed brown sugar
- 1 egg
- 2 tablespoons milk
- 1 teaspoon vanilla extract
- 1-1/4 cups all-purpose flour
- 1-1/4 cups graham cracker crumbs (about 20 squares)
- 1/2 teaspoon baking soda
- 1/4 teaspoon salt
- 1/8 teaspoon ground cinnamon
- 2 cups (12 ounces) semisweet chocolate chips
- 24 to 28 large marshmallows

In a mixing bowl, cream butter and sugars. Beat in the egg, milk and vanilla. Combine the flour, graham cracker crumbs, baking soda, salt and cinnamon; gradually add to creamed mixture. Stir in chocolate chips.

Drop by tablespoonfuls 2 in. apart onto ungreased baking sheets. Bake at 375° for 8-10 minutes or until golden brown. Remove to wire racks to cool.

S'more Sandwich Cookies

Place four cookies bottom side up on a microwave-safe plate; top each with a marshmallow. Microwave, uncovered, on high for 10-20 seconds or until marshmallows begin to puff (do not overcook). Top each with another cookie. Repeat with remaining cookies. **Yield: about 2 dozen.**

Vanilla-Butter Sugar Cookies

Frosted Cashew Cookies

Vanilla-Butter Sugar Cookies

I always bake these for Christmas. For Valentine's Day, I cut them out as hearts and write messages in the frosting. —*Cynthia Ettel, Glencoe, Minnesota*

- 1-1/2 cups butter, softened
- 1-1/2 cups sugar
- 2 eggs
- 2 tablespoons vanilla extract
- 4 cups all-purpose flour
- 1 teaspoon salt
- 1 teaspoon baking soda
- 1 teaspoon cream of tartar

FROSTING:

- 1-1/2 cups confectioners' sugar
- 3 tablespoons butter, softened
- 1 tablespoon vanilla extract
- 1 tablespoon milk
- Food coloring, optional
- Colored sugar

In a mixing bowl, cream butter and sugar. Add eggs and vanilla; beat well. Stir together dry ingredients; gradually add to creamed mixture until completely blended. Cover and refrigerate for 30 minutes.

On a lightly floured surface, roll dough to a 1/4-in. thickness. Cut with floured 2-1/2-in. cookie cutters. Using a floured spatula, transfer cookies to ungreased baking sheets. Bake at 350° for 10-12 minutes. Cool on wire racks.

For frosting, combine the sugar, butter, vanilla and milk; beat until creamy. Thin with additional milk to achieve desired spreading consistency if necessary. Add a few drops of food coloring if desired. Spread frosting over cookies and decorate with colored sugar. **Yield: 7 dozen.**

Toffee Malted Cookies

Frosted Cashew Cookies

My sister's sister-in-law discovered this recipe. We enjoy these cookies at Christmas, but they're rich and elegant for a special coffee.
—Sheila Wyum, Rutland, North Dakota

- 1/2 cup butter, softened
- 1 cup packed brown sugar
- 1 egg
- 1/3 cup sour cream
- 1/2 teaspoon vanilla extract
- 2 cups all-purpose flour
- 3/4 teaspoon *each* baking powder, baking soda and salt
- 1-3/4 cups salted cashew halves

BROWNED BUTTER FROSTING:

- 1/2 cup butter
- 3 tablespoons half-and-half cream
- 1/4 teaspoon vanilla extract
- 2 cups confectioners' sugar

Additional cashew halves, optional

In a mixing bowl, cream the butter and brown sugar. Beat in the egg, sour cream and vanilla; mix well. Combine dry ingredients; add to creamed mixture and mix well. Fold in cashews.

Drop by rounded teaspoonfuls onto greased baking sheets. Bake at 375° for 8-10 minutes or until lightly browned. Cool on a wire rack.

For the frosting, lightly brown butter in a small saucepan over low heat. Remove from the heat; add cream and vanilla. Beat in confectioners' sugar until smooth and thick. Frost cookies. Top each with a cashew half if desired. **Yield: about 3 dozen.**

Toffee Malted Cookies

As much as I delight in sharing these goodies, my family considers them keepers. It's a wonder I ever get them out the door to take to meetings! With their buttery, melt-in-your-mouth texture, they're always popular. *—Sharon Timpe, Mequon, Wisconsin*

- 1 cup butter, softened
- 1/2 cup sugar
- 1/2 cup packed brown sugar
- 2 eggs
- 1 package (3.4 ounces) instant vanilla pudding mix
- 1 teaspoon vanilla extract
- 2-1/4 cups all-purpose flour
- 1 cup quick-cooking oats
- 1 teaspoon baking soda
- 1/2 teaspoon salt
- 1 cup malted milk balls, chopped
- 3/4 cup English toffee bits *or* almond brickle chips

In a large mixing bowl, cream the butter and sugars. Add eggs, one at a time, beating well after each addition. Add pudding mix and vanilla. Combine the flour, oats, baking soda and salt; add to creamed mixture. Fold in the malted milk balls and the toffee bits (dough will be stiff).

Drop by rounded teaspoonfuls 2 in. apart onto ungreased baking sheets. Bake at 350° for 12-15 minutes or until golden brown. Cool for 2 minutes before removing to wire racks. **Yield: about 6 dozen.**

Fruit-Filled Spritz Cookies

Fruit-Filled Spritz Cookies

From the first time I baked these cookies, they've been a lip-smacking success. Old-fashioned and attractive, they make a perfect holiday pastry.
—Ingeborg Keith, Newark, Delaware

- 1-1/2 cups chopped dates
- 1 cup water
- 1/2 cup sugar
- 2 teaspoons orange juice
- 2 teaspoons grated orange peel
- 1 cup maraschino cherries, chopped
- 1/2 cup flaked coconut
- 1/2 cup ground nuts

DOUGH:

- 1 cup butter, softened
- 1 cup sugar
- 1/2 cup packed brown sugar
- 3 eggs
- 1/2 teaspoon almond extract
- 1/2 teaspoon vanilla extract
- 4 cups all-purpose flour
- 1/2 teaspoon baking soda
- 1/2 teaspoon salt

Confectioners' sugar

In a saucepan, combine the first five ingredients; bring to a boil, stirring constantly. Reduce heat; cook and stir for 8 minutes or until thickened. Cool completely. Stir in cherries, coconut and nuts; set aside.

In a mixing bowl, cream butter and sugars. Beat in eggs and extracts. Combine the flour, baking soda and salt; gradually add to creamed mixture.

Using a cookie press fitted with a bar disk, press a 12-in.-long strip of dough onto an ungreased baking sheet. Spread fruit filling over dough. Press another strip over filling. Cut into 1-in. pieces (there is no need to separate the pieces). Repeat with remaining dough and filling.

Bake at 375° for 12-15 minutes or until edges are golden. Recut into pieces if necessary. Remove to wire racks to cool. Dust with confectioners' sugar. **Yield: about 7-1/2 dozen.**

Swedish Butter Cookies 1st prize

It's impossible to eat just one of these treats. Naturally, they're a favorite with my Swedish husband and children—but anyone with a sweet tooth will appreciate them. My recipe is well-traveled among our friends and neighbors.
—Sue Soderland, Elgin, Illinois

- 1 cup butter, softened
- 1 cup sugar
- 2 teaspoons maple syrup
- 2 cups all-purpose flour

1 teaspoon baking soda
Confectioners' sugar

In a mixing bowl, cream butter and sugar. Add syrup; mix well. Combine flour and baking soda; gradually add to creamed mixture. Divide dough into eight portions. Roll each portion into a 9-in. log.

Place 3 in. apart on ungreased baking sheets. Bake at 300° for 25 minutes or until lightly browned. Cut into 1-in. slices. Remove to wire racks to cool. Dust with confectioners' sugar. **Yield: about 6 dozen.**

Swedish Butter Cookies

Lemon Snowballs

These crunchy little cookies with the bright taste of lemon are winners!

—Audrey Thibodeau, Fountain Hills, Arizona

- 1/2 cup butter, softened
- 2/3 cup sugar
- 1 egg
- 1/4 cup lemon juice
- 1 tablespoon grated lemon peel
- 1-3/4 cups all-purpose flour
- 1/4 teaspoon baking soda
- 1/4 teaspoon cream of tartar
- 1/4 teaspoon salt
- 1/2 cup finely chopped almonds
- Confectioners' sugar

In a mixing bowl, cream butter and sugar. Beat in egg. Add lemon juice and peel. Combine the flour, baking soda, cream of tartar and salt; stir into creamed mixture. Add almonds. Cover and refrigerate the dough for at least 1 hour or overnight.

Roll into 1-in. balls. Place on ungreased baking sheets. Bake at 350° for 10-12 minutes or until bottoms are lightly browned (cookies will not brown on top). Remove immediately to wire racks; cool for 5 minutes, then roll in confectioners' sugar. **Yield: about 3 dozen.**

Lemon Snowballs

Scandinavian Pecan Cookies

Scandinavian Pecan Cookies

We enjoyed these rich, buttery cookies at a bed-and-breakfast in Galena, Illinois, and the hostess was kind enough to share her simple recipe. The pretty nut-topped treats are so special you could give a home-baked batch as a gift.

—Laurie Knoke, DeKalb, Illinois

- 1 cup butter, softened
- 3/4 cup packed brown sugar
- 1 egg, *separated*
- 2 cups all-purpose flour
- 1/2 cup finely chopped pecans

In a mixing bowl, cream the butter and brown sugar. Beat in egg yolk. Gradually add flour. Shape into 1-in. balls. In a small bowl, beat egg white. Dip balls in egg white, then roll in pecans.

Place 2 in. apart on ungreased baking sheets; flatten slightly. Bake at 375° for 8-12 minutes or until edges are lightly browned. Cool on wire racks. **Yield: 4-5 dozen.**

Macadamia Chip Cookies

Macadamia Chip Cookies

If you like cookies with a crunch, you'll love these golden treats. Crushed peanut brittle adds a special surprise to the vanilla chips and brown sugar that flavor the dough. It's hard to believe something this easy to make tastes so terrific.

—Dorothy Kollmeyer, Dupo, Illinois

- 1 cup butter, softened
- 3/4 cup packed brown sugar
- 1/4 cup sugar
- 2 eggs
- 1 teaspoon vanilla extract
- 2-1/4 cups all-purpose flour
- 1 package (3.4 ounces) instant vanilla pudding mix
- 1 teaspoon baking soda

Vanilla Chip Maple Cookies

- 1/4 teaspoon salt
- 1 package (10 to 12 ounces) vanilla *or* white chips
- 2 jars (3-1/4 ounces *each*) macadamia nuts, chopped
- 1/2 cup finely crushed peanut brittle

In a mixing bowl, cream butter and sugars until smooth. Add eggs, one at a time, beating well after each addition. Beat in vanilla. Combine the flour, dry pudding mix, baking soda and salt; gradually add to creamed mixture and mix well. Stir in the chips, nuts and peanut brittle.

Drop by rounded tablespoonfuls 2 in. apart onto greased baking sheets. Bake at 375° for 10-12 minutes or until golden brown. Remove to wire racks to cool. **Yield: 5-1/2 dozen.**

Vanilla Chip Maple Cookies

Since my husband farms, I try to have simple meals and snacks available, as I never know when he and his father will come in from the fields. These cookies have a distinct maple flavor and stay moist and soft, although they're never in my cookie jar for long!

—Debra Hogenson, Brewster, Minnesota

- 1 cup shortening
- 1/2 cup butter, softened
- 2 cups packed brown sugar
- 2 eggs
- 1 teaspoon vanilla extract
- 1 teaspoon maple flavoring
- 3 cups all-purpose flour
- 2 teaspoons baking soda
- 2 cups vanilla *or* white chips
- 1/2 cup chopped pecans

FROSTING:

- 1/4 cup butter, softened
- 4 cups confectioners' sugar
- 1 teaspoon maple flavoring
- 4 to 6 tablespoons milk
- 3-1/2 cups pecan halves

In a mixing bowl, cream the shortening, butter and brown sugar. Add eggs, one at a time, beating well after each addition. Beat in vanilla and maple flavoring. Combine the flour and baking soda; gradually add to creamed mixture. Stir in vanilla chips and pecans.

Drop by rounded tablespoonfuls 2 in. apart onto ungreased baking sheets. Bake at 350° for 8-10 minutes or until golden brown. Cool for 2 minutes before removing to wire racks.

In a mixing bowl, cream butter and confectioners' sugar. Beat in maple flavoring and enough milk to achieve spreading consistency. Frost cooled cookies. Top each with a pecan half. **Yield: about 7 dozen.**

Chocolate Malted Cookies 1st prize

These cookies are the next best thing to a good old-fashioned malted milk. With malted milk powder, chocolate syrup plus chocolate chips and chunks, these are the best cookies I've ever tasted—and with six kids, I've made a lot of cookies over the years.
—Teri Rasey-Bolf, Cadillac, Michigan

- **1 cup butter-flavored shortening**
- **1-1/4 cups packed brown sugar**
- **1/2 cup malted milk powder**
- **2 tablespoons chocolate syrup**
- **1 tablespoon vanilla extract**
- **1 egg**
- **2 cups all-purpose flour**
- **1 teaspoon baking soda**
- **1/2 teaspoon salt**
- **1-1/2 cups semisweet chocolate chunks**
- **1 cup milk chocolate chips**

In a large mixing bowl, beat the shortening, brown sugar, malted milk powder, chocolate syrup and vanilla for 2 minutes. Add egg. Combine the flour, baking soda and salt; gradually add to creamed mixture, mixing well after each addition. Stir in chocolate chunks and chips.

Shape into 2-in. balls; place 3 in. apart on ungreased baking sheets. Bake at 375° for 12-14 minutes or until golden brown. Cool for 2 minutes before removing to a wire rack. **Yield: about 1-1/2 dozen.**

Fudge Puddles

The inspiration for these cookies came one year while I was out Christmas shopping. They became an instant favorite with my husband's family.
—Kimarie Maassen, Avoca, Iowa

- **1/2 cup butter, softened**
- **1/2 cup creamy peanut butter**

Chocolate Malted Cookies

- **1/2 cup sugar**
- **1/2 cup packed light brown sugar**
- **1 egg**
- **1/2 teaspoon vanilla extract**
- **1-1/4 cups all-purpose flour**
- **3/4 teaspoon baking soda**
- **1/2 teaspoon salt**

FUDGE FILLING:

- **1 cup milk chocolate chips**
- **1 cup (6 ounces) semisweet chocolate chips**
- **1 can (14 ounces) sweetened condensed milk**
- **1 teaspoon vanilla extract**

Chopped peanuts

In a large mixing bowl, cream the butter, peanut butter and sugars. Beat in egg and vanilla. Combine the flour, baking soda and salt. Gradually add to creamed mixture. Chill for 1 hour.

Shape into 1-in. balls. Place in lightly greased mini-muffin cups. Bake at 325° for 14-16 minutes or until lightly browned. Using the end of a wooden spoon handle, make a 3/8- to 1/2-in.-deep indentation in the center of each ball. Cool for 5 minutes before removing to wire racks to cool completely.

For filling, in a microwave or small saucepan, melt chocolate chips. Stir in milk and vanilla until smooth. Fill each shell with filling. Sprinkle with peanuts. (Leftover filling can be stored in the refrigerator and served warm over ice cream.) **Yield: 4 dozen.**

Chocolate Mint Cookies

My dad sandwiches mint patties between two tender chocolate cookies to create these chewy treats. The blend of chocolate and mint is a big hit at our house. Best of all, these cookies are easy and fun to make.
—Christina Burbage, Spartanburg, South Carolina

- 1-1/4 cups butter, softened
- 2 cups sugar
- 2 eggs
- 2 teaspoons vanilla extract
- 2 cups all-purpose flour
- 3/4 cup baking cocoa
- 1 teaspoon baking soda
- 1/2 teaspoon salt
- 32 round thin chocolate-covered mint patties

In a mixing bowl, cream butter and sugar. Add eggs, one at a time, beating well after each addition. Beat in vanilla. Combine the flour, cocoa, baking soda and salt; gradually add to the creamed mixture, beating until well combined.

Drop by tablespoonfuls 2 in. apart onto ungreased baking sheets. Bake at 350° for 8-9 minutes or until puffy and tops are cracked. Invert half of the cookies onto wire racks. Immediately place a mint patty on each, then top with remaining cookies. Press lightly to seal. Cool completely. **Yield: 32 sandwich cookies.**

Fudge Puddles

Chocolate Mint Cookies

Chocolate Surprise Cookies

Chocolate Meringues

Chocolate Surprise Cookies

It's fun watching folks' faces when they bite into the middle of these pretty cookies. The surprise is a burst of peanut butter. —Grace Crary, West Linn, Oregon

- 3/4 cup peanut butter
- 3/4 cup confectioners' sugar

CHOCOLATE DOUGH:

- 1/2 cup butter, softened
- 1/4 cup peanut butter
- 1/2 cup sugar
- 1/2 cup packed brown sugar
- 1 egg white
- 1 teaspoon vanilla extract
- 1-1/2 cups all-purpose flour
- 1/2 cup baking cocoa
- 1/2 teaspoon baking soda

ICING:

- 2 tablespoons shortening
- 1 cup confectioners' sugar
- 1/4 teaspoon vanilla extract
- 1 to 2 tablespoons milk

In a mixing bowl, cream peanut butter and confectioners' sugar until smooth. Roll into thirty 3/4-in. balls. Cover and refrigerate for 30 minutes.

Meanwhile, for dough, in a mixing bowl, cream the butter, peanut butter and sugars. Beat in egg white and vanilla. Combine the flour, cocoa and baking soda; gradually add to creamed mixture. Roll into thirty 1-1/2-in. balls.

Using floured hands, flatten chocolate balls and shape one around each peanut butter ball, sealing edges. Place 2 in. apart on greased baking sheets. Flatten with a glass dipped in sugar. Bake at 375° for 7-9 minutes or until cookies are set and tops are cracked. Cool for 1 minute, before removing to wire racks.

White Chocolate Oatmeal Cookies

For icing, in a small mixing bowl, cream shortening and confectioners' sugar. Beat in vanilla and enough milk to achieve spreading consistency. Pipe icing over cookies in a zigzag pattern. **Yield: 2-1/2 dozen.**

Editor's Note: Reduced-fat or generic brands of peanut butter are not recommended for this recipe.

Chocolate Meringues

These cookies are great for fancy occasions, but easy enough to make as a snack.
—Nancy Grace, San Diego, California

- 1 cup (6 ounces) semisweet chocolate chips
- 2 egg whites
- 1/2 teaspoon white vinegar
- 1/2 teaspoon vanilla *or* almond extract
- 1/4 teaspoon cream of tartar
- 1/8 teaspoon salt
- 1/2 cup sugar
- 1/2 cup flaked coconut
- 1/4 cup chopped almonds

In a microwave or heavy saucepan, melt chocolate chips; stir until smooth and set aside. In a mixing bowl, beat the egg whites, vinegar, vanilla, cream of tartar and salt on medium speed until soft peaks form. Add sugar, 1 tablespoon at a time, beating on high until stiff peaks form, about 5 minutes. Fold in melted chocolate until combined; fold in coconut and almonds.

Drop by tablespoonfuls 2 in. apart onto lightly greased baking sheets. Bake at 350° for 10-11 minutes or until firm. Remove to wire racks to cool. Store in an airtight container. **Yield: about 2-1/2 dozen.**

White Chocolate Oatmeal Cookies

My sons and grandsons manage our ranch, and they always seem to have one hand in the cookie jar—especially when I bake these crunchy morsels!
—Edith Pluhar, Cohagen, Montana

- 1 cup butter, softened
- 1/2 cup sugar
- 1/2 cup packed brown sugar
- 1 egg
- 3 teaspoons vanilla extract
- 1 teaspoon coconut extract
- 1-1/2 cups quick-cooking oats
- 1-1/4 cups all-purpose flour
- 1 teaspoon salt
- 1 teaspoon baking soda
- 1 cup flaked coconut, toasted
- 6 squares (1 ounce *each*) white baking chocolate, cut into 1/2-inch chunks
- Additional sugar

In a mixing bowl, cream butter and sugars. Add the egg and extracts; mix well. Combine the oats, flour, salt and baking soda; gradually add to creamed mixture. Stir in the coconut and chocolate.

Drop by tablespoonfuls 3 in. apart onto ungreased baking sheets. Flatten with a glass dipped in sugar. Bake at 350° for 8-9 minutes or until golden brown. Cool for 1 minute before removing to wire racks. **Yield: about 5 dozen.**

Triple Chocolate Kisses

Triple Chocolate Kisses

These crisp meringue cookies with a chocolate center are easy to make but look like you spent a lot of time on them. When our son and daughter-in-law moved into their first home on Valentine's Day, I prepared them a nice dinner and gave them a batch of these cute treats. —*Evelyn Lindburg, Shenandoah, Iowa*

- 2 egg whites
- 1/4 teaspoon cream of tartar
- 1/4 teaspoon almond extract
- 1/2 cup sugar
- 1 square (1 ounce) semisweet chocolate, grated
- 42 milk chocolate kisses

Baking cocoa

In a mixing bowl, beat egg whites, cream of tartar and extract on medium speed until soft peaks form, about 6 minutes. Gradually add sugar, 1 tablespoon at a time, beating on high until stiff peaks form. Fold in grated chocolate.

Insert a medium open-star tip in a pastry or plastic bag. Fill with the meringue. On lightly greased baking sheets, pipe forty-two 1-in. circles. Press a chocolate kiss into the center of each. Pipe meringue around each kiss in continuous circles from base to top until kiss is completely covered. Dust with cocoa.

Bake at 325° for 15-18 minutes or until the edges are lightly browned. Immediately remove to wire racks to cool. **Yield: 3-1/2 dozen.**

Peanut Butter Sandwich Cookies

I'm a busy mother of two children. I work in our school office and help my husband on our hog and cattle farm. When I find time to bake a treat, I want it to be special like this scrumptious recipe.
—*Debbie Kokes, Tabor, South Dakota*

- 1 cup butter-flavored shortening
- 1 cup creamy peanut butter
- 1 cup sugar
- 1 cup packed brown sugar
- 3 eggs
- 1 teaspoon vanilla extract
- 3 cups all-purpose flour
- 2 teaspoons baking soda
- 1/4 teaspoon salt

FILLING:

- 1/2 cup creamy peanut butter
- 3 cups confectioners' sugar
- 1 teaspoon vanilla extract
- 5 to 6 tablespoons milk

In a large mixing bowl, cream the shortening, peanut butter and sugars. Add eggs, one at a time, beating well after each addition. Add vanilla. Combine the flour, baking soda and salt; add to creamed mixture and mix well.

Shape into 1-in. balls and place 2 in. apart on ungreased baking sheets. Flatten to 3/8-in. thickness with a fork. Bake at 375° for 7-8 minutes or until golden. Remove to wire racks to cool.

For filling, in a large mixing bowl, beat the peanut butter, confectioners' sugar, vanilla and enough milk to achieve spreading consistency. Spread on half of the cookies and top each with another cookie. **Yield: 2 dozen sandwich cookies.**

Peanut Butter Chocolate Cookies

This recipe was featured in our Sunday paper, and I just had to try it. Kids of all ages really love the peanut butter surprise inside the cookie.
—June Formanek, Belle Plaine, Iowa

- 1/2 cup butter, softened
- 1/2 cup sugar
- 1/2 cup packed brown sugar
- 1 cup creamy peanut butter, *divided*
- 1 egg, lightly beaten
- 1 teaspoon vanilla extract
- 1-1/2 cups all-purpose flour
- 1/2 cup baking cocoa
- 1/2 teaspoon baking soda
- 3/4 cup confectioners' sugar

In a large mixing bowl, cream butter, sugars and 1/4 cup peanut butter. Add egg and vanilla; mix well. Combine the flour, cocoa and baking soda; add to creamed mixture and mix well.

In a bowl, blend confectioners' sugar with remaining peanut butter until smooth. Roll into 24 balls, 1 in. each. Divide dough into 24 pieces; flatten each into a 3-in. circle.

Place one peanut butter ball on each circle; bring edges over to completely cover it. (Dough may crack; reshape cookies as needed.) Place cookies with seam side down on ungreased baking sheets. Flatten each cookie slightly with the bottom of a glass dipped in sugar. Bake at 375° for 7-9 minutes or until set. Remove to wire racks to cool. **Yield: 2 dozen.**

Peanut Butter Sandwich Cookies

Peanut Butter Chocolate Cookies

Molasses Spice Cutouts

Cinnamon Sugar Cookies

Molasses Spice Cutouts

It hardly ever fails—when I send these cookies to school with our youngsters, I'm almost always asked for the recipe by their teachers! I'm happy to share it.
—Doris Heinmen, St. Cloud, Minnesota

- 1 cup butter, softened
- 1-1/2 cups sugar
- 1 cup light molasses
- 1/2 cup cold coffee
- 6 cups all-purpose flour
- 2 teaspoons baking soda
- 1 teaspoon salt
- 1/2 teaspoon ground nutmeg
- 1/4 teaspoon ground cloves

ICING (optional):

- 1 envelope unflavored gelatin
- 3/4 cup cold water
- 3/4 cup sugar
- 3/4 cup confectioners' sugar
- 3/4 teaspoon baking powder
- 1/2 teaspoon vanilla extract
- Colored sugar
- Decorator icing, optional

In a mixing bowl, cream butter and sugar; beat in molasses and coffee. Combine the flour, baking soda, salt and spices; add to molasses mixture and mix well. Cover and refrigerate dough 1-2 hours or until easy to handle.

On a lightly floured surface, roll dough to a 1/4-in. thickness. If needed, add a little additional flour before rolling. Cut with floured holiday cutters. Place on ungreased baking sheets. Bake at 350° for 12-15 minutes. Cool on wire racks.

For icing, if desired, combine gelatin and water in a small saucepan. Let stand for 5 minutes to soften. Add sugar. Heat and stir over very low heat until the gelatin and sugar dissolve. Transfer to a mixing bowl. Add

Licorice Cookie Strips

confectioners' sugar; beat until foamy. Add baking powder and vanilla; beat until very thick, about 10 minutes.

Frost cookies by inverting them and quickly swirling the tops in the icing; decorate with colored sugar. For traditional gingerbread men, use decorator icing to add features as desired. **Yield: about 7-8 dozen (2-1/2-in. cookies).**

Cinnamon Sugar Cookies

My mom always had these cookies on hand. They're so good with a cup of hot chocolate, coffee or milk.
—Leah Costigan, Otto, North Carolina

- 1 cup butter, softened
- 1 cup sugar
- 1 cup confectioners' sugar
- 1 cup vegetable oil
- 2 eggs
- 1 teaspoon vanilla extract
- 4-1/3 cups all-purpose flour
- 1 teaspoon salt
- 1 teaspoon baking soda
- 1 teaspoon ground cinnamon
- 1 teaspoon cream of tartar
- 1 cup finely chopped pecans, optional
- Colored sugar, optional

In a large mixing bowl, cream the butter, sugars and oil. Add eggs and vanilla; mix well. Add the flour, salt, baking soda, cinnamon and cream of tartar. Stir in the pecans if desired.

Roll into 1-in. balls. Place on greased baking sheets; flatten with the bottom of a glass dipped in sugar. Sprinkle with colored sugar if desired. Bake at 375° for 10-12 minutes. Remove to wire racks to cool. **Yield: about 8 dozen.**

Licorice Cookie Strips

If you like the flavor of licorice, you'll love these crispy cookies. When our six children were young, I often made them to send along for lunches or as after-school snacks. Flattening the dough logs with a fork gives them a pretty look. Once they're baked, it's a breeze to cut them into strips.
—Dolores Hurtt, Florence, Montana

- 1 cup butter, softened
- 1 cup sugar
- 1 cup packed brown sugar
- 1 egg
- 2-1/2 cups all-purpose flour
- 2 teaspoons aniseed
- 1 teaspoon baking soda
- 1/2 teaspoon salt
- 1/2 teaspoon ground cinnamon
- 1/2 teaspoon ground nutmeg
- 1/2 cup chopped nuts

In a mixing bowl, cream butter and sugars. Beat in egg. Combine dry ingredients; add to creamed mixture and mix well. Stir in nuts.

Divide dough into 10 portions; shape each into a 12-in. log. Place 3 in. apart on ungreased baking sheets. Flatten with a fork to 1/4-in. thickness.

Bake at 350° for 8-10 minutes or until golden brown. Cool for 5 minutes; cut diagonally into 1-in. slices. Remove to wire racks to cool completely. **Yield: about 8 dozen.**

Old-Fashioned Gingersnaps

Old-Fashioned Gingersnaps

I discovered this recipe many years ago, and it's been a favorite among our family and friends since. Who doesn't like cookies during the holidays?
—Francis Stoops, Stoneboro, Pennsylvania

- 1 cup butter, softened
- 1 cup sugar
- 1 egg
- 1/4 cup molasses
- 2 cups all-purpose flour
- 2 teaspoons baking soda
- 1 teaspoon ground cinnamon
- 1 teaspoon ground cloves
- 1 teaspoon ground ginger
- 1/4 teaspoon salt
- Additional sugar

In a mixing bowl, cream butter and sugar. Beat in egg and molasses. Combine the flour, baking soda, cinnamon, cloves, ginger and salt; gradually add to creamed mixture. Chill.

Roll into 1-1/4-in. balls and dip into sugar. Place 2 in. apart on ungreased baking sheets. Bake at 375° for about 10 minutes or until set and surface cracks. Cool on wire racks. **Yield: about 4 dozen.**

Cinnamon Snaps

Since I'm a longtime cinnamon fan, I decided to give traditional gingersnaps a delightfully different twist. My husband and son agree I spiced them up just right. *—Cathy Cain, Carmel, California*

- 3/4 cup shortening
- 1 cup packed brown sugar
- 1 egg
- 1/4 cup molasses
- 2-1/4 cups all-purpose flour
- 2 teaspoons baking soda
- 2 teaspoons ground cinnamon
- 1/2 teaspoon salt
- Additional sugar

In a mixing bowl, cream shortening and brown sugar. Add egg and molasses. Combine the flour, baking soda, cinnamon and salt; gradually add to creamed mixture. Roll into 1-in. balls, then roll in additional sugar.

Place 2 in. apart on ungreased baking sheets. Bake at 350° for 10-12 minutes or until cookies are set and tops are cracked. Remove to wire racks to cool. **Yield: 4-1/2 dozen.**

Fruitcake Cookies

This recipe's one people always ask for. They tell me it's habit-forming! I'm the kind of cook who starts with a basic recipe, then throws in extras to make it my own. I'm also the type who doesn't like making the same old things over and over. So it's good my husband is happy to eat just about anything I serve.
—Hazel Staley, Gaithersburg, Maryland

- 6 cups chopped pecans (about 1-1/2 pounds)
- 2 cups graham cracker crumbs

Cinnamon Snaps

- 1-1/2 cups raisins
- 1-1/4 cups chopped candied cherries (about 1/2 pound)
- 1-1/4 cups chopped candied pineapple (about 1/2 pound)
- 4-1/2 cups miniature marshmallows
- 1/2 cup evaporated milk
- 1/4 cup butter, cubed
- 1-1/2 cups flaked coconut

In a large bowl, combine the pecans, cracker crumbs, raisins, cherries and pineapple. In a large saucepan, combine the marshmallows, milk and butter. Cook over low heat, stirring constantly, until melted.

Pour over pecan mixture and mix well. Shape into 1-in. balls and roll in the coconut. **Yield: 7-8 dozen.**

Fruitcake Cookies

Raspberry Truffle Brownies

German Chocolate Brownies

Raspberry Truffle Brownies 1st prize

On the outside, they look like traditional brownies. When people bite in, though, are they surprised! It's almost like eating a rich, filled chocolate candy.
—Leslie Knicl, Mahomet, Illinois

- 1/2 cup butter, cubed
- 1-1/4 cups semisweet chocolate chips
- 2 eggs
- 3/4 cup packed brown sugar
- 1 teaspoon instant coffee granules
- 2 tablespoons water
- 3/4 cup all-purpose flour
- 1/2 teaspoon baking powder

FILLING:

- 1 cup (6 ounces) semisweet chocolate chips
- 1 package (8 ounces) cream cheese, softened
- 1/4 cup confectioners' sugar
- 1/3 cup seedless red raspberry jam

GLAZE:

- 1/4 cup semisweet chocolate chips
- 1 teaspoon shortening

In a heavy saucepan, melt butter and chocolate chips over low heat. Cool slightly. In a large bowl, beat eggs and brown sugar. Dissolve coffee crystals in water; add to egg mixture with melted chocolate. Mix well. Combine flour and baking powder; stir into chocolate mixture.

Spread in a greased 9-in. square baking pan. Bake at 350° for 30-35 minutes or until a toothpick comes out clean. Cool on a wire rack.

For filling, melt chocolate chips; cool. In a mixing bowl, beat cream cheese and confectioners' sugar until smooth. Beat in jam. Stir in melted chocolate; spread over cooled

Maple Butterscotch Brownies

brownies.

For glaze, melt chocolate chips and shortening. Drizzle over filling. Chill before cutting. Store in the refrigerator. **Yield: about 5 dozen.**

German Chocolate Brownies

Even as a young girl, I was always going through recipe books in search of something new to make. That's how I came across these brownies, a favorite for our family reunions and church dinners.
—Karen Grimes, Stephens City, Virginia

- 1/2 cup butter, cubed
- 1 package (4 ounces) German sweet chocolate, broken into squares
- 1/2 cup sugar
- 1 teaspoon vanilla extract
- 2 eggs, lightly beaten
- 1 cup all-purpose flour
- 1/2 teaspoon baking powder
- 1/4 teaspoon salt

TOPPING:

- 2 tablespoons butter, melted
- 1/2 cup packed brown sugar
- 1 cup flaked coconut
- 1/2 cup chopped pecans
- 2 tablespoons corn syrup
- 2 tablespoons milk

In a microwave or heavy saucepan, melt butter and chocolate; stir until smooth. Cool slightly. Add sugar and vanilla; mix. Beat in the eggs. Mix in the flour, baking powder and salt. Pour into a greased 9-in. square baking pan. Bake at 350° for 18-22 minutes or a toothpick inserted near the center comes out clean.

For topping, combine butter and brown sugar in a bowl. Add the coconut, pecans, corn syrup and milk; mix well. Drop by teaspoonfuls onto warm brownies; spread evenly. Broil several inches from the heat for 2-4 minutes or until top is browned and bubbly. **Yield: 16 brownies.**

Maple Butterscotch Brownies

Generally, I'll make a double recipe of these brownies—they go so fast no matter where I take them! They're very easy, plus they keep and freeze well.
—Grace Vonhold, Rochester, New York

- 1/2 cup butter, melted
- 1-1/4 cups packed brown sugar
- 2 eggs
- 1-1/2 teaspoons maple flavoring
- 1-1/2 cups all-purpose flour
- 1 teaspoon baking powder
- 1 cup chopped walnuts

Confectioners' sugar, optional

In a large mixing bowl, cream the butter and brown sugar. Add eggs, one at a time, beating well after each addition. Beat in maple flavoring. Combine flour and baking powder; add to egg mixture. Stir in walnuts.

Pour into a greased 9-in. square baking pan. Bake at 350° for 27-32 minutes or until a toothpick inserted near the center comes out clean. Cool. Dust with confectioners' sugar if desired. **Yield: 16 brownies.**

Macaroon Brownies

Macaroon Brownies 1st prize

My mother-in-law made these coconut-filled brownies for my bridal shower and wedding reception. After the first bite, I knew why my husband loves them!

—Christine Foust, Stoneboro, Pennsylvania

- 1 cup butter, softened
- 2 cups sugar
- 4 eggs
- 1 teaspoon vanilla extract
- 2 cups all-purpose flour
- 1/2 cup baking cocoa
- 1/2 teaspoon cream of tartar
- 1/2 cup chopped walnuts

MACAROON FILLING:

- 1 package (14 ounces) flaked coconut
- 1 can (14 ounces) sweetened condensed milk
- 2 teaspoons vanilla extract

FROSTING:

- 3/4 cup sugar
- 1/4 cup milk
- 2 tablespoons butter
- 1 cup miniature marshmallows
- 1 cup (6 ounces) semisweet chocolate chips
- 1 teaspoon vanilla extract

In a mixing bowl, cream butter and sugar. Add eggs and vanilla; mix well. Combine flour, cocoa and cream of tartar; gradually add to creamed mixture. Stir in nuts. Spread half into a greased 13-in. x 9-in. x 2-in. baking pan.

Combine the coconut, condensed milk and vanilla; carefully spread over chocolate layer. Top with the remaining chocolate mixture. Bake at 350° for 40-45 minutes or until a toothpick inserted near the center comes out clean. Cool on a wire rack.

For frosting, combine the sugar, milk and butter in a saucepan; cook and stir until sugar is dissolved. Add the remaining ingredients. Cook and stir until marshmallows and chips are melted. Cool until mixture reaches spreading consistency, about 25 minutes. Spread over the cooled brownies. Cut into bars. **Yield: 4 dozen.**

Best Cake Brownies

This recipe caught my eye because it uses a whole can of chocolate syrup! I had searched for years for a brownie everyone likes, and this is it. We often dig in before they've cooled.

—Jean Kennedy, Springfield, Oregon

- 1/2 cup butter, softened
- 1 cup sugar
- 4 eggs
- 1 can (16 ounces) chocolate syrup
- 1 teaspoon vanilla extract
- 1 cup all-purpose flour
- 1/2 teaspoon salt

GLAZE:

- 1 cup sugar
- 1/3 cup butter, cubed
- 1/3 cup milk
- 2/3 cup semisweet chocolate chips
- 2/3 cup miniature marshmallows

In a mixing bowl, cream butter and sugar. Add the eggs, one at a time, beating well after each addition. Beat in chocolate syrup and vanilla. Add the flour and salt until blended.

Pour into a greased 15-in. x 10-in. x 1-in. baking pan. Bake at 350° for 20-25 minutes or until a toothpick inserted near the center comes out clean (top of brownies will still appear wet). Cool on a wire rack for 15-20 minutes.

Meanwhile, in a small saucepan, combine the sugar, butter and milk. Bring to a boil; boil until the sugar is dissolved. Remove from the heat; stir in chocolate chips and marshmallows until melted. Pour over brownies and spread evenly. Refrigerate for 5 minutes before cutting. **Yield: about 3 dozen.**

Best Cake Brownies

Caramel Cashew Brownies

I always have my eye out for a good recipe, like the one for these marvelous golden brownies. It's hard to eat just one! —*Judy High, Berryville, Arkansas*

- 18 caramels
- 1/3 cup butter
- 2 tablespoons milk
- 3/4 cup sugar
- 2 eggs
- 1/2 teaspoon vanilla extract
- 1 cup all-purpose flour
- 1/2 teaspoon baking powder
- 1/4 teaspoon salt
- 1 cup chopped salted cashews

In a saucepan, cook and stir the caramels, butter and milk over low heat until the caramels are melted and mixture is smooth. Remove from the heat; stir in sugar. Stir eggs and vanilla into caramel mixture. Combine the flour, baking powder and salt; stir into caramel mixture until blended. Fold in cashews.

Transfer to a greased 9-in. square baking pan. Bake at 350° for 24-28 minutes or until a toothpick inserted near the center comes out clean. Cool on a wire rack. Cut into bars. **Yield: 25 brownies.**

Caramel Cashew Brownies

Frosted Fudge Brownies

Fudgy Nut Brownies

Frosted Fudge Brownies 1st prize

A neighbor brought over a pan of these rich brownies along with the recipe when I came home from the hospital with our baby daughter. I've made them ever since for family occasions, potlucks and parties.
—Sue Soderlund, Elgin, Illinois

- 1 cup plus 3 tablespoons butter, cubed
- 3/4 cup baking cocoa
- 4 eggs
- 2 cups sugar
- 1-1/2 cups all-purpose flour
- 1 teaspoon baking powder
- 1 teaspoon salt
- 1 teaspoon vanilla extract

FROSTING:

- 6 tablespoons butter, softened
- 2-2/3 cups confectioners' sugar
- 1/2 cup baking cocoa
- 1 teaspoon vanilla extract
- 1/4 to 1/3 cup milk

In a saucepan, melt butter. Remove from the heat. Stir in cocoa; cool. In a mixing bowl, beat eggs and sugar. Combine the flour, baking powder and salt; gradually add to egg mixture. Stir in vanilla and the cooled chocolate mixture; mix well.

Spread into a greased 13-in. x 9-in. x 2-in. baking pan. Bake at 350° for 25-28 minutes or until a toothpick inserted near the center comes out clean (do not overbake). Cool on a wire rack.

For frosting, in a mixing bowl, cream the butter, confectioners' sugar, cocoa and vanilla. Stir in enough milk to achieve spreading consistency. Spread over brownies. Cut into bars. **Yield: 2 dozen.**

Macadamia Chip Brownies

Fudgy Nut Brownies

I've prepared this special recipe for many an open house and potluck dinner. It came from an old roommate, who is now a grandmother. While in our early 20s, we never imagined we'd be sharing brownie recipes after all these years.

—Ruth Stern, Shadow Hills, California

- 2-1/2 cups (15 ounces) semisweet chocolate chips
- 1 cup butter, cubed
- 1 cup sugar
- 1/4 teaspoon salt
- 4 eggs, lightly beaten
- 2 teaspoons vanilla extract
- 3/4 cup all-purpose flour
- 1 cup coarsely chopped hazelnuts

TOPPING:

- 12 squares (1 ounce *each*) semisweet chocolate
- 1 tablespoon shortening
- 3 squares (1 ounce *each*) white baking chocolate

In a microwave or heavy saucepan, melt chocolate chips and butter; stir until smooth. Remove from the heat. Add sugar and salt; stir until dissolved. Cool for 10 minutes.

Stir in the eggs, vanilla, flour and nuts. Spread into a greased 15-in. x 10-in. x 1-in. baking pan. Bake at 350° for 25-30 minutes or until a toothpick inserted near the center comes out with moist crumbs (do not overbake). Cool completely on a wire rack.

For topping, in a microwave or heavy saucepan, melt semisweet chocolate and shortening; stir until smooth. Spread over brownies.

Melt white chocolate. Pour into a small heavy-duty resealable plastic bag; cut a small hole in corner of bag. Pipe thin lines 1 in. apart widthwise. Beginning about 1 in. from a wide side, gently pull a toothpick through the lines to the opposite side. Wipe toothpick clean, then pull toothpick through lines in opposite directions. Repeat over entire top at 1-in. intervals. Cut into bars. **Yield: about 2-1/2 dozen.**

Macadamia Chip Brownies

With two kinds of chocolate, plus the macadamia nuts, there's no need to frost these scrumptious bars! I like to make them for special occasions. I'm a retired home economist who loves to bake for fun.

—Lucile Cline, Wichita, Kansas

- 1/3 cup butter
- 4 squares (1 ounce *each*) white baking chocolate
- 2 eggs
- 1 cup sugar
- 1 teaspoon vanilla extract
- 1 cup all-purpose flour
- 1/4 teaspoon salt
- 1/2 cup chopped macadamia nuts
- 1/2 cup milk chocolate chips

In a saucepan over low heat, melt butter and white chocolate; remove from the heat. In a bowl, combine the eggs, sugar and vanilla. Add the chocolate mixture, flour and salt; mix well. Stir in nuts and chocolate chips.

Pour into a greased 9-in. square baking pan. Bake at 325° for 30-35 minutes or until top is lightly browned. Cool on a wire rack. Cut into bars. **Yield: 1-1/2 dozen.**

Black Forest Brownies

Black Forest Brownies

Although I enjoy sweets, other recipes have failed me. But not this one! It's easy, and the ingredients are always on hand. Even people who don't like most sweets can't pass up these luscious brownies.
—Toni Reeves, Medicine Hat, Alberta

- 4 eggs, beaten
- 2 cups sugar
- 1 cup butter, melted
- 1-1/2 teaspoons vanilla extract
- 1 teaspoon almond extract
- 1-1/3 cups all-purpose flour
- 1 cup baking cocoa
- 1 teaspoon baking powder
- 1/2 teaspoon salt
- 1 cup maraschino cherries
- 1/2 cup chopped nuts

ICING:

- 2 cups confectioners' sugar
- 6 tablespoons baking cocoa
- 1/4 cup milk
- 1/4 cup butter, softened
- 1 teaspoon vanilla extract
- 1/4 cup chopped nuts

In a large mixing bowl, beat the eggs, sugar, butter, vanilla and almond extract. Combine the flour, cocoa, baking powder and salt; stir into egg mixture until blended. Fold in cherries and nuts.

Pour into a greased 13-in. x 9-in. x 2-in. baking pan. Bake at 350° for 35 minutes or until a toothpick inserted near the center comes out clean.

Meanwhile, for icing, in a small mixing bowl, beat the confectioners' sugar, cocoa, milk, butter and vanilla until smooth. Frost brownies. Sprinkle with nuts. **Yield: 3 dozen.**

Cappuccino Cake Brownies

If you like your sweets with a cup of coffee, this recipe is for you! These no-nut brownies combine a mild coffee flavor with the richness of semisweet chocolate chips. *—Mary Houchin, Lebanon, Illinois*

- 1 tablespoon instant coffee granules
- 2 teaspoons boiling water
- 1 cup (6 ounces) semisweet chocolate chips
- 1/4 cup butter, softened
- 1/2 cup sugar
- 2 eggs
- 1/2 cup all-purpose flour
- 1/4 teaspoon ground cinnamon

In a small bowl, dissolve coffee in water; set aside. In a microwave or saucepan, melt chocolate chips; stir until smooth. In a small mixing bowl, cream butter and sugar. Beat in the eggs, melted chocolate and coffee mixture. Combine flour and cinnamon; add to the creamed mixture and mix well.

Pour into a greased 8-in. square baking dish. Bake at 350° for 25-30 minutes or until a toothpick inserted near the center comes out clean. Cool on a wire rack. Cut into squares. **Yield: 16 bars.**

Peanut Butter Swirl Brownies

Peanut butter and chocolate are always a delicious duo, but they're extra-special paired in this treat.
—Linda Craig, Hay River, Northwest Territories

- 1/2 cup butter, softened
- 2/3 cup sugar
- 1/2 cup packed brown sugar
- 2 eggs
- 2 tablespoons milk
- 3/4 cup all-purpose flour
- 1/2 teaspoon baking powder
- 1/4 teaspoon salt
- 1/4 cup creamy peanut butter
- 1/3 cup peanut butter chips
- 1/3 cup baking cocoa
- 1/2 cup semisweet chocolate chips

In a mixing bowl, cream butter and sugars. Add eggs and milk; mix well. Combine the flour, baking powder and salt; add to creamed mixture and mix well. Divide batter in half. To one portion, add peanut butter and peanut butter chips; mix well. To the other portion, add the cocoa and chocolate chips; mix well.

In a greased 9-in. square baking pan, spoon chocolate batter in eight mounds in a checkerboard pattern. Spoon seven mounds of peanut butter batter between the chocolate batter. Cut through batters with a knife to swirl.

Bake at 350° for 25-30 minutes or until a toothpick inserted near the center comes out clean. Cool on a wire rack. **Yield: 3 dozen.**

Cappuccino Cake Brownies

Peanut Butter Swirl Brownies

Chocolate Mint Brownies

Chocolate Cream Cheese Brownies

Chocolate Mint Brownies

One of the best things about this recipe is the brownies get moister if you leave them in the refrigerator a day or two. The problem at our house is no one can leave them alone for that long!
—Helen Baines, Elkton, Maryland

- 1 cup all-purpose flour
- 1/2 cup butter, softened
- 1/2 teaspoon salt
- 4 eggs
- 1 teaspoon vanilla extract
- 1 can (16 ounces) chocolate-flavored syrup
- 1 cup sugar

FILLING:

- 1/2 cup butter, softened
- 2 cups confectioners' sugar
- 1 tablespoon water
- 1/2 teaspoon mint extract
- 3 drops green food coloring

TOPPING:

- 1 package (10 ounces) mint chocolate chips
- 1/2 cup plus 1 tablespoon butter, cubed

In a large mixing bowl, combine the first seven ingredients. Beat on medium speed for 3 minutes. Pour batter into a greased 13-in. x 9-in. x 2-in. baking pan. Bake at 350° for 30 minutes (top of brownies will still appear wet). Cool completely.

For the filling, in a large mixing bowl, beat the butter, confectioners' sugar, water, mint extract and food coloring until creamy. Spread over cooled brownies. Refrigerate until set.

For the topping, melt chocolate chips and butter over low heat in a small saucepan. Let cool for 30 minutes, stirring occasionally. Spread over filling. Chill. Cut into squares. Store in refrigerator. **Yield: 5-6 dozen.**

Editor's Note: If mint chocolate chips are

Shortbread Squares

not available, place 2 cups (12 ounces) semisweet chocolate chips and 1/4 teaspoon peppermint extract in a plastic bag; seal and toss to coat. Allow chips to stand for 24-48 hours.

Chocolate Cream Cheese Brownies

Whenever I take these to a gathering, someone will usually announce, "Lisa brought those brownies"—and everyone knows exactly which ones they are!
—Lisa Godfrey, Temple, Georgia

- 1 package (4 ounces) German sweet chocolate
- 3 tablespoons butter
- 2 eggs
- 3/4 cup sugar
- 1/2 cup all-purpose flour
- 1/2 teaspoon baking powder
- 1/4 teaspoon salt
- 1 teaspoon vanilla extract
- 1/4 teaspoon almond extract
- 1/2 cup chopped nuts

FILLING:

- 2 tablespoons butter, softened
- 1 package (3 ounces) cream cheese, softened
- 1/4 cup sugar
- 1 egg
- 1 tablespoon all-purpose flour
- 1/2 teaspoon vanilla extract

In a microwave or saucepan, melt chocolate and butter; stir until smooth and set aside.

In a small mixing bowl, beat the eggs. Gradually add sugar, beating until thick and pale yellow. Combine the flour, baking powder and salt; add to egg mixture and mix well. Stir in the extracts and reserved melted chocolate. Add the nuts. Pour half of the batter into a greased 8-in. square baking dish; set aside.

For filling, in another small mixing bowl, beat the butter, cream cheese and sugar until light and fluffy. Add the egg, flour and vanilla; mix well. Pour over batter in pan. Spoon remaining batter over filling. With a knife, cut through batter to create a marbled effect.

Bake at 325° for 35-40 minutes or a toothpick inserted near the center comes out clean. Cool on a wire rack. Cut into bars. Store in the refrigerator. **Yield: about 2 dozen.**

Shortbread Squares

Here's a traditional shortbread recipe that's perfect with a cup of hot tea or coffee. It's a favorite during the holidays.
—Mrs. G.C. Mayhew, Grass Valley, California

- 1 pound butter, softened
- 1 cup sifted confectioners' sugar
- 3-1/2 cups all-purpose flour
- 1/2 cup cornstarch

In a mixing bowl, cream butter and sugar. Combine flour and cornstarch; gradually add to creamed mixture.

Pat into an ungreased 15-in. x 10-in. x 1-in. baking pan. Pierce several times with a fork. Bake at 325° for 40-45 minutes or until lightly browned. Cut while warm. **Yield: about 6 dozen.**

Chocolate Chip Cheesecake Bars

Chocolate Chip Cheesecake Bars

I received this recipe from a co-worker who made these heavenly bars for a potluck. Since they combine two favorite flavors—chocolate chip cookies and cheesecake—in one bite, they're always a hit.

—Jane Nolt, Narvon, Pennsylvania

- 3/4 cup shortening
- 3/4 cup sugar
- 1/3 cup packed brown sugar
- 1 egg
- 1-1/2 teaspoons vanilla extract
- 1-1/2 cups all-purpose flour
- 1 teaspoon salt
- 3/4 teaspoon baking soda
- 1-1/2 cups miniature chocolate chips
- 3/4 cup chopped pecans

FILLING:

- 2 packages (8 ounces *each*) cream cheese, softened
- 3/4 cup sugar
- 2 eggs
- 1 teaspoon vanilla extract

In a mixing bowl, cream shortening and sugars. Beat in egg and vanilla. Combine the flour, salt and baking soda; add to the creamed mixture and mix well. Fold in the chocolate chips and pecans. Set aside a third of the dough for topping. Press remaining dough into a greased 13-in. x 9-in. x 2-in. baking pan. Bake at 350° for 8 minutes.

Meanwhile, in a small mixing bowl, beat cream cheese and sugar until smooth. Add eggs and vanilla; mix well. Spoon over crust. Drop teaspoonfuls of reserved dough over filling. Bake at 350° for 35-40 minutes or until golden brown. Cool on a wire rack. Store in the refrigerator. **Yield: 3 dozen.**

Caramel-Chocolate Oat Squares

In the summer, we often have weekend guests who go boating with us. These sweet, chewy bars are the perfect treat to take along. I use my microwave, which doesn't heat up the kitchen.

—Kellie Ochsner, Newton, Iowa

- 3/4 cup butter, cubed
- 1-1/4 cups all-purpose flour
- 1-1/4 cups quick-cooking oats
- 3/4 cup packed brown sugar
- 1/2 teaspoon baking soda
- 1/4 teaspoon salt
- 24 caramels
- 1/4 cup milk
- 1 cup (6 ounces) semisweet chocolate chips
- 1/2 cup chopped walnuts, optional

In a microwave-safe bowl, heat butter, uncovered, on high for 30-45 seconds or until softened. Combine the flour, oats, brown sugar, baking soda and salt; stir into butter until blended.

Set a third of the mixture aside for topping. Press remaining mixture onto the bottom of an 8-in. square microwave-safe dish. Cook, uncovered, on high for 2-3 minutes or until crust is raised and set (crust will be uneven), rotating a half turn after each minute.

In a 1-qt. microwave-safe dish, heat the caramels and milk, uncovered, on high for 3-4 minutes or until melted and smooth, stirring every minute. Sprinkle chips and nuts if desired over crust. Pour caramel mixture over all.

Sprinkle with reserved oat mixture; press down lightly. Microwave, uncovered, on high for 3-4 minutes or until the caramel is bubbly, rotating a quarter turn every minute. Cool before cutting. **Yield: 16 servings.**

Editor's Note: This recipe was tested with an 850-watt microwave.

Caramel-Chocolate Oat Squares

Chewy Peanut Butter Bars

This recipe combines three of my favorite foods—peanut butter, coconut and chocolate—into one mouth-watering dessert. It's very rich and filling, so a small piece usually satisfies even a real sweet tooth.
—Mrs. Sanford Wickham, Holbrook, Nebraska

- 1 cup all-purpose flour
- 1/3 cup sugar
- 1/2 cup cold butter

FILLING:

- 2 eggs
- 1/2 cup corn syrup
- 1/2 cup sugar
- 1/4 cup crunchy peanut butter
- 1/4 teaspoon salt
- 1/2 cup flaked coconut
- 1/2 cup semisweet chocolate chips

In a bowl, combine flour and sugar; cut in the butter until crumbly. Press into a greased 13-in. x 9-in. x 2-in. baking pan. Bake at 350° for 14-16 minutes or until lightly browned.

In a mixing bowl, beat the eggs, corn syrup, sugar, peanut butter and salt until smooth. Fold in coconut and chocolate chips. Pour over crust. Bake 15-20 minutes longer or until golden. Cool on a wire rack. **Yield: 3 dozen.**

Chewy Peanut Butter Bars

Ginger Bars

Pumpkin Bars

Ginger Bars

We always had dessert when we visited my grand-parent's farm, and this was one of our favorites. During harvesttime, my brothers and sisters and I would take this or another treat out to the field for the workers.

—Deborah Haake, Minnetonka, Minnesota

- 1 cup shortening
- 1 cup sugar
- 2 eggs
- 1 cup water
- 1/2 cup molasses
- 2-1/2 cups all-purpose flour
- 1 teaspoon baking soda
- 1 teaspoon ground cinnamon
- 1/2 teaspoon ground cloves
- 1/2 teaspoon ground ginger
- 1/2 teaspoon salt
- Confectioners' sugar, optional

In a large mixing bowl, cream shortening and sugar until light and fluffy. Add eggs; beat well. Beat in water and molasses. Combine flour, baking soda, cinnamon, cloves, ginger and salt; add to molasses mixture and mix well.

Spread into a greased 15-in. x 10-in. x 1-in. baking pan. Bake at 350° for 20-22 minutes or until a toothpick inserted near the center comes out clean. Cool on a wire rack. Dust with confectioners' sugar if desired. Cut into bars. **Yield: 20 servings.**

Pumpkin Bars

What could be more appropriate for a Halloween treat than a pan of pumpkin-flavored bars? Actually, they're winners with my family anytime of the year.

—Brenda Keller, Andalusia, Alabama

- 4 eggs
- 1-2/3 cups sugar
- 1 cup vegetable oil

Shortbread Lemon Bars

- 1 can (15 ounces) solid-pack pumpkin
- 2 cups all-purpose flour
- 2 teaspoons ground cinnamon
- 2 teaspoons baking powder
- 1 teaspoon baking soda
- 1 teaspoon salt

ICING:

- 1 package (3 ounces) cream cheese, softened
- 2 cups confectioners' sugar
- 1/4 cup butter, softened
- 1 teaspoon vanilla extract
- 1 to 2 tablespoons milk

In a mixing bowl, beat the eggs, sugar, oil and pumpkin. Combine the flour, cinnamon, baking powder, baking soda and salt; gradually add to pumpkin mixture and mix well. Pour into an ungreased 15-in. x 10-in. x 1-in. baking pan. Bake at 350° for 25-30 minutes or until a toothpick inserted near the center comes out clean. Cool completely on a wire rack.

For icing, in a small mixing bowl, beat the cream cheese, sugar, butter and vanilla. Add enough milk to achieve desired spreading consistency. Spread over bars. Store in the refrigerator. **Yield: 2 dozen.**

Shortbread Lemon Bars

I've put together two family cookbooks over the years, and this recipe ranks among my favorites. These special lemon bars have a yummy shortbread crust and a refreshing flavor. I'm never afraid to make this dessert for guests since I know it will be a hit with everyone. —Margaret Peterson, Forest City, Iowa

- 1-1/2 cups all-purpose flour
- 1/2 cup confectioners' sugar
- 1 teaspoon grated lemon peel
- 1 teaspoon grated orange peel
- 3/4 cup cold butter

FILLING:

- 4 eggs
- 2 cups sugar
- 1/3 cup lemon juice
- 1/4 cup all-purpose flour
- 2 teaspoons grated lemon peel
- 2 teaspoons grated orange peel
- 1 teaspoon baking powder

TOPPING:

- 2 cups (16 ounces) sour cream
- 1/3 cup sugar
- 1/2 teaspoon vanilla extract

In a food processor, combine the flour, confectioners' sugar and lemon and orange peels. Add butter; cover and process until crumbly. Continue processing until mixture forms a ball. Pat into a greased 13-in. x 9-in. x 2-in. baking pan. Bake at 350° for 12-14 minutes or until set and the edges are lightly browned.

In a mixing bowl, beat all the filling ingredients until blended. Pour over hot crust. Bake for 14-16 minutes or until set and lightly browned.

In a bowl, combine topping ingredients. Spread over filling. Bake 7-9 minutes longer or until topping is set. Cool on a wire rack. Refrigerate overnight. Cut into bars just before serving. **Yield: 3 dozen.**

Zucchini Dessert Squares

Zucchini Dessert Squares

We planted one too many zucchini plants a few summers ago and harvested a lot of zucchinis that year. I was looking for ways to use them—this delicious dessert is the result.

—Nancy Morelli, Livonia, Michigan

- 4 cups all-purpose flour
- 2 cups sugar
- 1/2 teaspoon ground cinnamon
- 1/2 teaspoon salt
- 1-1/2 cups cold butter

FILLING:

- 8 to 10 cups cubed seeded peeled zucchini (4 to 5 pounds)
- 2/3 cup lemon juice
- 1 cup sugar
- 1 teaspoon ground cinnamon
- 1/2 teaspoon ground nutmeg

In a bowl, combine the flour, sugar, cinnamon and salt. Cut in butter until crumbly; reserve 3 cups. Pat remaining crumb mixture into the bottom of a greased 13-in. x 9-in. x 2-in. baking pan. Bake at 375° for 12 minutes.

Meanwhile, for filling, place zucchini and lemon juice in a saucepan; bring to a boil. Reduce heat; cover and cook for 6-8 minutes or until zucchini is crisp-tender. Stir in the sugar, cinnamon and nutmeg; cover and simmer for 5 minutes (mixture will be thin).

Spoon over crust; sprinkle with the reserved crumb mixture. Bake at 375° for 40-45 minutes or until golden. Cool on a wire rack. Store in the refrigerator. **Yield: 16-20 servings.**

Cranberry Date Bars

I first discovered this recipe at Christmas a couple years ago, but it's a great way to use frozen cranberries throughout the year. It seems I'm always baking a batch of these moist bars for some event.

—Bonnie Nieter, Warsaw, Indiana

- 1 package (12 ounces) fresh *or* frozen cranberries, thawed
- 1 package (8 ounces) chopped dates
- 2 tablespoons water
- 1 teaspoon vanilla extract
- 2 cups all-purpose flour
- 2 cups old-fashioned oats
- 1-1/2 cups packed brown sugar
- 1/2 teaspoon baking soda
- 1/2 teaspoon salt
- 1 cup butter, melted

GLAZE:

- 2 cups confectioners' sugar
- 2 to 3 tablespoons orange juice
- 1/2 teaspoon vanilla extract

In a covered saucepan over low heat, simmer cranberries, dates and water for 15 minutes or until the cranberries have popped, stirring occasionally. Remove from the heat; stir in vanilla and set aside.

In a large bowl, combine the flour, oats, brown sugar, baking soda and salt. Stir in butter until well blended. Pat half into an ungreased 13-in. x 9-in. x 2-in. baking pan. Bake at 350° for 8 minutes.

Spoon cranberry mixture over crust. Sprinkle with remaining oat mixture. Pat gently. Bake at 350° for 25-30 minutes or until browned. Cool. Combine glaze ingredients; drizzle over bars. **Yield: 3 dozen.**

Cranberry Date Bars

Frosted Banana Bars

These bars are always a hit at potlucks in the small farming community where my husband and I live. I also provide them for coffee hour after church. They don't last long. —*Debbie Knight, Marion, Iowa*

- 1/2 cup butter, softened
- 1-1/2 cups sugar
- 2 eggs
- 1 cup (8 ounces) sour cream
- 1 teaspoon vanilla extract
- 2 cups all-purpose flour
- 1 teaspoon baking soda
- 1/4 teaspoon salt
- 2 medium ripe bananas, mashed (about 1 cup)

FROSTING:

- 1 package (8 ounces) cream cheese, softened
- 1/2 cup butter, softened
- 2 teaspoons vanilla extract
- 3-3/4 to 4 cups confectioners' sugar

In a mixing bowl, cream butter and sugar. Add the eggs, sour cream and vanilla. Combine flour, baking soda and salt; gradually add to the creamed mixture. Stir in bananas.

Spread into a greased 15-in. x 10-in. x 1-in. baking pan. Bake at 350° for 20-25 minutes or until a toothpick inserted near the center comes out clean. Cool.

For frosting, in a mixing bowl, beat the cream cheese, butter and vanilla. Gradually beat in enough confectioners' sugar to achieve desired consistency. Frost bars. Store in the refrigerator. **Yield: 3-4 dozen.**

Frosted Banana Bars

Strawberry Jam Bars

Sour Cream Raisin Squares

Strawberry Jam Bars

I bake for a group of seniors every week, and this is one of the goodies they request most. I always keep the ingredients on hand for baking emergencies. Give these bars your own twist by replacing the strawberry jam with the fruit jam of your choice.

—Karen Mead, Pittsburgh, Pennsylvania

- 1/2 cup butter, softened
- 1/2 cup packed brown sugar
- 1 egg
- 1 package (18-1/4 ounces) white cake mix
- 1 cup finely crushed cornflakes
- 1 cup strawberry jam

In a mixing bowl, cream butter and brown sugar until smooth. Add egg; mix well. Gradually add dry cake mix and cornflakes. Set aside 1-1/2 cups for topping. Press remaining dough into a greased 13-in. x 9-in. x 2-in. baking pan.

Carefully spread jam over crust. Sprinkle with reserved dough; gently press down. Bake at 350° for 30 minutes or until golden brown. Cool completely on a wire rack. Cut into bars. **Yield: 2 dozen.**

Sour Cream Raisin Squares

My aunt shared this recipe with me, and my family has always enjoyed it. I love to make these bars for friends who visit or give them away as gifts.

—Leona Eash, McConnelsville, Ohio

- 1 cup butter, softened
- 1 cup packed brown sugar
- 2 cups all-purpose flour
- 2 cups quick-cooking oats
- 1 teaspoon baking powder
- 1 teaspoon baking soda
- 1/8 teaspoon salt

Raspberry Almond Bars

FILLING:

4	egg yolks
2	cups (16 ounces) sour cream
1-1/2	cups raisins
1	cup sugar
1	tablespoon cornstarch

In a mixing bowl, cream the butter and brown sugar. Beat in the flour, oats, baking powder, baking soda and salt (the mixture will be crumbly). Set aside 2 cups; pat remaining crumbs into a greased 13-in. x 9-in. x 2-in. baking pan. Bake at 350° for 15 minutes. Cool.

Meanwhile, combine the filling ingredients in a saucepan. Bring to a boil; cook and stir constantly for 5-8 minutes. Pour over crust; sprinkle with reserved crumbs. Bake 15 minutes longer or until set. Cool on a wire rack. Store in the refrigerator. **Yield: 12-16 servings.**

Raspberry Almond Bars

A co-worker's mother gave me this gem of a recipe a few years back. I can never decide what's more appealing—the attractive look of the bars or their incredible aroma while they're baking! Everyone who tries these asks for the recipe.

—Mimi Priesman, Pace, Florida

1/2	cup butter
1	package (10 to 12 ounces) vanilla *or* white chips, *divided*
2	eggs
1/2	cup sugar
1	teaspoon almond extract
1	cup all-purpose flour
1/2	teaspoon salt
1/2	cup seedless raspberry jam
1/4	cup sliced almonds

In a saucepan, melt butter. Remove from the heat; add 1 cup chips (do not stir). In a small mixing bowl, beat eggs until foamy; gradually add sugar. Stir in chip mixture and almond extract. Combine flour and salt; add to egg mixture just until combined. Spread half of the batter into a greased 9-in. square baking pan. Bake at 325° for 15-20 minutes or until golden brown.

In a small saucepan over low heat, melt jam; spread over warm crust. Stir remaining chips into the remaining batter; drop by teaspoonfuls over the jam layer. Sprinkle with almonds. Bake 30-35 minutes longer or until a toothpick inserted near the center comes out clean. Cool on a wire rack. Cut into bars. **Yield: 2 dozen.**

Apricot Bars

This recipe is down-home baking at its best. It's won blue ribbons at country fairs and cookie contests in several states! This treat is easy to make, and it's perfect for potluck suppers, bake sales, lunch boxes or just plain snacking. —*Jill Moritz, Irvine, California*

- 3/4 cup butter, softened
- 1 cup sugar
- 1 egg
- 1/2 teaspoon vanilla extract
- 2 cups all-purpose flour
- 1/4 teaspoon baking powder
- 1-1/3 cups flaked coconut
- 1/2 cup chopped walnuts
- 1 jar (10 to 12 ounces) apricot preserves

In a large mixing bowl, cream the butter and sugar. Add egg and vanilla; mix well. Combine flour and baking powder. Gradually add to creamed mixture. Fold in coconut and walnuts.

Press two-thirds of dough into a greased 13-in. x 9-in. x 2-in. baking pan. Spread with preserves; crumble remaining dough over preserves. Bake at 350° for 30-35 minutes or until golden brown. Cool in pan on wire rack. Cut into bars. **Yield: 3 dozen.**

Apple Snack Squares

As soon as I was old enough to stand on a chair, I started cooking. This recipe came from my sister-in-law. It's a favorite at our large family gatherings.
—*Julia Quintrell, Sumerco, West Virginia*

- 2 cups sugar
- 2 eggs
- 3/4 cup vegetable oil
- 2-1/2 cups self-rising flour
- 1 teaspoon ground cinnamon
- 3 cups diced peeled tart apples

Apricot Bars

- 1 cup chopped walnuts
- 3/4 cup butterscotch chips

In a bowl, combine the sugar, eggs and oil. Stir in flour and cinnamon (batter will be thick). Stir in apples and nuts.

Spread into a greased 13-in. x 9-in. x 2-in. baking pan. Sprinkle with chips. Bake at 350° for 35-40 minutes or until golden and a toothpick inserted near the center comes out clean. Cool before cutting. **Yield: 2 dozen.**

Editor's Note: As a substitute for *each* cup of self-rising flour, place 1-1/2 teaspoons baking powder and 1/2 teaspoon salt in a measuring cup. Add all-purpose flour to measure 1 cup. For the 1/2 cup flour, place 3/4 teaspoon baking powder and 1/4 teaspoon salt in a 1/2 cup measuring cup. Add all-purpose flour to measure 1/2 cup.

Cherry Chewbilees

This is a good dish to carry to potlucks and parties. It's a hit at home, too—my husband rates it as one of his favorite desserts.
—*Debbi Smith, Crossett, Arkansas*

CRUST:

- 1-1/4 cups all-purpose flour
- 1/2 cup packed brown sugar
- 1/2 cup butter-flavored shortening
- 1 cup chopped walnuts, *divided*
- 1/2 cup flaked coconut

Apple Snack Squares

FILLING:

- 2 packages (8 ounces *each*) cream cheese, softened
- 2/3 cup sugar
- 2 eggs
- 2 teaspoons vanilla extract
- 2 cans (21 ounces *each*) cherry pie filling

In a bowl, combine flour and brown sugar; cut in shortening until fine crumbs form. Stir in 1/2 cup nuts and coconut. Reserve 1/2 cup crumb mixture for topping. Press remaining mixture into the bottom of a greased 13-in. x 9-in. x 2-in. baking pan.

Bake at 350° for 12-15 minutes or until lightly browned. Meanwhile, for filling, beat the cream cheese, sugar, eggs and vanilla in a mixing bowl until smooth. Spread over the hot crust. Bake 15 minutes.

Spread pie filling on top. Combine remaining nuts and reserved crumbs; sprinkle over cherries. Bake 15 minutes longer. Cool. Refrigerate until serving. **Yield: 20 servings.**

Cherry Chewbilees

Peanut Mallow Bars

Butterscotch Cashew Bars

Peanut Mallow Bars

Searching for the perfect combination of salty and sweet sensations? Well, look no further! Salted peanuts and rich caramel topping join marshmallow creme and brown sugar in these irresistible, chewy bars. You won't be able to stop at just one!

—Claudia Ruiss, Massapequa, New York

- 1 cup chopped salted peanuts
- 3/4 cup all-purpose flour
- 3/4 cup quick-cooking oats
- 2/3 cup packed brown sugar
- 1/2 teaspoon salt
- 1/2 teaspoon baking soda
- 1 egg, lightly beaten
- 1/3 cup cold butter

TOPPING:

- 1 jar (7 ounces) marshmallow creme
- 2/3 cup caramel ice cream topping
- 1-3/4 cups salted peanuts

In a large bowl, combine the peanuts, flour, oats, sugar, salt and baking soda; stir in the egg. Cut in butter until crumbly. Press into a greased 13-in. x 9-in. x 2-in. baking pan. Bake at 350° for 8-10 minutes or until lightly browned.

Spoon marshmallow creme over hot crust; carefully spread evenly. Drizzle with the caramel topping; sprinkle with peanuts. Bake for 15-20 minutes or until lightly browned. Cool on a wire rack. Cut into bars. **Yield: 3 dozen.**

Butterscotch Cashew Bars

I knew these nutty bars were a success when I took them on our annual family vacation. My husband couldn't stop eating them—and my sister-in-law, who is a great cook, asked for the recipe. It makes a big batch, which is good, because they go quickly!
—Lori Berg, Wentzville, Missouri

- 1 cup plus 2 tablespoons butter, softened
- 3/4 cup plus 2 tablespoons packed brown sugar
- 2-1/2 cups all-purpose flour
- 1-3/4 teaspoons salt

TOPPING:

- 1 package (10 to 11 ounces) butterscotch chips
- 1/2 cup plus 2 tablespoons light corn syrup
- 3 tablespoons butter
- 2 teaspoons water
- 2-1/2 cups salted cashew halves

In a large mixing bowl, cream the butter and brown sugar. Combine flour and salt; add to creamed mixture just until combined. Press into a greased 15-in. x 10-in. x 1-in. baking pan. Bake at 350° for 10-12 minutes or until lightly browned.

Meanwhile, combine the butterscotch chips, corn syrup, butter and water in a saucepan. Cook and stir over medium heat until chips and butter are melted. Spread over crust. Sprinkle with cashews; press down lightly.

Bake for 11-13 minutes or until topping is bubbly and lightly browned. Cool on a wire rack. Cut into bars. **Yield: 3-1/2 dozen.**

Chewy Pecan Pie Bars

Chewy Pecan Pie Bars

This is one of my husband's favorite recipes, and I've been making it for many years. If you like pecan pie, you'll love the flavor of these bars.
—Judy Taylor, Shreveport, Louisiana

- 1/4 cup butter, melted
- 2 cups packed brown sugar
- 2/3 cup all-purpose flour
- 4 eggs
- 2 teaspoons vanilla extract
- 1/4 teaspoon baking soda
- 1/4 teaspoon salt
- 2 cups chopped pecans

Confectioners' sugar

Pour butter into a 13-in. x 9-in. x 2-in. baking pan; set aside. In a mixing bowl, combine the brown sugar, flour, eggs, vanilla, baking soda and salt. Stir in pecans. Spread over butter.

Bake at 350° for 30-35 minutes. Remove from the oven; immediately dust with confectioners' sugar. Cool before cutting. **Yield: about 2 dozen.**

Jewel Nut Bars

Jewel Nut Bars

These colorful bars, with the eye-catching appeal of candied cherries and the crunchy goodness of mixed nuts, are certain to become a holiday standby. I get lots of compliments on the rich, chewy crust and the combination of sweet and salty flavors.

—Joyce Fitt, Listowel, Ontario

- 1-1/4 cups all-purpose flour
- 2/3 cup packed brown sugar, *divided*
- 3/4 cup cold butter
- 1 egg
- 1/2 teaspoon salt
- 1-1/2 cups mixed nuts
- 1-1/2 cups green and red candied cherries, halved
- 1 cup (6 ounces) semisweet chocolate chips

In a bowl, combine flour and 1/3 cup brown sugar; cut in butter until mixture resembles coarse crumbs. Press into a lightly greased 13-in. x 9-in. x 2-in. baking pan. Bake at 350° for 15 minutes.

Meanwhile, in a mixing bowl, beat egg. Add salt and remaining brown sugar. Stir in the nuts, cherries and chocolate chips. Spoon evenly over crust. Bake at 350° for 20 minutes. Cool on a wire rack. Cut into bars. **Yield: 3 dozen.**

CAKES & CHEESECAKES

-HOCOLATE COOKIE TORTE, pg. 397

Cakes & Cheesecakes

Sweetheart Walnut Torte

I always donate one of these elegant, lightly sweet, heart-shaped tortes for our church bake sale. The congregation never gets to see it, however—the ladies in charge quickly put it aside for one of them to buy!
—Gladys Jenik, Orland Park, Illinois

- 1/2 cup butter, softened
- 1/2 cup sugar
- 4 egg yolks
- 1/3 cup milk
- 1/2 teaspoon vanilla extract
- 1 cup all-purpose flour
- 2 teaspoons baking powder
- 1/8 teaspoon salt

MERINGUE:

- 4 egg whites
- 1/8 teaspoon cream of tartar
- 3/4 cup sugar
- 1 cup chopped walnuts

Walnut halves

FILLING:

- 1 cup cold milk
- 1 package (3.9 ounces) instant chocolate pudding mix
- 1 cup heavy whipping cream, whipped

Grease two 9-in. heart-shaped pans. Line with waxed paper and grease the paper; set aside.

In a large mixing bowl, cream butter and sugar. Add the egg yolks, milk and vanilla; mix well. Combine the flour, baking powder and salt; gradually add to creamed mixture. Pour into prepared pans.

Sweetheart Walnut Torte

In a mixing bowl, beat egg whites and cream of tartar until soft peaks form. Gradually add sugar; beat until stiff and glossy. Fold in chopped nuts. Spread evenly over batter, sealing edges to sides of pan. Arrange walnut halves over meringue in one pan.

Bake at 300° for 55 minutes or until golden brown. Cool for 10 minutes; remove to wire racks. Invert so meringue side is up; cool completely.

In a large mixing bowl, beat milk and pudding mix until thickened. Fold in whipped cream. Place plain cake meringue side up on serving plate. Spread with half of the filling; top with remaining cake. Frost sides with remaining filling. **Yield: 12-16 servings.**

Cream Cheese Sheet Cake

Cream Cheese Sheet Cake

This buttery sheet cake with its fudgy chocolate glaze is a real crowd-pleaser. It's not uncommon to see folks going back for second and even third slices.
—Gaye Mann, Rocky Mount, North Carolina

- 1 cup plus 2 tablespoons butter, softened
- 2 packages (3 ounces *each*) cream cheese, softened
- 2-1/4 cups sugar
- 6 eggs
- 3/4 teaspoon vanilla extract
- 2-1/4 cups cake flour

FROSTING:

- 1 cup sugar
- 1/3 cup evaporated milk
- 1/2 cup butter
- 1/2 cup semisweet chocolate chips

In a mixing bowl, cream the butter, cream cheese and sugar. Add eggs, one at a time, beating well after each addition. Beat in vanilla. Add flour; mix well.

Pour into a greased 15-in. x 10-in. x 1-in. baking pan. Bake at 325° for 30-35 minutes or until a toothpick inserted near the center comes out clean. Cool completely.

For frosting, combine sugar and milk in a saucepan; bring to a boil over medium heat. Cover and cook for 3 minutes (do not stir). Stir in butter and chocolate chips until melted. Cool slightly. Stir; spread over cake. **Yield: 24-30 servings.**

California Lemon Pound Cake

Citrus trees grow abundantly in California, and I'm always looking for new recipes that use the fruit from the orange and lemon trees in my yard. This is one of my favorites!
—Richard Killeaney, Spring Valley, California

- 1 cup butter, softened
- 1/2 cup shortening
- 3 cups sugar
- 5 eggs
- 1 tablespoon lemon extract
- 1 tablespoon grated lemon peel
- 3 cups all-purpose flour
- 1 teaspoon salt
- 1/2 teaspoon baking powder
- 1 cup milk

GLAZE:

- 1/4 cup butter, softened
- 1 to 1-1/4 cups confectioners' sugar
- 2 tablespoons lemon juice
- 1 teaspoon grated lemon peel

In a large mixing bowl, cream butter, shortening and sugar until light and fluffy, about 5 minutes. Add eggs, one at a time, beating well after each addition. Stir in lemon extract and peel. Combine the flour, salt and baking powder; gradually add to creamed mixture alternately with the milk. Beat just until combined.

Pour into a greased 10-in. fluted tube pan. Bake at 350° for 70 minutes or a toothpick inserted near the center comes out clean. Cool for 10 minutes before removing from pan to a wire rack to cool completely.

For glaze, combine all ingredients and drizzle over cooled cake. **Yield: 22 servings.**

Maple Nut Cake

Our state is famous for its maple syrup. I like using maple syrup in desserts because it lends a distinctive flavor. —Emma Magielda, Amsterdam, New York

- 1/2 cup butter, softened
- 1/2 cup sugar
- 1 cup maple syrup
- 2 eggs
- 2-1/4 cups cake flour
- 3 teaspoons baking powder
- 1 teaspoon salt
- 1/2 cup milk
- 1/2 cup chopped nuts

FROSTING:

- 1 cup sugar
- 1/2 cup maple syrup
- 2 egg whites
- 1 teaspoon corn syrup
- 1/8 teaspoon salt
- 1/4 teaspoon cream of tartar

In a bowl, beat the butter, sugar, syrup and eggs until blended. Combine the flour, baking powder and salt; add to the egg mixture alternately with milk. Fold in nuts. Pour into two greased and floured 9-in. round baking pans. Bake at 350° for 18-25 minutes or until a toothpick inserted near the center comes out clean. Cool for 10 minutes before removing from pans to wire racks to cool completely.

In a heavy saucepan or double boiler, combine the frosting ingredients. With a portable mixture, beat on low speed for 1 minute. Continue beating over low heat until frosting reaches 160°, about 8-10 minutes. Pour into a large mixing bowl. Beat on high until stiff peaks form, about 7 minutes. Spread frosting between layers and over top and sides of cake. **Yield: 12-14 servings.**

Editor's Note: A stand mixer is recommended for beating the frosting after it reaches 160°.

California Lemon Pound Cake

Maple Nut Cake

Special Strawberry Torte

Chocolate Chip Pound Cake

Special Strawberry Torte

The reason this is such a favorite is it's a little different, yet quick and easy. Plus, it looks like you really fussed. —Alyce Kafka, Wagner, South Dakota

- 1 package (18-1/4 ounces) yellow cake mix
- 4 eggs, *separated*
- 2/3 cup plus 2 tablespoons sugar, *divided*
- 1/4 cup sliced almonds
- 2 cups whipped topping
- 3 to 3-1/2 cups sliced fresh strawberries

Prepare cake mix according to package directions, substituting four egg yolks for the whole eggs. Pour the batter into two greased and floured 9-in. round baking pans.

In a mixing bowl, beat egg whites until soft peaks form. Gradually add 2/3 cup sugar, 1 tablespoon at a time, beating until stiff peaks form. Carefully spread over batter; sprinkle with almonds and remaining sugar.

Bake at 350° for 40-45 minutes or until meringue is golden and a toothpick inserted near the center comes out clean. Cool for 10 minutes; remove from pans. Place cakes meringue side up on wire racks to cool completely.

Place one cake with meringue side up on a serving plate. Spread with half of the whipping topping and top with half of the strawberries. Layer with remaining cake, topping and berries. **Yield: 10-12 servings.**

Chocolate Chip Pound Cake

My mom has been making this cake for over 30 years. Dotted with chips and topped with a chocolate glaze, it is absolutely divine.
—Michele Strunks, Brookville, Ohio

1 cup butter, softened
2 cups sugar
4 eggs
1 teaspoon vanilla extract
4 cups all-purpose flour
4 teaspoons baking powder
1 teaspoon baking soda
2 cups (16 ounces) sour cream
2 cups (12 ounces) semisweet chocolate chips

GLAZE:

1/4 cup semisweet chocolate chips
2 tablespoons butter
1-1/4 cups confectioners' sugar
3 tablespoons milk
1/2 teaspoon vanilla extract

In a mixing bowl, cream butter and sugar. Add the eggs, one at a time, beating well after each addition. Beat in vanilla. Combine the flour, baking powder and baking soda; add to creamed mixture alternately with sour cream. Fold in chocolate chips.

Pour into a greased and floured 10-in. fluted tube pan. Bake at 350° for 60-65 minutes or until a toothpick inserted near the center comes out clean. Cool for 10 minutes before removing from pan to a wire rack to cool.

For glaze, in a saucepan, melt chocolate chips and butter over low heat. Remove from the heat; whisk in the confectioners' sugar, milk and vanilla until smooth. Working quickly, drizzle over cooled cake. **Yield: 12-14 servings.**

Hawaiian Sunset Cake

This three-layer orange cake is pretty enough for company, but it's so simple to fix that you'll find yourself making it all the time.

—Kara De la Vega, Suisun City, California

Hawaiian Sunset Cake

1 package (18-1/4 ounces) white *or* orange cake mix
1 package (3.4 ounces) instant vanilla pudding mix
1 package (3 ounces) orange gelatin
4 eggs
1-1/2 cups milk
1/2 cup vegetable oil

FILLING:

1 can (20 ounces) crushed pineapple, drained
2 cups sugar
1 package (10 ounces) flaked coconut
1 cup (8 ounces) sour cream
1 carton (8 ounces) frozen whipped topping, thawed

Toasted coconut, optional

In a large mixing bowl, combine the first six ingredients; mix well. Pour into three greased and floured 9-in. round baking pans. Bake at 350° for 25-30 minutes or until a toothpick inserted near the center comes out clean. Cool for 10 minutes before removing from pans to wire racks to cool completely.

In a bowl, combine the pineapple, sugar, coconut and sour cream. Remove 1 cup to another bowl; set aside. Place one cake on a serving plate; top with a third of the remaining pineapple mixture. Repeat layers twice. Fold whipped topping into reserved pineapple mixture. Spread over top and sides of cake. Sprinkle with toasted coconut if desired. Store in the refrigerator. **Yield: 12-16 servings.**

Sour Cream Chocolate Cake

Sour Cream Chocolate Cake

This luscious chocolate layer cake gets wonderful moistness from sour cream. Its irresistible topping and marvelous from-scratch goodness make it a classic! I keep the recipe handy for birthdays, holidays and other special occasions.

—Patsy Foster, Marion, Arkansas

- 4 squares (1 ounce *each*) unsweetened chocolate, melted and cooled
- 1 cup water
- 3/4 cup sour cream
- 1/4 cup shortening
- 1 teaspoon vanilla extract
- 2 eggs, beaten
- 2 cups all-purpose flour
- 2 cups sugar
- 1-1/4 teaspoons baking soda
- 1 teaspoon salt
- 1/2 teaspoon baking powder

FROSTING:

- 1/2 cup butter, softened
- 6 squares (1 ounce *each*) unsweetened chocolate, melted and cooled
- 6 cups confectioners' sugar
- 1/2 cup sour cream
- 6 tablespoons milk
- 2 teaspoons vanilla extract
- 1/8 teaspoon salt

In a mixing bowl, combine the first six ingredients; mix well. Combine the dry ingredients; gradually add to chocolate mixture. Beat on low speed just until moistened. Beat on high for 3 minutes.

Pour into two greased and floured 9-in. round baking pans. Bake at 350° for 30 minutes or until a toothpick inserted near the center comes out clean. Cool for 10 minutes before removing from pans to wire racks to cool completely.

In a mixing bowl, combine frosting ingredients. Beat until smooth and creamy. Spread over cake. Store in the refrigerator. **Yield: 12-16 servings.**

Peanut Butter Chocolate Cake 1st prize

In our chocolate-loving house, this cake disappears very quickly! Cream cheese and peanut butter make the frosting extra creamy.

—Dorcas Yoder, Weyers Cave, Virginia

- 2 cups all-purpose flour
- 2 cups sugar
- 2/3 cup baking cocoa
- 2 teaspoons baking soda
- 1 teaspoon baking powder
- 1/2 teaspoon salt
- 2 eggs
- 1 cup milk
- 2/3 cup vegetable oil
- 1 teaspoon vanilla extract
- 1 cup brewed coffee, room temperature

PEANUT BUTTER FROSTING:

- 1 package (3 ounces) cream cheese, softened
- 1/4 cup creamy peanut butter
- 2 cups confectioners' sugar
- 2 tablespoons milk
- 1/2 teaspoon vanilla extract
- Miniature semisweet chocolate chips, optional

In a mixing bowl, combine the dry ingredients. Add the eggs, milk, oil and vanilla; beat for 2 minutes. Stir in coffee (batter will be thin).

Pour into a greased 13-in. x 9-in. x 2-in. baking pan. Bake at 350° for 35-40 minutes or until a toothpick inserted near the center comes out clean. Cool completely on a wire rack.

For frosting, in a mixing bowl, beat cream cheese and peanut butter until smooth. Beat in the sugar, milk and vanilla. Spread over cake. Sprinkle with chocolate chips if desired. Store in the refrigerator. **Yield: 12-16 servings.**

Peanut Butter Chocolate Cake

Hot Fudge Sundae Cake

Hot Fudge Sundae Cake

My husband is a real chocolate lover, so I'm always on the lookout for great dessert recipes like this one, which I found years ago. —Hildy Adams, Alma, Michigan

- 1 package (11-1/2 ounces) milk chocolate chips
- 1/3 cup butter, cubed
- 4 eggs, *separated*
- 1/3 cup all-purpose flour
- 1/3 cup sugar
- 1/2 cup slivered almonds, toasted

HOT FUDGE SAUCE:

- 1/2 cup sugar
- 1/2 cup baking cocoa
- 1/2 cup heavy whipping cream
- 1/2 cup semisweet chocolate chips
- 1/4 cup butter, cubed
- 1 teaspoon vanilla extract

Vanilla ice cream

In a saucepan, melt chips and butter over low heat. Cool slightly. Whisk in egg yolks. Add flour just until combined. In a mixing bowl, beat whites until foamy. Gradually add sugar, beating until stiff peaks form. Fold into chocolate mixture. Fold in almonds.

Pour into a greased 10-in. pie plate or quiche dish. Bake at 350° for 25-30 minutes or until a toothpick comes out clean. Cool on a wire rack. For sauce, the combine sugar, cocoa and cream in a saucepan. Add semisweet chips and butter. Cook and stir over low heat until chips and butter are melted and mixture is smooth. Remove from the heat; stir in vanilla.

Cut cake into wedges; top with ice cream. Drizzle with warm sauce. **Yield: 12 servings.**

Toffee-Mocha Cream Torte 1st prize

When you want to impress someone, this scrumptious torte is just the thing to make!
—Lynn Rogers, Richfield, North Carolina

- 1 cup butter, softened
- 2 cups sugar
- 2 eggs
- 1-1/2 teaspoons vanilla extract
- 2-2/3 cups all-purpose flour
- 3/4 cup baking cocoa
- 2 teaspoons baking soda
- 1/4 teaspoon salt
- 1 cup buttermilk
- 2 teaspoons instant coffee granules
- 1 cup boiling water

TOPPING:

- 1/2 teaspoon instant coffee granules
- 1 teaspoon hot water
- 2 cups heavy whipping cream
- 3 tablespoons light brown sugar
- 6 Heath candy bars (1.4 ounces *each*), crushed, *divided*

In a mixing bowl, cream butter and sugar. Beat in eggs and vanilla. Combine the flour, cocoa, baking soda and salt; add to creamed mixture alternately with buttermilk. Dissolve coffee in water; add to batter. Beat for 2 minutes.

Pour into three greased and floured 9-in. round baking pans. Bake at 350° for 16-20 minutes or until a toothpick inserted near the center comes out clean. Cool for 10 minutes before removing from pans to wire racks to cool completely. For topping, dissolve coffee in water in a mixing bowl; cool. Add cream and brown sugar. Beat until stiff peaks form.

Place bottom cake layer on a serving plate; top with 1-1/3 cups of topping. Sprinkle with 1/2 cup of crushed candy bars. Repeat layers twice. Store in the refrigerator. **Yield: 12-14 servings.**

Chocolate Cookie Torte

I use this recipe for our family's get-togethers. It's easy to make and beautiful.
—Irene Bigler, New Cumberland, Pennsylvania

- 1/2 cup butter, softened
- 1 cup sugar
- 1 egg
- 1 egg yolk
- 1/2 teaspoon vanilla extract
- 2 cups all-purpose flour
- 1 teaspoon baking powder
- 1/2 teaspoon salt

Additional sugar

FROSTING:

- 2 cups (12 ounces) semisweet chocolate chips
- 1/2 cup half-and-half cream
- 2 cups heavy whipping cream, whipped
- 2 teaspoons vanilla extract

Chocolate sprinkles

In a mixing bowl, cream butter and sugar. Beat in egg, yolk and vanilla. Combine flour, baking powder and salt; gradually add to creamed mixture and mix well. Form into a long log; cut into eight equal pieces. Shape each into a ball; wrap in plastic wrap. Chill for 1 hour.

Roll balls in additional sugar; place between two sheets of waxed paper. Roll each into a 6-in. circle. Remove top sheet of waxed paper; flip the circles onto ungreased baking sheets. Remove waxed paper; prick dough with a fork. Bake at 350° for 10-12 minutes or until lightly browned. Carefully loosen cookies and cool on paper towels.

For frosting, melt chips with half-and-half; stir. Cool. Fold whipped cream and vanilla into chocolate mixture. Layer cookies, spreading 1/4 cup frosting between each layer. Spread the remaining frosting over sides and top. Decorate with sprinkles. Chill overnight before cutting. **Yield: 8-10 servings.**

Toffee-Mocha Cream Torte

Chocolate Cookie Torte

Cream-Filled Pumpkin Cupcakes

Cream-Filled Pumpkin Cupcakes 1st prize

Here's a deliciously different use for pumpkin. Bursting with flavor and plenty of eye-catching appeal, these sweet and spicy filled cupcakes are bound to dazzle your family any time of the year.
—Ali Johnson, Petersburg, Pennsylvania

- 4 eggs
- 2 cups sugar
- 3/4 cup vegetable oil
- 1 can (15 ounces) solid-pack pumpkin
- 2 cups all-purpose flour
- 2 teaspoons baking soda
- 1 teaspoon salt
- 1 teaspoon baking powder
- 1 teaspoon ground cinnamon

FILLING:

- 1 tablespoon cornstarch
- 1 cup milk
- 1/2 cup shortening
- 1/4 cup butter, softened
- 2 cups confectioners' sugar
- 1/2 teaspoon vanilla extract, optional

In a mixing bowl, combine the eggs, sugar, oil and pumpkin. Combine the flour, baking soda, salt, baking powder and cinnamon; add to pumpkin mixture and beat until well mixed. Fill paper-lined muffin cups two-thirds full. Bake at 350° for 18-22 minutes or until a toothpick comes out clean. Cool for 10 minutes before removing from pans to wire racks to cool completely.

For filling, combine cornstarch and milk in a small saucepan until smooth. Bring to a boil; cook and stir for 2 minutes or until thickened.

Remove from the heat; cool to room temperature. In a mixing bowl, cream shortening, butter and sugar. Beat in vanilla if desired. Gradually add the cornstarch mixture, beating until light and fluffy.

Using a sharp knife, cut a 1-in. circle 1 in. deep in the top of each cupcake. Carefully remove tops and set aside. Spoon or pipe filling into cupcakes. Replace tops. **Yield: about 1-3/4 dozen.**

Gingerbread with Lemon Sauce

I asked my mother-in-law for this recipe once I learned that this fluffy spice cake topped with tangy lemon sauce is my husband's favorite. Now I bake it whenever he needs an extra special treat. It never fails to make us both smile.

— Kristen Oak, Pocatello, Idaho

- 1 cup shortening
- 1 cup sugar
- 1 cup molasses
- 2 eggs
- 3 cups all-purpose flour
- 1-1/2 teaspoons baking soda
- 1-1/2 teaspoons salt
- 1 teaspoon ground ginger
- 1 teaspoon ground cinnamon
- 1 cup hot water

LEMON SAUCE:

- 1/2 cup sugar
- 2 teaspoons cornstarch
- Dash salt
- Dash nutmeg
- 1 cup water
- 2 egg yolks, beaten
- 2 tablespoons butter
- 2 tablespoons lemon juice
- 1/2 teaspoon grated lemon peel

In a large mixing bowl, beat the shortening, sugar, molasses and eggs until well blended. Combine the flour, baking soda, salt, ginger and cinnamon; add to molasses mixture alternately with hot water.

Pour into a greased 13-in. x 9-in. x 2-in. baking pan. Bake at 350° for 35-40 minutes or until a toothpick inserted near the center comes out clean. Cool on a wire rack.

Meanwhile, in a saucepan, combine the sugar, cornstarch, salt, nutmeg and water until smooth. Cook and stir over medium-high heat until thickened and bubbly. Reduce heat; cook and stir 2 minutes longer. Remove from the heat. Stir a small amount of hot filling into egg yolks; return all to pan, stirring constantly. Bring to a gentle boil; cook and stir 2 minutes longer. Remove from the heat. Gently stir in the butter, lemon juice and peel. Serve with warm cake. Refrigerate leftover sauce. **Yield: 20 servings.**

Gingerbread with Lemon Sauce

Upside-Down Raspberry Cake

Banana Pecan Torte

Upside-Down Raspberry Cake

This delicious cake is great for any occasion. I've received many compliments from family and friends.
—Joy Beck, Cincinnati, Ohio

- 1-1/2 cups fresh *or* frozen unsweetened raspberries, *divided*
- 1 cup butter, softened
- 1 cup sugar
- 3 eggs
- 2 teaspoons lemon juice
- 1 teaspoon vanilla extract
- 2 cups all-purpose flour
- 1-1/2 teaspoons baking powder
- 1/2 teaspoon salt
- 2/3 cup milk
- Confectioners' sugar

Line the bottom and sides of a 9-in. square baking pan with foil; coat with nonstick cooking spray. Place 1/2 cup raspberries in pan; set aside.

In a mixing bowl, cream butter and sugar. Add eggs, lemon juice and vanilla; mix well. Combine the flour, baking powder and salt; add to creamed mixture alternately with milk.

Fold in the remaining raspberries. Carefully spoon over berries in pan. Bake at 350° for 40-45 minutes or until a toothpick inserted near the center comes out clean. Cool for 10 minutes.

Invert cake onto a serving platter; carefully remove foil. Cool completely. Dust with confectioners' sugar. **Yield: 9 servings.**

Editor's Note: If using frozen raspberries, do not thaw before adding to batter.

Banana Pecan Torte

A friend shared this recipe with me. It's been in her family for years. Now, my family loves it, too.
—Linda Fryar, Stanton, Texas

Apple Pear Cake

- 1 cup butter, softened
- 2-1/2 cups sugar
- 4 eggs
- 2 cups mashed ripe bananas (about 4 medium)
- 2 teaspoons vanilla extract
- 3-1/2 cups all-purpose flour
- 2 teaspoons baking soda
- 3/4 teaspoon salt
- 1/2 cup buttermilk
- 1 cup chopped pecans, toasted

FROSTING:

- 1 package (8 ounces) cream cheese, softened
- 1/2 cup butter, softened
- 3-1/2 cups confectioners' sugar
- 1 teaspoon vanilla extract

Toasted chopped pecans

In a mixing bowl, cream butter and sugar. Add the eggs, one at a time, beating well after each addition. Beat in bananas and vanilla. Combine the dry ingredients; add to creamed mixture alternately with buttermilk. Stir in pecans.

Pour into three greased and floured 9-in. round baking pans. Bake at 350° for 30-35 minutes or until a toothpick inserted near the center comes out clean. Cool for 10 minutes before removing from pans to wire racks to cool completely.

For the frosting, beat cream cheese, butter and sugar in a small mixing bowl. Add vanilla. Spread between layers and on top of cake. Sprinkle with pecans. **Yield: 12-16 servings.**

Apple Pear Cake

When my sister baked this apple cake for me, I asked her for the recipe because it was very moist and tasted so good. I made it a short time later and added some pears. Now every time I make it, people want the recipe. —Mary Ann Lees, Centreville, Alabama

- 2 cups shredded peeled tart apples
- 2 cups shredded peeled pears
- 2 cups sugar
- 1-1/4 cups vegetable oil
- 1 cup raisins
- 1 cup chopped pecans
- 2 eggs, beaten
- 1 teaspoon vanilla extract
- 3 cups all-purpose flour
- 2 teaspoons baking soda
- 2 teaspoons ground cinnamon
- 1/2 teaspoon ground nutmeg
- 1/2 teaspoon salt

CREAM CHEESE FROSTING:

- 1 package (3 ounces) cream cheese, softened
- 3 cups confectioners' sugar
- 1/4 cup butter, softened
- 2 tablespoons milk
- 1/2 teaspoon vanilla extract

In a large bowl, combine the first eight ingredients. Combine dry ingredients; stir into the fruit mixture.

Pour into a greased 13-in. x 9-in. x 2-in. baking pan. Bake at 325° for 60-65 minutes or until a toothpick inserted near the center comes out clean. Cool on a wire rack.

For frosting, in a large mixing bowl, beat the cream cheese, confectioners' sugar and butter until smooth. Beat in the milk and vanilla; frost cake. Store in the refrigerator. **Yield: 12-15 servings.**

Caramel Apple Cupcakes

Bring these extra-special cupcakes to your next bake sale and watch how quickly they disappear—if your family doesn't gobble them up first! Kids will go for the fun appearance and tasty toppings while adults will appreciate the moist spiced cake underneath.
—Diane Halferty, Corpus Christi, Texas

- 1 package (18-1/4 ounces) spice *or* carrot cake mix
- 2 cups chopped peeled tart apples
- 20 caramels
- 3 tablespoons milk
- 1 cup finely chopped pecans, toasted
- 12 Popsicle sticks

Mix cake batter according to the package directions; fold in the apples. Fill 12 greased or paper-lined jumbo muffin cups three-fourths full.

Bake at 350° for 20 minutes or until a toothpick comes out clean. Cool for 10 minutes before removing from pans to wire racks to cool completely.

In a saucepan, melt the caramels with milk over low heat, stirring until smooth. Spread over cupcakes. Sprinkle with pecans. Insert a wooden stick into the center of each cupcake. **Yield: 1 dozen.**

Caramel Apple Cupcakes

Fresh Grapefruit Cake 1st prize

I find this dessert's particularly good for a backyard barbecue. It's a pleasing, unexpected use for grapefruit. My husband and son both enjoy it. Second helpings are very common.
—Debbie Register, Youngstown, Florida

- 2/3 cup butter, softened
- 1-3/4 cups sugar
- 2 eggs
- 1-1/2 teaspoons vanilla extract
- 1 teaspoon grated grapefruit peel
- 3 cups cake flour
- 2-1/2 teaspoons baking powder
- 1/2 teaspoon salt
- 1/2 cup fresh grapefruit juice
- 3/4 cup milk

FROSTING:

- 1-1/2 cups sugar
- 2 egg whites
- 1 tablespoon light corn syrup
- 1/8 teaspoon salt
- 1/3 cup fresh grapefruit juice
- 1 tablespoon grated grapefruit peel
- 2 teaspoons vanilla extract

In a large mixing bowl, cream butter and sugar until light and fluffy. Add eggs, one at a time, beating well after each addition. Stir in vanilla and peel; mix well. Combine the flour, baking powder and salt; add to creamed mixture alternately with grapefruit juice. Beat just until combined. Stir in milk.

Pour batter into 2 greased and floured 9-in. baking pans. Bake at 350° for 30-35 minutes or until a toothpick inserted near the center comes out clean. Cool for 10 minutes before removing from pans to wire racks to cool completely.

For frosting, combine the sugar, egg whites, corn syrup and salt in a large heavy saucepan over low heat or double boiler over simmering water. With a portable mixer, beat on low speed for 1 minute. Continue beating on low over low heat until frosting reaches 160°, about 8-10 minutes.

Pour into a large mixing bowl; gradually add the grapefruit juice, peel and vanilla. Beat on high until frosting forms stiff peaks, about 7 minutes. Spread between layers and frost entire cake. **Yield: 12-16 servings.**

Editor's Note: A stand mixer is recommended for beating the frosting after it reaches 160°.

Fresh Grapefruit Cake

Blueberry Oat Cake

This is my favorite blueberry recipe. Everyone in my family likes this moist cake, so I make it rather frequently. —*Linda Police, Dover, New Jersey*

- 2 eggs
- 2 cups buttermilk
- 1 cup packed brown sugar
- 1/2 cup vegetable oil
- 2 cups all-purpose flour
- 2 teaspoons baking powder
- 1 teaspoon baking soda
- 1 teaspoon ground cinnamon
- 1/2 teaspoon salt
- 2 cups quick-cooking oats
- 2 cups fresh *or* frozen blueberries
- 1 cup chopped walnuts, optional

Confectioners' sugar

In a mixing bowl, beat the eggs, buttermilk, brown sugar and oil. Combine the flour, baking powder, baking soda, cinnamon and salt; add to batter. Beat on low speed for 2 minutes. Fold in the oats, blueberries and walnuts if desired.

Transfer to a greased and floured 10-in. fluted tube pan. Bake at 375° for 45-50 minutes or until a toothpick comes out clean. Cool for 10 minutes before removing from pan to a wire rack to cool completely. Dust with confectioners' sugar. **Yield: 12-16 servings.**

Editor's Note: If using frozen blueberries, do not thaw before adding to batter.

Blueberry Oat Cake

Strawberry Cheesecake Torte

Strawberry Cheesecake Torte 1st prize

After I tasted this dessert at a party, a friend shared the recipe. It originally called for pound cake...and I decided to lighten it up by substituting angel food. The result was this delicious light torte.
—Kathy Martinez, Edwards, California

- **1 package (16 ounces) angel food cake mix**
- **1 tablespoon confectioners' sugar**
- **1 package (.3 ounce) sugar-free strawberry gelatin**
- **1/2 cup boiling water**
- **1/4 cup seedless strawberry jam**
- **1 package (8 ounces) reduced-fat cream cheese, cubed**
- **1/3 cup fat-free milk**
- **2 tablespoons lemon juice**
- **3 cups reduced-fat whipped topping**
- **1 package (3.4 ounces) instant cheesecake *or* vanilla pudding mix**
- **1 cup sliced fresh strawberries**
- **1 kiwifruit, peeled, halved and sliced**
- **1-1/2 teaspoons grated lemon peel**

Line a 15-in. x 10-in. x 1-in. baking pan with ungreased parchment paper. Prepare cake mix according to package directions. Spread batter evenly in prepared pan. Bake at 350° for 24-26 minutes or until top is lightly browned. Sprinkle sugar over a waxed paper-lined baking sheet. Immediately invert cake onto baking sheet. Gently peel off the parchment paper; cool completely.

Dissolve gelatin in boiling water. Stir in jam until melted. With a fork, poke cake at 1/2-in. intervals. Brush with gelatin mixture; chill for 10 minutes.

In a bowl, beat the cream cheese, milk and lemon juice. Add whipped topping and pudding mix; whisk well. Reserve 1 cup. Place remaining pudding mixture in a pastry bag with a large star tip.

Trim edges of cake. Cut widthwise into three equal rectangles; place one on serving plate. Spread 1/2 cup reserved pudding mixture in center. Pipe pudding mixture around top edge of cake. Repeat with second cake layer. Top with remaining cake layer. Pipe pudding mixture along top edges. Fill center with fruit. Sprinkle with lemon peel. Store in refrigerator. **Yield: 12 servings.**

Ice Cream Party Roll

This tempting take on the much loved cake roll features a from-scratch chocolate cake, vanilla ice cream and a layer of berry jam. Garnished with hot fudge and whipped topping, the slices are hard to resist. —*Laura Andrews, Mantee, Mississippi*

- 4 eggs, *separated*
- 3/4 cup sugar, *divided*
- 1/2 cup cake flour
- 1/3 cup baking cocoa
- 1 teaspoon baking powder
- 1/4 teaspoon salt
- 1/2 cup strawberry *or* raspberry jam
- 2 cups vanilla ice cream, softened
- Confectioners' sugar
- Hot fudge topping and whipped topping

Line a greased 15-in. x 10-in. x 1-in. baking pan with parchment paper; grease the paper and set aside. In a mixing bowl, beat egg whites until soft peaks form. Gradually add 1/4 cup sugar, beating until stiff peaks form. In another mixing bowl, beat egg yolks and remaining sugar until thick and lemon-colored, about 5 minutes. Combine the flour, cocoa, baking powder and salt; add to yolk mixture and mix well. Fold in egg white mixture.

Spread batter evenly in prepared pan. Bake at 375° for 10-12 minutes or until cake springs back when lightly touched. Cool for 5 minutes. Invert cake onto a kitchen towel dusted with confectioners' sugar. Gently peel off paper. Roll up cake in towel jelly-roll style, starting with a short side. Cool on a wire rack.

Unroll cake; spread jam to within 1/2 in. of edges. Top with ice cream. Roll up without towel. Place seam side down on a platter. Cover and freeze for at least 4 hours before slicing. May be frozen for up to 2 months. Sprinkle with confectioners' sugar; serve with hot fudge topping and whipped topping. **Yield: 12 servings.**

Ice Cream Party Roll

Strawberry Nut Roll

Desserts like this refreshing rolled shortcake are my favorite. The nutty cake, creamy filling and fresh strawberries make pretty swirled slices.

—Judy Hayes, Peosta, Iowa

- 6 eggs, *separated*
- 3/4 cup sugar, *divided*
- 1 cup ground walnuts, toasted
- 1/4 cup dry bread crumbs
- 1/4 cup all-purpose flour
- 1/8 teaspoon salt

Confectioners' sugar

FILLING:

- 1 pint fresh strawberries
- 1 cup heavy whipping cream
- 2 tablespoons sugar
- 1 teaspoon vanilla extract

Confectioners' sugar

In a large mixing bowl, beat egg whites until soft peaks form. Gradually add 1/4 cup sugar, one tablespoon at a time, beating on high until stiff peaks form. Set aside.

In another large mixing bowl, beat egg yolks and remaining sugar until thick and lemon-colored. Combine the walnuts, bread crumbs, flour and salt; add to yolk mixture. Mix well. Fold in egg white mixture. Line a greased 15-in. x 10-in. x 1-in. baking pan with parchment paper; grease the paper. Spread batter evenly into pan. Bake at 375° for 15 minutes or until cake springs back when lightly touched. Cool for 5 minutes.

Invert cake onto a kitchen towel dusted with confectioners' sugar. Gently peel off paper. Roll up in the towel jelly-roll style, starting with a short side. Cool on a wire rack.

Slice six large strawberries in half; set aside for garnish. Thinly slice remaining berries; set aside. In a large mixing bowl, beat cream until it begins to thicken. Gradually add sugar and vanilla, beating until stiff peaks form. Unroll cake; spread with filling to within 1/2. in of edges. Top with sliced berries. Roll up again.

Place seam side down on serving platter. Chill until serving. Dust with confectioners' sugar. Garnish with reserved strawberries. Refrigerate leftovers. **Yield: 12 servings.**

Strawberry Nut Roll

Orange Chiffon Cake

It wasn't until a few years ago that I started entering our county fair. Since then, my moist Orange Chiffon Cake has been awarded several blue ribbons.

—Marjorie Ebert, South Dayton, New York

- 6 eggs, *separated*
- 2 cups all-purpose flour
- 1-1/2 cups sugar
- 1 teaspoon salt
- 1/2 teaspoon baking soda
- 3/4 cup fresh orange juice
- 1/2 cup vegetable oil
- 2 tablespoons grated orange peel
- 1/2 teaspoon cream of tartar

Orange Chiffon Cake

ORANGE GLAZE:

1/2 cup butter
2 cups confectioners' sugar
2 to 4 tablespoons fresh orange juice
1/2 teaspoon grated orange peel

Let eggs stand at room temperature for 30 minutes. In a large mixing bowl, combine the flour, sugar, salt and baking soda. In a bowl, whisk the egg yolks, orange juice, oil and orange peel; add to dry ingredients. Beat until well blended.

In another large mixing bowl, beat egg whites and cream of tartar on high speed until stiff peaks form. Fold into orange mixture Gently spoon batter into an ungreased 10-in. tube pan. Cut through the batter with a knife to remove air pockets.

Bake on the lowest rack at 350° for 45-50 minutes or until top springs back when lightly touched. Immediately invert pan; cool completely. Run a knife around sides and center tube of pan. Invert cake onto a serving plate.

For glaze, melt butter in a small saucepan; add remaining glaze ingredients. Stir until smooth. Pour over top of cake, allowing it to drizzle down sides. **Yield: 16 servings.**

Sponge Cake with Blueberry Topping

This recipe puts the blueberries grown in our area to good use. It's a great summertime treat.
—Frances Colley, Coos Bay, Oregon

- 6 eggs, *separated*
- 1-1/2 cups sugar
- 3/4 cup orange juice
- 1-1/2 cups all-purpose flour
- 1-1/2 teaspoons baking powder
- 1/4 teaspoon cream of tartar

BLUEBERRY TOPPING:

- 1/2 cup sugar
- 2 teaspoons cornstarch
- 1 tablespoon grated orange peel
- 1/2 cup orange juice
- 2 cups fresh *or* frozen blueberries

SOUR CREAM TOPPING:

- 2 cups (16 ounces) sour cream
- 1 tablespoon confectioners' sugar
- 1 teaspoon vanilla extract

Grated orange peel, optional

In a large mixing bowl, beat egg yolks for 4-5 minutes or until thickened and light yellow. Gradually add sugar, beating for 1-2 minutes or until sugar is dissolved. Add orange juice beat for 2-3 minutes or until mixture slightly thickens. Combine flour and baking powder; gradually add to yolk mixture and mix well.

In a small mixing bowl, beat egg whites and cream of tartar until stiff peaks form. Fold into egg yolk mixture until well blended.

Pour into an ungreased 10-in. tube pan. Bake at 325° for 50-55 minutes or until the cake springs back when lightly touched. Immediately invert pan to cool.

For blueberry topping, in a large saucepan,

Sponge Cake with Blueberry Topping

combine the sugar, cornstarch and orange peel. Stir in orange juice until smooth. Bring to a boil; cook and stir for 2 minutes or until thickened. Remove from the heat. Stir in blueberries.

In a large bowl, combine the sour cream, confectioners' sugar and vanilla. Remove cooled cake from pan; cut into slices. Serve with warm blueberry topping and the sour cream topping. Garnish with orange peel if desired. **Yield: 12-16 servings.**

Editor's Note: If using frozen blueberries, do not thaw before adding to batter.

Apple-of-Your-Eye Cheesecake

My most-often-requested dessert, this exquisite cheesecake with apples, caramel and pecans wins me more compliments than anything else I make. My husband's co-workers say it's too pretty to cut, but agree it's well worth it to do so.

—Debbie Wilson, Sellersburg, Indiana

CRUST:

- 1 cup graham cracker crumbs
- 3 tablespoons sugar
- 1/2 teaspoon ground cinnamon
- 1/4 cup butter, melted
- 2 tablespoons finely chopped pecans

FILLING:

- 3 packages (8 ounces *each*) cream cheese, softened
- 3/4 cup sugar
- 3 eggs
- 3/4 teaspoon vanilla extract

TOPPING:

- 2-1/2 cups chopped peeled apples
- 1 tablespoon lemon juice
- 1/4 cup sugar
- 1/2 teaspoon ground cinnamon

Apple-of-Your-Eye Cheesecake

- 6 tablespoons caramel ice cream topping, *divided*

Sweetened whipped cream

- 2 tablespoons chopped pecans

Combine the cracker crumbs, sugar and cinnamon. Stir in the butter, then the pecans. Press onto the bottom of a lightly greased 9-in. springform pan. Place on a baking sheet. Bake at 350° for 10 minutes; cool.

In a mixing bowl, beat cream cheese and sugar until smooth. Add eggs; beat on low just until combined. Stir in vanilla. Pour over crust. Toss apples with lemon juice, sugar and cinnamon; spoon over filling. Return to baking pan.

Bake at 350° for 55-60 minutes or until center is almost set. Cool on a wire rack for 10 minutes. Carefully run a knife around edge of pan to loosen. Drizzle with 4 tablespoons caramel topping. Cool for 1 hour. Refrigerate overnight.

Remove sides of pan. Just before serving, garnish with whipped cream. Drizzle with remaining caramel topping; sprinkle with pecans. Store in the refrigerator. **Yield: 12 servings.**

Chocolate Chip Cookie Dough Cheesecake 1st prize

I created this recipe to combine two of my all-time favorites, cheesecake and chocolate chip cookie dough.
—Julie Craig, Jackson, Wisconsin

- 1-3/4 cups crushed chocolate chips cookies *or* chocolate wafer crumbs
- 1/4 cup sugar
- 1/3 cup butter, melted

FILLING:

- 3 packages (8 ounces *each*) cream cheese, softened
- 1 cup sugar
- 3 eggs, lightly beaten
- 1 cup (8 ounces) sour cream
- 1/2 teaspoon vanilla extract

COOKIE DOUGH:

- 1/4 cup butter, softened
- 1/4 cup sugar
- 1/4 cup packed brown sugar
- 1 tablespoon water
- 1 teaspoon vanilla extract
- 1/2 cup all-purpose flour
- 1-1/2 cups miniature semisweet chocolate chips, *divided*

In a small bowl, combine the first three ingredients. Press onto the bottom and 1 in. up the sides of a greased 9-in. pan; set aside.

In a large mixing bowl, beat cream cheese and sugar until smooth. Add eggs; beat on low just until combined. Blend in sour cream and vanilla. Pour over crust; set aside.

In a mixing bowl, cream butter and sugars on medium speed until light and fluffy. Add water and vanilla. Gradually add flour. Stir in 1 cup chips. Drop dough by teaspoonfuls over filling, gently pushing dough below surface (dough should be completely covered by filling). Place pan on a baking sheet.

Chocolate Chip Cookie Dough Cheesecake

Bake at 350° for 45-55 minutes or until center is almost set. Cool on a wire rack for 10 minutes. Carefully run a knife around edge of pan to loosen; cool 1 hour. Chill overnight.

Remove sides of the pan. Sprinkle with remaining chips. Refrigerate leftovers. **Yield: 12-14 servings.**

Frozen Chocolate Cheesecake Tart

When I made this irresistible cheesecake for dinner, my husband said it was the best dessert he had ever eaten. *—Heather Bennett, Dunbar, West Virginia*

- 2-1/4 cups crushed chocolate cream-filled sandwich cookies (about 22 cookies)
- 1/3 cup butter, melted

FILLING:

- 2 packages (8 ounces *each*) cream cheese, softened
- 1/3 cup confectioners' sugar
- 3 cups vanilla *or* white chips, melted and cooled
- 1/3 cup heavy whipping cream
- 1 teaspoon vanilla extract
- 1/2 cup miniature semisweet chocolate chips

Chocolate curls, optional

In a small bowl, combine cookie crumbs and butter. Press onto the bottom and up the sides of a greased 9-in. fluted tart pan with a removable bottom. Freeze for at least 1 hour.

In a large mixing bowl, beat cream cheese and sugar until smooth. Beat in the vanilla chips, cream, and vanilla until well combined. Stir in chocolate chips; pour over crust. Cover and freeze for 8 hours or overnight.

Uncover; chill 3-4 hours before serving. Garnish with chocolate curls if desired. Refrigerate leftovers. **Yield: 12 servings.**

No-Bake Cherry Cheesecake

I'm always tight on time. Using a prepared graham cracker crust and canned pie filling, I can extend a no-bake mix to make two light, fancy-looking pies in less than 15 minutes. —Pam Noffke, Tylor, Texas

- 1 package (11.1 ounces) no-bake cheesecake mix
- 1/2 cup butter, melted
- 2 tablespoons sugar
- 1-1/2 cups cold milk
- 1 package (8 ounces) cream cheese, softened
- 1 cup confectioners' sugar
- 2 cups whipped topping
- 1 graham cracker crust (9 inches)
- 2 cans (21 ounces *each*) cherry pie filling

In a bowl, combine the cheesecake crust mix, butter and sugar. Press onto bottom and up the sides of an ungreased 9-in. pie plate. Chill.

In a large mixing bowl, beat cheesecake filling mix and milk on medium speed for 3 minutes. In another mixing bowl, beat cream cheese and confectioners' sugar until smooth. Add to cheesecake mixture; beat well. Fold in whipped topping.

Spoon half the filling into chilled crust and remaining filling into purchased crust. Refrigerate for at least 1 hour. Top with pie filling. **Yield: 2 pies (6-8 servings each).**

No-Bake Cherry Cheesecake

Frozen Chocolate Cheesecake Tart

Orange Cream Cheesecake

Orange Cream Cheesecake 1st prize

I love serving this impressive-looking cheesecake with its pretty layers and silky-smooth texture. The combination of orange gelatin, cream cheese and whipped topping is simply irresistible.

—Madonna Faunce, Boise, Idaho

- 2 cups graham cracker crumbs
- 1 teaspoon ground cinnamon
- 1 teaspoon grated orange peel
- 1/2 cup butter, melted

FILLING:

- 1 package (3 ounces) orange gelatin
- 3 packages (8 ounces *each*) cream cheese, softened
- 1-1/4 cups sugar
- 1 can (5 ounces) evaporated milk
- 1 teaspoon lemon juice
- 1/3 cup orange juice concentrate
- 1 teaspoon vanilla extract
- 1 envelope unflavored gelatin
- 2 tablespoons cold water
- 2 tablespoons boiling water
- 1 carton (8 ounces) frozen whipped topping, thawed

TOPPING:

- 2 cups whipped topping
- 1/4 cup sugar

Lemon slices, orange peel strips, kumquats and lemon balm for garnish, optional

In a bowl, combine the cracker crumbs, cinnamon, orange peel and butter. Press onto the bottom of a greased 10-in. springform pan. Refrigerate for at least 30 minutes.

Prepare orange gelatin according to package directions. Set aside 1/2 cup at room temperature. Chill remaining gelatin until slightly thickened, 40-60 minutes.

In a mixing bowl, beat cream cheese and sugar for 2 minutes. Gradually beat in milk and lemon juice. Beat on medium-high speed 2 minutes longer. Gradually beat in orange juice concentrate and vanilla.

In a small bowl, sprinkle unflavored gelatin over cold water; let stand for 2 minutes. Stir in boiling water; stir until gelatin is completely dissolved. Stir into room temperature orange gelatin. Stir into cream cheese mixture, then fold in whipped topping. Pour into crust.

For topping, in a mixing bowl, beat whipped topping and sugar. Beat in refrigerated orange gelatin (mixture will be thin). Chill for 30 minutes. Gently spoon over filling (pan will be full). Refrigerate for 8 hours or overnight. Garnish if desired. **Yield: 10-12 servings.**

S'more Cheesecake

This luscious dessert is just as wonderfully tasty as the campfire snack that inspired it. It's a great way to savor a summer classic anytime of year.

—Robin Andrews, Cary, North Carolina

- 2-1/4 cups graham cracker crumbs (about 36 squares)
- 1/3 cup sugar
- 1/2 cup butter, melted

FILLING:

- 2 packages (8 ounces *each*) cream cheese, softened
- 1 can (14 ounces) sweetened condensed milk
- 2 teaspoons vanilla extract
- 3 eggs, lightly beaten
- 1 cup (6 ounces) miniature semisweet chocolate chips
- 1 cup miniature marshmallows

TOPPING:

- 1 cup miniature marshmallows
- 1/2 cup semisweet chocolate chips
- 1 tablespoon shortening

In a small bowl, combine cracker crumbs and sugar; stir in butter. Press onto the bottom and 1-3/4 in. up the sides of a greased 10-in. springform pan; set aside.

In a large mixing bowl, beat the cream cheese, milk and vanilla until smooth. Add eggs; beat on low just until combined. Stir in chocolate chips and marshmallows. Pour over crust. Place on a baking sheet.

Bake at 325° for 40-45 minutes or until center is almost set. Sprinkle with marshmallows. Bake 4-6 minutes longer or until marshmallows are puffed.

Meanwhile, melt chocolate chips and shortening; stir until smooth. Drizzle over marshmallows. Cool on a wire rack for 10 minutes. Carefully run a knife around edge of pan to loosen; cool 1 hour longer. Refrigerate overnight. Remove sides of pan. Refrigerate leftovers. **Yield: 12 servings.**

S'more Cheesecake

Tropical Cheesecake

Tropical Cheesecake

I don't bake many sweet items, but I like to put together this cheesecake for parties. Every time I serve it, I receive many compliments. The colorful fruit topping is refreshing, and the coconut gives each slice a delicious tropical taste. People think you've worked so hard when they see the coconut crust, but it's so easy to make! —Shawntel Kemp, Pickens, Oklahoma

CRUST:

- 1 cup flaked coconut
- 1/4 cup chopped almonds
- 2 tablespoons butter, melted

FILLING:

- 2 packages (8 ounces *each*) cream cheese, softened
- 1 cup sugar
- 3 tablespoons cornstarch
- 3 eggs, lightly beaten
- 1 cup (8 ounces) sour cream
- 3 tablespoons lemon juice
- 2 teaspoons vanilla extract
- 1/4 teaspoon almond extract

TOPPING:

- 1/3 cup apricot preserves
- 1/2 cup pineapple tidbits
- 2 to 4 kiwifruit, peeled, sliced and halved
- 1/4 to 3/4 cup flaked coconut, toasted

In a small bowl, combine the coconut and almonds; stir in butter. Press onto the bottom of a greased 9-in. springform pan. Place on a baking sheet. Bake at 350° for 10 minutes. Cool on a wire rack.

In a large mixing bowl, beat cream cheese and sugar until smooth. Add cornstarch and beat well. Add eggs; beat on low just until combined. Add the sour cream, lemon juice vanilla and almond extracts; beat just until blended. Pour over crust.

Return cheesecake to baking sheet. Bake at 350° for 45-50 minutes or until center is almost set. Cool on a wire rack for 10 minutes. Carefully run a knife around the edge of pan to loosen; cool 1 hour longer. Refrigerate overnight.

In a small saucepan, melt preserves, stirring to break up any apricot pieces. Remove sides of pan from cheesecake. Arrange pineapple and kiwi on top of cheesecake. Brush preserves over fruit and on sides of cheesecake. Press coconut onto the sides of the cheesecake. Refrigerate leftovers. **Yield: 10-12 servings.**

Tangy Lemon Cheesecake

This dessert gets added spark from a gingersnap crust and a luscious lemon sauce. The mix of sweet and tart is unexpected and delightful.

—Pam Persons, Towanda, Kansas

- 2-1/2 cups gingersnap cookies (about 40 cookies)
- 1/3 cup butter, melted

FILLING:

- 3 packages (8 ounces) cream cheese, softened
- 1 cup sugar
- 3 eggs, lightly beaten
- 1 tablespoon lemon juice
- 1 tablespoon vanilla extract

SAUCE:

- 1/2 cup sugar
- 2 tablespoons cornstarch
- 3/4 cup water
- 2 tablespoons butter
- 1/4 cup lemon juice
- 1 tablespoon grated lemon peel

In a small bowl, combine cookie crumbs and butter; mix well. Press onto the bottom and 2 in. up the sides of a greased 9-in. springform pan; set aside.

In a large mixing bowl, beat cream cheese and sugar until smooth. Add eggs, beat on low just until combined. Add lemon juice and vanilla; beat just until blended.

Pour into crust. Place on a baking sheet. Bake at 350° for 35-40 minutes or until center is almost set. Cool on a wire rack for 10 minutes. Carefully run a knife around the edge of pan to loosen; cool 1 hour longer.

In a saucepan, combine the sugar and cornstarch. Stir in water until smooth; bring to a boil. Reduce heat; cook and stir over medium heat for 2 minutes or until thickened. Remove from the heat; gently stir in butter, lemon juice and peel.

Refrigerate cheesecake and sauce overnight. Remove sides of pan from cheesecake. Serve sauce over cheesecake. Refrigerate leftovers. **Yield: 12 servings.**

Tangy Lemon Cheesecake

Peanut Butter Cheesecake

Peanut Butter Cheesecake

The first time I served this cheesecake, my friends all went wild over it. They were surprised when I told them the crust is made of pretzels. The pairing of sweet and salty, plus peanut butter and chocolate, left everyone asking for another slice.

—Lois Brooks, Newark, Delaware

- 1-1/2 cups crushed pretzels
- 1/3 cup butter, melted

FILLING:

- 5 packages (8 ounces *each*) cream cheese, softened
- 1-1/2 cups sugar
- 3/4 cup creamy peanut butter
- 2 teaspoons vanilla extract
- 3 eggs, lightly beaten
- 1 cup peanut butter chips
- 1 cup (6 ounces) semisweet chocolate chips

TOPPING:

- 1 cup (8 ounces) sour cream
- 3 tablespoons creamy peanut butter
- 1/2 cup sugar
- 1/2 cup finely chopped unsalted peanuts

In a small bowl, combine pretzels and butter. Press onto the bottom and 1 in. up the sides of a greased 10-in. springform pan. Place on a baking sheet. Bake at 350° for 5 minutes. Cool on a wire rack.

In a large mixing bowl, beat cream cheese and sugar until smooth. Beat in peanut butter and vanilla. Add eggs; beat on low speed just until combined. Stir in chips. Pour over crust.

Return pan to baking sheet. Bake at 350° for 50-55 minutes or until center is almost set. Cool on a wire rack for 15 minutes.

Meanwhile, in a mixing bowl, combine the sour cream, peanut butter and sugar; spread over filling. Sprinkle with nuts. Bake 5 minutes longer.

Cool on a wire rack for 10 minutes. Carefully run a knife around the edge of the pan to loosen; cool 1 hour longer. Refrigerate overnight. Remove sides of pan. Refrigerate leftovers. **Yield: 12-14 servings.**

Cranberry Cheesecake

The holidays wouldn't be complete without cranberries and eggnog. I use them both in this flavorful cheesecake. —*Nancy Zimmerman*
Cape May Court House, New Jersey

- 1 cup sugar
- 2 tablespoons cornstarch
- 1 cup cranberry juice
- 1-1/2 cups fresh *or* frozen cranberries

CRUST:

- 1 cup graham cracker crumbs (about 14 squares)
- 3 tablespoons sugar
- 3 tablespoons butter, melted

FILLING:

- 4 packages (8 ounces *each*) cream cheese, softened
- 1 cup sugar
- 3 tablespoons all-purpose flour
- 4 eggs, lightly beaten
- 1 cup eggnog
- 1 tablespoon vanilla extract

In a large saucepan, combine the first four ingredients; bring to a boil. Reduce heat; cook and stir over medium heat for 2 minutes. Remove from the heat; set aside.

In a small bowl, combine the cracker crumbs and sugar; stir in butter. Press onto the bottom of a greased 9-in. springform pan. Place on a baking sheet. Bake at 325° for 10 minutes. Cool on a wire rack.

In a large mixing bowl, beat cream cheese and sugar until smooth. Beat in flour. Add eggs, beat on low just until combined. Add eggnog and vanilla; beat just until blended. Pour two-thirds of the filling over crust. Top with half of the cranberry mixture (cover and chill remaining cranberry mixture). Carefully spoon remaining filling on top.

Return to baking pan. Bake at 325° for 60-70 minutes or until center is almost set. Cool on a wire rack for 10 minutes. Carefully run a knife around edge of pan to loosen; cool 1 hour longer. Refrigerate overnight.

Remove sides of pan. Spoon remaining cranberry mixture over cheesecake. **Yield: 12 servings.**

Editor's Note: This recipe was tested with commercially prepared eggnog.

Cranberry Cheesecake

Chocolate Truffle Cheesecake

Chocolate Truffle Cheesecake

If you delight in the taste of chocolate, then this is the cheesecake for you. Every creamy bite melts in your mouth. It's so impressive yet not difficult to prepare.
—Mary Jones, Cumberland, Maine

- 1-1/2 cups chocolate wafer crumbs
- 2 tablespoons sugar
- 1/4 cup butter, melted

FILLING:

- 1/4 cup semisweet chocolate chips
- 1/4 cup heavy whipping cream
- 3 packages (8 ounces *each*) cream cheese, softened
- 1 cup sugar
- 1/3 cup baking cocoa
- 3 eggs, lightly beaten
- 1 teaspoon vanilla extract

TOPPING:

- 1-1/2 cups (9 ounces) semisweet chocolate chips
- 1/4 cup heavy whipping cream
- 1 teaspoon vanilla extract

Whipped cream and miniature chocolate kisses for garnish

In a small bowl, combine cookie crumbs and sugar; stir in butter. Press onto the bottom and 1-1/2 in. up the sides of a greased 9-in. springform pan. Place on a baking sheet. Bake at 350° for 10 minutes. Cool on a wire rack.

Reduce heat to 325°. In a saucepan over low heat, melt chocolate chips, stirring until smooth. Remove from the heat; add cream and mix well. Set aside.

In a large mixing bowl, beat cream cheese and sugar until smooth. Add cocoa and beat well. Add eggs; beat on low just until combined. Stir in vanilla and reserved chocolate mixture just until blended. Pour over crust. Return pan to baking sheet. Bake for 45-50 minutes or until center is almost set.

For topping, melt chocolate chips in a saucepan over low heat, stirring until smooth. Remove from the heat. Stir in the cream and vanilla; mix well. Spread over the filling. Refrigerate overnight.

Carefully run a knife around edge of the pan to loosen. Remove sides of pan. Just before serving, garnish with whipped cream and miniature chocolate kisses if desired. **Yield: 12 servings.**

PIES

ARAMEL PEAR PIE, pg. 427

Pies

Farm Apple Pan Pie

You'll find this pie's very convenient for taking to a covered-dish supper, picnic, etc. But be prepared—people always ask for a copy of the recipe!
—Dolores Skrout, Summerhill, Pennsylvania

EGG YOLK PASTRY:

- 5 cups all-purpose flour
- 4 teaspoons sugar
- 1/2 teaspoon salt
- 1/2 teaspoon baking powder
- 1-1/2 cups shortening
- 2 egg yolks, lightly beaten
- 3/4 cup cold water

FILLING:

- 5 pounds tart apples, peeled and thinly sliced
- 4 teaspoons lemon juice
- 3/4 cup sugar
- 3/4 cup packed brown sugar
- 1 teaspoon ground cinnamon
- 1/2 teaspoon ground nutmeg
- 1/4 teaspoon salt

Milk
Additional sugar

In a large bowl, combine the flour, sugar, salt and baking powder; cut in shortening until the mixture resembles coarse crumbs. Combine yolks and cold water. Sprinkle over dry ingredients; toss with fork. If needed, add additional water, 1 tablespoon at a time, until mixture can be formed into a ball. Divide dough in half. On a lightly floured surface, roll half of dough to fit a 15-in. x 10-in. x 1-in. baking pan.

Farm Apple Pan Pie

Sprinkle apples with lemon juice; arrange half of them over dough. Combine the sugars, cinnamon, nutmeg and salt; sprinkle half over apples. Top with remaining apples; sprinkle with remaining sugar mixture.

Roll remaining pastry to fit pan; place on top of filling and seal edges. Brush with milk and sprinkle with sugar. Cut vents in top pastry. Bake at 400° for 50 minutes or until crust is golden brown and filling is bubbly. **Yield: 18-24 servings.**

Sweet Apple Pie

By pairing apples and candy, I came up with this creation—a kind of toffee apple in a pie crust!
—Irene Evenson, Minto, North Dakota

Pastry for double-crust pie (9 inches)
- **3/4 cup sugar**
- **1/4 cup all-purpose flour**
- **1/2 teaspoon ground cinnamon**
- **1/2 teaspoon ground nutmeg**

Dash salt
- **6 cups thinly sliced peeled tart apples (about 6 medium)**
- **1 cup English toffee bits *or* almond brickle chips**
- **2 tablespoons butter**

Heavy whipping cream, optional

Line a 9-in. pie plate with bottom pastry; trim pastry even with edge of plate. In a large bowl, combine the sugar, flour, cinnamon, nutmeg and salt; add apples and toss to coat. Stir in toffee bits. Pour into crust. Dot with butter.

Roll out remaining pastry to fit top of pie; make decorative cutouts in the pastry. Place pastry over filling. Trim, seal and flute edges. Top with cutouts; brush top pastry with cream if desired. Cover edges loosely with foil.

Bake at 425° for 30 minutes. Remove foil; bake 10-15 minutes longer or until crust is golden brown and filling is bubbly. Cool on a wire rack. Store in the refrigerator. **Yield: 6-8 servings.**

Apple Meringue Pie

I received this recipe from my mother-in-law, and it's one of my husband's favorites. It's a nice variation on traditional apple pie.
—Virginia Kraus, Pocahontas, Illinois

- **7 cups thinly sliced peeled tart apples**
- **2 tablespoons lemon juice**
- **2/3 cup sugar**

Sweet Apple Pie

- **2 tablespoons all-purpose flour**
- **1/3 cup milk**
- **2 egg yolks, beaten**
- **1 teaspoon grated lemon peel**

Pastry for single-crust pie (9 inches)
- **1 tablespoon butter**

MERINGUE:
- **3 egg whites**
- **1/4 teaspoon cream of tartar**
- **6 tablespoons sugar**

In a large bowl, toss apples with lemon juice. In a small bowl, whisk the sugar, flour, milk, egg yolks and lemon peel until smooth. Pour over apples and toss to coat.

Line a 9-in. pie plate with pastry; trim to 1/2 in. beyond edge of pie plate and flute edges. Pour filling into crust; dot with butter. Cover edges loosely with foil.

Bake at 400° for 20 minutes. Remove foil; bake 25-30 minutes longer or until apples are tender. Reduce heat to 350°.

In a mixing bowl, beat the egg whites and cream of tartar on medium speed until foamy. Gradually beat in sugar, 1 tablespoon at a time, on high just until stiff peaks form and sugar is dissolved. Spread evenly over hot filling, sealing edges to crust. Bake for 15 minutes or until golden brown. Cool on a wire rack. Store in the refrigerator. **Yield: 6-8 servings.**

Apple Blackberry Pie

After a blackberry-picking trip, my husband and I decided to include a few in an apple pie we were making. It was the best we'd ever tasted!
—Dorian Lucas, Corning, California

- 2 cups all-purpose flour
- 1 teaspoon sugar
- 1 teaspoon salt
- 1 teaspoon ground cinnamon
- 2/3 cup cold butter
- 4 to 6 tablespoons cold water

FILLING:

- 5 cups thinly sliced peeled tart apples (about 6 medium)
- 1 cup fresh blackberries
- 1/2 cup packed brown sugar
- 4-1/2 teaspoons cornstarch
- 1 teaspoon ground cinnamon
- 1 teaspoon ground nutmeg

In a large bowl, combine the flour, sugar, salt and cinnamon; cut in butter until crumbly. Gradually add water, tossing with a fork until dough forms a ball. Divide dough in half. Roll out one portion to fit a 9-in. pie plate; place pastry in plate and trim even with edge.

In a large bowl, combine apples and blackberries. Combine brown sugar, cornstarch, cinnamon and nutmeg; add to fruit mixture and toss to coat. Pour into crust.

Roll out remaining pastry to fit top of pie; place over filling. Trim, seal and flute edges. Cut slits in pastry. Add decorative cutouts if desired. Cover edges loosely with foil.

Bake at 450° for 10 minutes. Reduce heat to 350°; remove foil. Bake 40-50 minutes longer or until lightly browned and filling is bubbly. Cool on a wire rack. Store in the refrigerator. **Yield: 6-8 servings.**

Apple Meringue Pie

Apple Blackberry Pie

Fresh Blueberry Pie

Macaroon Cherry Pie

Fresh Blueberry Pie

I've been making this dessert for 30 years. Blueberries are abundant in our area, since Michigan is the leader in blueberry production.
—Linda Kernan, Mason, Michigan

- 3/4 cup sugar
- 3 tablespoons cornstarch
- 1/8 teaspoon salt
- 1/4 cup cold water
- 5 cups fresh blueberries, *divided*
- 1 tablespoon butter
- 1 tablespoon lemon juice
- 1 pastry shell (9 inches), baked

In a large saucepan, combine the sugar, cornstarch, salt and water until smooth. Add 3 cups blueberries. Bring to a boil over medium heat; cook and stir for 2 minutes or until thickened and bubbly.

Remove from the heat. Add the butter, lemon juice and remaining berries; stir until butter is melted. Cool. Pour into pastry shell. Refrigerate until serving. **Yield: 6-8 servings.**

Macaroon Cherry Pie

I use homegrown cherries in this bountiful pie with its unique crunchy coconut topping. But I've found that purchased tart cherries yield a dessert that's nearly as delicious. I always bake this pie around Presidents' Day or Valentine's Day, but it's popular with my family in any season.
—Lori Daniels, Beverly, West Virginia

Pastry for single-crust pie (9 inches)
- 3 cans (14-1/2 ounces *each*) pitted tart cherries
- 1 cup sugar
- 1/3 cup cornstarch
- 1/2 teaspoon ground cinnamon
- 1/4 teaspoon red food coloring, optional

TOPPING:

- 1 egg, lightly beaten
- 2 tablespoons milk
- 1 tablespoon butter
- 1/4 teaspoon almond extract
- 1/4 cup sugar
- 1/8 teaspoon salt
- 1 cup flaked coconut
- 1/2 cup sliced almonds

Line a 9-in. deep-dish pie plate with pastry. Trim to 1/2-in. beyond edge of plate; flute edges. Bake at 400° for 6 minutes; set aside.

Drain cherries, reserving 1 cup juice. Set cherries aside. In a large saucepan, combine sugar and cornstarch; gradually stir in cherry juice until blended. Bring to a boil over medium heat; cook and stir for 2 minutes or until thickened.

Remove from the heat; stir in cinnamon and food coloring if desired. Gently fold in cherries. Pour into crust. Cover edges loosely with foil. Bake at 400° for 20 minutes.

Meanwhile, in a large bowl, combine the first six topping ingredients. Stir in coconut and almonds. Remove foil from pie; spoon topping over pie. Bake at 350° for 20 minutes or until topping is lightly browned. Cool on a wire rack for 1 hour.

Chill for at least 4 hours before cutting. Refrigerate leftovers. **Yield: 6-8 servings.**

Cherry Blueberry Pie

I came up with this pie recipe that combines cherries and blueberries. It's especially good served warm with ice cream. —*Betty Williams, Scotts, Michigan*

Pastry for a double-crust pie (9 inches)

- 2 cups pitted sweet cherries
- 2 cups fresh blueberries *or* frozen unsweetened blueberries
- 3/4 cup sugar
- 1/4 cup all-purpose flour
- 1/8 teaspoon ground nutmeg
- 1 tablespoon butter

Additional sugar

Cherry Blueberry Pie

Line a 9-in. pie plate with bottom crust; trim pastry even with edge. Set aside.

In a large bowl, gently combine cherries and blueberries. Combine the sugar, flour and nutmeg; stir into fruit. Let stand for 10 minutes. Pour into crust; dot with butter. Roll out remaining pastry; make lattice crust. Seal and flute edges. Sprinkle with additional sugar. Cover edges of pastry loosely with foil.

Bake at 425° for 15 minutes. Reduce heat to 350°; bake 30-35 minutes longer or until pastry is golden brown and filling is bubbly. Cool on a wire rack. **Yield: 6-8 servings.**

Editor's Note: If using frozen blueberries, do not thaw before adding to batter.

Dutch Apricot Pie

Dutch Apricot Pie

I freeze several bags of apricots when they are in season, thinking of this pie all the while.
—Joanne Hutmacher, Lemoore, California

- 3/4 cup sugar
- 2 tablespoons quick-cooking tapioca
- 4 cups sliced fresh apricots (about 16)
- 1 tablespoon lemon juice
- 1 pastry for single-crust pie (9 inches)

TOPPING:

- 2/3 cup all-purpose flour
- 1/2 cup sugar
- 1/2 cup chopped pecans, toasted
- 1/4 cup butter, melted

In a small bowl, combine sugar and tapioca. Add apricots and lemon juice; toss to coat. Let stand for 15 minutes. Line a 9-in. pie plate with pastry. Trim pastry to 1/2 in. beyond edge of plate; flute edges. Pour filling into crust.

In a small bowl, combine the flour, sugar and pecans. Stir in butter. Sprinkle over filling. Cover edges loosely with foil. Bake at 350° for 15 minutes. Remove foil; bake 25-30 minutes longer or until crust is golden brown and filling is bubbly. Cool on a wire rack. Store in the refrigerator. **Yield: 8 servings.**

Golden Peach Pie

More than 15 years ago, I entered this lattice-top pie in the Park County Fair in Livingston. It won a first-place blue ribbon plus a purple ribbon for "Best All Around!" My large family and many friends all agree with the contest judges that it's very delicious.
—Shirley Olson, Polson, Montana

Pastry for double-crust pie (9 inches)

- 1 cup sugar
- 1/4 cup cornstarch
- 1/4 teaspoon ground nutmeg
- 1/8 teaspoon salt
- 2 teaspoons lemon juice
- 1/2 teaspoon grated orange peel
- 1/8 teaspoon almond extract
- 5 cups sliced peeled fresh peaches (about 5 medium)
- 2 tablespoons butter

Milk

Line a 9-in. pie plate with bottom pastry; trim even with the edge of plate. Set aside. In a large bowl, combine the sugar, cornstarch, nutmeg and salt; stir in lemon juice, orange peel and extract. Add the peaches; toss gently. Pour into crust; dot with butter.

Roll out remaining pastry to fit top of pie; make decorative cutouts in pastry. Set cutouts aside. Place top crust over filling. Trim, seal and flute edges. Brush pastry and cutouts with milk; place cutouts on top of pie. Cover the edges loosely with foil.

Bake at 400° for 40 minutes. Remove foil;

bake 10-15 minutes longer or until crust is golden brown and filling is bubbly. Cool on a wire rack. Store in the refrigerator. **Yield: 8 servings.**

Caramel Pear Pie

A dear friend shared the recipe for this attractive pie. The caramel drizzle and streusel topping make it almost too pretty to eat. Knowing this dessert is waiting is great motivation for our children to eat all their vegetables. —*Mary Kuehler, Lodi, California*

- **6** **cups sliced peeled ripe pears (about 6 medium)**
- **1** **tablespoon lemon juice**
- **1/2** **cup plus 3 tablespoons sugar, *divided***
- **2** **tablespoons quick-cooking tapioca**
- **3/4** **teaspoon ground cinnamon**
- **1/4** **teaspoon salt**
- **1/4** **teaspoon ground nutmeg**
- **1** **unbaked pastry shell (9 inches)**
- **3/4** **cup old-fashioned oats**
- **1** **tablespoon all-purpose flour**
- **1/4** **cup cold butter, cubed**
- **18** **caramels**
- **5** **tablespoons milk**
- **1/4** **cup chopped pecans**

In a large bowl, combine pears and lemon juice. In another bowl, combine 1/2 cup sugar, tapioca, cinnamon, salt and nutmeg. Add to pears; stir gently. Let stand for 15 minutes.

Pour into pastry shell. In a bowl, combine the oats, flour and remaining sugar. Cut in butter until crumbly. Sprinkle over pears. Bake at 400° for 45 minutes.

In a saucepan over low heat, melt caramels with milk. Stir until smooth; add pecans. Drizzle over pie. Bake 8-10 minutes longer or until crust is golden brown and filling is bubbly. Cool on a wire rack. Store in the refrigerator. **Yield: 6-8 servings.**

Golden Peach Pie

Caramel Pear Pie

Fluffy Strawberry Meringue Pie

Granny's Rhubarb Pie

Fluffy Strawberry Meringue Pie

The combination of the cool, creamy berry filling and the delightfully different meringue crust guarantees you'll hear, "Pass the pie, please," all around the table.
—Roxanna Shoffstall, Lakeview, Ohio

- 3 egg whites
- 1 teaspoon vanilla extract
- 1/4 teaspoon cream of tartar
- 1 cup sugar
- 1/2 cup crushed saltines (about 12 crackers)
- 1/2 cup chopped pecans
- 2 pints fresh strawberries, *divided*
- 4 cups miniature marshmallows
- 1 carton (8 ounces) frozen whipped topping, thawed

Red food coloring, optional

In a mixing bowl, beat egg whites, vanilla and cream of tartar on medium speed until soft peaks form. Gradually beat in sugar, 1 tablespoon at a time, on high until stiff glossy peaks form and sugar is dissolved. Fold in the crackers and pecans.

Spread onto the bottom and up the sides of a greased 10-in. deep-dish pie plate. Bake at 350° for 25-30 minutes or until meringue is lightly browned. Cool on a wire rack.

Set aside one strawberry for garnish. Slice half of the strawberries; set aside. In a bowl, mash the remaining strawberries; drain juice, reserving 1/2 cup. In a saucepan, combine marshmallows and reserved juice. Cook and stir over low heat until marshmallows are melted. Refrigerate until partially set.

Fold the sliced and mashed strawberries and whipped topping into marshmallow mixture. Add food coloring if desired. Spoon into meringue shell. Garnish with the reserved strawberry. Refrigerate for 3 hours or until set. Refrigerate leftovers. **Yield: 8-10 servings.**

County Fair Pie

County Fair Pie

This quick and easy pie is one of my family's favorites. I've taken it to lots of potlucks and have been asked for the recipe many times.

—Judy Acuff, Lathrop, Missouri

- 1 cup butter, softened
- 1 cup sugar
- 1/2 cup all-purpose flour
- 2 eggs
- 1 teaspoon vanilla extract
- 1 cup coarsely chopped walnuts
- 1 cup (6 ounces) semisweet chocolate chips
- 1/2 cup butterscotch chips
- 1 unbaked pastry shell (9 inches)

In a mixing bowl, beat the butter, sugar, flour, eggs and vanilla until well blended. Stir in nuts and chips.

Pour into pie shell. Bake at 325° for 1 hour or until golden brown. Cool on a wire rack. **Yield: 6-8 servings.**

Granny's Rhubarb Pie

This recipe originated with my grandmother, who baked many different rhubarb desserts. This was always a favorite of mine.

—Blanche Baninski, Minto, North Dakota

- 3 cups all-purpose flour
- 1-1/2 teaspoons salt
- 1 cup shortening
- 5 tablespoons water
- 1 egg
- 1 teaspoon white vinegar

FILLING:

- 3 cups cut fresh *or* frozen rhubarb (1/2-inch pieces)
- 2 cups sliced peeled tart apples
- 1 can (8 ounces) crushed pineapple, drained
- 1/4 cup honey
- 1 tablespoon lemon juice
- 1 cup sugar
- 3 tablespoons all-purpose flour
- 1 tablespoon butter

In a large bowl, combine flour and salt. Cut in shortening until mixture resembles coarse crumbs. Combine the water, egg and vinegar; stir into flour mixture until a ball forms.

Divide dough in half. Roll out one portion on a lightly floured surface; transfer to a 9-in. pie plate. Trim pastry even with edge.

In a large bowl, combine the rhubarb, apples, pineapple, honey and lemon juice. Combine sugar and flour; add to rhubarb mixture. Pour into crust. Dot with butter.

Roll out remaining pastry to fit top of pie. Place over filling; trim, seal and flute edges. Cut slits in pastry. Bake at 350° for 1-1/4 hours or until the pastry is golden brown and the apples are tender. **Yield: 6-8 servings.**

Editor's Note: If using frozen rhubarb, measure rhubarb while still frozen, then thaw completely. Drain in a colander, but do not press liquid out.

Lemon Sour Cream Pie

One bite and people marvel over this pie. Some even say it reminds them of cheesecake. The recipe was shared by a friend; now, I'm glad to do the same.
—Nancy Beran, St. Peter, Minnesota

- 1 cup sugar
- 1/4 cup cornstarch
- 1/8 teaspoon salt
- 1 cup milk
- 3 egg yolks, beaten
- 1/4 cup butter, cubed
- 1/4 cup fresh lemon juice
- 1 teaspoon grated lemon peel

MERINGUE:

- 3 egg whites
- 1/2 teaspoon vanilla extract
- 1/4 teaspoon cream of tartar
- 6 tablespoons sugar
- 1 cup (8 ounces) sour cream
- 1 pastry shell (9 inches), baked

Lemon peel strips, optional

In a large saucepan, combine the sugar, cornstarch and salt; gradually stir in the milk. Cook and stir over medium-high heat until thickened and bubbly, about 2 minutes. Reduce heat; cook and stir 2 minutes longer. Gradually stir 1/2 cup into egg yolks; return all to the pan. Bring to a gentle boil; cook and stir for 2 minutes. Remove from the heat; stir in butter, lemon juice and peel. Set aside.

For meringue, beat egg whites, vanilla and cream of tartar until foamy. Add sugar, 1 tablespoon at a time, beating until stiff peaks form; set aside.

Fold sour cream into the lemon mixture; pour into pastry shell. Cover with meringue, sealing to edges of pastry. Bake at 350° for 12-15 minutes or until golden. Garnish with lemon peel strips if desired. Cool completely. Store in the refrigerator. **Yield: 6-8 servings.**

Lemon Sour Cream Pie

Very Lemony Meringue Pie

As a winter resident of Florida, I have access to juicy, tree-fresh lemons. They're at their zesty best in this mouth-watering family pie recipe.
—Betty Bradley, Sebring, Florida

- 1-1/4 cups sugar
- 1/3 cup cornstarch
- 1 cup cold water
- 3 egg yolks
- 1 cup lemon juice
- 3 tablespoons butter
- 1 pastry shell (9 inches), baked

MERINGUE:

- 1 tablespoon cornstarch
- 1/3 cup cold water
- 3 egg whites
- 1 teaspoon vanilla extract

Dash salt

- 6 tablespoons sugar

In a saucepan, combine sugar and cornstarch; gradually stir in water until smooth. Cook and stir over medium heat until thickened and bubbly. Reduce heat; cook and stir 2 minutes longer. Remove from the heat. Stir in a small amount of hot filling into egg yolks. Return all to the pan, stirring constantly. Bring to a gentle boil; cook and stir 2 minutes longer.

Remove from the heat. Add lemon juice and butter; stir until butter is melted and mixture is blended. Pour hot filling into pastry shell.

In a saucepan, combine cornstarch and water until smooth. Cook and stir over medium-low heat until mixture comes to a boil and is thickened, about 2 minutes. Remove from the heat. In a mixing bowl, beat egg whites, vanilla and salt until foamy. Gradually beat in sugar, 1 tablespoon at a time, on medium speed until soft peaks form and sugar is dissolved. Gradually beat in cornstarch mixture, 1 tablespoon at a time, on high until stiff peaks form.

Spread evenly over hot filling, sealing edges to crust. Bake at 325° for 18-20 minutes or until meringue is golden. Cool on a wire rack for 1 hour. Chill for at least 3 hours before serving. Refrigerate the leftovers. **Yield: 8 servings.**

Very Lemony Meringue Pie

Maple Pecan Pie

Our Vermont maple syrup can't be beat, and I like to use it in a variety of recipes such as this pie.
—Mildred Wescom, Belvidere, Vermont

- 3 eggs
- 1/2 cup sugar
- 1 cup maple syrup
- 3 tablespoons butter, melted
- 1/2 teaspoon vanilla extract
- 1/4 teaspoon salt
- 1 cup pecan halves
- 1 unbaked pastry shell (9 inches)

In a bowl, whisk the eggs and sugar until smooth. Add the maple syrup, butter, vanilla, salt and pecans. Pour into pastry shell.

Bake at 375° for 40-45 minutes or until a knife inserted near the center comes out clean. Cool on a wire rack for 1 hour. Store in the refrigerator. **Yield: 8 servings.**

Maple Pecan Pie

Classic Custard Pie

Golden Squash Pie

Classic Custard Pie

This recipe came from the best cook in West Virginia—my mother! I just adjusted the recipe to suit my family's tastes. I make my custard pie for church and club functions. It's the most different pie of all the ones in my collection.
—Maxine Linkenauger, Montverde, Florida

- **1 pastry for single-crust *or* double-crust pie (9 inches)**
- **4 eggs**
- **2-1/2 cups milk**
- **1/2 cup sugar**
- **1 teaspoon vanilla extract**
- **1 teaspoon almond extract**
- **1/2 teaspoon salt**
- **1 teaspoon ground nutmeg**

Line pie plate with pastry; flute edges or prepare a braided crust (see Editor's Note). Bake at 400° for 10 minutes.

Meanwhile, beat eggs in a large bowl. Add remaining ingredients; mix well. Pour into crust. Cover edges with foil. Bake for 20-25 minutes or until a knife inserted near the center comes out clean. Cool completely. Store in the refrigerator. **Yield: 6-8 servings.**

Editor's Note: Pastry for a double crust is needed only if a braided crust is desired. **To prepare braided crust:** Trim pastry even with the edge of the pie plate; brush with water. From the top pastry, cut 12 strips, each 1/4 in. thick. Using three strips at a time, braid pastry on edge of crust, attaching ends together. Press down gently. Bake as directed.

Golden Squash Pie

Whether you take this yummy pie to a party or potluck, be prepared to share the recipe. An alternative to pumpkin pie, it bakes up high and flavorful.
—Patricia Hardin, Seymour, Tennessee

- 4 eggs
- 4 cups mashed cooked butternut squash
- 1 cup buttermilk
- 1/4 cup butter, melted
- 2 teaspoons vanilla extract
- 2 cups sugar
- 2 tablespoons all-purpose flour
- 1 teaspoon salt
- 1/2 teaspoon baking soda
- 2 unbaked pastry shells (9 inches)

Ground nutmeg, optional

In a large bowl, combine the eggs, squash, buttermilk, butter and vanilla. Combine the dry ingredients; add to the squash mixture and mix until smooth. Pour into pastry shells. Cover edges loosely with foil.

Bake at 350° for 35 minutes. Remove foil. Bake 25 minutes longer or until a knife inserted near the center comes out clean. Cool on a wire rack. Sprinkle with nutmeg if desired. Store in the refrigerator. **Yield: 2 pies (6-8 servings each).**

Old-Fashioned Chess Pie

This recipe dates back many years and has certainly stood the test of time. It's very rich, so small servings might be in order.

—Christine Batts, Murray, Kentucky

- 1 cup butter, softened
- 2 cups sugar
- 6 egg yolks
- 1 egg
- 1/3 cup cornmeal
- 1/4 cup all-purpose flour
- 1/3 cup milk
- 1 teaspoon vanilla extract
- 1 unbaked deep-dish pastry shell (9 inches)

Old-Fashioned Chess Pie

TOPPING:

- 2 cups sugar, *divided*
- 2/3 cup milk
- 1/2 cup butter

In a large mixing bowl, cream butter and sugar. Beat in egg yolks and egg. Add the cornmeal and flour; mix well. Beat in milk and vanilla (do not overbeat). Pour into the pastry shell. Bake at 325° for 55-65 minutes or until the filling is almost set. Cool on a wire rack.

In a large heavy saucepan, heat 1/2 cup sugar over low heat without stirring until partially melted, about 5 minutes. Cook and stir with a metal spoon until syrup is completely melted and golden, about 5 minutes. Stir in the milk, butter and remaining sugar (mixture will be lumpy). Cook over medium heat, stirring until a candy thermometer reads 234° (soft-ball stage). Remove from the heat.

Pour into a large mixing bowl without stirring. Cool, without stirring, to 190°. Beat on high speed until mixture turns light brown and creamy and a candy thermometer reads 130°-137°, about 5 minutes. Immediately spread over the pie. Store in the refrigerator. **Yield: 8-10 servings.**

Editor's Note: We recommend that you test your candy thermometer before each use by bringing water to a boil; the thermometer should read 212°. Adjust the recipe temperature up or down based on your test.

Strawberry Lover's Pie

Strawberry Lover's Pie 1st prize

The second question people ask when I serve them this pie is, "What's your recipe?" It comes right after their first question—"May I have another slice?"
—Lauretha Rowe, Scranton, Kansas

- **3 squares (1 ounce *each*) semisweet chocolate, *divided***
- **1 tablespoon butter**
- **1 pastry shell (9 inches), baked**
- **2 packages (3 ounces *each*) cream cheese, softened**
- **1/2 cup sour cream**
- **3 tablespoons sugar**
- **1/2 teaspoon vanilla extract**
- **3 to 4 cups fresh strawberries, hulled**
- **1/3 cup strawberry jam, melted**

In a large saucepan, melt 2 ounces chocolate and butter over low heat, stirring constantly; spread or brush over the bottom and up the sides of pastry shell. Chill.

Meanwhile, in a large mixing bowl, beat the cream cheese, sour cream, sugar and vanilla until smooth. Spread over chocolate layer; cover and chill for 2 hours.

Arrange strawberries tip end up atop the filling. Brush jam over strawberries. Melt the remaining chocolate and drizzle over all. **Yield: 6-8 servings.**

Very Raspberry Pie

We live along a 130-year-old railroad track—our house once was a train station—edged a couple weeks a year with wild raspberries that I pick for my pie.
—Kathy Jones, West Winfield, New York

RASPBERRY TOPPING:

- **6 cups fresh *or* frozen unsweetened raspberries, thawed**
- **1 cup sugar**
- **3 tablespoons cornstarch**
- **1/2 cup cold water**

CREAM FILLING:

- **1 package (8 ounces) cream cheese, softened**
- **1 cup whipped topping**
- **1 cup confectioners' sugar**
- **1 graham cracker crust (9 inches)**

Fresh mint, optional

Mash about 2 cups raspberries to measure 1 cup; place in a large saucepan. Combine the sugar, cornstarch and water until smooth. Gradually stir into pan. Bring to a boil; cook and stir for 2 minutes or until thickened. Strain to remove berry seeds if desired. Cool to room temperature, about 20 minutes.

Meanwhile, for filling, in a large mixing bowl beat cream cheese and confectioners' sugar until smooth. Fold in whipped topping. Spread over bottom of the crust. Top with remaining raspberries. Pour cooled raspberry sauce over top. Refrigerate until set, about 3 hours. Store in the refrigerator. Garnish with mint if desired. **Yield: 6-8 servings.**

Black Forest Pie

With three active children, I don't usually fuss with fancy desserts. This one is simple but impressive—it's the one I make to show how much I care. The tempting combination of chocolate and tangy red cherries is guaranteed to make anyone feel special.
—Trudy Black, Dedham, Massachusetts

- 3/4 cup sugar
- 1/3 cup baking cocoa
- 2 tablespoons all-purpose flour
- 1/3 cup milk
- 1/4 cup butter, cubed
- 2 eggs, lightly beaten
- 1 can (21 ounces) cherry pie filling, *divided*
- 1 unbaked pastry shell (9 inches)

Whipped topping, optional

In a small saucepan, combine the sugar, cocoa and flour. Stir in milk until smooth. Add butter. Cook and stir over medium-high heat until thickened and bubbly. Reduce heat; cook and stir 2 minutes longer.

Remove from the heat. Stir a small amount of hot filling into eggs; return all to pan, stirring constantly. Fold in half of the pie filling.

Pour into pastry shell. Bake at 350° for 35-40 minutes or until filling is almost set. Cool completely on a wire rack. Just before serving, top with remaining pie filling and whipped topping if desired. **Yield: 6-8 servings.**

Very Raspberry Pie

Black Forest Pie

Peanut Butter Pie

Peanut Butter Pie

This creamy pie is always a special treat at our house. I haven't met anyone who doesn't like it.
—Gloria Pittman, Shelby, North Carolina

- 1/3 cup creamy peanut butter
- 1 package (3 ounces) cream cheese, softened
- 2 tablespoons butter, softened
- 1 cup confectioners' sugar
- 1/4 cup milk
- 1 carton (8 ounces) frozen whipped topping, thawed
- 1 chocolate crumb crust (9 inches)
- 2 tablespoons chopped peanuts, optional
- Chocolate curls, optional

In a large mixing bowl, beat the peanut butter, cream cheese and butter until smooth. Add sugar and milk; fold in whipped topping. Pour into the crust.

Cover and freeze for at least 4 hours. Remove from the freezer just before serving. Garnish with peanuts and chocolate curls if desired. **Yield: 6 servings.**

DESSERTS

EMON WHIRLIGIGS WITH RASPBERRIES, pg. 459

Desserts

Chocolate Peanut Delight

Peanut lovers will appreciate this yummy dessert I dreamed up. A brownie-like crust is packed with nuts, topped with a fluffy peanut butter layer and covered with whipped topping and more nuts. It was so well received that I made it for a local restaurant where I used to work. —*Karen Kutruff, New Berlin, Pennsylvania*

- 1 package (18-1/4 ounces) chocolate cake mix
- 1/2 cup butter, melted
- 1/4 cup milk
- 1 egg
- 1 cup chopped peanuts, *divided*
- 1 package (8 ounces) cream cheese, softened
- 1 cup peanut butter
- 1 cup confectioners' sugar
- 1 can (14 ounces) sweetened condensed milk
- 1-1/2 teaspoons vanilla extract
- 1 carton (16 ounces) frozen whipped topping, thawed, *divided*
- 1/2 cup semisweet chocolate chips
- 4-1/2 teaspoons butter
- 1/2 teaspoon vanilla extract

In a large mixing bowl, combine dry cake mix, butter, milk and egg. Add 3/4 cup of peanuts. Spread into a greased 13-in. x 9-in. x 2-in. baking pan. Bake at 350° for 30 minutes or until a toothpick inserted near the center comes out clean. Cool on a wire rack.

Chocolate Peanut Delight

In a large mixing bowl, beat the cream cheese, peanut butter, sugar, condensed milk and vanilla until smooth. Fold in 3 cups whipped topping. Spread over the crust; top with the remaining whipped topping and peanuts.

Microwave chocolate chips and butter until melted, stirring until smooth. Stir in vanilla; drizzle over the dessert. Refrigerate for 2-3 hours before cutting. **Yield: 12-15 servings.**

Snappy Pumpkin Dessert

Snappy Pumpkin Dessert

Our town has a pumpkin-canning factory, so we're known as the "Pumpkin Capital of the World." New pumpkin recipes are always welcomed by our family. This one's a favorite.

—Nilah Fischer, Morton, Illinois

- 2-1/2 cups finely crushed gingersnaps (about 40 cookies)
- 1/2 cup butter, melted
- 1 package (8 ounces) cream cheese, softened
- 1/2 cup confectioners' sugar
- 2 tablespoons milk

TOPPING:

- 3 cups cold milk
- 2 packages (3.4 ounces *each*) instant vanilla pudding mix
- 1 can (15 ounces) solid-pack pumpkin
- 2-1/2 teaspoons pumpkin pie spice
- 2 cups whipped topping

Additional whipped topping, optional

In a large bowl, combine gingersnap crumbs and butter; press into an ungreased 13-in. x 9-in. x 2-in. baking pan. Bake at 325° for 10 minutes. Cool.

In a large mixing bowl, beat the cream cheese, confectioners' sugar and milk until smooth. Spread over the crust. In another large mixing bowl, whisk milk and pudding mix for 1 minute. Add pumpkin and pie spice; whisk until well blended.

Fold in whipped topping. Spread over the cream cheese layer. Refrigerate for at least 3 hours. Cut into squares; garnish with whipped topping if desired. **Yield: 12-15 servings.**

Valentine Berries And Cream 1st prize

Everyone was so impressed with this scrumptious chocolate-filled chocolate heart served at a banquet held by our adult Sunday school class. I got the recipe, and now I enjoy rave reviews from family and friends when I serve it.

—Tamera O'Sullivan, Apple Valley, Minnesota

- 8 squares (1 ounce *each*) semisweet chocolate
- 1 tablespoon shortening
- 2 packages (3 ounces *each*) cream cheese, softened
- 1/4 cup butter, softened
- 1-1/2 cups confectioners' sugar
- 1/3 cup baking cocoa
- 2 tablespoons milk
- 1 teaspoon vanilla extract
- 2-1/2 cups heavy whipping cream, whipped, *divided*
- 1-1/2 cups fresh strawberries, halved

Line a 9-in. heart-shaped or square baking pan with foil; set aside. In a large heavy saucepan over low heat, melt chocolate and shortening, stirring until smooth. Pour into prepared pan, swirling to coat the bottom and 1-1/2 in. up the sides.

Refrigerate for 1 minute, then swirl the

chocolate to reinforce sides of heart pan. Refrigerate for 30 minutes or until firm. Using foil, lift from pan; remove foil and place chocolate heart on a serving plate.

In a large mixing bowl, beat the cream cheese and butter until smooth. Combine confectioners' sugar and cocoa; add to creamed mixture along with milk and vanilla. Beat until smooth.

Gently fold two-thirds of the whipped cream into cream cheese mixture. Spoon into heart. Insert star tip #32 into a pastry or plastic bag; fill with the remaining whipped cream. Pipe around the edge of heart. Garnish with strawberries. **Yield: 8-10 servings.**

Mocha Fondue

People have such fun dipping pieces of cake and fruit into this heavenly melted chocolate mixture. It's an exquisite treat to serve at wedding and baby showers or for other special gatherings. I've found it to be a welcome part of any buffet.
—Gloria Jarrett, Loveland, Ohio

- 3 cups (18 ounces) milk chocolate chips
- 1/2 cup heavy whipping cream
- 1 tablespoon instant coffee granules
- 2 tablespoons hot water
- 1 teaspoon vanilla extract
- 1/8 teaspoon ground cinnamon
- 1 pound cake (16 ounces), cut into 1-inch cubes
- Strawberries, kiwi *or* other fresh fruit

In a heavy saucepan, melt chocolate with cream over low heat, stirring constantly. Dissolve coffee in water; add to chocolate mixture with vanilla and cinnamon. Mix well. Serve warm, using cake pieces and fruit for dipping. **Yield: 2 cups.**

Valentine Berries and Cream

Mocha Fondue

Heart's Delight Eclair

Cream Puff Dessert

Heart's Delight Eclair

This lovely and luscious treat is rumored to have been the favorite dessert of European royalty long ago. I know that it's won the hearts of everyone I've ever made it for. Enjoy!

—Lorene Milligan, Chemainus, British Columbia

- 1 package (17-1/4 ounces) frozen puff pastry, thawed
- 3 cups cold milk
- 1 package (5.1 ounces) instant vanilla pudding mix
- 2 cups heavy whipping cream
- 1 teaspoon vanilla extract, *divided*
- 1 cup confectioners' sugar
- 1 tablespoon water
- 1/4 teaspoon almond extract
- 1/2 cup semisweet chocolate chips
- 1 teaspoon shortening

On a lightly floured surface, roll each puff pastry sheet into a 12-in. square. Using an 11-in. heart pattern, cut each pastry into a heart shape. Place on greased baking sheets. Bake at 400° for 12-15 minutes or until golden brown. Remove to wire racks to cool.

Meanwhile, whisk milk and pudding mix until thickened. In a large mixing bowl, beat cream and 1/2 teaspoon of vanilla until stiff peaks form. Carefully fold into pudding.

Split puff pastry hearts in half. Place one layer on a serving plate. Top with a third of the pudding mixture. Repeat twice. Top with remaining pastry.

In a bowl, combine the confectioners' sugar, water, almond extract and the remaining vanilla until smooth. Spread over top.

Melt chocolate chips and shortening; pipe in diagonal lines in one direction over frosting. Beginning 1 in. from side of heart, use a sharp knife to draw right angles across the piped lines. Refrigerate until set. **Yield: 10-12 servings.**

Cream Puff Dessert

I recently took this rich dessert to a fellowship meeting at our church. Everyone loved it! In fact, so many people asked for the recipe that the church secretary printed it in our monthly newsletter.

—Lisa Nash, Blaine, Minnesota

- 1 cup water
- 1/2 cup butter
- 1 cup all-purpose flour
- 4 eggs

FILLING:

- 1 package (8 ounces) cream cheese, softened
- 3-1/2 cups cold milk
- 2 packages (3.9 ounces *each*) instant chocolate pudding mix

TOPPING:

- 1 carton (8 ounces) frozen whipped topping, thawed
- 1/4 cup milk chocolate ice cream topping
- 1/4 cup caramel ice cream topping
- 1/3 cup chopped almonds

In a large saucepan, bring water and butter to a boil over medium heat. Add flour all at once; stir until a smooth ball forms. Remove from the heat; let stand for 5 minutes. Add the eggs, one at a time, beating well after each addition. Beat until smooth.

Spread into a greased 13-in. x 9-in. x 2-in. baking dish. Bake at 400° for 30-35 minutes or until puffed and golden brown. Cool completely on a wire rack.

Meanwhile, in a large mixing bowl, beat the cream cheese, milk and pudding mix until smooth. Spread over puff; refrigerate for 20 minutes. Spread with whipped topping; refrigerate until serving. Drizzle with chocolate and caramel toppings; sprinkle with almonds. Store leftovers in the refrigerator. **Yield: 12 servings.**

Strawberry Shortcake Cups

Strawberry Shortcake Cups

Back when store-bought shortcake was an unheard-of thing, my grandmother passed this recipe down to my mother. Mother later shared it with me, and I've since given it to my daughter.

—Althea Heers, Jewell, Iowa

- 1 quart fresh strawberries
- 4 tablespoons sugar, *divided*
- 1-1/2 cups all-purpose flour
- 1 tablespoon baking powder
- 1/2 teaspoon salt
- 1/4 cup cold butter, cubed
- 1 egg
- 1/2 cup milk
- Whipped cream

Mash or slice the strawberries; place in a large bowl. Add 2 tablespoons sugar and set aside. In another bowl, combine the flour, baking powder, salt and remaining sugar; cut in butter until crumbly. In a small bowl, beat egg and milk; stir into flour mixture just until moistened.

Fill eight greased muffin cups two-thirds full. Bake at 425° for 12 minutes or until golden. Remove from the pan to cool on a wire rack.

Just before serving, split shortcakes in half horizontally. Spoon berries and whipped cream between layers and over the top. **Yield: 8 servings.**

Pecan Pumpkin Dessert

Pecan Pumpkin Dessert

I always fix this recipe for Thanksgiving. It was given to me by a friend, and I've shared it with many others. —Sue Williams, Mt. Holly, North Carolina

- 2 cans (15 ounces *each*) solid-pack pumpkin
- 1 can (12 ounces) evaporated milk
- 1 cup sugar
- 3 eggs
- 1 teaspoon vanilla extract
- 1 package (18-1/4 ounces) yellow cake mix
- 1 cup butter, melted
- 1-1/2 cups chopped pecans

FROSTING:

- 1 package (8 ounces) cream cheese, softened
- 1-1/2 cups confectioners' sugar
- 1 teaspoon vanilla extract
- 1 carton (12 ounces) frozen whipped topping, thawed

Line a 13-in. x 9-in. x 2-in. baking pan with waxed paper and coat the paper with nonstick cooking spray; set aside.

In a large mixing bowl, combine the pumpkin, milk and sugar. Beat in eggs and vanilla. Pour into prepared pan. Sprinkle with dry cake mix and drizzle with butter. Sprinkle with pecans.

Bake at 350° for 1 hour or until golden brown. Cool completely in pan on a wire rack. Invert onto a large serving platter; carefully remove waxed paper.

In a large mixing bowl, beat the cream cheese, confectioners' sugar and vanilla until smooth. Fold in whipped topping. Frost dessert. Store in the refrigerator. **Yield: 16 servings.**

Easy Rhubarb Dessert

This is a very tasty and attractive dessert. It's great served warm with ice cream.

—Mildred Mesick, Richmond, New York

- 4 cups sliced fresh *or* frozen rhubarb
- 1 package (3 ounces) raspberry gelatin
- 1/3 cup sugar
- 1 package (18-1/4 ounces) yellow *or* white cake mix
- 1 cup water
- 1/3 cup butter, melted

Ice cream, optional

Place rhubarb in a greased 13-in. x 9-in. x 2-in. baking dish. Sprinkle with the gelatin, sugar and cake mix. Pour water evenly over dry ingredients; drizzle with butter.

Bake at 350° for 1 hour or until rhubarb is tender. To serve, spoon into a bowl, then top with ice cream if desired. **Yield: 16-20 servings.**

Editor's Note: If using frozen rhubarb, measure rhubarb while still frozen, then thaw completely. Drain in a colander, but do not press liquid out.

Fried Sweet Potato Pies

With my dad being a farmer who grew them, sweet potatoes have graced our table for as long as I can recall. These, though, resulted from an experiment at a church bake sale when we had excess pastry. People couldn't get enough!

—Marilyn Moseley, Toccoa, Georgia

- 4-1/2 cups self-rising flour
- 3 tablespoons sugar
- 1/2 cup shortening
- 2 eggs
- 1 cup milk

FILLING:

- 3 cups mashed sweet potatoes
- 2 cups sugar
- 3 eggs, lightly beaten
- 1 can (5 ounces) evaporated milk
- 1/4 cup butter, melted
- 3 tablespoons all-purpose flour
- 1 teaspoon vanilla extract

Oil for deep-fat frying

Confectioners' sugar, optional

In a large bowl, combine flour and sugar; cut in shortening until mixture resembles coarse crumbs. Combine eggs and milk; add to crumb mixture, tossing with a fork until a ball forms. Cover and chill several hours.

In a large bowl, combine the seven filling ingredients; stir until smooth. Divide the dough into 25 portions. On a floured surface, roll each portion into a 5-in. circle. Spoon 2 tablespoons of filling on half of each circle. Moisten edges with water; fold dough over filling and press edges with a fork to seal. Prick tops with a fork 4-5 times.

In an electric skillet, heat 1/2 in. of oil to 375°. Fry pies, a few at a time, for 1 minute on each side or until golden brown. Drain on paper towels. Dust with confectioners' sugar if desired. Store in the refrigerator. **Yield: 25 pies.**

Editor's Note: As a substitute for the self-rising flour, place 6-3/4 teaspoons baking powder and 2-1/4 teaspoons salt in a measuring cup. Add all-purpose flour to measure 1 cup. Add 3-1/2 cups more of all-purpose flour to the recipe.

Easy Rhubarb Dessert

Fried Sweet Potato Pies

Raspberry Marshmallow Delight

Blueberry Angel Dessert

Raspberry Marshmallow Delight

This is one of our family's favorite desserts. It has a tangy, unique flavor. After a hard day of working on the farm, this fruity treat is most welcome.
—Gloria Iden, Kimmell, Indiana

- 1-1/4 cups graham cracker crumbs
- 1/4 cup butter, melted
- 50 large marshmallows
- 1 cup milk
- 1 carton (8 ounces) frozen whipped topping, thawed
- 2 packages (10 ounces *each*) frozen sweetened raspberries
- 1-1/4 cups water, *divided*
- 1/2 cup sugar
- 2 teaspoons lemon juice
- 6 tablespoons cornstarch
- Whipped cream and fresh raspberries, optional

Combine crumbs and butter; press into the bottom of a greased 13-in. x 9-in. x 2-in. baking pan. Bake at 350° for 10 minutes. Cool.

In a large saucepan over medium heat, stir marshmallows and milk until marshmallows are melted. Cool to room temperature. Fold in whipped topping; spread over crust.

In a large saucepan, bring raspberries, 1 cup water, sugar and lemon juice to a boil. Combine cornstarch and remaining water until smooth; stir into raspberry mixture. Boil and stir for 2 minutes or until thickened. Cool to room temperature. Spread over marshmallow layer.

Chill until firm, about 4 hours. Garnish with whipped cream and raspberries if desired. **Yield: 12-16 servings.**

Blueberry Angel Dessert

Make the most of angel food cake, pie filling and whipped topping by creating this light, impressive dessert that doesn't keep you in the kitchen for hours. It's the perfect way to end a summer meal. I frequently get requests for the recipe.

—Carol Johnson, Tyler, Texas

- 1 package (8 ounces) cream cheese, softened
- 1 cup confectioners' sugar
- 1 carton (8 ounces) frozen whipped topping, thawed
- 1 prepared angel food cake (16 ounces), cut into 1-inch pieces
- 2 cans (21 ounces *each*) blueberry pie filling

In a large mixing bowl, beat cream cheese and sugar until smooth; fold in whipped topping and cake cubes. Spread evenly into an ungreased 13-in. x 9-in. x 2-in dish; top with pie filling. Cover and refrigerate for at least 2 hours before cutting into squares. **Yield: 12-15 servings.**

Lemon Custard in Meringue Cups

My husband loves lemon meringue pie. This variation is a favorite of his. I like it, too—it's very easy to make but looks very elegant. I've served it at every occasion from a formal dinner party to just a casual get-together. Ever since I was a young girl, making desserts has been a favorite hobby. Over the years, I've filled two binders with recipes for them!

—Marie Frangipane, Eugene, Oregon

- 3 eggs, *separated*
- 1/2 teaspoon white vinegar
- 1/4 teaspoon vanilla extract
- 1/4 teaspoon salt, *divided*
- 2 cups sugar, *divided*

Lemon Custard in Meringue Cups

- 1/3 cup cornstarch
- 1-1/2 cups water
- 6 tablespoons fresh lemon juice
- 2 tablespoons butter
- 1 tablespoon grated lemon peel

Sweetened whipped cream

In a large mixing bowl, beat the egg whites, vinegar, vanilla and 1/8 teaspoon salt until soft peaks form. Gradually add 1 cup sugar, 2 tablespoons at a time, beating on high until stiff peaks form.

Line baking sheet with parchment paper. Spoon egg white mixture into eight mounds on paper. Shape into cups with a spoon. Bake at 300° for 35 minutes. Turn oven off and leave door closed; let shells dry in oven for at least 1 hour. Remove shells from paper. When thoroughly cooled, store in an airtight container.

For custard, in a large bowl, combine the cornstarch and the remaining salt and sugar; gradually add the water, stirring until smooth. Cook and stir over medium-high heat until thickened and bubbly. Reduce heat; cook and stir 2 minutes longer. Remove from the heat. Beat egg yolks. Stir a small amount of hot filling into egg yolks; return all to pan, stirring constantly. Bring to a gentle boil; cook and stir 2 minutes longer. Remove from the heat. Gently stir in the lemon juice, butter and peel.

Refrigerate until chilled. Just before serving, fill meringue shells with custard and top with whipped cream. **Yield: 8 servings.**

Brownie Baked Alaska

This cool and chocolaty dessert looks like I fussed, when really, it's easy to put together. No one can resist the combination of brownies and two kinds of ice cream with a light meringue topping.
—*Carol Twardzik, Spy Hill, Saskatchewan*

- 2 squares (1 ounce *each*) unsweetened chocolate
- 1/2 cup shortening
- 1 cup sugar
- 1 teaspoon vanilla extract
- 2 eggs
- 3/4 cup all-purpose flour
- 1/2 teaspoon baking powder
- 1/2 teaspoon salt
- 1 cup chopped walnuts, optional
- 1 quart strawberry ice cream, slightly softened
- 1 quart vanilla ice cream, slightly softened

MERINGUE:

- 5 egg whites
- 2/3 cup sugar
- 1/2 teaspoon cream of tartar

Brownie Baked Alaska

In a large saucepan, melt chocolate and shortening; remove from the heat. Stir in sugar and vanilla. Add eggs, one at a time, beating well after each addition. Combine the flour, baking powder and salt; stir into chocolate mixture. Add nuts if desired.

Spread into a greased 9-in. round baking pan. Bake at 350° for 20-25 minutes or until a toothpick inserted near the center comes out with moist crumbs (do not overbake). Cool for 10 minutes before removing from pan to a wire rack to cool completely.

Meanwhile, line an 8-in. or 9-in. round bowl (1-1/2 qts.) with foil. Quickly spread strawberry ice cream over bottom and up sides of bowl, leaving center hollow; cover and freeze for 30 minutes. Pack vanilla ice cream into center; cover and freeze.

To assemble, place the brownie base on a 10-in. ovenproof serving plate. Unmold ice cream onto brownie. Return to freezer while preparing meringue.

In a heavy saucepan or double boiler over simmering water, combine egg whites, sugar and cream of tartar. Heat over low heat while beating egg white mixture with a portable mixer on low speed for 1 minute, scraping down sides of bowl. Continue beating until mixture reaches 160°. Remove from the heat. Beat on high speed until stiff peaks form.

Quickly spread over ice cream and brownie. Bake at 500° for 2-5 minutes or until meringue is lightly browned. (Or return to freezer until ready to bake.) Transfer to a serving plate; serve immediately. **Yield: 12 servings.**

Chocolate Souffle

My family considers this recipe to be part of our heritage. It came from my Aunt Clara, whose cooking was a blend of her country and rural French roots.
—*Carol Ice, Burlingham, New York*

- 2 squares (1 ounce *each*) unsweetened chocolate
- 1/4 cup butter, cubed

Chocolate Souffle

- 5 tablespoons all-purpose flour
- 1/3 cup plus 1 teaspoon sugar, *divided*
- 1/4 teaspoon salt
- 1 cup milk
- 3 eggs, *separated*
- 1 teaspoon vanilla extract
- 1/4 teaspoon almond extract

SAUCE:

- 1 cup heavy whipping cream
- 1/4 cup confectioners' sugar
- 1/4 teaspoon vanilla extract

Baking cocoa *or* ground cinnamon, optional

In a large heavy saucepan, melt chocolate and butter over low heat, stirring until smooth. In a small bowl, combine the flour, 1/3 cup sugar and salt; add milk and stir until smooth. Stir into melted chocolate. Cook and stir over medium heat until thickened and bubbly. Reduce heat; cook and stir 2 minutes longer. Remove from the heat.

In a small bowl, beat egg yolks. Stir a small amount of filling into yolks; return all to the pan, stirring constantly. Add extracts.

In a small mixing, beat egg whites on medium speed until soft peaks form. Gradually beat in remaining sugar on high until stiff peaks form. With a spatula, stir a fourth of the egg whites into chocolate batter until no white streaks remain, then fold in remaining egg whites.

Grease the bottom of 1-1/2-qt. baking dish; add souffle batter. Place dish in a larger pan. Fill large pan with hot water to a depth of 1 in. Bake at 325° for 1 hour or until a knife inserted near the center comes out clean.

For topping, in a small mixing bowl, beat the cream until it begins to thicken. Add confectioners' sugar and vanilla; beat until soft peaks form. Serve souffle warm with a dollop of sauce. Sprinkle with cocoa or cinnamon if desired. **Yield: 6 servings.**

Lemony Apple Dumplings

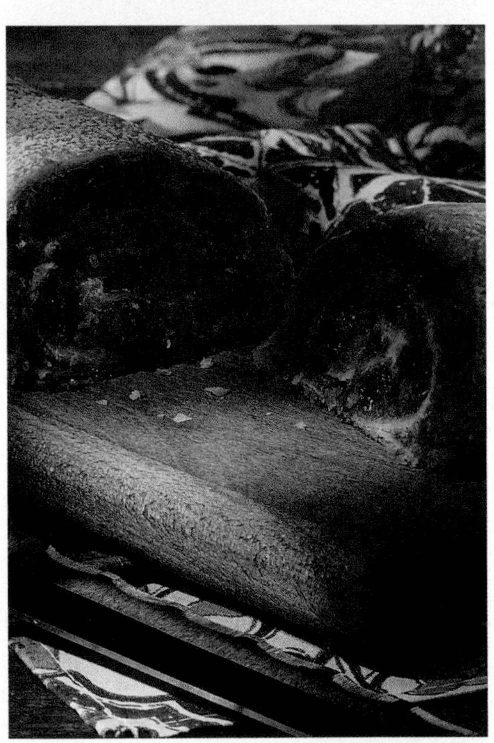

Apple Strudel

Lemony Apple Dumplings

The first time I made this recipe, I was serving guests who had two little daughters. The girls proclaimed the treat yummy and cleaned their plates.
—Kristy Deloach, Baker, Louisiana

- 1-1/2 cups all-purpose flour
- 1-1/4 teaspoons salt, *divided*
- 1/3 cup shortening
- 4 to 5 tablespoons cold milk
- 1/2 cup packed brown sugar
- 3 tablespoons butter, softened
- 1/2 teaspoon ground cinnamon
- 4 medium tart apples, peeled and cored
- 1 egg white, beaten

LEMON SAUCE:

- 1/2 cup sugar
- 4 teaspoons cornstarch
- 1 cup cold water
- 3 tablespoons butter
- 4 teaspoons lemon juice
- 2 teaspoons grated lemon peel
- 1/8 teaspoon salt

Combine flour and 1 teaspoon salt. Cut in shortening until crumbly. Gradually add milk, tossing with a fork until dough forms a ball; set aside. Stir together the brown sugar, butter, cinnamon and remaining salt to form a paste. Divide and press into center of each apple; pat any extra filling on outside of apples.

On a floured surface, roll pastry into a 14-in. square. Cut into four 7-in. squares. Place one apple in center of each square. Brush edges of pastry with egg white. Fold up corners to center; pinch to seal.

Place in a greased 9-in. square baking dish. Bake at 375° for 35-40 minutes or until golden brown. Combine sugar and cornstarch in a saucepan. Stir in water. Bring to a boil; cook and stir for 2 minutes. Remove from the

Gingered Apricot-Apple Crumble

heat; stir in remaining ingredients until smooth. Serve warm over warm dumplings. **Yield: 4 servings.**

Apple Strudel

This is one of my favorite recipes during autumn. The aroma of this dessert is absolutely wonderful on a cool, crisp day. —*Helen Lesh, Forsyth, Missouri*

- 1 cup cold butter
- 2 cups all-purpose flour
- 1 cup (8 ounces) sour cream
- 1/4 teaspoon salt

FILLING:

- 2 cups dry bread crumbs
- 1/4 cup butter, melted
- 4 medium tart apples, peeled and chopped
- 2 cups sugar
- 1 cup golden raisins
- 1/2 cup chopped pecans
- 2 teaspoons ground cinnamon

Confectioners' sugar, optional

In a medium bowl, cut butter into flour until mixture resembles coarse crumbs. Add sour cream and salt; mix well. Shape the dough into a ball; cover and refrigerate overnight.

For filling, combine the bread crumbs and butter. Add the next five ingredients; mix well and set aside. Divide dough into thirds; turn onto a floured surface. Roll each into a 15-in. x 12-in. rectangle; spread filling to within 1 in. of edges. Roll up from one long side; pinch seams and ends to seal.

Carefully place each loaf seam side down on an ungreased baking sheet. Bake at 350° for 55-60 minutes or until light brown. Cool completely on wire racks. Dust with confectioners' sugar if desired. **Yield: 3 loaves.**

Gingered Apricot-Apple Crumble 1st prize

Hot or cold, plain or topped with ice cream, this crumble is tasty. —*Sylvia Rice, Didsbury, Alberta*

- 1 cup apricot nectar
- 3/4 cup finely chopped dried apricots
- 1/3 cup honey
- 1/4 cup maple syrup
- 2 tablespoons lemon juice
- 8 cups sliced peeled tart apples (about 8 large)
- 3 tablespoons all-purpose flour
- 1 teaspoon ground cinnamon
- 1/2 teaspoon ground ginger
- 1/2 teaspoon ground cardamom

TOPPING:

- 3/4 cup all-purpose flour
- 1/2 cup quick-cooking oats
- 1/2 cup chopped pecans, optional
- 1/4 cup vegetable oil
- 1/4 cup maple syrup

In a large bowl, combine the first five ingredients; set aside. Arrange apples in an ungreased 13-in. x 9-in. x 2-in. baking dish. Combine the flour and spices; stir into apricot mixture. Spoon over apples.

Combine topping ingredients; sprinkle over fruit. Bake, uncovered, at 350° for 50-60 minutes or until topping is golden brown and fruit is tender. **Yield: 12 servings.**

Caramel Apricot Grunt

We enjoyed this recipe at my grandmother's house for years. It's perfect for dessert or church socials.
—Shari Dore, Brantford, Ontario

- 2 cans (15-1/4 ounces *each*) apricot halves, undrained
- 2 teaspoons quick-cooking tapioca
- 1/3 cup packed brown sugar
- 1 tablespoon butter
- 1 tablespoon lemon juice

DUMPLINGS:

- 1-1/2 cups all-purpose flour
- 1/2 cup sugar
- 2 teaspoons baking powder
- 2 tablespoons cold butter
- 1/2 cup milk

TOPPING:

- 1/4 cup packed brown sugar
- 2 tablespoons water

Half-and-half cream, optional

In a large saucepan, combine apricots and tapioca; let stand for 15 minutes. Add the brown sugar, butter and lemon juice. Cook and stir until mixture comes to a full boil. Reduce heat to low; keep warm.

For dumplings, in a large bowl, combine the flour, sugar and baking powder; cut in butter until crumbly. Add milk; mix just until combined. Pour warm fruit mixture into an ungreased 2-qt. baking dish (mixture will be very thick). Drop the batter into six mounds onto fruit mixture. Cover and bake at 425° for 15 minutes or until a toothpick inserted into a dumpling comes out clean (do not lift the cover while baking).

In a small saucepan, bring brown sugar and water to a boil; cook until sugar is dissolved. Spoon over dumplings; bake, uncovered, 5 minutes longer. Serve with cream if desired. **Yield: 6 servings.**

Caramel Apricot Grunt

Blackberry Dumplings

As long as I can remember, my mother has been making Blackberry Dumplings. They finish cooking while you eat—and they really do make you hurry through dinner! *—Liecha Collins, Oneonta, New York*

- 1 quart fresh *or* frozen (loose-pack) blackberries
- 1 cup plus 1 tablespoon sugar, *divided*
- 3/4 teaspoon salt, *divided*
- 1/2 teaspoon lemon extract
- 1-1/2 cups all-purpose flour
- 2 teaspoons baking powder
- 1/4 teaspoon ground nutmeg
- 2/3 cup milk

Half-and-half cream *or* whipped cream, optional

In a Dutch oven, combine the blackberries, 1 cup sugar, 1/4 teaspoon salt and lemon extract. Bring to a boil; reduce heat and simmer for 5 minutes.

Meanwhile, in a large bowl, combine the flour, baking powder, nutmeg and remaining sugar and salt. Add milk; stir just until mixed. (Dough will be very thick.)

Drop by tablespoonfuls into six mounds onto hot blackberry mixture; cover and simmer for 15 minutes or until a toothpick inserted in a dumpling comes out clean (do not lift the lid while cooking). Spoon into serving dishes. Serve with cream or whipped cream if desired. **Yield: 6-8 servings.**

Northern Cherry Puffs

This is one of my family's favorite cherry recipes.
—Barbara Hanmer, Benzonia, Michigan

- 1 cup fresh *or* frozen pitted dark sweet cherries, thawed and drained
- 1 tablespoon lemon juice
- 1-1/2 teaspoons almond extract, *divided*
- 1/4 teaspoon red food coloring, optional
- 1/3 cup shortening
- 2/3 cup sugar
- 1 egg
- 1 cup all-purpose flour
- 1/2 teaspoon baking powder
- 1/2 teaspoon salt
- 1/3 cup milk

SAUCE:

- 1/2 cup sugar
- 4-1/2 teaspoons cornstarch
- 1/4 cup water
- 2 cups fresh *or* frozen pitted dark sweet cherries
- 1/4 teaspoon red food coloring, optional

Whipped cream *or* vanilla ice cream

In a bowl, combine cherries, lemon juice, 1/2 teaspoon extract and food coloring if desired. Spoon into four greased 10-oz. custard cups.

In a mixing bowl, cream shortening and sugar. Beat in egg and remaining extract. Combine dry ingredients; add to the creamed mixture alternately with milk. Spoon over cherries.

Bake, uncovered, at 375° for 20-25 minutes or until golden brown. Cool in cups for 10 minutes.

In a large saucepan, combine sugar and cornstarch. Stir in water until blended. Add cherries and food coloring if desired. Bring to a boil over medium heat; cook and stir for 2 minutes or until thickened. Invert puffs onto dessert plates; top with warm cherry sauce and whipped cream. **Yield: 4 servings.**

Blackberry Dumplings

Northern Cherry Puffs

Date Pudding Cobbler

Peach Pizza Pie

Date Pudding Cobbler

There were eight children in my family when I was a girl, and all of us enjoyed this cobbler. I now serve it for everyday and special occasions alike.

—Carolyn Miller, Guys Mills, Pennsylvania

- 1 cup all-purpose flour
- 1-1/2 cups packed brown sugar, *divided*
- 2 teaspoons baking powder
- 1 tablespoon cold butter
- 1/2 cup milk
- 3/4 cup chopped dates
- 3/4 cup chopped walnuts
- 1 cup water
- Whipped cream and ground cinnamon, optional

In a large bowl, combine the flour, 1/2 cup brown sugar and baking powder. Cut in butter until crumbly. Gradually add the milk, dates and walnuts.

In a large saucepan, combine water and remaining brown sugar; bring to a boil. Remove from the heat; add the date mixture and mix well.

Transfer to a greased 8-in. square baking dish. Bake at 350° for 25-30 minutes or until top is golden brown and fruit is tender. Serve warm. **Yield: 6-8 servings.**

Peach Pizza Pie

We have very good peach orchards in our state, so I'm always on the lookout for recipes with peaches in them. My family and friends have enjoyed this dessert for many years.

—Ann Kidd, Lewes, Delaware

- 1/2 cup butter, softened
- 1/4 cup confectioners' sugar
- 1 cup all-purpose flour
- 4 to 5 cups sliced fresh peaches

Apricot Peach Cobbler

GLAZE:

- 2 tablespoons sugar
- 1 tablespoon cornstarch
- 1/8 to 1/4 teaspoon ground mace, optional
- 1/2 cup orange juice
- 1/2 cup red currant jelly

Whipped cream, optional

In a mixing bowl, cream butter and sugar until light and fluffy, about 5 minutes. Add flour and mix well. Pat into a greased 12-in. pizza pan; prick with a fork. Bake at 350° for 10-15 minutes or until golden. Cool completely.

Arrange peach slices on crust. In a large saucepan, mix sugar, cornstarch and mace if desired. Add orange juice and jelly. Bring to a boil over medium heat; cook and stir for 2 minutes or until thickened.

Remove from the heat and cool slightly, about 5 minutes. Spoon over peaches. Chill for 1 hour or until set. Garnish with whipped cream if desired and serve immediately. **Yield: 12-15 servings.**

Apricot Peach Cobbler

Whenever I'm baking with apricots, I recall picking them fresh from my aunt's tree more than 25 years ago. This comforting cobbler has a crumb topping that is super. —Tobi Breternitz, Bay Port, Michigan

- 1 can (29 ounces) sliced peaches
- 1 can (15-1/4 ounces) apricot halves
- 1/2 cup sugar
- 2 tablespoons cornstarch
- 1/2 teaspoon ground cinnamon
- 1/4 teaspoon ground nutmeg
- 1 tablespoon butter

TOPPING:

- 1/2 cup all-purpose flour
- 1/2 cup sugar
- 3/4 teaspoon baking powder
- 1/4 teaspoon salt
- 1 egg
- 2 tablespoons butter, softened

HONEY CREAM:

- 1 cup heavy whipping cream
- 2 tablespoons honey
- 1/2 teaspoon ground cinnamon

Drain peaches, reserving 1/2 cup syrup. Drain apricots, reserving 1/2 cup syrup. Cut apricots in half; set fruit aside.

In a large saucepan, combine the sugar, cornstarch, cinnamon, nutmeg and reserved syrups until smooth. Bring to a boil; cook and stir for 2 minutes or until thickened. Remove from the heat; stir in butter until melted. Stir in peaches and apricots. Transfer to a greased 8-in. square baking dish.

For topping, in a bowl, combine flour, sugar, baking powder and salt. Add egg and butter; mix well. Spoon over fruit. Bake at 350° for 40-45 minutes or until golden brown.

In a mixing bowl, beat the cream, honey and cinnamon until stiff peaks form. Serve with warm cobbler. **Yield: 6-8 servings.**

Colorado Peach Cobbler

Colorado Peach Cobbler

My husband and I live on our ranch/wheat farm. I've served this dessert for family, hired help and guests many times. I've used other fruits that are in season, but we like peaches best.

—Clara Hinman, Flagler, Colorado

- 1 cup sugar
- 2 tablespoons all-purpose flour
- 1/4 teaspoon ground nutmeg
- 4 cups sliced peeled fresh peaches

TOPPING:

- 1 cup sugar
- 1 cup all-purpose flour
- 1 teaspoon baking powder
- 1 teaspoon salt
- 1/3 cup cold butter
- 1 egg, beaten

Ice cream, optional

In a large bowl, combine the sugar, flour and nutmeg. Add peaches; stir to coat. Pour into a greased 11-in. x 7-in. x 2-in. baking pan.

For topping, in a small bowl, combine the sugar, flour, baking powder and salt; cut in the butter until the mixture resembles fine crumbs. Stir in egg. Spoon over peaches.

Bake at 375° for 35-40 minutes or until filling is bubbly and topping is golden. Serve hot or cold with ice cream if desired. **Yield: 8-10 servings.**

Pear Crisp

Since he's a livestock truck driver, my husband often starts work around 2 or 3 a.m. A piece of this crisp will keep him going until breakfast.

—Joanne Korevaar, Burgessville, Ontario

- 8 medium ripe pears, peeled and thinly sliced
- 1/4 cup orange juice
- 1/2 cup sugar
- 1 teaspoon ground cinnamon
- 1/4 teaspoon ground allspice
- 1/4 teaspoon ground ginger

TOPPING:

- 1 cup all-purpose flour
- 1 cup old-fashioned oats
- 1/2 cup packed brown sugar
- 1/2 teaspoon baking powder
- 1/2 cup cold butter

Fresh mint and additional pear slices, optional

Toss pears with orange juice; place in a greased 13-in. x 9-in. x 2-in. baking dish. Combine the sugar, cinnamon, allspice and ginger; sprinkle over the pears.

In a large bowl, combine the flour, oats, brown sugar and baking powder; cut in butter until crumbly. Sprinkle over pears.

Bake at 350° for 35-40 minutes or until topping is golden brown and fruit is tender. Serve warm. Garnish with mint and additional pears if desired. **Yield: 12 servings.**

Poached Pear Surprise

Pears are my husband's favorite fruit, so he immediately declared this dessert a keeper. It's elegant but easy, satisfying yet light. Plus, it's fun to watch the looks on the faces of our grandkids and great-grandkids when they discover the surprise filling inside. —Barbara Smith, Cannon Falls, Minnesota

- 4 medium ripe pears
- 1 cup water
- 1/2 cup sugar
- 1 teaspoon vanilla extract
- 1/3 cup finely chopped walnuts
- 2 tablespoons confectioners' sugar
- 1 teaspoon milk

CHOCOLATE SAUCE:

- 1/3 cup water
- 1/3 cup sugar
- 1/4 cup butter
- 1-1/3 cups semisweet chocolate chips

Fresh mint, optional

Core pears from bottom, leaving stems intact. Peel pears. Cut 1/4 in. from bottom to level if necessary. In a saucepan, bring water and sugar to a boil. Add pears; reduce heat. Cover and simmer for 10-15 minutes or until tender. Remove from the heat; stir vanilla into sugar syrup. Spoon over pears. Cover and refrigerate until chilled.

Meanwhile, combine the walnuts, confectioners' sugar and milk; set aside. For chocolate sauce, in a small saucepan, bring the water, sugar and butter to a boil. Remove from the heat; add chocolate chips, stirring until melted.

To serve, drain pears well; spoon nut mixture into cavities. Place on dessert plates; top with some of the chocolate sauce. Insert a mint leaf near stem if desired. Serve with the remaining chocolate sauce. **Yield: 4 servings.**

Pear Crisp

Poached Pear Surprise

Almond Plum Kuchen

Lemon Whirligigs with Raspberries

Almond Plum Kuchen

You'll find this dessert both easy and very tasty. Everyone who tries it comments on how the orange and plum flavors go together so well and complement each other. We like it best when it is served warm with ice cream. —*Norma Enders, Edmonton, Alberta*

- 1-1/2 cups all-purpose flour
- 3/4 cup packed brown sugar
- 1/2 cup ground almonds
- 1 tablespoon grated orange peel
- 3/4 cup cold butter

FILLING:

- 3 eggs
- 3/4 cup sugar
- 1/2 cup all-purpose flour
- 1/2 cup ground almonds
- 1 tablespoon grated orange peel
- 1/2 teaspoon baking powder
- 7 to 8 cups quartered fresh plums

TOPPING:

- 1/4 cup sugar
- 1/4 cup all-purpose flour
- 1/4 cup butter, softened
- 1/2 cup sliced almonds

In a large bowl, combine the first four ingredients; cut in butter until the mixture resembles coarse crumbs. Press into a greased 13-in. x 9-in. x 2-in. baking dish. Bake at 375° for 15 minutes.

Meanwhile, in a mixing bowl, beat eggs and sugar until thick and lemon-colored, about 5 minutes. Stir in the flour, almonds, orange peel and baking powder. Arrange plums over crust; pour egg mixture over plums.

Combine the first three topping ingredients; sprinkle over filling. Top with almonds. Bake for 40-45 minutes or until golden brown. **Yield: 12 servings.**

Rhubarb Elderberry Crisp

Lemon Whirligigs with Raspberries

Golden whirligigs with a tart lemon flavor float on a ruby raspberry sauce in this delectable dessert.
—Vicki Ayres, Wappingers Falls, New York

- 2/3 cup sugar
- 2 tablespoons cornstarch
- 1/4 teaspoon ground cinnamon
- 1/8 teaspoon salt
- 1/8 teaspoon ground nutmeg
- 1 cup water
- 3 cups fresh raspberries

WHIRLIGIGS:

- 1 cup all-purpose flour
- 2 teaspoons baking powder
- 1/2 teaspoon salt
- 3 tablespoons shortening
- 1 egg, lightly beaten
- 2 tablespoons half-and-half cream
- 1/4 cup sugar
- 2 tablespoons butter, melted
- 1 teaspoon grated lemon peel

Heavy whipping cream and additional raspberries, optional

In a saucepan, combine the first five ingredients. Add water; bring to a boil. Cook and stir for 2 minutes or until thickened. Place raspberries in an ungreased 1-1/2-qt. shallow baking dish; pour sauce over top. Bake at 400° for 10 minutes. Set aside.

For the whirligigs, combine the first three ingredients; cut in shortening until crumbly. Combine egg and cream; stir into dry ingredients to form a stiff dough. Shape into a ball; place on a lightly floured surface. Roll into a 12-in. x 6-in. rectangle. Combine the sugar, butter and peel; spread over dough. Roll up jelly-roll style, starting at a long side. Cut into 10 slices; pat each slice slightly to flatten.

Place whirligigs on top of berry mixture. Bake at 400° for 15 minutes or until whirligigs are golden. Garnish servings with cream and raspberries if desired. **Yield: 10 servings.**

Rhubarb Elderberry Crisp

Rhubarb and elderberries are quite abundant around these parts, so I combined the two in this crisp.
—Carolyn Scouten, Wyalusing, Pennsylvania

- 1 cup all-purpose flour
- 3/4 cup quick-cooking oats
- 1-1/2 cups sugar, *divided*
- 1 teaspoon ground cinnamon
- 1/2 cup cold butter
- 3 cups diced fresh rhubarb *or* frozen rhubarb
- 2 cups elderberries *or* blackberries
- 2 tablespoons cornstarch
- 1 cup water
- 1 teaspoon vanilla extract

In a bowl, combine flour, oats, 1/2 cup sugar and cinnamon; cut in butter until mixture is crumbly. Set aside half for topping.

Press remaining crumb mixture into an ungreased 11-in. x 7-in. x 2-in. baking dish. Top with rhubarb and berries. In a saucepan, combine cornstarch and remaining sugar. Stir in water until smooth. Bring to a boil; cook and stir for 2 minutes or until thickened. Remove from the heat; stir in vanilla.

Pour over the fruit. Sprinkle with the reserved crumb mixture. Bake at 350° for 50-55 minutes or until golden brown. Serve warm or cold. **Yield: 10 servings.**

Rhubarb Granola Crisp

Rhubarb Granola Crisp

When my husband and I moved to our house in town, the rhubarb patch had to come along! This is a hit whether I serve it warm with ice cream or cold.

—Arlene Beitz, Cambridge, Ontario

- 4 cups chopped fresh *or* frozen rhubarb, thawed and drained
- 1-1/4 cups all-purpose flour, *divided*
- 1/4 cup sugar
- 1/2 cup strawberry jam
- 1-1/2 cups granola cereal
- 1/2 cup packed brown sugar
- 1/2 cup chopped pecans
- 1/2 teaspoon ground cinnamon
- 1/2 teaspoon ground ginger
- 1/2 cup cold butter
- Ice cream, optional

In a large bowl, combine the rhubarb, 1/4 cup flour and sugar; stir in jam and set aside. In another bowl, combine the granola, brown sugar, pecans, cinnamon, ginger and remaining flour. Cut in butter until the mixture resembles coarse crumbs.

Press 2 cups of the granola mixture into a greased 8-in. square baking dish; spread rhubarb mixture over the crust. Sprinkle with remaining granola mixture.

Bake at 375° for 30-40 minutes or until filling is bubbly and topping is golden brown. Serve warm with ice cream if desired. **Yield: 9 servings.**

Editor's Note: If using frozen rhubarb, measure rhubarb while still frozen, then thaw completely. Drain in a colander, but do not press liquid out.

Oat-Fashioned Strawberry Dessert

Thanks to this dessert, our house is a popular place in summertime. I make it for family get-togethers, picnics and potlucks, too. It's a treat on a breakfast or brunch buffet as well.

—Linda Forrest, Belleville, Ontario

- 4 cups sliced fresh strawberries
- 1-1/4 cups whole wheat flour
- 1-1/4 cups quick-cooking oats
- 2/3 cup packed brown sugar
- 1/4 teaspoon baking soda
- 1/8 teaspoon salt
- 2/3 cup cold butter
- 2 tablespoons sugar
- 1/4 to 1/2 teaspoon ground cinnamon

Drain strawberries on paper towels; set aside. In a large bowl, combine the flour, oats, brown sugar, baking soda and salt. Cut in butter until mixture resembles coarse crumbs. Reserve 1-1/2 cups for topping. Pat remaining crumb mixture into a greased 9-in. square baking pan.

In a bowl, combine sugar and cinnamon; stir in strawberries. Spoon over the prepared crust. Sprinkle with the reserved crumb mixture. Bake at 350° for 35-40 minutes or until golden brown. Serve warm. **Yield: 9 servings.**

Chocolate and Fruit Trifle 1st prize

Layers of devil's food cake, a creamy pudding mixture, red berries and green kiwi are perfect for the holidays. I like making it in a clear glass trifle bowl to show off its festive colors.
—Angie Dierikx, State Center, Iowa

- 1 package (18-1/4 ounces) devil's food cake mix
- 1 can (14 ounces) sweetened condensed milk
- 1 cup cold water
- 1 package (3.4 ounces) instant vanilla pudding mix
- 2 cups heavy whipping cream, whipped
- 2 tablespoons orange juice
- 2 cups fresh strawberries, chopped
- 2 cups fresh raspberries
- 2 kiwifruit, peeled and chopped

Prepare cake batter according to package directions; pour into a greased 15-in. x 10-in. x 1-in. baking pan. Bake at 350° for 20 minutes or until a toothpick inserted near the center comes out clean. Cool completely on a wire rack. Crumble enough cake to measure 8 cups; set aside. (Save remaining cake for another use.)

In a large mixing bowl, combine milk and water until smooth. Whisk in pudding mix for 2 minutes or until slightly thickened. Fold in the whipped cream. To assemble, spread 2-1/2 cups pudding mixture in a 4-qt. glass bowl. Top with half of the crumbled cake; sprinkle with 1 tablespoon orange juice. Arrange half of the berries and kiwi over cake.

Repeat pudding and cake layers; sprinkle with remaining orange juice. Top with remaining pudding mixture. Spoon remaining fruit around edge of bowl. Cover and refrigerate until serving. **Yield: 12-16 servings.**

Oat-Fashioned Strawberry Dessert

Chocolate and Fruit Trifle

Creamy Caramel Flan

Minty Cocoa Mousse

Creamy Caramel Flan 1st prize

If you're unfamiliar with flan, think of it as a tasty variation on custard. One warning, though—it's very filling. A small slice goes a long way!
—Pat Forte, Miami, Florida

- 3/4 cup sugar
- 1 package (8 ounces) cream cheese, softened
- 5 eggs
- 1 can (14 ounces) sweetened condensed milk
- 1 can (12 ounces) evaporated milk
- 1 teaspoon vanilla extract

In a large heavy saucepan, cook and stir sugar over medium-low heat until sugar is melted and golden, about 15 minutes. Quickly pour into an ungreased 2-qt. round baking or souffle dish, tilting to coat the bottom; let stand for 10 minutes.

In a large mixing bowl, beat cream cheese until smooth. Beat in eggs, one at a time, until thoroughly combined. Add remaining ingredients; mix well. Pour over caramelized sugar.

Place the dish in a larger baking pan. Pour boiling water into larger pan to a depth of 1 in. Bake at 350° for 50-60 minutes or until center is just set (mixture will jiggle). Remove dish from a larger pan to a wire rack; cool for 1 hour. Refrigerate overnight.

To unmold, run a knife around edges and invert onto a large rimmed serving platter. Cut into wedges or spoon onto dessert plates; spoon sauce over each serving. **Yield: 8-10 servings.**

Minty Cocoa Mousse

Junior Mints give the refreshing mint taste to this scrumptious smooth-as-silk mousse. It's one of my best desserts because it's a snap to prepare, yet the flavor is beyond compare.
—Melissa Tarbox, Allen, Texas

- 2 tablespoons baking cocoa
- 2 tablespoons milk
- 1 cup chocolate-covered peppermint candies
- 2 tablespoons butter
- 1 carton (8 ounces) frozen whipped topping, thawed, *divided*
- 1/2 teaspoon vanilla extract

Fresh mint and additional whipped topping, optional

In a large saucepan, combine cocoa and milk until smooth. Add mints and butter; cook and stir over low heat until smooth. Cool for 15 minutes.

Stir in 1 cup whipped topping and vanilla. Fold in the remaining whipped topping. Spoon into dessert dishes. Refrigerate until serving. Garnish with mint and whipped topping if desired. **Yield: 4 servings.**

Raisin Bread Pudding

Raisin Bread Pudding

My sister gave me the recipe for this delicious bread pudding that's dotted with raisins. It's a big hit with everyone who's tried it. A homemade vanilla sauce goes together quickly on the stovetop and is yummy drizzled over warm servings of this old-fashioned tasting treat. *—Sherry Nice, McComb, Ohio*

- 8 slices bread, cubed
- 4 eggs
- 2 cups milk
- 1/4 cup sugar
- 1/4 cup butter, melted
- 1/4 cup raisins
- 1/2 teaspoon ground cinnamon

SAUCE:

- 2 tablespoons butter
- 2 tablespoons all-purpose flour
- 1 cup water
- 3/4 cup sugar
- 1 teaspoon vanilla extract

Place bread cubes in a greased 3-qt. slow cooker. In a large bowl, beat eggs and milk; stir in the sugar, butter, raisins and cinnamon. Pour over bread; stir. Cover and cook on high for 1 hour. Reduce heat to low; cook for 3-4 hours or until a thermometer reads 160°.

Just before serving, melt butter in a saucepan. Stir in the flour until smooth. Gradually add the water, sugar and vanilla. Bring to a boil; cook and stir for 2 minutes or until thickened. Serve with warm bread pudding. **Yield: 6 servings.**

Old-Fashioned Rice Custard

I don't remember where or how I found this dessert. When I took it to a family reunion many years ago, however, a great-uncle was sure I'd used my great-grandmother's recipe! I like to have it warm for dinner. Then, the next morning, I'll enjoy the cold leftovers for my breakfast.
—Shirley Leister, West Chester, Pennsylvania

- 1/2 cup uncooked long-grain rice
- 4 cups milk, *divided*
- 1/4 cup butter, cubed
- 3 eggs
- 3/4 cup sugar
- 1 teaspoon vanilla extract
- 1/4 teaspoon salt
- 1/2 teaspoon ground nutmeg

In a large heavy saucepan or double boiler, combine rice and 2 cups milk. Cook, stirring occasionally, over boiling water until rice is tender and most of the water has evaporated, about 45 minutes. Stir in butter.

In a large mixing bowl, beat eggs. Blend in the sugar, vanilla, salt and remaining milk; stir into the hot rice mixture.

Pour into a lightly greased 2-qt. baking dish and top with nutmeg. Bake at 350° for 50 minutes or until firm. **Yield: 6-8 servings.**

Old-Fashioned Rice Custard

Raspberry White Chocolate Mousse

Raspberry sauce is an appealing base for this fluffy white chocolate mousse. The treasured treat is surprisingly easy and a delightful change of pace from heavier cakes and pies.
—Mary Lou Wayman, Salt Lake City, Utah

- 1 package (10 ounces) frozen sweetened raspberries, thawed
- 2 tablespoons sugar
- 1 tablespoon frozen orange juice concentrate, thawed
- 2 cups heavy whipping cream
- 6 ounces white baking chocolate, chopped
- 1 teaspoon vanilla extract
- 1/4 cup milk chocolate chips
- 1 teaspoon vegetable oil

In a blender, combine the raspberries, sugar and orange juice concentrate; cover and process until smooth. Press through a sieve; discard seeds. Refrigerate sauce.

In a large saucepan, cook and stir cream and white chocolate over low heat until chocolate is melted. Stir in vanilla. Transfer to a large mixing bowl. Cover and refrigerate for 6 hours or until thickened, stirring occasionally. Beat cream mixture on high speed until light and fluffy, about 1-1/2 minutes (do not overbeat).

Just before serving, melt chocolate chips and oil in a microwave or saucepan, stirring until smooth. Spoon 2 tablespoons of raspberry sauce on each plate. Pipe or spoon 1/2 cup chocolate mousse over sauce; drizzle with melted chocolate. Refrigerate leftovers. **Yield: 8 servings.**

Pretty Plum Parfaits 1st prize

With a plum tree in our backyard, I'm always eager to try new plum recipes. But none of them have beat this wonderful dessert! Light, refreshing and easy to whip up, these fruit parfaits are an ideal summer treat. —Norma Reynolds, York, Pennsylvania

- 9 to 12 medium medium ripe red *or* purple plums (2 pounds), sliced
- 1/2 cup red currant jelly
- 1/2 cup packed brown sugar
- 1 orange peel strip (1 to 3 inches)
- 1 cinnamon stick (3 inches)
- 1 cup heavy whipping cream
- 1 tablespoon confectioners' sugar
- 1/2 teaspoon vanilla extract

Fancy cookies and additional whipped cream and plum slices, optional

In a large heavy saucepan, combine the plums, jelly, brown sugar, orange peel and cinnamon stick. Bring to a boil. Reduce heat; simmer, uncovered, for 10-15 minutes or until plums are tender, stirring occasionally. Remove from the heat; cool slightly. Discard orange peel and cinnamon stick, coarsely mash plums. Cover and refrigerate.

Just before serving, in a small mixing bowl, beat cream until it begins to thicken. Add sugar and vanilla; beat until peaks form. Place about 1/4 cup plum mixture each in four chilled parfait glasses; top with 1/4 cup whipped cream. Repeat layers. Top with remaining plum mixture. Garnish with a cookie, dollop of whipped cream and plum slice if desired. **Yield: 4 servings.**

Raspberry White Chocolate Mousse

Pretty Plum Parfaits

Pumpkin Crunch Parfaits

Pumpkin Trifle

Pumpkin Crunch Parfaits

Here's a fun dessert that your youngsters can help make. It's a great treat for Halloween or Thanksgiving.
—Lorraine Darocha, Berkshire, Massachusetts

- 3/4 cup cold milk
- 1 package (3.4 ounces) instant vanilla pudding mix
- 2 cups whipped topping
- 1 cup canned pumpkin
- 1/2 teaspoon pumpkin pie spice
- 1 cup chopped pecans
- 1-1/2 cups crushed gingersnaps (about 32 cookies)
- Additional whipped topping

In a large mixing bowl, whisk milk and pudding mix for 2 minutes. Stir in the whipped topping, pumpkin and pumpkin pie spice; mix well. Fold in pecans.

Spoon half of the mixture into parfait glasses; top with half of the gingersnap crumbs. Repeat layers. Top with additional whipped topping. **Yield: 6 servings.**

Pumpkin Trifle 1st prize

This trifle is convenient and tastes like a traditional pumpkin pie, even though you don't have to make a crust or bake it.
—Melody Hurlbut, St. Agatha, Ontario

- 2 to 3 cups leftover crumbled unfrosted spice cake, muffins *or* gingerbread
- 2-1/2 cups cold milk
- 1 can (15 ounces) solid-pack pumpkin
- 4 packages (3.4 ounces *each*) instant butterscotch pudding mix
- 1 teaspoon ground cinnamon
- 1/4 teaspoon ground nutmeg

Strawberry Banana Trifle

1/4 teaspoon ground ginger
1/4 teaspoon ground allspice
2 cups heavy whipping cream
Maraschino cherries, optional

Set aside 1/4 cup cake crumbs for topping. Divide remaining crumbs into four portions; sprinkle one portion into a trifle bowl or 3-qt. serving bowl.

In a large mixing bowl, combine the milk, pumpkin, pudding mixes and spices; beat until smooth. Spoon half into the serving bowl. Sprinkle with a second portion of crumbs. In a small mixing bowl, beat cream until stiff peaks form; spoon half into bowl.

Sprinkle with a third portion of crumbs. Top with the remaining pumpkin mixture, then remaining portion of crumbs and whipped cream. Sprinkle the reserved crumbs around the edge of bowl. Garnish with cherries if desired. Cover and chill at least 2 hours before serving. **Yield: 12-15 servings.**

Strawberry Banana Trifle

No matter where I take this dessert, the bowl gets emptied in minutes. It's fun to make because everyone "oohs" and "ahhs" over how pretty it is.
—Kim Waterhouse, Randolph, Maine

1 cup sugar
1/4 cup cornstarch
3 tablespoons strawberry gelatin powder
1 cup cold water
1 pint fresh strawberries, sliced
1-3/4 cups cold milk
1 package (3.4 ounces) instant vanilla pudding mix
3 medium firm bananas, sliced
1 tablespoon lemon juice
6 cups cubed angel food cake
2 cups heavy whipping cream, whipped
Additional strawberries *or* banana slices, optional

In a saucepan, combine the sugar, cornstarch and gelatin; stir in water until smooth. Bring to a boil; cook and stir for 2 minutes or until thickened. Remove from the heat. Stir in strawberries; set side.

In a large bowl, whisk milk and pudding mix for 2 minutes; set aside. Toss bananas with lemon juice; drain and set aside.

Place half of the cake cubes in a trifle bowl or 3-qt. serving bowl. Layer with half of the pudding, bananas, strawberry sauce and whipped cream. Repeat layers. Cover and refrigerate for at least 2 hours. Garnish with additional fruit if desired. **Yield: 14 servings.**

Caramel Fried Ice Cream

For birthday parties or outdoor barbecues, this is a hit. I sometimes substitute strawberry or Neopolitan for the vanilla ice cream.
—Darlene Markel, Sublimity, Oregon

- 1 quart vanilla ice cream
- 1/4 cup heavy whipping cream
- 2 teaspoons vanilla extract
- 2 cups flaked coconut, finely chopped
- 2 cups finely crushed cornflakes
- 1/2 teaspoon ground cinnamon

CARAMEL SAUCE:

- 1 cup sugar
- 1/2 cup butter, cubed
- 1/2 cup evaporated milk

Oil for deep-fat frying

Using a 1/2-cup ice cream scoop, place eight scoops of ice cream on a baking sheet. Cover and freeze for 2 hours or until firm. In a bowl, combine whipping cream and vanilla. In another bowl, combine coconut, cornflakes and cinnamon.

Remove scoops of ice cream from freezer; wearing plastic gloves, shape the ice cream into balls. Dip balls into cream mixture, then roll in coconut mixture, making sure to coat entire surface. Place coated balls on a baking sheet. Cover and freeze at least 3 hours or until firm.

For caramel sauce, heat sugar in a heavy saucepan over medium heat until partially melted and golden, stirring occasionally. Add butter. Gradually add milk, stirring constantly. Cook and stir for 8 minutes or until sauce is thick and golden; keep warm.

Heat oil in an electric skillet or deep-fat fryer to 375°. Fry ice cream balls until golden, about 30 seconds. Drain on paper towels. Serve immediately with caramel sauce. **Yield: 8 servings.**

Caramel Fried Ice Cream

Strawberry Brownie Bombe

A friend and I dreamed up this recipe. We use it to entertain and for special family dinners. For an extra touch, you can dip the strawberries in chocolate.
—Joanne Watts, Kitchener, Ontario

- 1 package fudge brownie mix (13-inch x 9-inch pan size)
- 1/2 cup chopped walnuts
- 1/2 cup strawberry preserves
- 1 quart strawberry ice cream, softened
- 2 cups heavy whipping cream
- 3 drops red food coloring, optional
- 1/4 cup confectioners' sugar

Fresh strawberries and mint, optional

Prepare brownie mix according to package directions for cake-like brownies. Stir in walnuts. Pour the batter into two greased and waxed paper-lined 9-in. round baking pans. Bake at 350° for 25-30 minutes or until a toothpick inserted near the center comes out clean. Cool completely in pans.

Line a 1-1/2-qt. metal bowl with foil. Cut

Strawberry Brownie Bombe

and fit one brownie layer to evenly line the inside of a bowl (brownie may crack). Spread preserves over brownie layer. Freeze for 15 minutes. Fill brownie-lined bowl with ice cream; smooth top. Cover and freeze for 3 hours or until ice cream is firm.

Place remaining brownie layer on a serving plate. Remove bowl from freezer; uncover. Invert onto brownie layer; remove bowl and foil. Return to freezer.

In a large mixing bowl, beat cream and food coloring until cream begins to thicken. Add the sugar; beat until stiff peaks form. Set aside 1-1/2 cups. Spread remaining whipped cream over top and sides of bombe.

Cut a small hole in the corner of a pastry or plastic bag and insert star tip. Fill with reserved whipped cream; pipe border at base of bombe. Holding the bag straight up and down, form stars on top. Garnish with strawberries and mint if desired. **Yield: 16 servings.**

Editor's Note: Unfrosted bombe may be frozen for up to 3 days.

Frozen Mocha Marbled Loaf

Mint Chip Ice Cream

Frozen Mocha Marbled Loaf

It's really simple to make this showstopping marbled dessert. And, it's great for company since it is prepared ahead of time, then frozen. Frosty slices have a creamy blend of chocolate and coffee that's delightful anytime of year.

—Cheryl Martinetto, Grand Rapids, Minnesota

- 2 cups finely crushed chocolate cream-filled sandwich cookies (about 22 cookies)
- 3 tablespoons butter, melted
- 1 package (8 ounces) cream cheese, softened
- 1 can (14 ounces) sweetened condensed milk
- 1 teaspoon vanilla extract
- 2 cups heavy whipping cream, whipped
- 2 tablespoons instant coffee granules
- 1 tablespoon hot water
- 1/2 cup chocolate syrup

Line a 9-in. x 5-in. x 3-in. loaf pan with foil. In a bowl, combine cookie crumbs and butter. Press firmly onto bottom and 1-1/2 in. up the sides of prepared pan.

In a large mixing bowl, beat cream cheese until light and fluffy. Add milk and vanilla; mix well. Fold in whipped cream. Spoon half of the mixture into another bowl and set aside. Dissolve coffee in hot water; fold into remaining cream cheese mixture. Fold in chocolate syrup.

Spoon half of the chocolate mixture over crust. Top with half of the reserved cream cheese mixture. Repeat layers. Cut through layers with a knife to swirl the chocolate (pan will be full). Cover and freeze for 6 hours or overnight. To serve, lift out of the pan; remove foil. Cut into slices. **Yield: 12 servings.**

Mint Chip Ice Cream

We have a milk cow, so homemade ice cream has become a regular treat for our family. This has a mild mint flavor that goes well with the mini chocolate chips. —Farrah McGuire, Springdale, Washington

- 1-3/4 cups milk
- 3/4 cup sugar
- Pinch salt
- 3 eggs, lightly beaten
- 1-3/4 cups heavy whipping cream
- 1 teaspoon vanilla extract
- 1/4 teaspoon peppermint extract
- 4 drops green food coloring, optional
- 1/2 cup miniature semisweet chocolate chips

In a small saucepan, heat the milk to 175°; stir in the sugar and salt until dissolved. Whisk in a small amount of the hot mixture to the eggs. Return all to the pan, whisking constantly. Cook and stir over low heat until mixture reaches at least 160° and coats the back of a metal spoon. Remove from the heat.

Frosty Chocolate Mousse

Cool quickly by placing pan in a bowl of ice water; stir for 2 minutes. Stir in the whipping cream, extracts and food coloring if desired. Press plastic wrap onto surface of custard. Refrigerate for several hours or overnight.

Stir in the chocolate chips. Fill ice cream freezer cylinder two-thirds full; freeze according to the manufacturer's directions. Refrigerate remaining mixture until ready to freeze. Transfer the ice cream to a freezer container; freeze for 2-4 hours before serving. **Yield: 1-1/2 quarts.**

Frosty Chocolate Mousse

This is a wonderful dessert that whips up fast. It's very smooth and silky and is a perfect complement to any meal. —Myra Innes, Auburn, Kansas

- 1-1/2 cups heavy whipping cream
- 1/2 cup sugar
- 1/2 cup sifted baking cocoa
- 1/2 teaspoon rum extract
- 1/2 teaspoon vanilla extract

In a large mixing bowl, combine all ingredients. Beat until mixture mounds softly. Spoon into dessert dishes. Freeze for at least 2 hours before serving. **Yield: 4 servings.**

Strawberry Ice

When we pick strawberries at a local farm, this is what many of the berries are used for. It's a great summertime treat.

—Kim Hammond, Watsonville, California

- 5 cups fresh *or* frozen unsweetened strawberries, thawed
- 2/3 cup sugar
- 2/3 cup water
- 1/4 cup lemon juice

Place the strawberries in a blender or food processor; cover and process until smooth. In a saucepan, bring sugar and water to a boil. Cook and stir until sugar is dissolved, about 5 minutes; cool slightly. Add to blender along with the lemon juice; cover and process until combined.

Pour into a shallow freezer container; cover and freeze for 4-6 hours or until almost frozen. Just before serving, whip mixture in a blender or food processor. **Yield: 6 servings.**

Peach Ice Cream

Adding peaches to a mouth-watering vanilla ice cream recipe I got from my mother-in-law resulted in this fabulous flavor. My boys say it's the greatest and think it tastes best served outdoors under a shade tree!

—Lisa Tenbarge, Haubstadt, Indiana

- 1 cup milk
- 1 cup sugar
- 1 egg, beaten
- 3-1/3 cups heavy whipping cream
- 1/4 cup instant vanilla pudding mix
- 1-1/2 cups finely chopped fresh *or* frozen peaches, thawed
- 2 teaspoons vanilla extract

In a large saucepan, heat the milk to 175°; stir in the sugar until dissolved. Whisk a small amount of the hot mixture into the egg.

Strawberry Ice

Return all to the pan, whisking constantly. Cook and stir over low heat until mixture reaches at least 160°; and coats the back of a metal spoon. Remove from the heat. Cool quickly by placing pan in a bowl of ice water; stir for 2 minutes. Press plastic wrap onto surface of custard. Refrigerate for several hours or overnight.

When ready to freeze, stir in the cream, pudding mix, peaches and vanilla. Pour into the cylinder of an ice cream freezer. Freeze according to manufacturer's directions. Refrigerate remaining mixture until ready to freeze. Transfer ice cream to a freezer container; freeze for 2-4 hours before serving. **Yield: 1-1/4 quarts.**

Lemon Lime Dessert

This make-ahead treat offers a wonderfully refreshing blend of citrus flavors. Topped with a smooth lemon sauce, it's the perfect ending to any meal. Using an electric mixer makes it easy to combine the lime sherbet and vanilla ice cream.

—Marsha Schindler, Fort Wayne, Indiana

- 1-1/2 cups graham cracker crumbs (about 24 squares)
- 14 tablespoons butter, melted, *divided*

Peach Ice Cream

- 1-1/4 cups sugar, *divided*
- 1/2 gallon vanilla ice cream, softened
- 1 quart lime sherbet, softened
- 2 eggs, beaten
- 1/4 cup lemon juice

In a bowl, combine the cracker crumbs, 7 tablespoons butter and 1/4 cup sugar; mix well. Press into an ungreased 13-in. x 9-in. x 2-in. dish; freeze. In a mixing bowl, combine ice cream and sherbet; pour over the crust. Freeze until firm.

In a heavy saucepan, combine eggs and remaining sugar. Stir in the lemon juice and remaining butter. Cook over low heat until mixture is thickened and reaches 160°. Cover and refrigerate until cool.

Spread over ice cream mixture. Cover and freeze for 3 hours or overnight. May be frozen for up to 2 months. Just before serving, remove from the freezer and cut into squares. **Yield: 12-15 servings.**

Lemon Lime Dessert

Strawberry Peach Melba

Praline Sundae Topping

Strawberry Peach Melba

"Looks Fantastic!" is what I hear when I set out this cool, fruity dessert. It combines my three all-time favorites—peaches, strawberries and ice cream. It's so simple I can assemble it for company after we all finish the main course.
—Marion Karlin, Waterloo, Iowa

- 3 cups fresh *or* frozen whole strawberries
- 1 cup confectioners' sugar
- 1/4 cup water
- 1 teaspoon lemon juice
- 2 teaspoons cornstarch
- 1 tablespoon cold water
- 1 teaspoon vanilla extract
- 4 slices *or* scoops vanilla ice cream
- 1 can (15 ounces) sliced peaches, drained
- Whipped topping

In a large saucepan, mash strawberries; add sugar, water and lemon juice. Cook and stir until mixture comes to a boil. Combine the cornstarch and cold water until smooth; stir into the strawberry mixture. Cook and stir for 2 minutes or until thickened. Remove from the heat; stir in vanilla.

Strain to remove the pulp. Place the pan in an ice-water bath to cool, stirring occasionally. Serve strawberry sauce over ice cream; top with peaches and whipped topping. **Yield: 4 servings.**

Praline Sundae Topping

Necessity can be the mother of recipes, too! I came up with this delicious one as a way of using up the extra evaporated milk I had from making fudge.
—Valerie Cook, Hubbard, Iowa

- 1/4 cup butter, cubed
- 1-1/4 cups packed brown sugar

16 large marshmallows
2 tablespoons light corn syrup
Dash salt
1 cup evaporated milk
1/2 cup chopped pecans, toasted
1 teaspoon vanilla extract
Ice cream

Melt butter in a large saucepan. Add the brown sugar, marshmallows, corn syrup and salt. Cook and stir over low heat until marshmallows are melted and mixture comes to a boil. Boil for 1 minute.

Remove from the heat; cool for 5 minutes. Stir in evaporated milk, pecans and vanilla; mix well. Serve warm or cold over ice cream. Store in the refrigerator. **Yield: 2-1/2 cups.**

Pecan Delights

A relative visiting from Oklahoma brought these and the recipe with her. Who can resist rich, chewy caramel over crunchy pecans drizzled with sweet chocolate? These candies have become a holiday favorite to both make and eat!

—Linda Jonsson, Marion, Ohio

2-1/4 cups packed brown sugar
1 cup butter, cubed
1 cup light corn syrup
1/8 teaspoon salt
1 can (14 ounces) sweetened condensed milk
1 teaspoon vanilla extract
1-1/2 pounds whole pecans
1 cup (6 ounces) semisweet chocolate chips
1 cup milk chocolate chips
2 tablespoons shortening

Pecan Delights

In a large saucepan, combine the first four ingredients. Cook over medium heat until all sugar is dissolved. Gradually add milk; mix well. Cook until a candy thermometer reads 248° (firm-ball stage).

Remove from the heat; stir in vanilla. Fold in the pecans. Drop by tablespoonfuls onto a greased or parchment-lined baking sheet. Chill until firm. Loosen from paper.

In a microwave or heavy saucepan, melt chocolate chips and shortening, stirring until smooth. Drizzle over each cluster. Cool. **Yield: about 4 dozen.**

Editor's Note: We recommend that you test your candy thermometer before each use by bringing water to a boil; the thermometer should read 212°. Adjust your recipe temperature up or down based on your test.

English Toffee Bars

English Toffee Bars 1st prize

My mother and I get together every year around Christmastime to make this delicious chocolate-coated toffee, using a recipe she got years ago in a cooking class. It's a tradition I plan to continue with my daughters and grandchildren. Our families and friends wait with mouths watering for their packages.
—Dianne Brooks, Augusta, Kansas

- 1 tablespoon plus 1-3/4 cups butter, softened, *divided*
- 2 cups sugar
- 1 tablespoon light corn syrup
- 1 cup chopped pecans
- 1/4 teaspoon salt
- 16 ounces milk chocolate candy coating

Butter a 15-in. x 10-in. x 1-in. baking pan with 1 tablespoon butter; set aside. In a heavy 3-qt. saucepan, melt the remaining butter. Add sugar and corn syrup; cook and stir over medium heat until a candy thermometer reads 295° (soft-crack stage). Remove from the heat; stir in pecans and salt.

Quickly pour into prepared pan. Let stand for 5 minutes. Using a sharp knife, score into lines. Let stand at room temperature until cool.

Separate into squares, using a sharp knife if necessary. In a microwave or heavy saucepan, melt candy coating, stirring often. Dip squares, one at a time, in coating. Place on waxed paper until set. **Yield: 2-1/4 pounds.**

Editor's Note: We recommend that you test your candy thermometer before each use by bringing water to a boil; the thermometer should read 212°. Adjust your recipe temperature up or down based on your test.

Angel Food Candy

It was my dad who inspired me to first try making this candy. He remembered it from when he was a boy. The ultimate compliment was when he told me my version tasted even better!
—Shelly Matthys, New Richmond, Wisconsin

- 1/2 teaspoon butter
- 1 cup sugar
- 1 cup dark corn syrup
- 1 tablespoon white vinegar
- 1 tablespoon baking soda
- 1 pound milk chocolate candy coating

Butter a 13-in. x 9-in. x 2-in. baking pan with 1/2 teaspoon butter; set aside. In a heavy saucepan, combine the sugar, corn syrup and vinegar. Cook over medium heat, stirring constantly, until sugar is dissolved. Cook without stirring until the temperature reaches 300° (hard-crack stage) on a candy thermometer. Do not overcook.

Remove from the heat and quickly stir in baking soda. Pour into prepared pan. Do not spread candy; mixture will not fill pan. When cool, break into bite-size pieces.

In a microwave or heavy saucepan, melt chocolate, stirring until smooth. Dip candy into melted chocolate; place on waxed paper until the chocolate is set. Store candy tightly covered. **Yield: 1-1/2 pounds.**

Editor's Note: We recommend that you test your candy thermometer before each use by bringing water to a boil; the thermometer should read 212°. Adjust your recipe temperature up or down based on your test.

Chocolate Pecan Caramels

I haven't missed a year making this candy for the holidays since a friend gave me the recipe many, many years ago!

—June Humphrey, Strongsville, Ohio

- 1 tablespoon plus 1 cup butter, softened, *divided*
- 1-1/2 cups coarsely chopped pecans, toasted
- 1 cup (6 ounces) semisweet chocolate chips
- 2 cups packed brown sugar
- 1 cup light corn syrup
- 1/4 cup water
- 1 can (14 ounces) sweetened condensed milk
- 2 teaspoons vanilla extract

Line a 13-in. x 9-in. x 2-in. baking pan with foil; butter the foil with 1 tablespoon butter. Sprinkle with pecans and chips; set aside.

In a heavy saucepan, melt remaining butter over medium heat. Add brown sugar, corn syrup and water. Cook and stir until mixture comes to a boil. Stir in milk. Cook, stirring constantly, until a candy thermometer reads 248° (firm-ball stage).

Remove from the heat and stir in vanilla. Pour into prepared pan (do not scrape saucepan). Cool completely before cutting. **Yield: about 2-1/2 pounds (about 6-3/4 dozen).**

Editor's Note: We recommend that you test your candy thermometer before each use by bringing water to a boil; the thermometer should read 212°. Adjust your recipe temperature up or down based on your test.

Chocolate Pecan Caramels

Angel Food Candy

Three-Chip English Toffee

Double Chocolate Fudge

Three-Chip English Toffee 1st prize

With its melt-in-your-mouth texture and rich flavor, this is the ultimate toffee! Drizzled on top are three different kinds of melted chips, plus a sprinkling of walnuts. Packaged in colorful tins, these pretty pieces make great gifts.—Lana Petfield, Richmond, Virginia

- 1 teaspoon plus 2 cups butter, *divided*
- 2 cups sugar
- 1 cup slivered almonds
- 1 cup milk chocolate chips
- 1 cup chopped walnuts
- 1/2 cup semisweet chocolate chips
- 1/2 cup vanilla *or* white chips
- 1-1/2 teaspoons shortening

Butter a 15-in. x 10-in. x 1-in. baking pan with 1 teaspoon butter. In a heavy saucepan over medium-low heat, bring sugar and remaining butter to a boil, stirring constantly. Cover and cook for 2-3 minutes.

Uncover; add almonds. Cook and stir with a clean spoon until a candy thermometer reads 300° (hard-crack stage) and mixture is golden brown.

Pour into prepared pan (do not scrape sides of saucepan). Surface will be buttery. Cool for 1-2 minutes. Sprinkle with milk chocolate chips. Let stand for 1-2 minutes; spread chocolate over the top. Sprinkle with walnuts; press down gently with the back of a spoon. Chill for 10 minutes.

In a microwave or heavy saucepan, melt semisweet chips, stirring until smooth. Drizzle over walnuts. Refrigerate for 10 minutes. Melt vanilla chips and shortening; stir until smooth. Drizzle over walnuts. Cover and refrigerate for 1-2 hours. Break into pieces. **Yield: about 2-1/2 pounds.**

Editor's Note: We recommend that you test your candy thermometer before each use by bringing water to a boil; the thermometer should read 212°. Adjust your recipe temperature up or down based on your test. If toffee separates during cooking, add 1/2 cup hot water and stir vigorously. Bring back up to 300° and proceed as recipe directs.

Double Chocolate Fudge

If you love chocolate, here's a recipe that's sure to please. This rich treat is a favorite of our family all year long and especially around the holidays.
—Marilyn Jordan, Hoosick Falls, New York

- 1-1/2 teaspoons plus 2 tablespoons butter, *divided*
- 4-1/2 cups sugar
- 1 can (12 ounces) evaporated milk
- Pinch salt
- 1 jar (7 ounces) marshmallow creme
- 2 cups (12 ounces) semisweet chocolate chips
- 3 packages (4 ounces *each*) German sweet chocolate, broken into pieces
- 2 cups chopped walnuts, optional

Line a 15-in. x 10-in. x 1-in. baking pan with foil. Grease the foil with 1-1/2 teaspoons butter; set aside.

In a large saucepan, combine the sugar, milk, salt and remaining butter. Cook and stir over medium heat until sugar is dissolved. Bring to a rapid boil; boil for 5 minutes, stirring constantly.

Remove from the heat; stir in marshmallow creme until melted. Stir in chips and German sweet chocolate until melted. Add walnuts if desired; mix well. Pour into prepared pan. Refrigerate overnight or until firm.

Using foil, remove fudge from pan; carefully peel off foil. Cut into 1-in. squares. Store in the refrigerator. **Yield: 5 pounds.**

Cinnamon Peanut Brittle

Cinnamon Peanut Brittle

I made this sweet and crunchy candy for Christmas and sent some with my husband to work. His co-workers liked it so much they asked for more. It has a lovely glossy appearance, is packed with peanuts and gets a different flavor from cinnamon.
—Grace Miller, Mansfield, Ohio

- 1 cup sugar
- 1/2 cup light corn syrup
- 2 cups salted peanuts
- 1 teaspoon butter
- 1/2 teaspoon ground cinnamon
- 1 teaspoon baking soda
- 1 teaspoon vanilla extract

In a 2-qt. microwave-safe and heatproof bowl, combine sugar and corn syrup. Heat, uncovered, on high for 4 minutes; stir. Heat 3 minutes longer. Stir in the peanuts, butter and cinnamon. Microwave, uncovered, on high for 30-60 seconds or until mixture turns a light amber color (mixture will be very hot).

Quickly stir in baking soda and vanilla until light and foamy. Immediately pour onto a greased baking sheet and spread with a metal spatula. Refrigerate for 20 minutes or until firm; break into small pieces. Store in an airtight container. **Yield: 1-1/4 pounds.**

Editor's Note: This recipe was tested in an 850-watt microwave.

True Love Truffles

A few years ago, I began giving these smooth, minty truffles in tins as Christmas gifts. Now I can't go a year without sharing them. They also make a perfect Valentine's treat for someone dear.

—Kim Weiesnbach, Claremore, Oklahoma

- 1 tablespoon plus 3/4 cup butter, *divided*
- 1-1/2 cups sugar
- 1 can (5 ounces) evaporated milk
- 2 packages (4.67 ounces *each*) mint Andes candies (56 pieces total)
- 1 jar (7 ounces) marshmallow creme
- 1 teaspoon vanilla extract
- 22 ounces white baking chocolate, *divided*
- 1/2 cup semisweet chocolate chips
- Green food coloring, optional

Butter a 15-in. x 10-in. x 1-in. pan with 1 tablespoon butter; set aside. In a heavy saucepan, combine the sugar, milk and remaining butter. Bring to a boil over medium heat, stirring constantly. Reduce heat; cook and stir until a candy thermometer reads 236° (soft-ball stage). Remove from the heat. Stir in candies until melted and mixture is well blended. Stir in marshmallow creme and vanilla until smooth. Spread into prepared pan; cover and refrigerate for 1 hour.

Cut into 96 pieces; roll each into a ball (mixture will be soft). Place on a waxed paper-lined baking sheet.

In a heavy saucepan or microwave-safe bowl, melt 18 oz. of white chocolate and chocolate chips, stirring until smooth. Dip balls in melted chocolate; place on waxed paper to set. Melt the remaining white chocolate; add food coloring if desired. Drizzle over truffles. Store in an airtight container. **Yield: 8 dozen.**

Editor's Note: We recommend that you test your candy thermometer before each use by bringing water to a boil; the thermometer should read 212°. Adjust your recipe temperature up or down based on your test.

True Love Truffles

Cashew Caramel Fudge

This yummy confection makes a great present! Cashews and caramel are such a delicious combination. I especially enjoy making this fudge for a holiday treat.

—Cathy Grubelink, Raton, New Mexico

- 2 teaspoons plus 1/2 cup butter, softened, *divided*
- 1 can (5 ounces) evaporated milk
- 2-1/2 cups sugar
- 2 cups (12 ounces) semisweet chocolate chips
- 1 jar (7 ounces) marshmallow creme
- 24 caramels, quartered
- 3/4 cup salted cashew halves
- 1 teaspoon vanilla extract

Line a 9-in. square baking pan with foil; butter the foil with 2 teaspoons butter. Set aside.

In a large heavy saucepan, combine the milk, sugar and remaining butter. Cook and stir over medium heat until sugar is dissolved.

Bring to a rapid boil; boil for 5 minutes, stirring constantly. Remove from the heat; stir in chocolate chips and marshmallow creme until melted. Fold in the caramels, cashews and vanilla; mix well.

Pour into prepared pan. Cool. Using foil, lift fudge out of pan. Discard foil; cut fudge into 1-in. squares. Store in an airtight container. **Yield: about 3 pounds.**

Cashew Caramel Fudge

Chocolate Peanut Sweeties

Inspired by my passion for peanut butter and chocolate, I combined a trusted recipe for peanut butter eggs with the salty crunch of pretzels. Now our kids have fun helping me make and eat these heavenly treats.

—Gina Kintigh, Connellsville, Pennsylvania

- **1 cup peanut butter**
- **1/2 cup butter, softened**
- **3 cups confectioners' sugar**
- **60 miniature pretzels (about 3 cups)**
- **1-1/2 cups milk chocolate chips**
- **1 tablespoon shortening**

In a small mixing bowl, beat peanut butter and butter until smooth. Beat in confectioners' sugar until combined. Shape into 1-in. balls; press one on each pretzel. Place on waxed paper-lined baking sheets. Refrigerate until peanut butter mixture is set, about 1 hour.

In a microwave-safe bowl or heavy saucepan, melt chocolate chips and shortening, stirring until smooth. Dip the peanut butter ball into chocolate. Return to baking sheet, pretzel side down. Refrigerate for at least 30 minutes before serving. Store in an airtight container in the refrigerator. **Yield: 5 dozen.**

Chocolate Peanut Sweeties

Maple Peanut Delights

Maple Peanut Delights 1st prize

This wonderful candy recipe makes a big batch—enough to fill several Christmas gift boxes and still have treats left for my husband and our grandchildren. —*Katie Stutzman, Goshen, Indiana*

- 1 package (8 ounces) cream cheese, softened
- 1/2 cup butter, softened
- 6 cups confectioners' sugar
- 1 teaspoon maple flavoring
- 2 pounds dark chocolate candy coating
- 1 cup chopped peanuts

In a large mixing bowl, beat the cream cheese, butter, confectioners' sugar and flavoring until smooth. Cover and refrigerate for 1 hour.

Shape into 1-in. balls. In a microwave or heavy saucepan, melt candy coating, stirring often. Dip balls in coating; sprinkle with peanuts. Place on waxed paper-lined baking sheets. Refrigerate. **Yield: about 8 dozen.**

Buttery Almond Crunch

The texture of this delectable candy is crisp but not as hard as peanut brittle. Some people say it reminds them of the toffee center of a well-known candy bar.
—*Mildred Clothier, Oregon, Illinois*

- 1 tablespoon plus 1/2 cup butter, softened, *divided*
- 1/2 cup sugar
- 1 tablespoon light corn syrup
- 1 cup sliced almonds

Line an 8-in. square pan with foil; butter the foil with 1-1/2 teaspoons butter. Set aside.

Spread the sides of a heavy saucepan with 1-1/2 teaspoons butter. Add the sugar, corn syrup and remaining butter. Bring to a boil over medium-high heat, stirring constantly. Cook and stir until mixture is golden brown, about 3 minutes. Stir in almonds. Quickly pour into prepared pan.

Refrigerate until firm. Invert pan and remove foil. Break candy into pieces. **Yield: 10 ounces.**

Buttery Almond Crunch

REFERENCES

References

Selecting the perfect recipe to prepare is just the beginning. This chapter gathers many extras you'll need for success in the kitchen, including tips on storing food, using herbs and a glossary with over 80 cooking terms and their definitions. Look to the inside covers for Food Equivalent chart and the Ingredient Substitution chart.

Food Storage Guidelines

Pantry Storage

Check the sell-by or use-by dates on pantry items. Discard items that are past those dates. In the pantry, store opened items tightly closed and place in a cool, dry place. Times given in the charts on pages 486-487 are for pantry storage of opened items.

Refrigerated Foods

The use-by date on refrigerated items is only for the unopened item. Use the times given in the chart for opened foods. Keep the refrigerator temperature between 34°-40°. In the refrigerator, store leftovers in covered refrigerator containers or wrap them in plastic wrap or foil. Resealable plastic bags also are great for storage.

Frozen Foods

For the best quality, foods should be frozen in a freezer that maintains 0° and is at least two-thirds full. Cool cooked food quickly before freezing. Store food in containers that are moisture-proof and vapor-proof, such as foil, freezer bags, freezer wrap and plastic freezer containers. Remove as much air as possible when packaging the food. Label and date packages before freezing. Spread out the packages for quicker freezing, and then stack them after they are solidly frozen.

Defrost foods in the refrigerator, microwave oven or cold water. Generally, small items will defrost overnight in the refrigerator. Most items take 1 or 2 days. Bulky, large items will take even longer to thaw. To defrost in a microwave oven, follow the manufacturer's directions. To defrost in cold water, place food in a watertight plastic storage bag. Place the bag in cold water. Change the water every 30 minutes until the food is thawed.

	OPENED FOOD ITEM	REFRIGERATOR TEMP. 34° TO 40°	FREEZER TEMP. 0°
DAIRY	**BUTTER**	1 to 3 months	6 to 9 months
	CHEESE		
	Brie	1 week	6 months
	Cottage/Ricotta	1 week	not suitable
	Cream Cheese	2 weeks	not suitable
	Cheddar, Brick, Swiss, Monterey Jack	3 to 4 weeks	6 months
	Mozzarella	1 week	6 months
	Parmesan/Romano, Grated	2 months	6 months
	CREAM		
	Ultrapasteurized	1 month	not suitable
	Heavy Whipping or Half-and-Half	3 days	2 to 4 months
	EGGS		
	Whole, In the shell	4 to 5 weeks	not suitable
	Whites or Yolks, Uncooked	2 to 4 days	12 months
	MILK		
	Milk	7 days	3 months
	Buttermilk	7 to 14 days	3 months
	Evaporated or Sweetened Condensed	4 to 5 days	2 months
	MARGARINE	4 to 5 months	12 months
	SOUR CREAM	7 to 21 days	not suitable
	YOGURT	7 to 14 days	1 to 2 months
MEATS–BEEF, PORK, LAMB	**FRESH**		
	Chops	3 to 5 days	4 to 6 months
	Ground or Stew Meat	1 to 2 days	3 to 4 months
	Roasts	3 to 5 days	4 to 12 months
	Sausage, Fresh	1 to 2 days	1 to 2 months
	Steaks	3 to 5 days	6 to 12 months
	Leftover Cooked Meats/Casseroles	1 to 4 days	2 to 3 months
	PROCESS MEATS		
	Bacon	7 days	1 month
	Ham	3 to 5 days	1 to 2 months
	Luncheon Meats	3 to 5 days	1 to 2 months
POULTRY	**CHICKEN/TURKEY**		
	Whole	1 to 2 days	1 year
	Parts	1 to 2 days	9 months
	Leftover, Cooked	1 to 4 days	1 to 4 months
FISH & SEAFOOD	**LEAN FISH** (Fillets/Steaks)		
	Cod, Sole, Halibut, Orange Roughy, Flounder	1 to 2 days	6 months
	FATTY FISH (Fillets/Steaks)		
	Catfish, Perch, Salmon, Whitefish	1 to 2 days	2 to 3 months
	CRAB, COOKED	1 to 2 days	3 months
	SCALLOPS/SHRIMP		
	Uncooked	1 to 2 days	3 to 6 months
	Cooked	3 to 4 days	3 months
	LEFTOVER, COOKED SEAFOOD	3 to 4 days	3 to 6 months

STAPLES

OPENED FOOD ITEM	PANTRY STORAGE TEMP. 70°	REFRIGERATOR TEMP. 34° TO 40°	FREEZER TEMP. 0°
BAKING POWDER	18 months		
BAKING SODA	18 months		
BOUILLON CUBES	1 year		
BREAD	2 to 7 days	4 to 7 days	3 months
CANNED GOODS			
Fish and Seafood		2 days	
Fruit		1 week	
Pasta Sauces		5 days	
Vegetables		2 to 3 days	
CEREAL			
Cook before eating	6 months		
Ready to eat	2 to 3 months		
CORNMEAL	12 months		
CORNSTARCH	18 months		
FLOUR			
All-Purpose	15 months		
Whole Wheat	6 months		
FRUIT, DRIED	6 months		
HONEY	12 months		
JAM AND JELLY		12 months	
KETCHUP OR CHILI SAUCE		4 to 6 months	
MAYONNAISE		2 months	
MUSTARD		6 to 12 months	
NUTS	3 to 6 months	3 to 6 months	6 to 12 months
OILS			
Canola or Corn Oil	6 months		
Olive Oil	4 months		
PEANUT BUTTER	2 to 3 months		
PICKLES		1 to 2 months	
PIES			
Custard		2 to 3 days	not suitable
Fruit, Unbaked			8 months
Fruit, Baked		4 to 5 days	1 to 2 months
Pumpkin		4 to 5 days	2 months
RICE			
Brown	1 month	6 months	
White	2 years		
SALAD DRESSINGS		3 months	
SALSA		1 month	
SHORTENING	8 months		
SOY SAUCE		12 months	
SUGAR			
Brown	4 months		
Granulated	2 years		
WORCESTERSHIRE SAUCE	12 months		

Guide to Common Herbs

Dried herbs need to be stored in tightly closed containers in a cool, dark, dry place. Keep them away from the heat of the oven or stovetop. For best flavor, use dried herbs within 6 months of purchase. When fresh herbs are available, substitute them by using three times the amount of the dried herb called for in the recipe. For example, if a recipe calls for 1 teaspoon dried basil, substitute 1 tablespoon minced fresh basil.

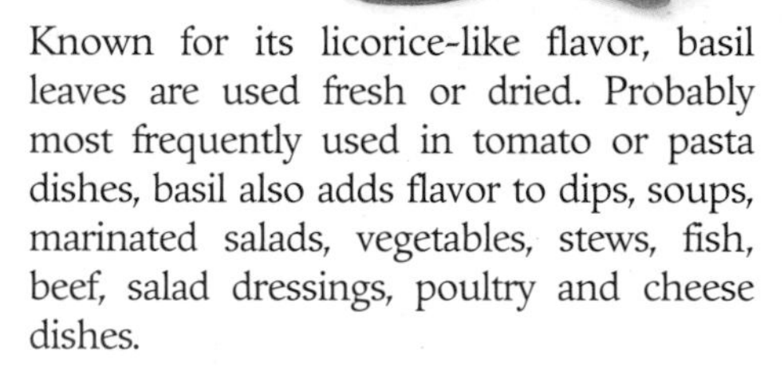

Basil

Known for its licorice-like flavor, basil leaves are used fresh or dried. Probably most frequently used in tomato or pasta dishes, basil also adds flavor to dips, soups, marinated salads, vegetables, stews, fish, beef, salad dressings, poultry and cheese dishes.

Bay Leaf

Bay leaf is most often found as a dried whole leaf, but sometimes can be found as fresh leaves. Bay leaf is most effective when allowed to simmer or marinate in the recipe for several hours. Try 1 to 2 bay leaves in soups, stews, pot roasts, poultry dishes, gravies, sauces and pickle brines. Bay leaves are always discarded before serving.

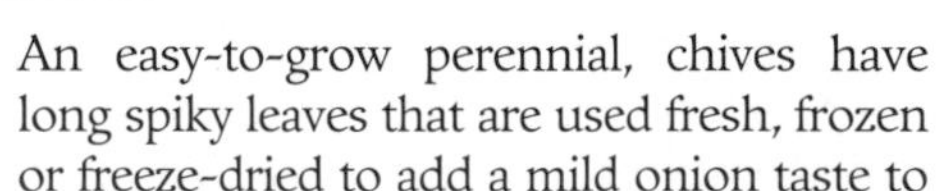

Chives

An easy-to-grow perennial, chives have long spiky leaves that are used fresh, frozen or freeze-dried to add a mild onion taste to egg dishes, poultry and fish or to garnish cream soups, salads and cooked vegetables. Preserve your own garden chives by snipping into 1/4-inch lengths and freezing in airtight storage containers.

Cilantro

Also known as coriander or Chinese parsley, the zesty-flavored green leaves of this herb are used fresh in Mexican-style dishes. Cilantro leaves add distinctive flavor to salsas, Southwestern-style appetizers, dips, sauces, chili, pesto and rice and bean dishes. Cilantro is best added to dishes just before serving to retain its fresh flavor.

Dill

Both the green tops (dill weed) and seeds (dill seed) have a distinctive caraway flavor. Dill weed is used fresh or dried to season pickle brines, salad dressings, sauces, dips, fish, shellfish and egg dishes. It also makes a pretty garnish. Dill seed is most often used in pickle brines and salad dressings.

Garlic

This strong-flavored, pungent herb is available fresh, dried and in powder form and adds life to a variety of foods, including dips, soups, salad dressings, flavored butters, casseroles, sauces, stews, grilled foods, marinades and meat, bean, rice or vegetable dishes.

Marjoram

Used fresh or dried, marjoram's green leaves have a strong sweet aroma much like oregano. Add to meat, poultry, fish, egg, homemade sausage and vegetable dishes. It's especially good with Italian-style foods.

Mint

Available fresh and dried, mint has a spicy flavor and aroma. Use it in stews, sauces, salads and mint jelly. Mint is often used as a garnish for fruits, desserts and beverages such as iced tea.

Oregano

The dark green leaves of oregano are used fresh or dried in Italian, Mexican and Greek dishes. Oregano flavors soups, stews, chili, poultry, ground beef, seafood, marinades, salad dressings, sauces, hot or cold pasta dishes and pizza.

Parsley

Available in curly and flat-leaf varieties, fresh parsley adds a refreshing flavor and spark of green garnish to soups, salads, salad dressings, sauces, fish, poultry, poultry stuffings and potato, grain, bean and pasta dishes. Flat-leaf or Italian parsley has a stronger flavor than the traditional curly variety. Dried parsley is mild in flavor and color.

Rosemary

Known for its needle-like leaves, rosemary has a distinctive fragrant evergreen scent and bold flavor. Fresh or dried rosemary complements lamb, pork, poultry, marinades, potato dishes, herb butters and homemade savory breads.

Sage

The pale green leaves of sage can be enjoyed fresh or dried and rubbed into a fluffy powder. Sage is well-known for adding a distinctive flavor to poultry stuffings, poultry, roasted red meats, meat pies, soups, stews and Italian dishes.

Tarragon

Tarragon's long slender leaves have a mild licorice-like flavor and are used fresh or dried. Tarragon flavors chicken, poultry marinades, pasta salads, potato salads, vegetables, sauces, salad dressings, fish and egg dishes.

Thyme

Thyme has a bold earthy taste and a strong aroma. There are many varieties of fresh thyme, including the popular lemon-flavored plant. Use fresh or dried thyme to season fish, potato dishes, soups, stuffings, stews, rice pilaf, wild rice dishes, poultry and meat marinades.

Glossary

Al Dente: An Italian term meaning "to the tooth" used to describe pasta that is cooked but still firm.

Au Jus: Natural, unthickened juices that collect while roasting meats.

Bake: To cook in an oven surrounded by dry heat. When baking, preheat the oven before placing the food in it.

Baste: To moisten foods while cooking by brushing with pan juices, butter, margarine, oil or a reserved marinade.

Batter: A mixture made of flour and a liquid such as milk. It may also include other ingredients such as sugar, butter, shortening or oil, eggs, leaveners and flavorings. The consistency of batters ranges from thin to thick. Thin batters are pourable, such as pancakes or cakes. Thick batters can be dropped from a spoon, such as quick breads.

Beat: To rapidly mix with a spoon, fork, wire whisk or electric mixer.

Betty: A baked fruit dessert that alternates layers of sweetened fruit with cake, cookies or bread crumbs.

Blanch: To cook for a few minutes in boiling water. This technique is used to help remove peels, to partially cook foods as a preparation step in a recipe or to prepare foods for freezing.

Blend: To combine several ingredients with a spoon, electric mixer, blender or food processor.

Boil: To heat liquids until bubbles form that cannot be stirred down. In the case of water, the temperature will reach 212° at sea level.

Bone: To remove raw or cooked meat from bones.

Braise: To cook slowly in a small amount of liquid in a covered pan on the stovetop or in the oven. Generally used for less tender cuts of meat.

Breading: A coating of fine bread crumbs or crackers used on meat, fish or vegetables.

Broil: To cook foods about 4 to 6 inches from a heat source.

Brown: To cook foods in a small amount of fat over medium to high heat until the food becomes brown, sealing in the juices and developing rich pan drippings.

Brown Bits: Little flecks of browned food that are left in the bottom of a pan after browning or cooking meat or poultry.

Buckle: A baked, cake-like fruit dessert made with berries. Named because the cake sometimes buckles under the weight of the topping.

Butterfly: To split foods, such as chicken breast, boneless meat or shrimp, lengthwise in half, leaving the meat attached along one side.

Caramelize: To heat sugar in a skillet or saucepan over low heat until melted and golden brown. Also refers to cooking onions in butter until soft, caramel-colored and rich in flavor.

Chill: To cool foods to below room temperature (40° or less) by placing in the refrigerator, freezer or an ice bath.

Chop: To cut foods into 1/4-inch to 1/2-inch pieces.

Clarify: To remove sediment and suspended particles from a liquid. Clarified butter has the milk solids removed, which allows the clarified butter to be heated to a higher temperature without smoking.

Coat: To dip or roll foods in flour, sugar or a sauce until covered.

"Coats Spoon": To leave a thin, even, smooth film on the back of a metal spoon. This is a doneness test for stirred custards.

Cobbler: A fruit dessert with a biscuit topping. The topping can be either in a single layer or dropped over the fruit to give a cobblestone effect.

Combine: To place several ingredients in a single bowl or container and thoroughly mix.

Cooking in Liquid: To simmer meat covered with liquid for a long time. Generally used for less tender cuts of meat to tenderize the meat.

Cool: To bring foods to room temperature (about 70°).

Core: To remove the seed area of an apple or pear using a coring tool or a small knife.

Cream: To beat softened butter, margarine or shortening alone or with sugar using a spoon or mixer until light and fluffy.

Crimp: To seal the edge of a double-crusted pie by pinching or pressing the crusts together with your fingers, fork or other utensil.

Crisp: A baked fruit dessert that has a crumb topping over fruit. The topping generally has flour, sugar and butter and may or may not have oats, nuts and spices. The topping gets crisp while baking.

Crisp-Tender: A stage of vegetable cooking where the vegetables are cooked until they are crunchy yet tender enough to be pierced with a fork.

Crush: To reduce foods to crumbs, paste or powder. Herbs can be crushed in a mortar and pestle. Garlic cloves and fresh gingerroot can be crushed with the side of a knife.

Cube: To cut foods into 1/2-inch to 1-inch square pieces.

Cut in: To break down and distribute cold butter, margarine or shortening into a flour mixture using a pastry blender or two knives.

Dash: A measurement less than 1/8 teaspoon that is used for herbs, spices or hot pepper sauce. This is not an accurate measurement.

Deep-Fat Fry: To cook foods in enough hot oil so that the food floats in the oil.

Dice: To cut foods into small cubes (1/8-inch to 1/4-inch cubes).

Direct Heat: To cook foods on an outdoor grill directly over coals or heat source.

Dissolve: To stir a solid food with a liquid until none of the solid remains, such as yeast with warm water or gelatin in boiling water.

Dollop: A small mound of soft food such as whipped cream or whipped topping.

Dot: To break up butter into small pieces and distribute over the top of a pie or dough.

Dough: A thick mixture made of flour and a liquid that is not pourable. It may include ingredients such as sugar, butter, shortening or oil, eggs, leaveners and flavorings. It may be stiff enough to be worked with by hand (kneading bread dough, for example).

Dredge: To lightly coat foods with flour or bread crumbs.

Drippings: The juices and melted fat that collect in the bottom of the pan as meat is cooked. The juices and some of the fat from the drippings can be used in gravies and sauces.

Drizzle: To slowly spoon or pour a thin stream of an icing, melted butter or other liquid over food.

Dust: To lightly sprinkle with confectioners' sugar, baking cocoa or flour.

Dutch Oven: A multipurpose cooking pot that can range in size from 5 to 8 quarts and is used to roast meats, cook soups and stews, boil pasta or steam vegetables.

Egg Wash: A mixture of beaten egg, egg yolk or egg white and water that is brushed over breads, rolls, pastries or pie crusts before baking. Egg washes give the final baked product a shiny brown finish.

Emulsify: To combine through a whisking action two liquids that traditionally separate, such as oil and vinegar, into a uniform mixture.

Extracts: The distilled essential oils from plant materials, which are then dissolved in alcohol. Common examples are vanilla and almond.

Filet: A boneless cut of meat.

Fillet: A boneless piece of fish.

Flake: To separate foods into small pieces. The term is frequently used when describing the doneness of fish.

Flavorings: Chemical compounds that replicate the flavor of a particular food or plant and do not originate from the plant material. Common examples are maple, banana and coconut.

Flute: To make a V-shape or scalloped edge on pie crust with thumb and fingers.

Fold: A method of mixing to combine light or delicate ingredients such as whipped cream or egg whites with other ingredients without beating. A rubber spatula is used to gently cut down through the ingredients, move across the bottom of the bowl and bring up part of the mixture.

Food Coloring: Used to tint foods. Food coloring is available in liquids, gels or pastes.

Full Rolling Boil: To boil a liquid in which the bubbles created by the boil cannot be stirred down.

Freeze: To store foods in the freezer.

Frost: To cover a cake, cupcake or cookie with a spreadable frosting.

Fry: To cook foods in a small amount of fat over medium to high heat.

Garnish: A decorative and edible accompaniment to give a dish more eye appeal and sometimes a flavor boost.

Glaze: To coat the exterior of sweet or savory foods with a thin, glossy mixture.

Grate: To rub ingredients such as citrus peel, spices and chocolate over a grater to produce very fine particles.

Grease: To rub the inside of a baking dish or pan with shortening, butter or oil, or to coat with nonstick cooking spray to keep the contents from sticking.

Grease and Flour: To rub the inside of a baking dish or pan with a thin layer of shortening, butter or oil, or coat with nonstick cooking spray and then dust with flour. The excess flour is shaken out of the pan. Cakes baked in round baking pans or fluted tube pans generally require the pan to be greased and floured.

Grill: To cook foods outside on a grid over hot charcoals or a gas flame. Also refers to an indoor countertop electrical appliance.

Grind: To transform a solid piece of food into smaller pieces using a food processor, blender or mortar and pestle.

Headspace: An area left unfilled between the top of the food in a home canning jar or freezer container and the bottom of the lid.

Hull: To remove the green stem and leaves of strawberries.

Ice: To spread a thin frosting over cakes or cookies.

Indirect Heat: To cook foods on an outdoor grill over a drip pan with the coals banked (or other heat source) on one or both sides of the drip pan. Indirect heat is used for cooking larger cuts of meat or less tender cuts of meat.

Jelly Roll: A dessert made by spreading a filling, jelly or whipped cream over a sponge cake baked in a 15-inch x 10-inch x 1-inch pan and rolling into a log. Jelly-roll style is used when any food is filled and rolled into a log shape.

Julienne: To cut foods into long, thin matchstick shapes about 2 inches long and 1/2 inch thick.

Knead: To work dough by using a pressing and folding action to make it smooth and elastic.

Line: To cover a baking sheet with a piece of parchment paper, waxed paper or foil to prevent sticking.

Marble: To swirl light and dark batters in a cake, bar cookie, pie or cheesecake. The batters should not be combined into one color; there should still be two distinct batters after marbling.

Marinate: To tenderize and/or flavor foods, usually meat or raw vegetables, by placing in a liquid mixture of oil, vinegar, wine, lime or lemon juice, herbs and spices.

Mince: To cut foods into very fine pieces (no larger than 1/8 inch).

Mix: To stir or beat two or more ingredients together with a spoon, a fork or a mixer until well combined.

Moisten: To add enough liquid to dry ingredients while stirring gently to make a wet, but not runny, mixture. Often used in muffin and quick bread recipes.

Pan-Broil: To cook tender cuts of meat, uncovered, in a skillet on the stovetop without the addition of any fat or liquid.

Pan-Dressed: Fish or small game with the internal organs and head removed, making it ready for cooking.

Pan-Fry: To cook tender cuts of meat, uncovered, in a skillet on the stovetop with the addition of fat but no liquid.

Parboil: To boil foods, usually vegetables, until partially cooked. Most often used when vegetables are finished using another cooking method or chilled for marinated salads or appetizer dips.

Partially Set: The consistency of chilled gelatin (resembles unbeaten egg whites) before fruits, vegetables and nuts can be added without floating.

Peel: To remove the skin from fruits and vegetables. To remove the peel, use a small sharp knife, a grater, a vegetable peeler or zester. Also, the outer portion of a citrus fruit is known as the peel.

Pinch: A measurement less than 1/8 teaspoon of a seasoning or spice that is easily held between the thumb and index finger. This is not an accurate measurement.

Pipe: To force a soft mixture such as whipped cream, frosting or meringue through a pastry bag for a fancy shape.

Pit: To remove the seed from fruit. Also refers to the seed in cherries, peaches, nectarines and avocados.

Plump: To soak dried fruit such as raisins and cherries in liquid until softened.

Poach: To cook meat, fish, eggs or fruits in simmering liquid. The liquid can be flavored with salt, bay leaves, onion, celery and/or white wine if desired.

Preheat: To bring an oven up to the baking temperature before baking.

Press: Often called a cookie press. Used to extract cookie dough in decorative shapes.

Prick: To pierce food or pastry with the tines of a fork to prevent them from bursting or rising during baking. Also used when roasting ducks and geese to remove excess fat under the skin.

Process: To combine, blend, chop or puree foods in a food processor or blender.

Proof: To check the quality of yeast before using. To proof yeast, dissolve yeast and a little sugar in warm water (110° to 115°) and let stand for 5 minutes. If the yeast is alive, there will be a thick foam on the surface. To proof also refers to letting yeast dough rise after it's been shaped and before baking.

Pulse: To process foods in a food processor or in a blender using short bursts of power. This is accomplished by quickly turning the machine on and off.

Punch Down: To use a fist to deflate risen yeast dough after the first rising.

Puree: To mash solid foods into a smooth mixture using a food processor, food mill, blender or sieve.

Reduce: To thicken sauces and gravy by boiling down and evaporating a portion of the liquid in an uncovered pan.

Refrigerate: To place in the refrigerator to chill.

Roast: To cook meat or vegetables with a dry heat as in cooking in an oven without the addition of liquid. Also refers to large cuts of meat that are intended to be roasted.

Rounded Teaspoon or Tablespoon: To mound dough slightly in measuring spoon.

Roux: A French term for a mixture of flour and fat that is cooked together until golden brown and used to thicken gumbo, soups and sauces.

Saute: To cook or lightly brown foods in butter, margarine or oil until tender.

Scald: To heat milk or cream over low heat until just before it boils. Look for small bubbles around the edge of the liquid.

Score: To make thin slashes on the surface of breads to decorate and allow steam to escape during baking.

Seed: To remove seeds from fruits and vegetables.

Seize: To become thick and lumpy. Seizing refers to when a small amount of liquid comes in contact with melted chocolate.

Separate: To remove the egg white from the egg yolk.

Shred: To cut or tear foods into long, thin strips, such as cooked chicken. In the case of soft cheese, carrots or potatoes, a metal shredder is used.

Shuck: To remove the meat of oysters, clams, etc. from their shells. Also refers to removing the husk from an ear of corn.

Sift: To pass dry ingredients such as flour or confectioners' sugar through a fine-mesh strainer or sifter to remove lumps, add air and combine several dry ingredients.

Simmer: To cook liquids alone or a combination of ingredients with liquid just under the boiling point (180° to 200°). The surface of the liquid will have some movement and there may be small bubbles around the side of pan.

Skim: To remove with a spoon a layer of fat or foam that rises from the top of cooking liquids.

Snip: To cut herbs into small pieces using a kitchen shears.

Soft Peaks: The stage of beating egg whites or heavy whipping cream when the beater is lifted from the mixture and the points of the peaks curl over.

Soften: To bring butter, margarine or cream cheese to a soft consistency by holding at room temperature for a short time.

Spice Bag: A container made out of cheesecloth to hold whole spices and/or herbs. The bag makes it easy to remove and discard the spices or herbs before serving.

Steam: To cook foods covered on a rack or in a steamer basket over a small amount of boiling water. Most often used for vegetables.

Steep: To place dry foods, such as tea leaves, in hot water to extract flavor and/or color.

Stew: To cover food with liquid and slowly cook over low heat in a tightly covered pot. This cooking method tenderizes tough cuts of meat and allows flavors to blend.

Stiff Peaks: The stage of beating egg whites or heavy whipping cream when the beater is lifted from the mixture and points of peaks stand straight up.

Stir: To blend a combination of ingredients by hand using a spoon in a circular motion.

Stir-Fry: To quickly saute meats and vegetables while stirring constantly in a wok or skillet.

Stock: A long-simmered broth made from meat, poultry, fish and/or vegetables with herbs and spices.

Strain: To separate solids from liquid by pouring through a sieve or colander.

Stud: To insert seasonings like whole cloves into the surface of food, such as a ham.

Stuff: To fill a cavity in fish, poultry or pork chops with a bread or rice, vegetable, fruit or nut mixture.

Tear: To use your hands to pull food apart into unevenly sized pieces, such as when tearing salad greens.

Thread: To place pieces of meat and vegetables onto skewers as when making kabobs.

Toss: To quickly and gently mix ingredients with a spoon or fork. Often done with flour and candied fruit in baked goods.

Truss: To tie the legs and wings of poultry close to the body before roasting. If poultry is stuffed, the openings are closed with skewers that are tied or closed with string.

Warm: To hold foods at a low temperature, usually around 200°, without further cooking.

Water Bath: To place a baking dish containing food, such as a custard or souffle, in a large dish. The larger dish is filled with hot or boiling water. The food is then baked in the water bath to promote even cooking.

Weave: To thread food on a skewer using a back and forth motion. The term is also used to describe the action when making a lattice top for a pie.

Whip: To beat rapidly by hand or with an electric mixer to add air and increase volume.

Whisk: A multi-looped, wire mixing utensil with a handle used to whip sauces, eggs, cream, etc. to a smooth, airy consistency. Also means to whip ingredients together.

Zest: *See Peel.*

ALPHABETICAL INDEX

Alphabetical Index

A

B

C

D

E

F

G

H

I

J

L

M

N

O

P

Q

R

S

T

U

V

W

Z

GENERAL INDEX

General Recipe Index